Theories of
Social Casework

Theories of Social Casework

Edited by
Robert W. Roberts
Robert H. Nee

The University of Chicago Press   Chicago and London

Papers written for the Charlotte Towle Memorial
Symposium on Comparative Theoretical Approaches
to Casework Practice

International Standard Book Number: 0–226–72105–1
Library of Congress Catalog Card Number: 70–123358
The University of Chicago Press, Chicago 60637
The University of Chicago Press, Ltd., London
© 1970 by The University of Chicago
All rights reserved. Published 1970
Second Impression 1971
Printed in the United States of America

Reason and heart will give you words
Homer

Contents

A Tribute to Charlotte Towle

This volume is a fitting way to honor Charlotte Towle, for she was a leader in the move to teach social casework generically rather than by fields of practice. That the writers of most of these chapters were her friends attests to the range and depth of her scholarly interests. It is easy to envisage with what perceptiveness she would have examined these papers and gone quickly to the nuggets and to the clarification of the formulations that were unfamiliar to her. She foresaw the current interest in comparative theory and in her preface to Florence Hollis's *Casework: A Psychosocial Therapy* she wrote, "We will be in a better position to appraise new directions in casework practice, and to define and clarify issues, as this work excites controversy. It is less important that we all think alike than that we know our likenesses and differences, so that we may speak intelligibly from group to group, within social work and within the interprofessional scene."[1]

Recently I have been rereading some of Charlotte Towle's works so that I might comment on her as a theorist. Perhaps someone who knows her only from her publications can do that best, for those of us who were her colleagues learned daily from her penetrating and ofttimes witty comments, and the person seems to come between me and the page.

Her writings may be grouped under three major topics: social work practice, social work education, and social work philosophy; but these topics are not as separate as they may sound. One is impelled to ask: On what did she not write? Although she did not acquire the tools of the researcher, her formulations were the theoretical underpinnings for the major study of Lilian Ripple and associates, *Motivation, Capacity, and Opportunity: Studies in Casework Theory and Practice.* She was our foremost writer on education for social work, her work culminating in *The Learner in Education for the Professions.* Helen H. Perlman has edited and commented on twenty of Charlotte Towle's papers for the University of Chicago Press, and these have appeared both in hard cover and in paperback editions.

---

1. Florence Hollis, *Casework: A Psychosocial Therapy* (New York: Random House, 1964), p. xiv.

Published material is open to the public and available for study by all who seek to learn. Yet Charlotte Towle contributed to theory in areas on which she did not publish. A significant number of colleagues and students were the recipients of these formulations, and so they are worthy of comment. I shall mention three of these. Charlotte Towle was long associated with members of other professions, notably with psychiatrists, and developed material on the consultation process that she presented in several institutes. I believe that the content was immeasurably influential in practice. Just as she wrote and taught about differential diagnosis in casework, she sought to understand differences in learning patterns of students; and for her advanced students she formulated a beginning classification of learning patterns. I hope that this material, along with formulations of other educators, will appear in the literature. Her conviction about the desirability of a social worker's teaching human growth and behavior from the perspective of the normal stresses of life led her to develop such a course. The rich content is possessed by students and faculty members who were in those classes, though she published only the aims of the course and a general outline.

One remembers her capacity for penetrating analysis. Reread, for instance, her review of volume 1 of the *Social Work Curriculum Study* of 1959. Her convictions and commitments shine clearly. I think I was impressed most, though, by the opposite characteristic. She saw so much in so little material that it was like a sunburst of ideation in all directions. The integration of what she knew and felt was so complete that she was free to be creative. She wrote of the *Curriculum Study:*

It is well established that creativity is largely a matter of new integrations. This implies perpetuation of that which was vital in the old. Creativity involves some departure from the established order and, therefore, a considerable sloughing-off of the old. What is retained is decisive, making for progress or retrogression. So we can well ask: How vital are the discards to the attainment of the aims of social work education? We should examine the innovations carefully. Are they truly innovations or, as often occurs in times of stress, do they bespeak a revival of an outworn past? Finally, we need to ask: Are our shortcomings inherent in our system or in our conduct of it? For greater efficiency, does our system need nurture or renovation?[2]

These are timely questions to which the authors in this volume addressed themselves.

Charlotte Towle had a love for and sense of history and she often wrote and spoke of the need for "the attainment of orderly thinking that approximates the scientific method." It is fitting that the first chapter should be entitled "Casework and Science: A Historical Encounter." I believe that future readers may consider the publication of these papers a benchmark in the evolution of theory and building for practice. They were prepared by eminent exponents of each approach and they are of a high theoretical level. The symposium for which they were prepared may come to occupy a place in history similar to that of the Milford Conference. Meanwhile, it is my hope that the study of the papers may bring to the reader vicariously some of the intellectual stimulation that participants of the Charlotte Towle Memorial Symposium experienced in discussing them.

DOROTHY AIKIN

---

2. *Social Service Review* 33 (December 1959):362.

Introduction

Social work is a new profession, born of the twentieth century. Unlike the older professions which developed specializations in their maturity, social work grew out of multiple specializations in diverse fields of practice. It was not until 1957, in fact, that the National Association of Social Workers was formed to unite into one professional organization the many groups committed to particular specialties.

Social casework, the earliest and best defined social work method, has a history similar to that of its parent profession. Casework began with the diverse humanitarian efforts of volunteers in the nineteenth century. It was not until 1917, however, that Mary Richmond wrote the first text on casework, *Social Diagnosis*. Twelve years later, the Milford Conference undertook the task of conceptualizing a common base for casework as practiced in many specialized settings. In the ensuing years, casework theoreticians spent much of their energy trying to develop a generic theory that would synthesize the interests of many specialities into a common professional identity. The exception to this preoccupation with generic theory was the theoretical schism between the diagnostic and functional schools during the forties. After surviving that controversy, casework theoreticians renewed their search for similarities between divergent viewpoints and virtually ignored differences in theory and practice.

In the 1950s, the profession reached a point of security in its identity that permitted a critical examination of its traditional practices. Casework became committed in fact, as well as in word, to the scientific method, and empirical studies proliferated. Many of these studies addressed the question of casework's effectiveness. Given the paucity of scientific understanding of the social problems casework was attempting to solve, such evaluative studies were premature and potentially harmful to a young profession. Despite this, attempts to assess casework's efficiency led to two positive consequences. Dissatisfied with the way some researchers had interpreted casework theory, theoreticians became more precise, specific, and internally consistent in their conceptualization of practice. Second, casework theory became more of an open system and increasingly receptive to new inputs. These new inputs included not only findings from empirical studies but also perspectives from behavioral sciences which were formerly overlooked by casework theorists. In combination, these factors have resulted in a proliferation of theoretical approaches to casework practice.

For the most part, these developments have been gradual and piecemeal and there have been few efforts to systematically compare the differences and similarities among the various theoretical approaches. Serious students of casework have thus been confronted with the Herculean task of surveying vast bodies of professional literature and of independently trying to integrate discrete products of an evolutionary growth into comprehensible theoretical wholes. Fair comparisons have been almost impossible to make, even by scholars who have achieved independent integrations, because each theoretical position was itself in process. Major contributions from competing schools appeared at different points in time, and theoreticians had not always addressed similar issues or topics in their writings.

Although it is desirable that theoretical (as well as empirical) knowledge grow through a cumulative process, there is also a need for periodic theoretical stock-taking and integration. Unfortunately—especially in a profession committed to action in an era of violent social change—social work scholars seldom have the opportunity to come together to assess the position of theory development at a given time. Disciplined and rigorous comparisons have thus been impossible because individual casework theories are dynamic and in a process of constant development.

In seeking a way to honor the memory of Charlotte Towle, it was felt that a symposium to appraise the current status of casework theory would be a most appropriate memorial. The idea was enthusiastically accepted by former Dean Alton A. Linford and the faculty of the School of Social Service Administration, the University of Chicago. The Charlotte Towle Memorial Fund Committee agreed to finance the symposium.

The plan for the symposium was to have major casework scholars, known to be identified with important theoretical approaches, write position papers and then to meet for three days of intensive discussion from May 1 to 3, 1969. Decisions about who should be asked to write papers were made by committee vote. Criteria for invitations were based on the scholars' demonstrated excellence in theory building and on their professional commitment to a specific, rather than an eclectic, point of view.

Decisions about which theoretical approaches should be included were more difficult to make. This was because many of today's casework theoreticians, unlike those in the past, are less interested in creating or adding to a general casework theory and are working at more microcosmic levels of theoretical specification. Some of the issues of current concern (such as casework advocacy), although important to today's practice realities, are not wide enough in scope to be considered a distinct theoretical approach. Others are involved with conceptualizing practice for use with such elite client groups (e.g., autistic children) that it is difficult to ascertain how far their productions can be generalized.

A final decision was made to include the four theoretical approaches which are considered general approaches (the psychosocial, the functional, the problem-solving, and the behavioral modification approaches) and three "middle-range" approaches (family-group treatment, crisis-oriented brief treatment, and adult socialization). These latter approaches, although addressed to specific groups within the general client population, were included because the size of the client group for whom they are designed is considerable and because many of the concepts and principles of these approaches have obvious utility for casework with other client groups or problem situations.

To insure that the papers would be roughly comparable in content, and thus permit rigorous and critical comparisons, the contributors were given a suggested outline for their papers. This outline consisted of topics which had either been included traditionally in theories of casework or seemed logically indicated. There was no attempt to force the outline on the authors, but they were asked to defend the omission of any topic if it did not seem pertinent to their point of view. After some initial discomfort, all the contributors found that they could write within the framework suggested. The order in which they covered the topics, however, varied with the proclivities of the writer and of the nature of the particular theory.

To help the reader understand the appropriate bases for comparison of the papers, the suggested outline given to the authors follows:

1. General characteristics of the theoretical approach under discussion and a brief statement about the origins of the approach.
2. Behavioral science foundations (a description of the major theoretical and empirical underpinnings of the practice theory).
3. The initial phase (a discussion of how professional workers engage clients in treatment). This should include a statement of the goals, the content, and the process of the early stages of client-worker-agency interaction.
4. Assessment of the client in his situation (i.e., diagnosis or its equivalent). This should include a detailed and specific statement of whether differential assessments are made, how they are made (if they are made), what classification scheme (if any) is used, and the possible effects of such a scheme on the exclusion or inclusion of major types of social work clients.
5. Treatment principles and methods. Treatment should be discussed in terms of goals, content, and method or process. If relevant, a classification of treatment approaches should be presented with reference to the diagnostic classification scheme included.
6. The target group (a definition, in terms of major social problems, types of clients, and fields of practice, of those who are considered appropriate clients for workers using this theoretical approach).
7. Unsolved problems (a discussion of the major theoretical problems and issues).
8. Bibliography—Specification of approximately ten major references.

In addition to the position papers, this volume contains two other major contributions to casework theory. The first, by Carel Germain, was the keynote address given at the one public meeting of the symposium. Her assignment was to prepare a paper on the historical development of casework theory since Mary Richmond. Rather than surveying the major contributions of individuals through the years, Mrs. Germain has produced an interpretation of the relationship between casework theory and the philosophies of science underlying the behavioral sciences from which practice theory was built.

The final chapter is by Bernece Simon, who accepted the difficult task of leading the three days of discussions. Since Mrs. Simon is a leading theoretician in comparative casework theory, she was not asked to limit herself to summarizing the discussions. Instead, she has written a comprehensive overview of casework theory. She presents a paradigm for the systematic analysis of any theory of social casework, a critical examination of casework theory as presented in the papers, and a synthesis of the major issues and topics pursued in the three days of meetings. The first part of her chapter is recommended as a guide for comparative analysis of the seven theoretical approaches and can profitably be read as an introduction to the seven position papers.

The task of editing this volume was considerably lightened by the quality of the papers and the cooperation of the authors. In addition to accepting responsibility for writing papers, they participated freely and graciously in a critical examination of their ideas during the symposium. Their generosity of mind and spirit was responsible for the success of the symposium and for the intellectual enrichment of its participants.

Special recognition is due to Dean Alton A. Linford for his support of the symposium, and to other members of the planning committee: Professors Dorothy Aikin, Rachel Marks, and Bernece Simon. Ernestina Alexander, assistant dean for continuing education and special events, was in large measure responsible for the uncustomary smoothness which characterized the operation of the symposium from beginning to end.

Thanks are also due Elizabeth Butler, Janet Kohrman, Friedericka Mayers, and Philip Hovda, who served as recorders at the discussions, and to Fe Logan, Jimmie Reed, and Esther Silverman, who have helped with secretarial and editing functions.

A final debt is acknowledged to the family, friends, and

colleagues of Charlotte Towle who have contributed to her memorial fund. It was their generosity which made this volume and the symposium possible. We sincerely hope that this production will serve as a long-lasting testament to the theoretical, educational, and personal contributions of a great social work theoretician and teacher—Charlotte Towle.

ROBERT W. ROBERTS
ROBERT H. NEE

Theories of
Social Casework

1 | Casework and Science: A Historical Encounter

Carel Germain

It is especially fitting that the subject of casework's relations with science be considered here at the University of Chicago, whose School of Civics and Philanthropy was founded in 1907 as one of the first university-sponsored schools of social work in the country. This is of particular importance since university-based graduate education for the scholarly disciplines itself came into being under the pressures of science, has lived its whole life in an increasingly scientific age, and is today largely a scientific institution.[1] Thus, from its inception, the Chicago school stood in contrast to its contemporaries which, in their aloofness to university affiliation, long supported a more technical and sometimes proprietary type of training. Moreover, the school's early and illustrious dean, Edith Abbott, proclaimed the need for men and women in social welfare to be "trained in the scientific method and inspired by the scientific spirit."[2] The *Social Service Review,* under the editorship of the faculty of the University of Chicago's School of Social Service Administration, has, since its first issue in 1927, carried on its masthead the words "A quarterly devoted to the scientific and professional interests of social work." Through the long and honorable years of its existence, this school has achieved a dominant position in the application of scientific knowledge and scientific method throughout American social work. It has maintained this position through its research and teaching activities, the practice of its graduates, and the widespread influence of its distinguished faculty, both past and present. And so it is particularly appropriate to examine the historical connections of casework and science here at Chicago.

Carel Germain is associate professor of social work, School of Social Work, University of Connecticut, Hartford.

Responsibility for the content of this chapter is mine, yet I have been long indebted to two scholars of the Columbia University School of Social Work in whom the humanism and the scientific commitment of social work are brightly reflected. From Professor Emeritus Lucille N. Austin I learned social casework not as final truth but as a quest for deeper understanding and wider knowledge. From Professor Irving Miller I caught an abiding interest in the history of ideas and their meaning for social work.

1. Bernard Berelson, *Graduate Education in the United States* (New York: McGraw-Hill Book Co., 1960), p. 12.
2. Edith Abbott, *Social Welfare and Professional Education*, rev. ed. (Chicago: University of Chicago Press, 1941), p. 12.

There have been, over the course of forty years, several historical analyses[3] of the development of casework, all of which have helped contribute to the formation of our professional identity. In Erikson's terms, they provide us with a sense of meaningful continuity with our past, so that we can recognize ourselves in our predecessors and can understand the historical conditions and experiences that made us what we are as a professional group. It is less certain that these histories provide us with any sense of what we are about to become, and thus with a continuity linked to the future which also must be a part of our collective identity. An accelerated rate of social change and the consequent upsurge of new social problems and needs have been eroding our sense of direction and our inner professional identity. Erikson tells us that when traditional identities become outworn as new developments encroach upon them, crisis compels men to wage holy wars against those who seem to question or threaten their unsafe ideological bases.[4] Thomas Kuhn, writing of the history of science, speaks of crisis in a discipline as arising from the failure of existing rules to solve the problems with which the discipline deals. Such a crisis usually demands large-scale destruction of the current model for the discipline's activities, and it is normally accompanied by a proliferation of competing theories and by great professional insecurity.[5] Today we appear to be facing an analogous crisis in our identity as caseworkers, complete with a holy war among ourselves, discontent within, challenge from without, and beginning shifts in how we see problems and

3. See, for example, Virginia Robinson, *A Changing Psychology in Social Casework* (Chapel Hill: University of North Carolina Press, 1930), part 1; Annette Garrett, "Historical Survey of the Evolution of Casework," *Journal of Social Casework* 30 (June 1949):219–29; Shirley Hellenbrand, "Main Currents in Social Casework 1918–1936," D.S.W. diss., Columbia University School of Social Work (University Microfilms Publication #65–13953, Ann Arbor, Michigan); Helen Harris Perlman, "Social Work Method: A Review of the Past Decade," *Social Work* 10 (October 1965).
4. Erik Erikson, "The Problem of Ego Identity," in *Identity and the Life Cycle,* Psychological Issues 1 (New York: International Universities Press, 1959), p. 158.
5. Thomas Kuhn, *The Structure of Scientific Revolutions,* Phoenix ed. (Chicago: University of Chicago Press, 1962), p. 67.

design intervention—all accompanied by professional insecurity.

Because of new problems it seems worthwhile to attempt still another version of the past. A study of the history of social casework in the light of its scientific commitment may help to explain the present crisis. It may also provide some perspective for increasing our accessibility to change and our willingness to plan anew. We are justified in making yet another interpretation of the past, I think, since philosophers of history have shown that there is no single version of an era or of a group which is uniquely valid. However, the question always remains whether historical analysis discovers actual realities about the past or merely creates imagined ones by applying particular constructs to the data.[6] As we understand it today, social casework's commitment to science embraces a body of knowledge derived from the foundation sciences and from empirical experience; a scientific method or particular approach to phenomena; and a set of scientific attitudes including the open-mindedness and objectivity which reflect the spirit of scientific inquiry. Significant throughout its development has been casework's linkage of this commitment with humanistic values and human purposes. I believe that tracing the origins, development, and outcomes of casework's commitment to science will reveal one valid image of our past. Indeed, this commitment may well be the continuing thread which leads to the future.

Since time began there has probably been some degree of concern for the man in distress. Concern and help might have been on the basis of kinship; it might have depended on whether the victim were friend or foe, insider or outsider; it often depended on religious, moral, political, and economic considerations of the era. Charity did not, however, become "scientific" in addition to all its other attributes until the late nineteenth century, and then, characteristically, the description was most often applied to philanthropy in America.[7] Scientific philanthropy, derived from earlier Eu-

---

6. Raymond Aron, "Evidence and Inference in History," *Evidence and Inference*, ed. Daniel K. Lerner (Glencoe: Free Press, 1959), p. 25.

7. The earliest sources of scientific charity can be located in the orderly management of poor relief in Hamburg and Elberfeld. Still more immediate sources can be found in the work and thought of English re-

ropean sources, took root in this country in a general climate of optimism which included the belief that science would cure all social ills and lead to unlimited progress. The Charity Organization movement was introduced in the late 1870s as a means for making almsgiving scientific, efficient, and preventive. Charity Organization Societies (COS) developed and spread rapidly over the next twenty-five years, and modern social casework, as their later offspring, became the twentieth-century heir of the movement's scientific aspirations. Optimistically, the key to prevention and cure was thought to lie in scientific laws and methods.[8] Speakers and

---

formers including the Webbs and Arnold Toynbee and charity organization workers such as Sir Charles Lock, who influenced the activities of settlement and charity organization workers in the United States. As early as 1881, Toynbee (the uncle of the famed historian) said in a lecture to an Oxford University audience, "To make benevolence scientific is the great problem of the present day." See *The Industrial Revolution of the 18th Century in England* (London: Longmans, Green & Co., 1908). This statement was quoted by Edith Abbott in her address at the 161st Convocation of the University of Chicago (see Abbott, *Social Welfare*, p. 2).

8. In 1889 a paper entitled "Scientific Charity," by Mrs. Glendower Evans (see *National Conference of Charities and Corrections Proceedings* 1889:24), likened the application of science to charity to the use of a physician in illness, urging that the same intelligence and scientific spirit which created power over the physical world be used to understand and modify social forces. Cooperation between the offices of visiting and almsgiving was declared to be the first essential of an efficient or a scientific charity. A few years later Professor Wilcox of Cornell University urged a closer relation between universities and charity organization societies as potential sociological laboratories. Such a relationship, he felt, would increase the scholarliness and scientific base of charity work; the union of theory and practice would give scientific value to work upon social questions (see Walter Wilcox, "Social Science and Statistics," *NCCC Proceedings* 1894:86); Daniel Fulcomer, lecturer in social science at the University of Chicago and acting chairman of the Conference Committee on Instruction in Sociology in Institutions of Learning, felt that the evils of charity would disappear with increased knowledge of a science of man. (See *NCCC Proceedings* 1894:67). In 1890 Charles D. Kellogg, the general secretary of the New York COS and one of the bright group of young men who passed through Professor Francis Peabody's Harvard class in social philosophy (see Frank Bruno, *Trends in American Social Work*, [New York: Columbia University Press, 1948], p. 133) said statistics would throw light on the causes, present condition, and wisest treatment of poverty and pauperism (see *NCCC Proceedings* 1890:31–35). D. O. Kellogg of the Philadelphia COS had said ten years earlier, "Charity is a

writers connected with scientific philanthropy urged the application of scientific data collection and classification to identify and control such results of poverty as pauperism, crime, and disease. The National Conference of Charities and Corrections[9] served as a forum for the communication of the ideas and values connected with scientific charity. (Later the conference shared this function with the newly developed professional associations, journals, and training schools.) Various men and women of ideas interacted with what Znaniecki has called a social circle, an audience, to whom they addressed themselves and who in turn provided them with respect and esteem.[10] In this way, over the years opinions were formed and guided, group solidarity was promoted, and the developing commitment to a scientific outlook was shaped by debate and discussion.

Close to the end of the nineteenth century, and after twenty-five years of struggle by the conference to make charity scientific, Mary Richmond began her almost regular attendance and frequent contributions to that body.[11] More than any of her predecessors or contemporaries, Mary Richmond is credited with laying the foundation for a scientific approach in casework, an achievement marked by the publication of Social Diagnosis.[12]

---

science, the science of social therapeutics, and has laws like all other sciences." It was this statement made before a meeting of American Social Science Association that caught the interest of David Coit Gilman, President of Johns Hopkins University, and led to the part he played in establishing the Baltimore COS. (See Muriel Pumphrey, "Mary Richmond and the Rise of Professional Social Work in Baltimore," D.S.W. diss., Columbia University School of Social Work, University Microfilms Publication #17,076, Ann Arbor, Michigan, p. 108.)

9. This body was renamed the National Conference of Social Work in 1917. In 1950 it received its present name, National Conference of Social Welfare.

10. This discussion draws on the formulations of Florian Znaniecki, The Social Role of the Man of Knowledge (New York: Columbia University Press, 1940).

11. Mary Richmond read papers in 1895, 1897, 1901, 1907, 1908, 1910, 1911, 1912, 1915, 1917, 1918, and 1920.

12. Mary Richmond, Social Diagnosis (New York: Russell Sage Foundation, 1917). Charlotte Towle wrote that Mary Richmond's outstanding contribution was the formulation of a scientific method, but that because it was misinterpreted and misapplied it negated for some years

The example of Mary Richmond highlights very well the social influences on spokesmen for the scientific commitment as well as their influences on one another and on the developing occupation group. Richmond worked closely at the Baltimore COS with its president, David Coit Gilman, who, at the same time, was also the first president of the Johns Hopkins University, where American graduate education with its emphasis on science had made its initial appearance. Other fellow workers at the COS were a host of Hopkins faculty and doctoral graduates serving as board members, friendly visitors, and even as general secretaries.[13] Clearly, each of these men by training and bent was committed to the development of a scientific foundation in the provision of charity, and Richmond was guided in her reading, thinking, and learning during the Baltimore years by these and other academicians. We see in *Social Diagnosis,* for example, the demand for an exhaustive collection and weighing of facts from the premise that uncovering the cause will reveal the cure, a premise that reflected nineteenth-century science and scientism.

Derived as it was from the mechanistic physics of Newton, in which the universe was assumed to be run by mathematical laws, science in this era—the late nineteenth and early twentieth centuries—emphasized the doctrine of single causation. A linear relation was envisioned between cause and effect, in

---

Richmond's concept of casework as a democratic process. (Charlotte Towle, "Social Casework," *Social Work Yearbook* [New York: Russell Sage Foundation, 1947].)

13. Pumphrey, "Mary Richmond," pp. 110–12 and 388; within the group were Herbert B. Adams, professor of history and a conference participant; Richard T. Ely, professor of political economy; G. Stanley Hall, professor of psychology, who later, as president of Clark University, brought Freud to this country for his series of lectures in 1909. Another colleague was Jeffrey Brackett, president of the conference in 1904, who later left the Baltimore COS to direct the Boston School of Social Work, newly founded by Simmons College and Harvard University. His assistant was Zilpha Smith, also a conference contributor and closely identified with the ideas of scientific philanthropy in Boston charity organizations. Miss Smith had been Mary Richmond's teacher by correspondence in the early Baltimore years. Still another associate and Hopkins Ph.D. was Phillip Ayres, who later became an associate secretary of the New York COS under Edward Devine and the first Director of the New York School of Social Work.

which an effect was considered traceable to one cause. There-fore uncovering the cause of a social ill would suggest the cure. So, too, observation of all the facts in a situation would lead to certain and absolute knowledge. This point of view was consistently reflected in the scientific commitment as for-mulated by writers and conference spokesmen in the early years.[14]

Supporting nineteenth-century meliorism, and its faith in unlimited scientific progress, was the newly emerging phi-losophy of pragmatism. As a reaction against social Dar-winism and the Puritan Myth in various systems of thought, pragmatism was a philosophy linked to social reform; as a reflection of the American empirical spirit, it was a phi-losophy congruent with the scientific outlook and the scien-tific method. Pragmatism may therefore have furnished another condition in which social casework moved to em-brace the scientific ethos. Or perhaps it was only that case-work's scientific interest was a parallel development. In any event, the sociology of knowledge suggests an interrelation-ship between the system of ideas then beginning to be called social casework and the social-historical context from which it arose. Certainly, the morning years of casework were those in which the pragmatic temper flourished. They were also

---

14. In 1895, for example, Professor William Brewer of Yale said in a conference paper, "The universe is governed by law. Science investigates the ways of nature and deduces the laws governing her work. These laws are God's laws; and man's work, to be successful, must be in accordance with them. The closer the accordance, the more effective the work. . . . The efficient and economic management of charity and correction on the scale we have now to deal with must be conducted as an applied science . . . directed along lines marked by fixed laws of nature." (William Brewer, "The Relation of Universities to Charity and to Reformatory Work," *NCCC Proceedings* 1895:143.)

In 1905, the chairman of the Conference Committee on Needy Fam-ilies in Their Homes stated that two basic principles of charity organi-zation, "the painstaking inquiry into, and the recording of, as many facts as possible bearing on the problem at hand, are precisely the methods by which modern inductive science has achieved its astonishing results." (James Jackson: *NCCC Proceedings* 1905:344.)

As late as 1920, Arthur J. Todd, the director of the Training Course for Social and Civic Work in the University of Minnesota, in his book *The Scientific Spirit and Social Work* (New York: Macmillan Co., 1920), p. 83, wrote, "Science [in social work] is hunting out cause and effect in all their ramifications."

the years of the Progressive Era when social workers joined with others to effect the great social reforms of the age.

The early commitment to a scientific outlook began to intensify rapidly, first as the charity organization societies gradually became bureaucratized, and next as the new group of paid agents themselves began to push toward professionalization. The striving for status impelled them to achieve a scientific methodology, and this intersected with the organizational need to achieve scientific efficiency.[15] Thus the transformation of charity workers into caseworkers began and the commitment to science became clear. In 1921, Mary Richmond was granted an honorary M.A. degree by Smith College for "establishing the scientific basis of a new profession."[16] Three years earlier Smith College had established a training school for psychiatric social work in response to the increased demand for workers to handle the emotional problems of returning World War I veterans and their families. Thenceforth, casework was extended to persons above the poverty line. The new school also reflected a growing interest in wartime developments in psychiatry and a turning away by casework from behaviorist psychology. Even though the initial adoption of a scientific outlook in philanthropy had paralleled the appearance of pragmatism, the identification was more with scientism and naive notions of induction and causality than with those aspects of pragmatism which supported environmental change. To understand how this came about, it is necessary to go back and trace the development of the method by which the scientific commitment was implemented.

Richmond's writings carry many quotations from William Osler, the famous Johns Hopkins surgeon, whom she deeply

15. Roy Lubov, *The Professional Altruist* (Cambridge: Harvard University Press, 1965).

These pressures were reinforced by the growing professionalization and specialization in the total American occupational structure, by the developing prestige of science, and by the increasing specialization of knowledge in all areas of thought. See, for example, Bernard Barber, *Science and the Social Order* (Glencoe: Free Press, 1952), p. 160.

16. Joanna Colcord and Ruth Z. S. Mann, *The Long View: Papers and Addresses by Mary E. Richmond* (New York: Russell Sage Foundation, 1930), p. 427.

admired. It is known that two of her closest advisors in Baltimore were prominent physicians at Hopkins, and medical students were friendly visitors all during Richmond's tenure as general secretary of the COS.[17] It seems reasonable to suppose that these many associations contributed to her development of the medical or disease metaphor of social diagnosis and treatment. It was during the Baltimore years that she wrote, for example, of pauperism as "a disease" and of the friendly visitor as a "social physician or general practitioner of charity" who is called upon to "heal" complex conditions.[18] Although her writings contain references to what the teacher does with pupils[19] and to how the lawyer uses forms of evidence,[20] it was the medical or disease metaphor which was ultimately selected, developed, and refined by Mary Richmond and by later generations of casework theorists. In addition to the prevailing scientism and Richmond's professional associations, other social influences also fostered the adoption of this model. Most notable of these seems to have been the roles played by Dr. Richard Cabot and Ida Cannon of the Massachusetts General Hospital[21] in the development of medical casework. Workers in other medical settings, in order to differentiate themselves from nursing staff and to enhance their status in the host institutions, also identified with the higher status profession of medicine, the physician's body of knowledge, and his method of diagnosis and treatment.[22] In these ways, over the 1920s the medical model was adopted and, with it, a study-diagnosis-treatment framework that supplied a scientific method by which to implement the scientific commitment. For a profession on

---

17. Pumphrey, "Mary Richmond," pp. 232, 313–15.

18. Ibid., p. 300.

19. Mary Richmond, *What Is Social Casework?* (New York: Russell Sage Foundation, 1922).

For a somewhat later view of casework as teaching, see M. Antoinette Cannon, "Underlying Principles and Common Practices in Social Work," *National Conference on Social Welfare Proceedings* 1928:564–68.

20. Mary Richmond, *Social Diagnosis.*

21. Ida M. Cannon, *Social Work in Hospitals: A Contribution to Progressive Medicine,* rev. ed. (New York, 1923); Richard Cabot, *Social Service and the Art of Healing* (New York, 1909).

22. Lubov, *Professional Altruist,* chap. 2, "From Friendly Visiting to Social Diagnosis."

the way up this was a welcome advance, especially for one which had been accused by Abraham Flexner in 1915 of having no transmissible knowledge and skill of its own to warrant professional aspirations.[23]

In 1929 the Milford Conference published the report of its attempts over the twenties to identify the generic components of casework practice. Despite variations in specific settings, it was hoped that a professional unity could be established and maintained. The report underscored the scientific commitment by expressing the conviction that casework's growth would depend on its becoming increasingly scientific through adaptations of knowledge from other sciences and through analysis of its own scientific aspects. Although it did make possible the later introduction of generic courses and a body of common knowledge into the social work curriculum, the report led to unforeseen ideological tensions between education and practice which then impeded the very theory development it espoused.[24]

Two later issues played back and forth in theory and practice and had their own impacts on the scientific commitment

---

23. Abraham Flexner, "Is Social Work a Profession?" *NCCC Proceedings* 1915:576–90.

In our day, it is ironic to recall Flexner's disdain for the liaison or management function of the caseworker in the light of the growing prominence currently being given to the broker and advocate roles within the caseworker's repertoire of professional roles.

24. *The Milford Conference Report: Social Casework Generic and Specific* (New York: American Association of Social Workers, 1929), p. 27.

Our concern today is with the complementary aspects of the generic and specific issue rather than with their oppositional aspects, so that a generic practice theory may be developed. See Alfred J. Kahn, "Current Conceptualizations of Social Work Practice and Their Implications for Social Work Education," paper delivered to the Annual Program Meeting of the Council on Social Work Education, 18 January 1962. See also Harriett M. Bartlett, "The Generic-Specific Concept in Social Work Education and Practice," in *Issues in American Social Work,* ed. Alfred J. Kahn (New York: Columbia University Press, 1959), pp. 159–90. The author points out that because of the fallacious assumption that there was a common practice, rather than only a common core of knowledge to be transmitted in education, casework failed to analyze practice itself. In this sense, time was lost in extracting generic knowledge and common principles applicable to all fields of practice and in defining specific knowledge to be imparted in specific fields.

and on the medical model by which it was implemented: the concern about cause and function and the diagnostic-functional controversy. Like the generic-specific concept, they are being recast today in new ways. In his 1929 presidential address to the National Conference, Porter Lee, who was also the leader of the Milford Conference and director of the New York School of Social Work, discussed the transformation of social work from cause to function and his concern with the increasing preoccupation with techniques, method, and efficiency which had accompanied the rational organization of services. The achievement of a cause, such as a new way of meeting human need, he said, depends on methodical function to implement it. But social work, although it must develop and administer its service as an efficient, science-based activity, must also retain its capacity to inspire enthusiasm for a cause.[25] In subsequent years some of our most venerated and venerable colleagues have decried casework's over-concern with function, in the sense of method, and its abdication of cause, in the sense of social action.[26]

In retrospect, it is easy to see that one of the unplanned outcomes of adopting the medical model to implement the scientific commitment was to direct attention to presumed individual defect, thus obscuring institutional or social inadequacies. The model tended, in use, to obliterate awareness and concern with social systems and social processes. Contrary to Mary Richmond's own involvement with environmental issues, yet inherent in the model, was a focus on individual processes which all but ignored the social context in which they are embedded.[27] Although social casework, in the thirties and beyond, did attempt to overcome a one-

25. Porter Lee, "Presidential Address," *NCCC Proceedings* 1929:3–20.
26. For example, Bertha Reynolds and Philip Klein. For recent expressions of their views, see, e.g., Bertha Reynolds, *An Uncharted Journey* (New York: Citadel Press, 1963); Philip Klein, *From Philanthropy to Social Welfare* (San Francisco: Jossey-Bass, 1968). (See especially chap. 10, "Casework, the Major Technique," pp. 147–59.)
27. Even the Milford Conference Report had departed from the earlier view of the family as the unit of attention to one "in which the individual, his adjustment and development is accepted as the essential problem." *Milford Conference Report,* chap. 7.

sided approach by conceiving the unit of attention to be person-situation,[28] the model itself implied that the problem or need exists within the individual, who must be understood, treated, and, it is hoped, cured. Thus, try as we might, an inherent bias in the model kept us—over the long run and with exceptions—more concerned with the person than with the situation. A dichotomy was preserved that was unnatural to begin with. Although social theory was not as fully developed as psychological theory in those early years, the profession—again with exceptions—did not explore what social theory was available. Part of this was due to the distortion ground into the conceptual lens by the medical-disease model; but social influences can be recognized as well. World War I had brought the Progressive Era to a close, national concern with social reform diminished, and casework's interest in the environment waned.[29] The postwar twenties saw the beginning of a culturewide interest in the unique inner world of individual experience, while interest in the shared external world and in directed social change faded. The mental hygiene movement was born and spread and engaged caseworkers as spectators or active participants. The new psychiatry of the twenties, especially in child guidance, seemed to offer a promising avenue of scientific thinking and method development.

One wonders whether the cause-function issue, the preoccupation with method, procedures, and function over the twenties, could have somehow paved the way for a view of casework in the thirties which was not to be treatment in the disease sense, but was rather to be a service offered in terms of agency function. Beginning in the early thirties, social workers at the University of Pennsylvania School of Social Work constructed an approach to casework practice in these terms, based on the psychoanalytic concepts of Otto Rank. Rank, in

---

28. See, for example, Gordon Hamilton, *Theory and Practice of Social Casework*, rev. ed. (New York: Columbia University Press, 1951); Ada Eliot Sheffield, *Social Insight in Case Situations* (New York and London: D. Appleton Century Co., 1937), especially chap. 6; see also Florence Sytz, "The Unit of Attention in the Casework Process," *Family* 27 (1946): 135–39.

29. See, for example, Mary Jarrett, "The Psychiatric Thread Running through All Casework," *NCCC Proceedings* 1919.

his disavowal of the mechanistic determinism characteristic of nineteenth-century science, seemed to abjure a science of treatment altogether in favor of developing a philosophy of helping. To Rank's view of the will, of the difficulties in taking help, of the meaning of beginning and ending, the Pennsylvania School added the concept of agency function as the limiting aspect against which the client tested his ability to ask for and to use help. Functional casework relinquished the commitment to science and to scientific knowledge as the base for practice.[30] However, some years later, in 1944, Dr. Jessie Taft suggested that a scientific base and an area of research for functional casework could be found in the study of structure and process; that is, in the helping relationship itself as shaped and controlled by agency function.[31]

Although there were uneasy strains arising from the twenty years of ideological controversy between the two approaches, there was positive consequences as well. Functional casework highlighted the influences exerted by the agency on practice. Today, having the advantage of modern organizational theory, caseworkers conceive of the agency as a social system exhibiting processes that constrain or support helping procedures. No longer viewed as a fixed set of limiting arrangements, the agency is more often seen as an object of change or even as an instrument for change. It is also well known that functional workers explored and developed the use of fees and time dimensions in casework service. Stunning new insights into the nature and importance of the casework relationship were gained, beginning first with the work of Virginia Robinson of the Pennsylvania School.[32] Although Mary Richmond and others after her had stressed the importance of the action of mind on mind, the change came in the sense of identification of worker and client as two similar human beings, with psychological commonalities. With reduction of the difference that had been felt and maintained between

30. Jesse Taft, "The Relation of Function to Process in Social Case Work," *Journal of Social Work Process* 1 (November 1937):3.

31. Jessie Taft, *A Functional Approach to Family Casework* (Philadelphia: University of Pennsylvania Press, 1944), p. 3. See also Kenneth Pray, "A Restatement of the Generic Principles of Social Casework Practice," *NCSW Proceedings* 1947:227–39.

32. Robinson, *Changing Psychology in Social Casework*.

giver and receiver, the worker now stood beside the client, not above him.

During this era of the thirties and its search for scientific ways to help more effectively, many caseworkers were increasingly drawn to the ideas of Freud and the technology of psychoanalysis. The individualizing emphasis in casework derives as much from psychoanalytic thought as from democratic-Judeo-Christian ideas.[33] The beginning experience of these caseworkers in the use of Freudian concepts and techniques and the experience of functional caseworkers in the use of Rankian principles made these years fruitful for the development of a psychological method of helping. During the post-depression years the new principles and techniques were further elaborated and refined by private agency workers. Time and energy for the task had been freed when the private agencies relinquished their traditional relief-giving functions to the new public agencies and became quite clearly agencies for family counseling services. In the war and postwar years, the principles and processes of study, diagnosis, and treatment were again enriched by the shift in emphasis from "id psychology" to ego psychology. Although the depression and the war had served to redirect attention to environmental forces, it was not until the fifties and sixties that an actual reengagement with the social sciences took place. Even now, a socially based counterpoint to the present helping technology has not yet developed. Concepts from the social sciences, although they permit us to describe and define the situation ever more richly, offer only limited prescriptions for intervention. Psychoanalytic theory, in contrast, had not only been rich in insights but had also offered a kit of treatment techniques which met the needs of a professional group oriented to individualized services and seeking a method for providing them.

Here we must pause to recognize the work of Gordon Hamilton. Although her first paper had been delivered to the National Conference in 1923 and her editorials in *Social*

33. Jerome Bruner, for example, states, "Freud's sense of the continuity of the human condition, of the likeness of the human plight has made possible a deeper sense of the brotherhood of man" (Jerome Bruner, "The Freudian Conception of Man and the Continuity of Man," *Daedalus* 87 [1958]:77–84).

Work continued to influence theory and practice into the early sixties, it is her contributions of the thirties and forties and fifties that will be considered here. Building on the scientific orientation which had shaped the earlier approaches, yet going beyond the mechanistic nineteenth-century scientism of Mary Richmond, Hamilton moved casework theory toward a receptive engagement with some of the constructs beginning to emerge in twentieth-century science. In embracing the new ideas in science and absorbing their manifold implications, she formulated many of the concepts and principles on which contemporary casework rests. For example, where we had been intent on understanding reality through the examination of parts or units conceived in linear cause and effect sequences, Hamilton urged the expansion of our thought ways to include the examination of significant wholes which manifest properties not observable in their parts.[34] An organismic approach to casework was defined by Hamilton as the person-in-situation configuration, or as the psychosocial domain of practice. Influenced by the Gestalt emphasis in psychology, she drew attention to the interaction of phenomena as part of a larger whole or field, to a consideration of multiple causality in human events, and to an emphasis on growth, development, and change. Hamilton taught that, in addition to understanding the client's feelings, the worker must engage him as an active participant in change. This was a new conception of the client as acting for himself rather than being acted upon. In these and other ways Gordon Hamilton influenced the humanistic and scientific aspects of social work; she indicated a direction for the ongoing development of casework in our contemporary world that required an altogether new comprehension of reality and a different kind of engagement with it.

---

34. "The whole and its parts are mutually related, the whole being as essential to an understanding of the parts as the parts are to an understanding of the whole"; Gordon Hamilton, "The Underlying Philosophy of Social Casework," *NCSW Proceedings* 1941. See also Hamilton's other addresses in *NCSW Proceedings* 1923, 1931, 1934, 1937, 1943, 1955; her editorial in *Social Work,* January 1962 and her foreword to *Social Perspectives on Behavior,* ed. Herman D. Stein and Richard A. Cloward (Glencoe: Free Press, 1958).

Despite the range of Hamilton's thought and its influence, much of practice seemed still to view person and situation as units which had first to be understood in their separateness and then connected and related by bridging concepts not yet discovered. Perhaps this continuing difficulty derived in part from life experience. Our language, cultural habits of thought, and schooling prepared us for perceiving and conceiving the world in linear terms and resulted in a trained incapacity for viewing it as organized complexity in systemic terms. Even where we could see configurations, our only mode for intervention was based on linearity. On another level, the difficulty may have derived from the understandable human reluctance to relinquish the discreteness of organism from environment. Having been removed from our central position in the universe by Copernicus and on earth by Darwin, we resist a view in which we seem to fade into the milieu altogether, particularly since Western thought has long separated man from the rest of nature. There is also the fact that work with intrapsychic problems has appeared to offer more dignity and gratification to the worker than has dealing with the more difficult and less tractable problems of outer reality. Perhaps the major impediment to effecting change in professional action, in keeping with Hamilton's advanced thought, lay in the practice model itself and its underlying assumptions. The model appeared to give priority to understanding the individual, and environment was viewed as a linear appendage. Thus entrenched modes of thinking and acting were not sufficiently altered to utilize newer knowledge and to deal with the needs, problems, and strivings of contemporary life. Today's tentative explorations of perspectives from general system theory offer promise of expanding and enriching the unit of attention, not only conceptually but for action as well.[35]

35. Sister Mary Paul Janchill, "Systems Concepts in Casework Theory and Practice," *Social Casework* 50 (February 1969):74–82; Carel B. Germain, "Social Study: Past and Future," *Social Casework* 49 (July 1968): 403–9; Roy R. Grinker et al., *Psychiatric Social Work: A Transactional Case Book* (New York: Basic Books, 1961); Donald E. Lathrope, "Use of Social Science in Social Work Practice: Social Systems," *Trends in Social Work Practice and Knowledge* (New York: National Association of Social

What seems to have happened in areas of practice during recent decades was a slow conversion of the scientific commitment into an ideological one, in which the commitment served to justify a particular stance, to express a preferred position. As ideology, the scientific commitment then tended to preserve the traditional perspective on phenomena quite independently of the validity or invalidity of the perspective. On the one hand, an ideological use of the commitment may have supported the authority and prestige of those associated with the traditional, invoking closure to theoretic exploration and innovation. On the other hand, ideology appears to have advanced professionalization, group cohesiveness and increased skill in techniques.

In any case, embracing the psychotherapeutic infusion of the medical model as the most promising means of fulfilling the scientific commitment during the thirties and beyond did have some negative consequences. It created the perplexing problem of specifying the scope and distinguishing features of social casework and resulted in tendencies which seem to have contributed to our present crisis state. For example, in addition to the tendency to define problems largely in personality terms, emphasis was placed on transference aspects of relationship, while less attention was given to cultural and social influences on communication. High value was accorded to the client's motivation, verbal skills, and interest in introspection—so that the new psychological procedures were often less effective with clients having problems that were socially perceived rather than self-perceived, or clients whose own expectations for help were not understood or met. Although the procedures were effective with particular groups of self-selected clients, those whose personal or cultural characteristics did not coincide with the requirements of the practice model and its service arrangements tended to be excluded.

Workers, 1966); Gordon A. Hearn, ed., *The General Systems Approach: Contributions toward a Holistic Conception of Social Work* (New York: Council on Social Work Education, 1968). These newer attempts build on earlier efforts to utilize systems theory. See Gordon A. Hearn, *Theory Building in Social Work* (Toronto: University of Toronto Press, 1959); Werner A. Lutz, *Concepts and Principles Underlying Social Work Practice,* Social Work Practice in Medical Care and Rehabilitation Settings, monograph 3 (New York: National Association of Social Workers, 1958).

The problems have admittedly been stated in their extreme form, and it is recognized that ways to overcome them have been constantly sought by casework practitioners, theorists, and educators.[36] Increasingly, the sixties saw the introduction of practice innovations including family treatment, use of group methods, planned brief treatment, therapeutic milieu approaches, and experimentation with a variety of organizational arrangements and new theoretical systems. These have culminated in some of the conceptual approaches to practice presented in this volume. Nevertheless, the problems have been thrown into bold relief to highlight the uneven development as well as the resistances and confusions that arise because the new approaches are felt by some to lack fit with the dominant practice model. This is because they may require different hypotheses and assumptions concerning the object of help, the role of the helper, the arena of help, and the nature of the helping processes; so their objectives and techniques cannot be derived from the traditional approach to practice.[37]

There were also positive consequences in the quest for ways to make help more effective by making it more scientific. The decades of the thirties and forties saw much productive work go forward in the classification of treatment measures. Some classifications were based on the dynamics of the procedures and others were based on goals and

---

36. Charlotte Towle's efforts were among the most prominent. For example, in an address before the National Conference in 1941 she said, "The worker, who staunchly maintains that he can help only the person who can use a certain kind of relationship, frequently is saying that he can relate himself only to that individual who least needs help. . . . While this stand may be reconciled with the function of some agencies, it cannot be reconciled with our profession's purpose as a whole." (Charlotte Towle, "Underlying Skills of Casework Today," *NCSW Proceedings* 1941:254–66.) In 1946 Miss Towle wrote, "We know also that unmodifiable adverse social circumstances are decisive and that the tender ministrations of an understanding relationship cannot compensate for basic environmental lacks, meager services, and restrictive agency policies." (Charlotte Towle, "Social Casework in Modern Society," *Social Service Review* 20 [June 1946]:165–79.)

37. Morris S. Schwartz and Charlotte Green Schwartz, *Social Approaches to Mental Patient Care* (New York: Columbia University Press, 1964). See especially chap. 6, "Broadening the Conceptions of Help," pp. 84–91.

method.[38] The sweep of treatment typologies reflects many of the historical changes and accretions in the knowledge base and theoretical perspectives. All schemes dichotomize the direct and indirect, that is, the psychological and environmental modes; yet the classification constructed by Lucille N. Austin recognized explicitly that positive experiences both in the transference and in real life situations bring about better adaptations and thus change.[39] In addition to

---

38. Grete L. Bibring, "Psychiatry and Social Work," *Journal of Social Casework* 28 (June 1947):203–10; Florence Hollis, "The Techniques of Casework," *Journal of Social Casework* 30 (June 1949):235–44. These are classifications based on the dynamics of treatment means. For typologies based on goals and method, see Eleanor Cockerill et al., "A Conceptual Framework for Social Casework," mimeographed (Pittsburgh: University of Pittsburgh School of Social Work, 1952); Fern Lowry, "The Client's Needs as the Basis for Differential Approach in Casework Treatment," in *The Differential Approach in Casework Treatment* (New York: Family Welfare Association of America, 1936), pp. 1–13; Louis Lehrman, "Science, Art and Social Casework," mimeographed (Pittsburgh: University of Pittsburgh School of Social Work, 1957); *Scope and Methods of the Family Service Agency*, Report of the Committee on Methods and Scope (New York: Family Service Association of America, 1953); *Methods and Process in Social Casework*, Report of a Staff Committee, Community Service Society of New York (New York: Family Service Association of America, 1958).

Classifications based on the dynamic nature of the treatment procedures had a profound influence on all schemes, since they were incorporated into those that were differently based on goal and methods. Indeed, their delineation of techniques derived from psychoanalytic procedures led to types of treatment based on differing levels or depths ultimately leading, it was then thought, to unconscious content. By the fifties there was healthy recognition of the limitation of content to conscious and preconscious material. All schemes acknowledged the person-situation as the unit of attention in varying degrees of specificity. Several were concerned with family interaction as a backdrop for the individual and some were frankly concerned only with the individual as a patient. A few included the differential management of relationship as a dimension in each method. Problem classifications, or diagnostic typologies, are implicit in some of the treatment classifications insofar as criteria for selection include specification of the problem or of the personality type or of the situation for which the method is deemed suitable.

39. Lucille N. Austin, "Trends in Differential Treatment in Social Casework," *Journal of Social Casework* 29 (June 1948):203–11; Lucille N. Austin, "Social Caseworkers," *American Journal of Orthopsychiatry* 26 (1956):47–57.

social therapy as a separate method. Austin considered appropriate activity in the environment to be a technique within each of the several submethods of psychotherapy. Such activity is conceptualized as the worker's fostering experiences in the life situation or structuring the situation in ways that will promote growth or complete the maturation process. This trenchant concept is being opened up further today in terms of sublimation, identification, and natural life processes which lead to new definitions of problems, objectives, and tasks.[40]

Valuable efforts were made in these decades to construct diagnostic classifications, seemingly a more difficult task and one of ongoing importance.[41] By the fifties, Lilian Ripple and Ernestina Alexander developed a schematic classification related to treatment implications in gross terms for many areas of practice, although their scheme had not actually been designed for that purpose.[42] It emerged from their much larger research project investigating the relationships (in family agencies) between the client's capacity, motivation, and opportunity and his continuance in treatment. Presenting problems appeared to be intervening variables that required classification.

40. Louise Bandler, "Some Casework Aspects of Ego Growth Through Sublimation," and Bernard Bandler, "The Concept of Ego-Supportive Psychotherapy"; both articles appear in *Ego Oriented Casework*, ed. Howard Parad (New York: Family Service Association of America, 1963); Eunice F. Allan, "The Super Ego in Ego-Supportive Casework Treatment," *Smith College Studies in Social Work* 33 (June 1963).
41. Ernest Greenwood, "Social Science and Social Work: A Theory of Their Relationship," *Social Service Review* 29 (March 1955):20–23; Samuel Finestone, "Issues Involved in Developing Diagnostic Classifications for Casework," *Casework Papers, 1960, from the National Conference on Social Welfare* (New York: Family Service Association of America, 1960); Lola G. Selby, "Typologies for Caseworkers: Some Considerations and Problems," *Social Service Review* 32 (1958):341–49.
42. Lilian Ripple and Ernestina Alexander, "Motivation, Capacity and Opportunity as Related to the Use of Casework Service: Nature of the Client's Problem," *Social Service Review* 30 (March 1956):38–54. Separate classifications of problems specific to particular fields of practice have also been developed. See, for example, Esther Glickman, *Child Placement through Clinically Oriented Casework* (New York: Columbia University Press, 1957); Jeannette Regensburg, "Psychoanalytic Contributions to Casework Treatment of Marital Problems," *Social Casework* 35 (December 1954).

From the standpoint of building scientific knowledge, many casework theorists believe there is need for a classification of helping measures matched to a problem classification so that needs and tasks are linked. Such articulated schemes might provide the opportunity to validate helping procedures in relation to assessment, planning, and predicted outcomes, and to generate new techniques and interventive modes. They might increase the effectiveness and rapidity of help by allowing the worker to structure help in clearly defined steps and to gear client and worker tasks to a diagnostically based sequence of objectives. In recent years, casework accomplished a degree of matching on the level of clinical types in work with clients manifesting anxiety hysteria, character disorder, depression, schizophrenia, retardation, etc. Limitations in these schemes arise because they do not account for social and cultural variability, or for biological variability in terms of growth and decline, illness, or disability.

Beginning somewhat before these classification attempts, but also continuing into the present with new vigor, was the work of conceptualizing the domain of practice. The first edition of Hamilton's book appeared in 1940. In the past decade three additional conceptualizations have appeared. In 1957 Helen Harris Perlman published *Casework: A Problem-solving Process*.[43] Florence Hollis's book *Casework: A Psychosocial Therapy*[44] appeared in 1964, and Ruth Smalley's work *Theory for Social Work Practice*[45] in 1967. The many and varied contributions to casework theory and practice made by these distinguished leaders are apparent in their symposium papers.[46]

---

43. Helen Harris Perlman, *Social Casework: A Problem-solving Process* (Chicago: University of Chicago Press, 1957).
44. Florence Hollis, *Casework: A Psychosocial Therapy* (New York: Random House, 1964).
45. Ruth Elizabeth Smalley, *Theory for Social Work Practice* (New York: Columbia University Press, 1967).
46. Hollis's work represents diagnostic theory and practice, Smalley's is the most recently formulated presentation of the functional approach to casework, and Perlman's eclectic approach attempts to blend the theoretical foundations of the diagnostic and functional positions into a common base.

In constructing the scientific base of substantive knowledge during the fifties there was a host of contributions in the use of ego psychology,[47] social science,[48] family concepts,[49] and specific accretions from fields of practice[50] and from casework research.[51] Research has been urged upon us from the earliest years[52] and has had a reciprocal relationship to the scientific commitment, arising from the commitment and in turn shaping it. As practiced by social caseworkers, re-

47. Annette Garrett, "Modern Casework: The Contribution of Ego Psychology," *Ego Psychology and Dynamic Casework*, ed. Howard J. Parad (New York: Family Service Association of America, 1958). Isobel Stamm, "Ego Psychology in the Emerging Theoretical Base of Casework," *Issues in American Social Work*, ed. Alfred J. Kahn (New York: Columbia University Press, 1959), pp. 80–109. Bernece K. Simon, "Relationship between Theory and Practice in Social Casework: 1. Ego Assessment, 2. Ego-Supportive Casework Treatment," Social Work Practice in Medical Care and Rehabilitation Settings, monograph 4 (New York: National Association of Social Workers, 1960).

48. For example, Herman Stein, "The Concept of the Social Environment in Social Work Practice," *Smith College Studies in Social Work* 30 (1960):187–210; Otto Pollak, *Integrating Social Science and Psychoanalytic Concepts* (New York: Russell Sage Foundation, 1956).

49. For example, Frances Scherz, "What Is Family-Centered Casework?" *Social Casework* 34 (October 1953):343–49.

50. For examples in the field of corrections, see Eliot Studt, "An Outline for Study of Social Authority Factors in Casework," *Social Casework* 35 (June 1954):231–38; Harris B. Peck and Virginia Bellsmith, *Treatment of the Delinquent Adolescent* (New York: Family Service Association of America, 1954); in the field of health services, Lydia Rapoport, "Work with Families in Crisis: An Exploration in Preventive Intervention," *Social Work* 7 (1962):48–56; Howard J. Parad, "Preventive Casework: Problems and Implications," in *The Social Welfare Forum, 1961*, Papers from the National Conference on Social Welfare (New York: Columbia University Press, 1961); in the field of child guidance, Yonata Feldman, "A Casework Approach toward Understanding Parents of Emotionally Disturbed Children," *Social Work* 3 (July 1958):23–29; in the development of "reaching out" as a concept, Alice Overton, "Aggressive Casework," *Journal of Social Work* (July 1952).

51. See Henry Maas, ed., *Five Fields of Social Service* (New York: National Association of Social Workers, 1966), for reports of research bearing upon casework theory and practice, and Mary E. Macdonald, "Social Work Research: A Perspective," in *Social Work Research*, ed. Norman A. Polansky (Chicago: Chicago University Press, 1960).

52. See, for example, Mary Jarrett, "The Need for Research in Social Casework by Experienced Social Workers Who Are Themselves Doing the Casework," *Journal of Social Forces* 11 (May 1925).

search is the clearest, and perhaps even the only area of casework directly accessible to the experimental method of science. Its potential contribution to the scientific knowledge base is vast and in the sixties we have had glimpses of its promise. Charlotte Towle, in her teaching and writing, made substantive contributions in several areas of knowledge. Earlier she had helped lead the way in the use of analytic concepts and in later years she directed attention to other important areas.[53]

For forty years the ideological tensions between cause and function have continued and Charlotte Towle addressed the issue in 1961. In a classic paper she said that generic social work, consideration of the individual within his social context, and the adequate meeting of needs through the close interrelations of social movements were problems "that had defied solution and must all become causes in a near tomorrow."[54]

That "near tomorrow" is already today, and may indeed be already yesterday, for the problems Towle identified have been overtaken by others still more intransigent. Thinking and feeling human beings are appalled by the absurdities which now distort and destroy men's lives. Some retreat into passivity or alienation. Others slip into delinquency, illness,

---

53. In a paper read before the National Conference in 1940, Charlotte Towle spoke of the need for social casework to be implemented with a social-research point of view. ("Some Basic Principles of Social Research in Social Casework," *NCSW Proceedings* 1940.) Six years later she wrote of casework's historical struggle for an orderly way of thinking which would approximate the scientific method, that is, study-diagnosis-treatment, adding that diagnostic hypotheses must be tested against treatment success, and underscored the part played by worker-bias in perception, thought, and action. (Towle, "Social Casework in Modern Society.") Her contributions to social work education in class and field are to be found in *The Learner in Education for the Professions* (Chicago: University of Chicago Press, 1954); "The Classroom Teacher as Practitioner," *Social Service Review* 22 (September 1948); "The Contribution of Education for Social Casework to Practice," *Social Casework* 31 (October 1950). Other contributions include: "Underlying Skills of Casework Today," *Social Service Review* 15 (1941):456–71; "Factors in Treatment," *Proceedings National Conference on Social Welfare, 1936;* rev. ed. (New York: National Association of Social Workers, 1957).
54. Charlotte Towle, "Social Work: Cause and Function, 1961," *Social Casework* 42 (October 1961):385–96.

or other forms of deviance. All stand in jeopardy of losing meaningful connections with others and with the world of nature whose qualities support and refresh human nature. A sense of receding autonomy and a flawed identity in a mass society are sources of chronic stress to countless numbers. In the constantly changing conditions of a technological society, the arena for help may no longer be man against himself in intrapsychic terms but man against malevolent forces and irrationalities in his environment. Carol Meyer has said that if social casework is to assume its potential role in such a society it must expand its knowledge base—reexamine its structural arrangements and its helping principles so that it can intervene in ways which take account of the unity of personality and society.[55] The humanization of our superurban life becomes the cause and the range of casework roles and tasks, and the flexibility of agency arrangements, become the function. This indeed could well be the union of cause and function envisaged by Charlotte Towle for that "near tomorrow" which is today.

Judging from the professional distress reflected in our literature at our conferences, and in our graduate schools, casework might seem instead to be facing its end, doomed by the contingencies of its past. The scientific commitment had seemed to promise social casework a secure position in the profession. Instead, our commitment has given us no protection against accusations of obsolescence in this most scientific of times. According to some it has not even afforded a base for social significance in this period of surging change. What has led us to this crisis state when we have been so devotedly committed to science, to society's instrument for unending progress and mastery over human problems?

My own notions about the crisis are these: Following upon our commitment in the ending years of the last century, science and the philosophy of science moved on in new ways and new directions and with new perspectives, whereas social casework remained committed to a view of science and the

---

55. Carol Meyer, "Casework in a Changing Society," in *National Conference on Social Welfare, Social Work Practice* (New York: Columbia University Press, 1966), pp. 3–19.

scientific method that became outmoded both in the light of science itself and of the changing human condition. Most would agree that casework as a scientific art cannot be patterned on the method of the sciences. Yet it can and does construct metaphors based on scientific concepts and in doing so must utilize new concepts and themes in science and not those no longer acceptable to science itself.

What comes to the fore in the new science is growth, change, development—including purposeful, directed change by man himself in which the potential for innovation poses new risks and new responsibilities.[56] Today's science deals with organized complexity at all levels and involves concepts alien to the older mechanistic science. Nineteenth-century scientific thought, in which casework's commitment and practice model are rooted, did not deal with problems of growth, change, and potentiality, with systems in mutual interaction, and with man as inseparable from environment in an ecological frame of reference. Both modern science and modern art seek to eliminate the dichotomy of object and space, of person and situation. What have been viewed as objects discrete from space are now described in terms of relationships, patterns, and transactions. This holds also for a professional practice which is both a science and an art.

Rene Dubos, the eminent biologist, has stated that the oversimplified models of orthodox science are not appropriate for understanding the complex nature of the cohesive forces which maintain man in an integrated state physically, psychologically, and socially within his ecological environment.[57] Properties and activities associated with living processes are expressions of the interplay of systems rather than of the characteristics of individual parts. To be in accord with the modern scientific viewpoint, then, requires that casework view and handle phenomena in terms of directions, flow, action, and transaction rather than in terms of cause. This means a concern with adaptation, growth, progressive forces, and purposive activity. What is suggested is

56. Peter Drucker, *Landmarks of Tomorrow* (New York: Harper & Row, 1959; paperback edition, 1963), p. 15.
57. Rene Dubos, "Science and Man's Nature," *Daedalus* 94 (Winter 1965):223–44.

more in the nature of a scientific orientation to practice than
the application of a procrustean scientific method or model.
A modern scientific orientation supports attitudes favoring
multiple bases for defining problems, a variety of helping
modes, and an array of realistic objectives which pose tasks
not only for the worker but for the client. Finestone has
stated that such an orientation for social casework is com-
prised of (1) attitudes favoring scientific inquiry, including
concern for evidence and for reliable and valid inference;
(2) facility in the discipline of scientific inquiry, including
systematic and logical thinking; (3) ability to move between
the concrete and the abstract, relating empirical data and
general theory; (4) ability to link values of human welfare to
the processes of scientific inquiry.[58] Plainly this is an open
system of thought. It does not support reliance on any one
approach to understanding and responsible action. The
Massachusetts Institute of Technology physicist Martin
Deutsch speaks cogently of the danger that lies in fixity. "If
one is too strongly attached to one's preconceived model, one
will of necessity miss all radical discoveries. It is amazing to
what degree one may fail to register mentally an observation
which does not fit the initial image. On the other hand, if
one is too open-minded and pursues every hitherto unknown
phenomenon, one is almost certain to lose one's self in
trivia."[59]

A degree of conservatism does serve to protect a discipline
against faddism. Perhaps this component is better described
as a scientific caution calling for prediction of the probable
outcomes of professional action and careful assessment of
actual outcomes. Thus creativity and innovation can be freed
while the hazards of trivia and faddism are minimized. Charlotte Towle wrote of the special problems in this: The caseworker "cannot be a free lance worker, experimenting at will
and departing from the established order as inspiration
prompts him. His freedoms will always be freedoms within
rigid limits set by his responsibility for human beings im-

58. Samuel Finestone, "The Scientific Component in the Casework Field
Curriculum," *Social Casework* 36 (May 1955):195–202.
59. Martin Deutsch, "Evidence and Inference in Nuclear Research," in
Evidence and Inference, ed. Daniel Lerner (Glencoe: Free Press, 1958),
p. 102.

mediately under his care or tutelage."[60] There are also other limitations, in the application of scientific ideas to a humanistic profession, having to do with the indeterminacy and unpredictability of subject matter, the unreliability of man himself as an observational instrument, the need for professional action before verified knowledge has been developed, and the presence of ethical values which must determine the area of professional concern and the objectives to be pursued.

It is clear that social casework is struggling to develop a greater flexibility in order to meet a wider range of needs across a wider variety of people and situations. That seven approaches to practice, with differing degrees of difference among them, can be presented in this symposium is proof In each approach the problem is defined differently and the helping processes are applied in different ways toward different tasks and objectives. Several approaches borrow concepts from the traditional model but combine them in novel ways for new principles and techniques. Others begin from new premises, build on different theoretical bases, and utilize different streams of knowledge. Any two of the differing approaches might well be deemed incompatible, yet together they form a consortium of practice approaches for casework compatible with ideas and images current in the humanities and sciences. Eventually the varied approaches might even attain harmony on both empirical and theoretical grounds under some set of overarching constructs—for example, those of general system theory. In any case, Kuhn states that science progresses not by simple accretions of knowledge but through the conflict of opposing theories.[61] He thus echoes Whitehead's belief that opportunity and not disaster inheres in the clash of ideas. It is hoped, then, that casework will avoid premature exclusion of variant approaches or too hasty closure on theoretical and empirical developments. Evolving models require not only a social circle within the profession which is prepared to reexamine the presumed fixity and rightness of what we do but.also a social environment favorable to innovation in meeting new problems and requirements. Both conditions seem to be met: Our younger mem-

---

60. Towle, *Learner in Education for the Professions,* p. 234.
61. Kuhn, *Structure of Scientific Revolutions.*

bers not only are receptive but are asking for change; our scholars are committed to the development of new knowledge and the exploration of ideas; the most talented of our practitioners are courageously experimenting; and the contemporary climate in the larger society demands creativity and innovation in the social services.

We have been scanning the past for its uses and the future for its inklings. Whatever the actuality of our historical past might have been, the question is not whether the various approaches supplant the dominant practice model, but whether we can perceive and develop what it is that each will add to the caseworker's opportunities for service within changing social realities which forever create new congeries of "common human needs."

If Charlotte Towle were speaking, I think she might urge us to search together for new ways to serve in the face of ceaseless and unexpected change—having the courage to endure risk and uncertainty, the tolerance to examine new ideas, the caution to evaluate innovations carefully, the willingess to search out and encourage creativity, and the wisdom to retain and renew the pragmatically useful from our past. She herself said, "This is a time for the social work profession to have faith in its cause, to reaffirm its humanistic values, and to work positively for conditions of life that will promote man's humanity to man . . . the union of cause and function within social work will be a natural outgrowth of the progressive union of science and humanism."[62]

---

62. Towle, "Cause and Function."

2 | The Psychosocial Approach to the Practice of Casework

Florence Hollis

GENERAL CHARACTERISTICS

"When we think of fundamental concepts we are inclined to imagine a static practice. The truth is that casework concepts are dynamic. They change, grow and develop as they are shaped by new experience and knowledge." Thus Gordon Hamilton began her article "Basic Concepts in Social Casework,"[1] which in 1937 delineated the major outlines of an approach to casework which later came to be called the "diagnostic" school of thought. In these sentences Miss Hamilton described one of the major characteristics of the psychosocial approach—that it is an open system of thought which constantly changes and grows as new data become available and as new propositions, concepts, hypotheses, and theories emerge.

In a later article, "The Underlying Philosophy of Social Casework" (1941),[2] Hamilton described the major differences as she saw them between the point of view for which she was the major spokesman and the functional approach. From this article the term "diagnostic" emerged. In her own writings —and this was also true of the writings of others who shared her views—Hamilton used such terms as the "organismic" approach, the "differential treatment" approach, and the "psychosocial" approach. Recently the last term has become the preferred one because it symbolizes the main components of this point of view more fully than the others do, though still imperfectly.

The distinguishing premises of psychosocial casework are given in these two articles by Hamilton, but the system of thought has continued "to change and grow." I will picture it as it exists some thirty years later.

Today the psychosocial view is essentially a system theory approach to casework. The major system to which diagnosis and treatment are addressed is the person-in-situation gestalt or configuration. That is to say, to be understood, the person

Florence Hollis is professor of social work, Columbia University School of Social Work, New York.

1. Gordon Hamilton, "Basic Concepts in Social Casework," *Family* 18 (July 1937):147.

2. Gordon Hamilton, "The Underlying Philosophy of Social Casework," *Family* 23 (July 1941):139–48.

to be helped—or treated, if you prefer—must be seen in the context of his interactions or transactions with the external world; and the segment of the external world with which he is in close interaction must also be understood. This may be his family or particular members of it, his social group, his educational milieu, his employment milieu, or some other social system of which he is a part. At times the family system itself is seen as "the client." It has been recognized throughout that changes in one part of the person-in-situation configuration bring changes in other parts and that interchanges between the various components are continuously in process, with mutual modifications occurring as a moving equilibrium is—sometimes precariously—maintained. The organismic view of the individual is, of course, a systems formulation. The frame of reference found most useful for understanding the dynamics of the individual's personality system in the psychosocial approach is Freudian personality theory, with emphasis upon the ego and its adaptive capacities.

A second emphasis of the psychosocial approach is that treatment must be differentiated according to the need of the client. This requires that the worker attempt to understand the client's need and respond to him in an individualized way according to his understanding of that need. "Need" as met in social work is expressed as a social dilemma—a discrepancy in interadaptation between the person and the others with whom he is associated or between the person, or family, and the social resources which normally permit the individual to function with a reasonable degree of comfort and satisfaction. When such discrepancies exist we believe it is necessary to locate the most salient multiple interacting factors contributing to discomfort. Discomfort may derive either from inadequacies in personal functioning or from a deficient or harmful social situation, or from varying degrees of both. We believe that defining these factors is necessary for the worker to respond to the client in ways most likely to meet his individualized needs. This involves fact gathering and a professional opinion called diagnosis or assessment.

Casework treatment is conceptualized as a blend of processes directed as diagnostically indicated toward modification in the person or his social or interpersonal environment or both, and of the exchanges between them. For the most part these processes consist of communications among the client or clients, the worker, and significant others, and of the provision of certain concrete services. Contacts may be with an individual, several individuals, or a family, or with nonfamily groups. These communications can be classified, and progress has been made in developing generalizations about the relationship between certain blends of them and the worker's diagnostic understanding of the person-situation gestalt. The objective of treatment may be to enable change to occur in the individual(s) or in the situation or in both. Emphasis in work with the individual himself is placed upon the client's developing understanding of his situation, of significant others, and of himself, upon the support he may secure in an accepting relationship, upon the general effect of his relationships with the worker, upon his adaptive capacities, and on the relief he may feel from expressing his fears, anxieties, and hostilities in treatment interviews. Advice and guidance, although sometimes used, on the whole play a minor role. It is assumed that personality change and growth can occur in response to casework treatment and that environmental changes brought about by treatment can facilitate adaptation.

This point of view emphasizes the nature of the relationship between client and worker which develops from these verbal and nonverbal communications. It is assumed that in many cases the nature of this relationship is a major determinant of the degree to which the client is helped.

Among the values stressed in the psychosocial approach are: (1) The worker must accept the client by having a commitment to his welfare, caring about him, and respecting him. Optimally this includes feelings of warmth for him. (2) The relationship must be "other-centered," with the worker giving precedence to the client's needs. (3) Insofar as possible the worker must understand the client with scientific objectivity, removing personal bias in evalution and response. (4) The worker must recognize the client's right to make his own decisions and the value of encouraging his self-directiveness. (5) The worker must recognize the interdependence of his client and others and realize that there may be times when the client's self-direction may need to be limited to protect others or himself from harm.

An underlying premise of this approach is that casework is both art and science. Intuitive insights and spontaneity are combined with continuous effort to develop and systematize knowledge and understanding of objective truths about man and his social expressions, relationships, and organizations.

It is assumed that man is not only acted upon but is capable of spontaneous activity; that he has some measure of control over his own fate both by adapting to and by changing his external realities; and that the caseworker can help in this. It is also assumed that adults can still change and develop toward fuller self-realization. The greater the client's active involvement in the change process the greater his mastery of the interadaption process is likely to be.

Origins of this Approach

The psychosocial approach is often traced to Mary Richmond's formulations. However, the approach changed drastically as it was influenced by the socioeconomic events of the twenties and thirties, as well as by the growth of personality and social theory. Freudian theory began to feed into this point of view about 1926. Early contributors were Marion Kenworthy of the New York School of Social Work, Betsey Libbey of the Family Society of Philadelphia, who gave leadership through agency and institute teaching; and Gordon Hamilton, teacher, theorist, and writer. Bertha Reynolds, Charlotte Towle, Florence Day, Fern Lowry, Lucille Austin, Annette Garrett, and many others contributed in the mid-thirties and later. The psychosocial view originated on the east coast, with Smith and the New York School taking the lead; selected psychiatric clinics and family agencies in Boston, New York, and Philadelphia contributed from practice. With migration of personnel and ideas westward it gradually spread over the country, influenced in part by the presence of psychoanalytically trained psychiatrists, who not only contributed personality theory but influenced treatment objectives and methods. The differentiation between psychoanalysis and casework became an important theme in the late forties, with Bibring and Austin, in particular, adding to the work already noted.

BEHAVIORAL SCIENCE FOUNDATION

The psychosocial approach has drawn from many sources. First, of course, there has been a constant flow of material from practice. Much of this consisted of reports on individual cases or small groups of cases. Practice theory was constructed on this, largely by casework teachers. Some master's theses made contributions, and there were occasional agency-based studies. Doctoral dissertations did not make much of a contribution until the early fifties. Better designed and implemented studies became more numerous in the fifties, and since then the flow of both agency- and school-based work has been steady.

As was already noted, psychoanalysis is the major system of personality theory drawn upon. Sigmund Freud, Abraham, Anna Freud, Alexander, French, Aichorn, Federn, Kardiner and, more recently, Erikson, Hartmann, Kris, and Rapaport are among the many names that come to mind, though dozens of other analysts had great influence as writers, agency consultants, or classroom and clinical teachers.

Among psychologists, Piaget's writings have been prominent. Lewin has contributed; Dollard and Allport have been followed with interest. The work of Henry Murray and his associates has been drawn on, and ideas from Gestalt psychology have been incorporated.

Social science has also exerted a great influence. Knowledge of the family has been taken from many sources and social influences on child rearing and studies of marital and sexual behavior have been of special interest. Cultural anthropology has been used, especially as it bears upon the development of personality and the influence of culture on personality. Relationships between emotional and behavioral disturbance and cultural factors, and the effects of different patterns of child rearing, have contributed. Ethnic and nationality differences have long been considered important. In the last decade, material on the many ramifications of social class and of race has been given much attention. Concepts of role behavior have been incorporated to varying degrees, as have data concerning small group behavior.

Beginning with the work of Werner Lutz,[3] which introduced Parsonian concepts to the field, there has been growing interest in writings about system theory. Many system concepts very aptly express ideas which have been intrinsic to the psychosocial approach but have not been as well conceptualized and interrelated as they can be by the use of the system approach. Interest is growing in communication theory.

THE INITIAL PHASE

The length of the "initial phase" of treatment varies with the length of treatment itself. In planned very short term work it may consist of only the first part of a single interview; where the total treatment consists of two or three interviews, it may be the entire first interview. When treatment is planned for a substantial period, the first three to five interviews constitute the "initial phase." This phase includes a number of components. Although some of these components usually precede others, they do not constitute an ordered sequence. Whether they go on simultaneously or in sequence is determined by the client's need and the worker's judgment.

The principal tasks during this initial phase include: (a) arriving at an understanding with the client of why the contact is taking place, (b) establishing a relationship with the client which will enable him to use the worker's help, (c) engaging the client in treatment, (d) beginning treatment itself, and (e) gathering the information needed for the psychosocial diagnosis and the guidance of treatment.

Understanding of Reasons for Contact

When the client himself applies for service it is simple to ask why he has come. Unless his reply shows that he has completely misunderstood the agency's function, the interview can proceed to further exploration of what he sees as his problem. If it does show a misunderstanding, or the matter is ambiguous, the worker will need to explain the agency services to the client or gain more information about his

3. Werner Lutz, *Concepts and Principles Underlying Casework Practice* (Washington, D.C.: National Association of Social Workers, 1956).

problem in order either to proceed with the contact or to refer him elsewhere.

When referral or application is made by someone other than the client being interviewed, there must be both an interview with the referring person and an interview with the client. In the first, the worker ascertains that there appears to be a problem that falls within the function of the agency (or the service offered by the individual practitioner, in the case of private practice); he then asks the referring person to communicate his concern to the potential client and ask him to make an appointment, or does so himself. In either case the worker must then clarify with the client himself whether or not he desires contact with the agency. This usually involves discussion of the reason seen by the referring person, sufficient information about the agency's service to help the client understand its potential use to him, and clarification of whether the client acquiesces with the referral, rejects it, or describes his problem in some other way which still constitutes a basis for continuing the contact.

In situations where the worker believes that casework service is needed even though the client does not recognize the need, a decision must be made as to how far the worker will go in trying to persuade the client to continue contact. This will vary with the agency's definition of its function, with the nature of the client's problem (especially the degree to which it involves the need for protection of the client himself, of others in the family, or of the community), and with the extent to which the worker believes he can be helpful. In recent years there has been an increased sense of responsibility for reaching people, especially those in the multi-problem group (many of whom are also in poverty), who do not seek or easily accept casework service, even though a caseworker could help with their problems. In these circumstances it is particularly important that the worker give the client a clear explanation of the reason for his intruding upon the client's time.

Establishing a Relationship

Simultaneously with this first step comes the second task, establishing a relationship which will enable the client to use the worker's help. Two ingredients are foremost in this at the very beginning—the client's trust in the worker's competence and his trust in the worker's goodwill.[4] The client's perception of the latter is strongly dependent upon the worker's true interest in helping him, his objectivity, his warmth, and his acceptance of the client and respect for him. The worker's way of greeting the client, his tone of voice, facial expression, and posture, as well as his verbal expression and the actual content of his communications, will all contribute to the client's perception of his goodwill. The worker's competence will have to be demonstrated by communications that convey his understanding of the client's needs and feelings, by the skill with which he enables the client to communicate, by his knowledge of resources when these are involved, and by the appropriateness of any treatment steps he takes in the first and several succeeding interviews.

Although the worker's goodwill and competence are *necessary* for the creation of a sound working relationship between client and worker they are not *sufficient* to create it. The client also brings attitudes and preconceptions. He may have had specific experiences with social workers which shape his anticipations and responses. What he has heard from friends and relatives will affect him. The very situation of dependence in having to ask for help of any kind puts people on guard. There is fear of domination or manipulation, fear that a price will have to be paid for accepting help, fear of being considered inferior. Factors of class and race may intensify these feelings. In addition, specific transference reactions are often activated by the dependent situation. Awareness by the worker of the possibility of these reactions is necessary if they are gradually to be replaced by mutual trust. In words and acts the worker must demonstrate his respect for the client's rights and his desire to enhance the client's self-direction rather than to impinge upon it. Often the problem must be brought into the open and specifically discussed.

---

4. Norman Polansky and Jacob Kounin, "Client Reactions to Initial Interviews: A Field Study," *Human Relations* 9 (1956):237–64.

Engaging the Client in Treatment

The process of engaging the client in treatment may be simple or quite complicated. It always has two primary aspects—motivation and resistance. These may both be high at the same time. Motivation has to do with how much the client wants to change and how willing he is to contribute to bringing about change. This in turn is related initially to how much discomfort the client feels in the situation which brought him to the agency, and to how much optimism he has about the possibility of favorable change. Too much discomfort may bring such a sense of helplessness that there is little hope, and hence apathy and weak motivation. Too little discomfort gives little reason for interest in change. One of the tasks of the initial period may be helping the client to arrive at a degree of discomfort and hope favorable to motivation.[5] If the client is too anxious or too discouraged, the worker may be able to relieve the anxiety somewhat during the initial period; and if there is real reason to hope that the situation can be improved this should certainly be communicated to the client. On the other hand, when the referral is made by someone other than the client, or when the client is inappropriately seeing the solution only in the change of some factor outside himself or in change brought about by the worker rather than by himself, work may need to be done on his understanding the problem more realistically. This is by no means to deny that there are situations in which the client is correct in perceiving the problem as primarily outside himself, and situations in which change in these externals must be made at least in part by the worker rather than by the client. The client's hope that he can be helped may also be affected by his knowledge—or lack of knowledge—of what the caseworker can offer. When the client lacks adequate information this should of course be clarified.

The other side of the coin of motivation is resistance. A person with *low* motivation to be sure will be resistant to

5. Lilian Ripple, Ernestina Alexander, and Bernice W. Polemis, *Motivation, Capacity, and Opportunity: Studies in Casework Theory and Practice,* Social Service Monographs, 2d ser., no. 3 (Chicago: School of Social Service Administration, University of Chicago, 1964), p. 43.

help, but it can also happen that *both* motivation and resistance are high. Resistance often depends in large part on anxiety about what is involved in taking help and what is involved in change. Treatment which involves change in any aspect of the client himself will naturally meet with more resistance than treatment which is entirely or primarily a matter of external change. Comments by the worker that even fleetingly raise the client's anxiety level, whether reality anxiety or instinctual anxiety, will increase resistance. When the client is not self-referred, resistance is apt to be higher; and it will be higher still if he does not know about the agency or about the nature of casework or, worse still, if he has negative impressions of the agency from his own previous experience or because of what he has heard from others.

Another variable in resistance is the nature of the problem itself. Insofar as the problem involves feelings of guilt or shame, fear of criticism, fear of social disapproval, or anxiety, resistance will be high. Factors in the client's own personality are also of great importance. The client with a low self-image, a severe superego, or chronically high anxiety will ordinarily be anxious and therefore, at least initially, resistant.

Several steps can be taken to lessen initial resistance. Discussing the client's negative or ambivalent feelings about seeking or accepting help is often of value, especially when the worker expresses his acceptance of them as a natural, even a healthy reaction. It is also important to find out what conceptions or misconceptions the client may have about the nature of service, and to clarify what the casework process will be like in relation to his particular needs. Ordinarily the worker can make it clear that his service is optional, and that he accepts the client's right to decide whether or not he wants service. If the worker has strong reason to believe that he could be of substantial service to the client despite his resistance, he may want to urge a trial period, delaying a final decision until the client has had an opportunity to learn more about the help that can be offered. In protective cases this option cannot be offered, though all the other procedures referred to can and should be used.

In most instances, special care must be taken in the initial phase not to arouse undue anxiety, but rather to relieve guilt and anxiety as far as is possible. However, diagnostic think-

ing may sometimes indicate that some anxiety must be
aroused or brought to the surface to motivate the client to
continue in a situation when the worker feels this is important. In such cases the worker must carefully assess the
client's ability to handle his anxiety and guard against pressure that will not make it more likely that the client will
use help.

With the multiproblem family or with clients who because
of poverty, lack of education, or prior experiences have a
negative picture of social agencies, resistance is apt to be
especially high. Such families are often referred by others,
motivation is often low, self-esteem may be low, and hence
both anxiety and resistance may be high. Extraordinary
measures may then have to be taken to change the client's
view of the caseworker from the critical intruder to the
accepting and potentially helpful worker. Much has been
written about this problem.[6]

In recent years the term "contract" has come into wide
usage to describe the end result of these three aspects of the
initial phase of work. Although practice varies in the extent
to which this "contract" or agreement is expliticly stated or
is implicit in the mutual understanding of the decision to
continue contact, there is growing preference for an explicit
statement.

Treatment in the Initial Period

It has long been held by most writers identified with the
diagnostic or psychosocial approach that treatment begins in
the first interview. In the early fifties there was considerable
controversy about this, with a few writers contending that
one could not "treat" at all until after a "diagnosis" had been
made. Today most workers would agree that a form of relatively nonspecific treatment is involved even in the first interview. The worker usually offers some form of sustainment
and an opportunity for ventilation which is of potential
therapeutic value. He also, to varying degrees, encourages
the client to reflect upon his situation and himself in order

---

6. See especially Louise S. Bandler, "The Families" in *The Drifters,* edited by Eleanor Pavenstadt (Boston: Little, Brown & Co., 1967); Alice
Overton et al., *Casework Notebook* (St. Paul: Greater St. Paul Community Chests and Councils, 1957).

to begin to understand one or both more fully. A study[7] of
a group of thirty-four marriage-counseling cases in four different agencies found that in the first interview somewhat
more than half the worker's communication was commonly
devoted to exploration for informational purposes and to
ventilation; about a tenth of the worker's comments were of
a sustaining nature, and almost a third were designed to encourage client reflection. Treatment does begin immediately, and exploration for greater understanding continues
throughout treatment. There is reason to believe that in
many long-term cases the continuing treatment pace has
already been reached as early as the third or fourth interview, though specific long-range objectives may not yet be
clear.[8] In planned short-term treatment and in crisis situations, of course, definitive treatment must begin more
quickly.

Psychosocial Study
Obviously it is in the initial phase that the worker gains his
first understanding of the kind of help his client needs. He
must learn what the client sees as his problem, what he thinks
can be done about it, what he himself has tried to do about
it, and what he sees as having brought about his present
difficulty. The worker will continuously try to arrive at his
own understanding of what the client's trouble is, what factors contribute to it causatively, and what assets in the client-
situation gestalt can enable the client to improve his situation and help the worker facilitate this improvement through
the casework treatment process.

To answer these questions one needs information. The
client will produce much of this information spontaneously,
but the worker is responsible for guiding the flow of the interview so that the most pertinent and useful information will
be secured in the limited time available. As Gordon Hamilton once put it, "If a question is not pertinent, it is imperti-
nent!" How can a caseworker determine what is pertinent?
He begins with the fact that the minimum unit of atten-

7. Florence Hollis, *A Typology of Casework Treatment* (New York: Family Service Association of America, 1968), p. 28.
8. Ibid., p. 22.

tion is a person-in-interaction-with-his-situation. That is, the unit of attention is a set of interacting forces—a system. Depending on how the problem is presented, this immediate system may be a family system or part of a family system, or it may be a family-cum-school system, an individual-cum-employment system, an individual or family-cum-health care system, cum housing, cum peer group—friend, gang, or combinations of these—and so on. In any case, the process of understanding begins with what the client sees as his problem, then moves into understanding some aspect of the client himself and some aspect of the rest of the system within which he locates his trouble—and of the ways in which these facets interrelate, interact, transact, and affect each other. How far this process goes will depend upon the nature of the problem, the services the agency or individual worker can offer, the complexity of the problem, and the willingness of the client to provide information.

Because the psychosocial approach has emphasized the effort to ascertain the client's need beyond what he presents as his initial problem and has stressed the effort to understand causation, several types of questions are often raised about the extensiveness of the study. (1) How far do you go into past history? (2) How deeply do you explore the personality? And (3) How much do you examine facets of the client's life about which he is not asking for help?

How far do you go into past history? The caseworker usually wants to know at what point the immediate problem began and what the client sees as its immediate antecedents. The client may locate this in the immediate past or may say it has been going on for a long time and himself reach a number of years into the past. If the worker knows that this sort of difficulty usually does not reach its present proportions in as brief a time as the client at first describes, the worker explores further to see if the client will recall or recognize earlier components in the problem. Only if the problem appears to be or is likely to be due in part to factors in an individual's personality or early personal experiences would one be likely to ask about these.

Considerable change has occurred in this area over the years. In the early thirties the vanguard of casework was the psychiatric social worker, especially the worker in the child guidance clinic. The importance of early childhood experiences was stressed in these agencies and extensive detailed developmental histories were taken routinely. This approach influenced many family agency workers, especially those who were finding the Freudian explanations of human behavior useful. Hence, the "diagnostic" workers tended to stress the need for an early well-rounded picture of the childhood of any client whose major problem appeared to be his own adjustment. Differential seeking of history, however, has always been recognized in diagnostic theory, and it received additional emphasis from the mid-thirties on. It is chiefly when the client's actions and responses in his current situation seem inappropriate that it becomes pertinent to inquire about aspects of his past life which our knowledge of human development leads us to believe may be influencing this inappropriateness and which therefore might help the worker understand his reactions and know what help to offer.

Except in work with young children and in certain psychiatric settings, there is today very little detailed exploration of the preschool years during the initial treatment period, and only rarely later in the contact when this is especially indicated. On the other hand, in problems of individual adjustment, knowledge of family relationships—especially of the latency and adolescent periods—is frequently pertinent. More emphasis is now being put on other kinship relationships which may have been important in the wider family, and more attention is being paid to cultural factors, including ethnic, class, and racial influences. There is also increasing emphasis on the client's values and role expectations both for himself and for others as these may have been influenced by reference groups—family and peers—and by cultural background factors.

How deeply do we explore the personality? This question usually means How much do you go into the unconscious? Casework from the psychosocial point of view rarely attempts to bring material from the true unconscious to the forefront of the mind. In the initial phase the content largely concerns matters that are fully conscious, though some suppressed preconscious material may also emerge, especially in interpersonal problems. With psychotics and clients on the border of psychosis, material which in the less damaged person would be deeply repressed is apt to be expressed immediately. This is part of the person's illness, whatever his presenting problem may be. In such situations, the worker's effort is directed toward keeping the client in contact with current realities, not toward exploring further the normally repressed ideation.

How much do we examine facets of the client's life about which he is not asking for help? This depends on the type of agency to which a client comes, on the extent to which problems not recognized by the client spontaneously make themselves apparent, on how serious such other problems appear to be, and on whether they fall within the scope of casework itself or are such that the client might benefit from referral to another social agency or another discipline. Certainly if, in exploring the nature of the presented problem, one found it an aspect of a different or larger problem one would be obligated to seek enough information about the broader problem to make some assessment of it and of whether the client would accept help with it either from the resource to which he first came or from one to which he could be referred.

In recent years there has also been considerable experimentation by workers of the "diagnostic" persuasion with various forms of planned short-term treatment. Here the worker purposely narrows his focus either to the presenting problem or to matters closely associated with it, in the expectation that if the client is enabled to deal better with that part of his life with which he already feels that he needs help, he will be better able to cope with the rest of his life on his own. In this approach exploration of problems other than the presenting one occurs only very early in the initial period and is used to establish a mutually agreed upon focus for treatment.

ASSESSMENT OF THE CLIENT IN HIS SITUATION

It is from its position on the assessment phase of casework that the psychosocial school of thought got the name "diagnostic," by which it is popularly known. We believe that diagnosis is essential. It is essential because it gives a realistic basis for *differentiation*—individuation based on broad knowledge of the individual-situation complex in the context of our general knowledge of individuals, situations, and their interactions. What kind of diagnosis are we trying to formulate? Certainly not a mere categorical label pinned on the client at the end of the exploratory period. Webster gives two quite different definitions for the word diagnosis—1. The art or act of recognizing disease from its symptoms. 2. Scientific determination, critical scrutiny, or its resulting judgment. The second meaning is far broader than the first and best describes how we regard the assessment process. It is the effort to deduce from the material available, seen against the background of what we know of human behavior and social realities, what the client's trouble is, what contributes to it, where changes can be brought to occur which will lessen or eradicate his trouble, and what steps the caseworker can take to forward this objective.

To start with an example: A client who is working claims that he is going into debt because his rent is too high and he cannot find another place to live. To find the source of his trouble one must first compare his rental with the normal range of rentals for his income. Without this one cannot know whether the problem is in fact a disproportionately high rent or is some misconception on the client's part. It may be that his income is too low to cover his necessities even though his rent is not abnormaly high. Here again a norm is applied in arriving at an opinion about the adequacy of his income. If in fact the income is adequate and the rent too high the problem is still not defined. Why has he not moved to a less expensive place? If he says he has tried but has been unable to find such a place, several alternatives are open. What is the rental situation in the community? Is it really extremely difficult to find suitable living quarters for the amount the client can afford? If so, he may need help in looking for a cheaper rental.

If the measurement of the rental situation against our knowledge of reality tells us it is not very difficult to find suitable quarters, the question becomes, Why can he not solve this realistic problem for himself? Now the possibilities broaden and the various systems in which the problem might lie must be explored until a reasonable definition of the problem is reached. The worker is now considering what factors might cause a person to be unable to locate suitable living quarters when his income is sufficient and housing in his price range is available. What about the social system? Is his race or ethnic group or social class or the size of his family making it difficult for him? Here the worker uses both the client's description of his house hunting experiences and his own knowledge of social attitudes usually found in the neighborhood. If the answer does not seem to lie here, the worker asks himself, "Does the trouble lie partially or wholly within the individual himself? Does he seem to lack knowledge of where and how to look? If so, why might this be? Is he a newcomer? Does he have difficulty speaking English? Is there a lack of intelligence?" If no clues are found in these possibilities, does he lack initiative? If so, is it because he is physically ill? Depressed? Discouraged? Mentally ill? Again observations are evaluated against knowledge of ordinary behavior, and causative elements are looked for in terms of our knowledge of what is likely to cause the trouble the client defines himself as having. If the trouble now appears to be partially within the person—in the personality system—we must look more closely not only into his own personality but also into his family system, or perhaps into his friendship system or his employment system, looking always at his interactions—or transactions—with the other individuals in these systems.

To go further would labor the point. The diagnostic process consists of a critical scrutiny of a client-situation complex and the trouble concerning which help is sought or needed for the purpose of understanding the nature of the difficulty with increasing detail and accuracy. The specific client-situation complex must be viewed repeatedly against a series of approximate norms—of average expectancies—concerning behavior of the client and of others, concerning pertinent aspects of his social situation, and concerning concrete realities.[9]

These inferences will be mainly of three types: dynamic,

9. For further discussion of the function of norms see Florence Hollis, *Casework: A Psychosocial Therapy* (New York: Random House, 1964), pp. 184–87.

etiological, and classificatory. (1) In the *dynamic* diagnosis we examine, among other things, how different aspects of the client's personality interact to produce his total functioning. We look at the interplay between the client and other people and at other systems and the interactions within them to understand how change in one part of a system may affect another part or how one system may affect another. The dynamics of family interaction are particularly important here and form a large part of what is often referred to as a family diagnosis. (2) *Etiological* factors are looked for, whether these lie in the current interactions or in preceding events which still actively affect the present and are among the causes of the client's dilemma. Usually, causation is seen as the convergence of a multiplicity of factors in the person-situation configuration. The dynamic and etiological aspects of the diagnosis together provide both a "linear" and an interactional or "transactional" view of causation. Where antecedents exist they are noted; they are usually seen as multiple. At the same time the continuous action between and among the various causative components in the transactional sense is an integral part of understanding the nature of the client-situation gestalt. (3) Effort is made to *classify* various aspects of the client's functioning, including, where pertinent and possible, a clinical diagnosis.

To arrive at these three types of understanding, the client-situation configuration is viewed from the perspective of various social and psychological frames of reference. Both individual and group behavior are part of a sociocultural fabric. Individual behavior, and the reverberating effect of one person on another, are influenced by socially conditioned behavioral expectations. It has long been recognized that cultural factors, especially those rooted in religious and ethnic background as transmitted by the family, have a profound influence on ego and superego development and on the response of others, both within the family and outside it, to the ways of the individual. More recently, class and racial factors have been better understood; knowledge of the sociocultural component in thought processes, in mental development, in psychological disturbances, and in choice of symptomatology is constantly expanding. The influence of social expectations related to chronological age is being given prominence along with the intrapsychic and physical components which have long been accredited.

We are also coming to understand more fully the nature and dynamics of role expectations as they influence the individual's shaping of his own behavior, his expectations of how others will act, his interpretations of their actions, and consequently his response to their actions and their response to his. Certain aspects of the dynamics of behavior within groups are also becoming better known and are used especially in understanding the forces at work in family life.

Since the personality theory used in the psychosocial approach is primarily Freudian, the personality system is conceptualized as a set of interacting forces designated as id, ego, and superego. The functioning of the many aspects of the ego, including how the individual's defenses operate, is considered of primary importance in assessing the adequacy of the client's efforts to deal with his difficulty and the extent to which he is contributing to his own problem. Ego functioning must be understood even when the causes of the problem lie primarily in the situation rather than in the client's personality. More often than not, wherever the cause may lie, the client himself will have to be active in bettering his situation, and in this process his ego functioning is central. When aspects of the client's personality appear to be a major part of his difficulty it becomes important also to understand his libidinal and aggressive drive functioning and the nature of his superego. The interplay of these forces in his personality, of course, produces his total functioning as we observe it in his behavior.

In recent years the characteristics of individuals in crises of various types have also been studied by practitioners associated with the psychosocial school of thought. Since this is developed at length in another chapter,[10] I need only mention it as a body of knowledge used by caseworkers of this school of thought in both diagnosis and treatment planning.

The *classification* aspect of diagnosis is most frequently a subject of controversy and perhaps also of misunderstanding. In psychosocial casework, one does *in addition* to the foregoing try to arrive at a diagnosis in the narrower sense of

---

10. Lydia Rapoport, chapter 7 of this volume.

"recognizing a disease from its symptoms." This is a form of classification, or—as those who do not like it sometimes call it—"categorization." The latter term implies putting something in a pigeonhole—sometimes without adequate reason —and keeping it there forever. It also implies mistaking the part for the whole and treating in narrow, fixed terms, by some formula that has been generally accepted as appropriate for the given category. I would agree that the wastebasket is the best place for that type of categorization.

Properly used, classification never applies to the whole person. Rather, it applies to various aspects of his functioning and his place in the world. An individual can be classified in dozens of ways. Only a few will be pertinent to understanding how to help him with his trouble, and these will not be the same in different cases. For the most part, for instance, his political classification will not be important, but one can think of certain problems in which it would be. Classification according to socioeconomic class, race, ethnic background, and religion is often important—so often, in fact, that provision is usually made for this data on agency face sheets. Social class status is often represented by education plus occupation and income. If physical disease is suspected, this classification is arrived at by a doctor. Intelligence is usually implicitly if not explicitly classified. When this is of crucial significance and hard to determine, a psychologist's opinion is sought. Breakdowns or inadequacies in social functioning tend to be classified according to the area in which the problem exists, as for instance a "parent-child adjustment problem," or a "learning problem."

The situational aspect of the person-situation complex has not been conceptualized in classificatory terms unless one thinks of simple, generally applicable terms representing qualitative differences quantitatively, such as degrees of adequacy or inadequacy of various aspects of the situation or situation-systems or degrees of opportunity or denial of opportunity. Housing, or the school system, or the employment system as it impinges on the client could be described in such terms.

Classifications have also been devised for families as a whole. The problem of overlapping categories continues to loom large in "family diagnosis." Many different systems are in use.

A more complicated form of classification occurs in the area of personality disturbance, where we have borrowed some terms from psychiatry. This is often referred to as the "clinical diagnosis." Obviously it is important that the worker, whatever the problem may be, recognize the possibility of psychosis in his client if signs of this emerge. Schizophrenia or severe depression, for instance, are frequently the causative factors of social dysfunctioning and also have specific implications for the form casework should take. When psychosis is suspected, psychiatric consultation should be sought. In many problems, especially where the major difficulty is interpersonal, it is also important to distinguish between psychoneurosis, neurotic character disorder, and character disorders of the nonneurotic type. Within either psychoneurosis or neurotic character disorder, it is useful to further classify, when possible, whether the predominant pattern appears to be hysteria, an oedipal problem, obsessive compulsiveness, or depression.

As is well known, personality functioning does not fit neatly even into these clinical categories. They represent types and degrees of interaction between the id, ego, and superego in the context of various degrees of psychosexual maturation or regression. Since the relative strength of any of these components varies along a continuum, these categories represent commonly found models of different possible combinations of interacting components. Individual cases will approximate these points to varying degrees. Some will lie midway between categories. Depending upon the severity of the disorder, the problem focus, and the type of casework treatment which might be offered, it may be either optional or imperative to secure a psychiatric opinion about the personality structure and its implications for treatment.

The use of the "clinical diagnosis" as part of the psychosocial diagnosis has led some writers recently to refer to the psychosocial approach as the "medical model" or the "disease model" of casework. This view overlooks several aspects of the model: (1) the breadth of the diagnosis—that is, its concern for the impact of the "situation" as well as for dysfunctional aspects of the client's mode of adaptation; (2) the dynamic part of the diagnosis; and (3) that, as has been well articulated by Hamilton and many others, it is as important to assess strengths as to locate weaknesses in the person-situation gestalt.

Diagnosis of whatever type—dynamic or etiological, or the classification of social or psychological facets of the total configuration—is an ongoing process constantly open to revision as new aspects of the person-situation complex emerge. Although some formulation should be arrived at early in the contact, this is by no means final; it must constantly be revised as the client's response to the worker's treatment and his own life events throw additional light upon any aspect of the total complex.

Goals and Treatment Planning

So far we have been concerned with diagnosis. An equally important part of the assessment process looks forward to how improvement can be brought about or how the discomfort can be reduced. Here we must look at client motivation and client strengths, and at how the situational components can be modified in order to assess the possibility of modifying the elements which have been etiologically identified as contributing causatively to the problem. If little can be done about causative factors, are there compensatory opportunities and gratifications that can be drawn upon to shift the balance of discomfort or malfunctioning? Are there strengths in the personality which might counterbalance or even modify the components of the personality responsible for dysfunctioning? What goals of treatment can be delineated? What treatment procedures will be needed to move toward these goals? The dynamic part of the diagnosis will have assessed strengths as well as weaknesses; now these are looked at for their potential in bringing about improvement. Motivation—the client's own objectives and the strength of his desire to move toward them—are major determinants in what the worker will offer. Goals are a composite of what the client sees and desires for himself and what the worker sees as possible and helpful. The available time, agency function, and worker skill are all components in the worker's view of what is possible. It would be irresponsible for the caseworker to participate in moving toward a goal desired by the client if this goal, in the worker's opinion, is either unattainable or harmful to the client or others. It would also be irresponsible not to attempt to enlist the client's interest in moving toward a goal which the worker considers attainable and in the client's interest, even though at the outset he does not recognize this as desirable or as possible. On the other hand, except in protective cases, the worker has no right to attempt to *impose* his goals upon the client.

Goals may be either ultimate or proximate; both are important. Ultimate goals are often vague and general at the outset. Proximate goals should be clear and specific; they involve the themes that are to be worked on and the specific objectives to be attained in the immediate future.

The treatment processes by which the worker will attempt to help the client move toward these goals can also be foreseen to some degree at this point, and movement will be accelerated if the worker is clear in his mind about them. Again it must be emphasized that this is a fluid process. We are dealing with moving life processes, not static entities. Goals, themes, and procedures must be subject to constant revision as the living process with which we are dealing changes or reveals itself in new ways. Communication between client and worker should be open and clear; the worker should be constantly alert, perceptive, and responsive to the client's reactions and desires.

TREATMENT PRINCIPLES AND METHODS
Objectives
The ultimate objective of the caseworker using the psychosocial approach is the very broad one of alleviating the client's distress and decreasing the malfunctioning in the person-situation system. Or, to put it positively, it is to enhance the client's comfort, satisfaction, and self-realization. This may require enhancing the adaptive skills of his ego and the functioning of the person-situation system. Change may be needed in either the person or the situation, and often in both.

This very general statement must be made specific. First, in what aspect of the person-situation configuration are we attempting to bring improvement? This is governed partly by where the client sees the need for help—either initially or as a development within the treatment process itself. It is governed partly by the worker's view of the problem and what goals he and the client, through casework, can hope to achieve. It is governed very largely by the client's motivation and capacities and by the modifiableness of the situation. It is also governed in part by the function of the agency to which the client has applied, the time available, and the individual worker's skill.

At the heart of the psychosocial approach, from its beginning in the work of Mary Richmond and throughout its history, is its emphasis on both the individual and his situation as factors to be understood in diagnosis and as elements in which change can be brought about by casework treatment. It has also been recognized throughout that, because of the interaction between the individual and his situation, changes in the environment affect the functioning of the individual and changes in the individual affect the functioning of elements in his environment. This is obviously a system theory concept.

The general goal of treatment becomes much more specific as it is shaped by the worker's understanding of the etiology and dynamics of the client's trouble and of the aspects of the person-situation configuration which appear to be modifiable. If the problem is lack of resources the aim becomes seeing that the resource is supplied, be it money, food, housing, employment, medical care, special schooling, a visiting homemaker, a foster home, adoptive parents, or any of the many other needs an individual or family may have.

Whether this need can best be met by the worker's intervention through the services of his own agency or through the mobilization of other resources, or whether the worker's efforts should be directed toward helping the client secure these things for himself depends upon the interrelationship between the person and this aspect of his situation. To what extent can the resource be made available through his own efforts? To what extent is he capable at this point of manipulating his own environment, with help from the worker in understanding it and in acquiring confidence in his ability to act on his own behalf?

When the dysfunctioning in the person-situation gestalt is primarily interpersonal, the aim naturally is to bring about better interpersonal adaptations. Where possible, this includes work with two or more persons involved in the disturbance. In present-day psychosocial casework this means attention to both the *interpersonal system*—parent-child, husband-wife, family—and to the *personality systems* of the individuals who compose the interpersonal system. The interpersonal system functions as the composite of a set of transactions—of actions occurring between the persons who make up the system. For these transactions to change there must be changes in the perceptions of the participants and in their responses to each other. These perceptions and responses both depend upon and create the quality of communication between the individuals in any interpersonal system. Faulty communication is recognized as a major source of family dysfunctioning, and improvement in communication is often a specific goal of treatment. Change in communication requires changes in the perceptions and responses of the individuals who compose the interpersonal system—that is, changes in the individuals' personality systems. Perception is an ego function. The nature of any specific perception depends upon the actual external event plus the ego's interpretation of the event. This interpretation, as distinguished from the *actual* event, depends upon the cultural perspective in which the individual places the event, his role expectations, distortions due to transference reactions, displacements, projections, and other defenses, the nature of his superego and ego ideal in certain types of events, and often the strength of any drive affected by the event.

The individual's *response* to an event, in turn, is shaped not only by his perception of it but by other ego qualities (such as intelligence, judgment, impulse control, defenses), superego and ego ideal, the maturity of his object relationships, and the strength and quality of his aggressive drive. In other words, although in interpersonal problems we are concerned with modifying the family or other interpersonal systems, there is no escaping the aim of modifying the personalities—or, if you prefer, personality systems—of the individuals involved. This can be done by interviewing individuals separately or together, or by a combination of the two approaches.

This leads us to the important question of what *kind* of changes in the client's personality we attempt to encourage. As is well known, there are many definitions of personality change. I shall use the following—that a change in personality has occurred whenever a new way of responding or behaving has been sufficiently incorporated into the personality to enable the individual to respond consistently in a changed way to repetitions of the same event or its equivalent. This is a very broad definition. It means that if a person learns to perceive certain situations differently, his personality, to that small degree, has changed. This is true if his self-perception changes, or his control, or his executive ability, or his defenses, or if changes occur in his superego, his ego ideal, his capacity for mature feelings for other people, his hostile tendencies, or his use of his aggressiveness. The term personality change does not imply direction, nor does it specify quantity. The change may be very specific and very small, such as the change in an ego when it learns how to interact more productively with a specific agency. It may be very great, as when broad maturation occurs in psychosexual development, in superego and ego ideal, and in general ego functioning. How far along this continuum do the goals of psychosocial casework go?

With children the goals may be very broad and profound. Treatment is often directed primarily toward bringing changes in the child's human environment—his parents, other family members, his school—or, when necessary, toward providing parent substitutes—adoptive parents, foster parents, or institutional care. Through these "indirect" means one hopes to provide the child with a setting within which healthy maturation can occur. Direct work with the child in some settings attempts to undo earlier injurious life experiences and to provide health-inducing experiences through the relationship with the caseworker or through relationships with other children and the worker in treatment groups. In other settings the aim of direct work with the child is limited to helping him to learn to cope with definite troublesome aspects of his life or to specifically defined personality modifications.

With adults the goal is usually limited and specific. It revolves around a change in the individual's capacity to deal with certain sectors of his life—such as his marriage, his parenthood, or his work. After the worker acquires some understanding of what aspect of the client's personality functioning is making it difficult for him to interact productively with spouse, child, or employers, he assesses the possibility of change in this area and evaluates what stress or change this in turn may introduce into the client's entire personality system. On the basis of this assessment, specific objectives for client and worker emerge. Common objectives are the modification of perceptions of others or of self, greater self-regard and greater self-confidence, a firmer sense of personal identity, modification in the use of defeating defenses (especially in the particular interpersonal relationship in which the discomfort is located), more realistic judgment, lessening of anxiety, greater capacity to act, better impulse control, greater realism in some aspect of ego ideal or superego, a reduction in hostility, and an increase in the capacity for mature love. As with the other conflicts, hostility and love are usually worked on in terms of particular relationships. Insofar as growth occurs in any of these respects it may well affect other relationhsips not specifically discussed in the casework interviews.

You may well ask, What limitations are there on what the caseworker does? One limitation is inherent—in casework we deal with specific sectors of the life experience with which the client is seeking help or is willing to accept it. A second limitation is that we are not using the technique of attempting to bring unconscious early life experiences to the surface of the mind. We do not use free association in the true sense of the word and we do not encourage a deeply regressive transference. We often understand some of what is going on in the unconscious, and we certainly use theory about the unconscious in our work. We also, in interpretations, make connections previously unrecognized by the client between experiences and behavior. But the focus of interviews is upon conscious material and material that has previously been preconscious rather than unconscious. The formulations of Kris and Rapaport expanding the concept of the preconscious

form the basis for this position.[11] Some practitioners belong-
ing to this school of casework would go further than the
writer does in thinking that it is within the function of the
caseworker actively to solicit material that has previously
been unconscious. Exception must always be made for work
with the psychotic. Here, the effort is to direct the client's
attention to reality despite his own inclination to discuss
material which in a healthier person would be unconscious.

The discussion of the aims of casework treatment has inevitably involved concepts concerning the relationship between the aims of treatment and of diagnosis. As the foregoing surely indicates, this relationship in the psychosocial
approach is not a simple one-to-one correspondence between
a clinical diagnosis or a problem classification and a single
prescribed goal. The diagnosis is designed to give a broad and
detailed picture of the dynamics and etiology of the total
current person-situation gestalt. It is a ground plan designed
to show what the trouble is, what factors in both person and
situation contribute to it, and how these factors interact. It
guides the worker to elements in the situation that need to be
modified because they contribute to the problem or because
they might provide a way of ameliorating it. It may reveal
"points of reverberation" within the system which if changed
are especially likely to bring further change in the totality.
It guides the worker in estimating how much change can
be hoped for and in foreseeing how change in one aspect
of the total gestalt will affect the rest of the system.

To reemphasize certain key points: treatment objectives
and methods constitute part of an open system. One does not
make fixed, unchangeable decisions about these things at the
end of an exploratory period. Rather, one hypothesizes that
certain objectives and methods will be helpful and acceptable
to the client. If new understanding of the client's needs
emerges, a modified hypothesis is formed and treatment proceeds along modified lines. To some degree this may occur
repeatedly as treatment progresses. Nevertheless, at any one
moment the worker should have clear reasons for what he
offers for the client's use.

---

11. For further discussion of this question see Hollis, *Casework*, pp.
131–49.

Treatment Process

This brings us to the means by which change is brought about in casework and the ways in which diagnosis guides the worker in his choice of means. The simplest approach to this is to summarize first the ways in which the worker may become active in the environment and then the ways in which he works directly with the client, following the old Richmond division of indirect treatment (environmental) and direct treatment—"the influence of mind upon mind."[12]

When the worker intervenes actively in the environment he may play many different roles. One group of these interventions consists of obtaining needed resources. When the worker is a staff member of an agency whose functions include providing the needed resources, his role is *provider* of the resource. At other times his role is *locator* of a resource or *interpreter* of the client's need. In more difficult situations he may be a *mediator* on the client's behalf with an unresponsive or poorly functioning resource, or even an active *advocate* when a legitimate resource is resistive to the client's need. Today the worker frequently must take this responsibility to secure financial assistance for which the client is eligible, proper health care, housing, and sometimes appropriate educational resources. At times the worker goes even further and *creates* or helps to create resources.

When some change in the environment rather than a resource is needed, the worker may take the role of *modifier* of the situation. Typical of this are school or employment situations where the worker may be able to straighten out misunderstandings by talking with school or employment personnel, or modify someone's behavior toward the client by supplying information about him or interpreting his actions. When the climate is favorable the worker sometimes makes suggestions or gives advice about the interactions involved.

When casework intervention is needed, the process is rarely limited to intervention in the environment. It usually also involves "direct" work with the client himself. The client is most often being put in touch with a resource *system* which he will need to go on using. He himself must acquire skill in

12. Mary E. Richmond, *What Is Social Case Work?* (New York: Russell Sage Foundation, 1922), pp. 87–125.

so relating himself to this system that it will yield the help for which it was created. This means learning what help he is eligible for and how to establish eligibility, learning how to avoid creating unnecessary antagonisms which will slow down response to his need, and learning to use existing channels for overcoming inefficiency and even malpractice when they exist. At times the client himself creates obstacles, and securing better transactions with the resource system may involve better understanding on his part both of the situation and of himself and his own responses. This is true to an even greater extent when situational *modification* rather than providing resources is involved.

Again taking the school or employment problem as an illustration, transactions between the client and these systems are involved. Often the child or adult is contributing to the problematic interaction and must modify his own perception of the situation and his responses to it if the situational intervention of the worker is to result in lasting improvement.

In familial and other interpersonal problems the approach may be entirely a "direct" one, each person in the interpersonal system becoming to some degree one of the worker's clients. Treatment is conducted sometimes entirely through individual interviews, sometimes in interviews in which two or more of the individuals involved are seen together and interact with each other as well as with the caseworker. The use of both interviewing modes in the same case is increasing. Family unit treatment, or treatment of the family as a group, one of the approaches increasingly used by workers of the psychosocial school of thought, will not be included here since chapter 6 of this volume is devoted entirely to this subject.

A number of different classifications of casework treatment processes have been developed from the viewpoint of the psychosocial caseworker. The best known are those of Hamilton,[13] Bibring,[14] and Austin,[15] and that developed by the

---

13. Gordon Hamilton, *Theory and Practice of Social Casework,* 2d ed. (New York: Columbia University Press, 1951), pp. 241–52.
14. Grete L. Bibring, "Psychiatry and Social Work," *Journal of Social Casework* 28 (June 1947).
15. Lucille N. Austin, "Trends in Differential Treatment in Social Casework," *Journal of Social Casework* 29 (June 1948).

FSAA committee in 1953[16] and elaborated and modified by a staff committee of the Community Service Society of New York in 1958.[17] The author has also made several attempts at such classification. This series of classifications reflects the changing issues and the development of theory in this school of thought. Different schemes are useful for different purposes. For the present I should like to describe the one with which I have recently been working and which has been used in a series of studies pertinent to the subject under discussion.[18]

This classification considers casework treatment as consisting of a series of verbal and nonverbal communications, and classifies these communications according to several dimensions. The first dimension concerns who is communicating, that is, client or collateral or worker. Following the original Richmond terminology, client-worker interchanges constitute "direct treatment," whereas collateral-worker interchanges constitute "indirect treatment." In multiple client interviews, client-client interchanges also occur, and in some multiple person interviews there are client-collateral communications. The second major dimension has to do with the dynamic which the communication appears either to attempt to evoke, if it is a worker communication, or to employ if it is a client communication. Other dimensions have to do with the subject matter of each communication and with the "change objective" of worker communication or "change context" of a client or collateral communication.

The treatment process is conceived as a blend in which different proportions of the different processes are present in the totality of a case, in different phases of the same case, and in different interviews within a given phase.

For the present discussion the dimension of the *dynamic* of the communication is of particular interest. This has six subdivisions; three involve processes of reflection capable of enlarging the client's understanding in some way, and three

16. *Scope and Methods of the Family Service Agency* (New York: Family Service Association of America, 1953).
17. *Method and Process in Social Casework* (New York: Family Service Association of America, 1958).
18. Hollis, *Typology of Casework Treatment.*

employ nonreflective dynamics. The nonreflective dynamics are (a) communications in which the worker attempts to sustain the client through expressions of interest, sympathy and understanding, desire to help, confidence in the client, and acceptance of him; (b) communications that directly promote or discourage client behavior through expression of the worker's opinions or attitudes; (c) communications that encourage exploration or ventilation of content concerning the nature of the client or his situation and their interactions, or on the client's part, describe, explain, or ventilate content.

The reflective[19] categories are communications of a type usually employed to contribute to or encourage reflective consideration, awareness, or understanding of (d) the client's person-situation gestalt in the present or adult past; (e) the psychological patterns and dynamics of the client's behavior; or (f) aspects of the client's early life that are thought to be relevant to his present behavior.[20]

The distinction between the sustainment and direction categories and the three reflective categories is of particular importance. The communications classified under sustainment are those in which the worker expresses interest in the client, sympathetic understanding, desire to help, confidence in the client, and acceptance or approval of him. The various types of reflective communications may also have as one of their ultimate *effects* the reducing of anxiety or the increasing of self-confidence, effects similar to those brought about by sustainment; but the *means* by which this is achieved in reflective communications is the client's acquiring greater *understanding* of some aspect of the person or the situation or of their interactions. Similarly, reflective communications sometimes promote or discourage various types of client behavior; but, again, if this happens it is because the client has acquired a different understanding of himself or his situation and their interactions, whereas communications

---

19. The term "reflective" is used in the sense of "involving mental consideration," "contemplation."
20. The following short titles will be used for convenience: (a) sustainment; (b) direction; (c) exploration-ventilation or description-ventilation; (d) person-situation reflection; (e) pattern-dynamic reflection; (f) early-life reflection.

classified as direction do not involve reflection, but only the dynamic of the direct influence of the worker's expressed opinion about how the client should act or has acted as communicated verbally or nonverbally.

The first four types of communication occur in client-worker, collateral-worker, client-client, and client-collateral interchanges. Pattern-dynamic reflection and early-life reflection, on the other hand, are most unlikely to occur except in client-worker and client-client interchanges.

This classification is relatively new, but through its use in content analysis of both workers' detailed process recordings and tape recordings in a number of small studies, important light has been thrown on various aspects of the psychosocial casework process in direct treatment.[21]

Two studies have dealt with the general distribution of worker communications over the "dynamics" dimension. Fortunately, two additional comparable studies have been made using an adaptation of the Community Service Society classification worked out by Reid.[22] Both Reid and Mullen, who used the typology just presented, are familiar with both of these classification systems and were able to work out a table of equivalents which makes it possible to compare findings arrived at in studies using either system. Although there is some degree of error in making these equivalences, the margin is probably small.

All four of these studies[23] found that from 80 to 85 percent of all recorded worker communications fell within the category of exploration-ventilation or of person-situation reflection. Of the remaining worker content, 5 to 7 percent could

---

21. The classification has not yet been used in a study of indirect (environmental) treatment.

22. William J. Reid, "Characteristics of Casework Intervention," *Welfare in Review* 5 (October 1967):11–19.

23. Reported by Edward J. Mullen in "Casework Communication," *Social Casework* 49 (November 1968):551. Mullen draws from William J. Reid and Ann Shyne, *Brief and Extended Casework* (New York: Columbia University Press, 1969), from his own dissertation, "Casework Treatment Procedures as a Function of Client Diagnostic Variables" (Columbia University School of Social Work, 1968), from Helen Pinkus, "Casework Techniques Related to Selected Characteristics of Clients and Workers" (DSW diss., Columbia University of Social Work, 1968), and from Hollis, *Casework*.

not be classified for one reason or another; 3 to 8 percent was sustainment; 2 to 5 percent was direction; 1 to 5 percent was pattern-dynamic reflection; and 1 to 2 percent was early-life reflection. The cases in these studies were all drawn from family service agencies and psychiatric agencies, in which one would expect to find a higher proportion of pattern-dynamic and early-life reflection than in other agency settings. The family agency cases dealt primarily with marital and parent-child problems.

If one compares the exploration-ventilation and the person-situation reflection communications in the four studies one finds the relative amounts vary from 37 percent exploration-ventilation and 46 percent person-situation reflection in one study to 51 percent exploration-ventilation and 31 percent person-situation reflection in another. Some of this difference may be due to discrepancies in equating the categories in the two systems. The Reid-Shyne study and the Pinkus study, both using the Reid-Community Service Society systems, show a marked difference in the distribution between these two categories. Comparison of the Pinkus study, which was heavily weighted with psychiatric agency cases, with the Reid-Shyne study, based entirely on family service cases, indicates that there is more exploration-ventilation and less person-situation reflection in the psychiatric setting. There also appears to be somewhat less direction and somewhat more pattern-dynamic reflection in the psychiatric setting than in the family agency setting. Early-life reflection, on the other hand, is extremely small in both types of agency.

Client patterns were examined in only one study,[24] using family agency cases. This indicates that less than 1 percent of client communications are in the combined categories of pattern-dynamic and early-life reflection. An average of 75 percent are descriptive-ventilative and 24 percent person-situation reflection.

There have been a number of other findings from these and related studies. One study[25] finds that in general the client talks three to four times as much as the worker. An-

24. Hollis, *Casework*, pp. 18–26.
25. Ibid., p. 20.

other finds[26] that difference in worker style accounts for more variation between cases than any other variable. The Mullen study shows a series of thirty significant relationships between the worker's assessments of the client's ego functioning and the proportion of worker communications that fall into direction, exploration-ventilation, various subcategories of person-situation reflection, and pattern-dynamic reflection. All these relationships were in a direction consistent with that generally advised in theory for the relationship between diagnosis and treatment.

Direct treatment in general, then, in the types of cases so far studied, can be described as including the following components: (1) an ongoing exploratory process in which new understanding of the client-situation complex as it moves through time is constantly being acquired; (2) a large amount of ventilation by the client in a treatment atmosphere of worker acceptance and objective understanding; (3) reflective discussion of various aspects of the client-situation complex in about 30 percent of the combined client-worker communications; (4) pattern-dynamic and early-life reflections, usually constituting an extremely small part of the treatment process; sustainment of a verbal nature, infrequent in number of communications but a continuing component of treatment; (6) directive communications, small in number. These proportions vary in different cases and different phases of the same case. They vary according to worker style and according to the nature of the trouble with which the client is seeking help; they vary with the client's willingness and ability to respond to the worker's communications; and they vary with the worker's diagnostic assessment of the client-situation configuration. Other variables are also involved, especially agency setting and the time available or set for treatment.

Diagnosis and Treatment

We have already discussed the relationship between diagnosis and the aims or goals of treatment, pointing out that there is no simple one-to-one correspondence between a clinical diagnosis or a problem classification and these goals. The

---

26. Reid and Shyne, *Brief and Extended Casework*, p. 15.

same can be said about their relationship to treatment methodology.

But this is by no means to say there is no relationship between diagnosis and treatment. It is rather to point to the complexity of the relationship. In casework treatment we are dealing with many-faceted, living, changing, and moving personality and social systems. The components of these systems are constantly affecting each other. Change in one not only brings change in specific other parts of the interlocking elements, but reverberates throughout the entire complex. In the diagnostic process we try to look at all the pertinent aspects. The dynamic-etiological part of the diagnosis looks at the nature of the components of the person-situation gestalt and the relationships that exist both within the personality system and the various situational systems and among them compositely. This is comparable to a fluoroscopic view of a living organism, which not only helps the worker to see what is contributing to the difficulty and how, but also to judge at what points in person or situation change is likely to help and is possible, and what effects, good and bad, these changes are likely to have on other parts of the total complex. Borrowing from system theory we can also say that in diagnosis we look for "points of reverberation," that is, those possible changes which will have the greatest effect in the total gestalt. Still borrowing, we can evoke the principle of "equifinality." Study may suggest alternate types of change that may improve functioning. Workers may choose different approaches and yet reach similar goals. This does not mean that all approaches are equally appropriate but rather that in many instances, within a given range of approaches, several might be effective.

When it is possible to make a clinical diagnosis, this, too, is always an important component in guiding treatment. It provides an approximate model of the probable nature of the personality system of the individual we are trying to help. It is a summation of the information about the personality of the client or clients provided by the examination of dynamic and etiological factors at work in the total situation. It alerts us to the probability that certain qualities beyond those observed may also be present, because it places the individual in a group about whom these other things tend to be true. The combination of dynamic, etiological, and clinical diagnosis gives the fullest possible guidelines to what treatment steps are most likely to be effective. In combination these three guide the worker in estimating how much change can be brought about by the client and how much requires the direct intervention of the worker. They enable the worker to judge whether the client's relationship capacity is sufficiently mature—that is, whether his concern for others is sufficiently developed—for him to be open to help in understanding the needs and viewpoints of others, or whether he is still so narcissistic or dependent that this is not likely to happen. They indicate whether a firm, giving relationship must be established with the worker and some of the client's own needs met before he can attend to others. Narcissism may be so extreme that the client may be able to understand others only in the context of how such understanding will benefit himself. The degree of severity or laxity of the superego will guide the worker in how soon he can safely encourage the client to look at his own mistakes and their consequences. It will also indicate whether the client is likely to engage in constructive self-criticism or to pull out of treatment if this is attempted early in the contact. The frequency with which directive communications are appropriate is also related to ego and superego factors as well as to the nature of the problem.

The diagnostic picture of the ego provides most important guidelines concerning the client's readiness, ability, and need to reflect in the various ways available; what anxiety can be expected; and what defenses he is likely to use. The extent to which sustainment is needed is directly related to the degree to which he is anxious or to which he lacks confidence in himself or in the worker, as well as to the nature of the situational pressure with which he is trying to cope.

The content of worker communications, whether questions, comments, explanations, or interpretations, will, of course, directly reflect the worker's own understanding both of the client and of details of his situation and day by day interactions or transactions. It is not necessary to repeat all that was discussed in the diagnostic section of this chapter.

Clearly, understanding of each part of the personal and social systems involved in the client's trouble contributes, detail by detail, to making treatment sensitive to his need.

THE TARGET GROUP

Psychosocial or diagnostic casework is a broad approach which seeks to adapt its methodology to the needs of the individual coming for help—which is not to claim that it has been entirely successful in doing this. Its original strength was in the family, medical, and psychiatric fields. Many school social workers and child welfare workers have found it most useful.

It has always addressed itself to environmental problems as well as to those of an interpersonal and intrapsychic nature. Because of its differential approach it is used with a wide range of clinical types as well as a wide range of social difficulties.

Although in the thirties and forties this school of thought was primarily interested in neurotic individuals, in the fifties and sixties much attention has been given to the various character disorders. Similarly, much attention has been given to the multiproblem family, and recently, as class factors have come to the fore, effort is being made to find better ways of reaching those in the poverty group whose problems suggest that they need casework help. Some work has been done with alcoholics and drug addicts. Some caseworkers using this approach are also working with delinquent children and adults in corrective settings.

The psychosocial approach has in the past depended heavily upon the motivation of the client and the voluntary nature of the treatment relationship. Adaptations are therefore necessary where motivation is low or nonexistent, as is often true at the outset with those with severe character disorders, alcoholics, drug addicts, and delinquents. Comparatively little attention has been given to mentally deficient clients or to the mental patient who is either acutely ill or seriously regressed. The fields of education and psychiatry have primary responsibility for these groups, but their families often need casework help.

UNSOLVED PROBLEMS

The crucial question is not so much target groups as unsolved problems. We especially need more understanding of how to work with those with severe character disorders, addicts and delinquents, and severely disorganized families. We know somewhat more about alcoholics, but here too there are many unsolved problems. Indeed, I do not by any means want to imply that there is any "target group" concerning whom there are no unsolved problems. Like all other theoretical approaches to human and social ills, there is far more to be learned than is already known. Here are a few of the major questions that come to mind:

To what extent is the worker unconsciously giving verbal or nonverbal cues which influence the client?

To what extent do nonverbal communications, consciously or unconsciously given, affect the outcome of treatment?

What elements in the worker's personality, such as warmth or charisma, affect treatment, and how?

What elements in worker style, such as directness or activity, affect treatment, and how?

Under what conditions is time-limited treatment effective?

What differentials determine the circumstances in which single or multiple client interviews or combinations of these are most effective?

What differentials indicate the circumstances in which treatment in nonfamily groups of various types is either preferable to individual and family interviews or should be used at the same time?

What sociocultural differentiations are significant for treatment and in what way do these require adaptations in treatment approach?

To what extent is client education a factor in choice of treatment procedures?

How do racial differences between client and worker affect treatment?

The above questions are not a list of the problems confronting casework as a whole, but rather those that occur to me as salient in relation to a particular casework approach. General problems of prevention, service delivery, agency auspices, training, and manpower, are the common challenge of all casework and all social work, not of any particular school of thought.

As a matter of fact, our biggest unsolved problem is research itself. We are still at a very primitive stage in our formal study of theory and practice. We use instruments and designs borrowed from the social and behavioral sciences, which may or may not measure what we use them to measure or what we need to have measured. We have not yet developed ways of studying our processes without unduly interfering with them. We do not sufficiently control extraneous variables, or the quality of our input. We have very few sophisticated researchers who are also sophisticated casework practitioners and theoreticians. Our greatest unsolved problem is to develop research designs and tools adapted to the study of questions of true salience. We need designs and tools which will produce findings that are not so open to methodological criticism that no one who is truly knowledgable about both research and casework can have confidence in them. There is much work ahead and we must learn to do it competently for ourselves.

Bibliography

Hamilton, Gordon. *Psychotherapy in Child Guidance*. New York: Columbia University Press, 1947.
————. *Theory and Practice of Social Case Work*. New York: Columbia University Press, 1940; 2d ed., 1951.
Hollis, Florence. *Casework: A Psychosocial Therapy*. New York: Random House, 1964.
Kasius, Cora, ed. *Principles and Techniques in Social Casework: Selected Articles, 1940–1950*. New York: Family Service Association of America, 1950.
Lutz, Werner. *Concepts and Principles Underlying Casework Practice*. Washington, D.C.: National Association of Social Workers, 1956.
Parad, Howard, ed. *Ego Psychology and Dynamic Casework*. New York: Family Service Association of America, 1958.
Parad, Howard, and Miller, Roger R., eds. *Ego-Oriented Casework*. New York: Family Service Association of America, 1963.
Pavenstadt, Eleanor, ed. *The Drifters*. Boston: Little, Brown and Company, 1967.
Richmond, Mary E. *What Is Social Casework?* New York: Russell Sage Foundation, 1922.

Ripple, Lilian; Alexander, Ernestina; and Polemis, Bernice W. *Motivation, Capacity, and Opportunity: Studies in Casework Theory and Practice.* Social Service Monographs, 2d ser., no. 3. Chicago: School of Social Service Administration, University of Chicago, 1964.

Towle, Charlotte. *Common Human Needs.* Washington, D.C.: Government Printing Office, 1945.

Turner, Francis J., ed. *Differential Diagnosis and Treatment in Social Work.* New York: Free Press, 1968.

3 | The Functional Approach to Casework Practice

Ruth E. Smalley

GENERAL CHARACTERISTICS OF THE FUNCTIONAL APPROACH: A BRIEF STATEMENT OF THE ORIGINS OF THIS APPROACH

General Characteristics of the Functional Approach

The "functional approach"[1] to social work practice was first developed in the 1930s by faculty members of the School of Social Work of the University of Pennsylvania as a theoretical approach to the practice of social casework. However, application of this viewpoint or theory to all of the major processes in social work, both primary and secondary, was made early and has continued to be made by faculty and alumni of this school, and by others. Such statements of functional social work theory and practice are available in the professional literature.[2]

Three characteristics of functional social work which differentiated it from diagnostic social work (the only clearly formulated theoretical approach to social casework developed at the time the functional theory was first stated), follow. They continue to constitute emphases which characterize functional social work theory and practice today.[3]

Understanding of the Nature of Man

The diagnostic school worked from a psychology of illness, with the worker responsible for diagnosing and treating a pathological condition and with the center for change residing in the worker. The functional group worked from a psychology of growth and saw the center for change not in the worker but in the client, with the worker engaging in a relationship process which released the client's own power for choice and growth. The functional group used the term

Ruth E. Smalley is professor emeritus and retired dean, School of Social Work, University of Pennsylvania, Philadelphia.

1. Much of what is presented under topics 1–6 is drawn from Ruth E. Smalley, *Theory for Social Work Practice* (New York: Columbia University Press, 1967).
2. Ibid.; see notes on chapter 6, item 4, p. 311.
3. Although I identify functional social work here "negatively" through its difference from diagnostic social work as I understand it, I later develop a frame of reference for its practice positively—as a practice form in its own right.

"helping" in referring to its method, the diagnostic group used "treating" or "treatment." The functional group's view of human nature also took into account to a greater extent, in the early years of its development, the effect of social and cultural forces in human development.

Understanding of the Purpose of Social Work

The diagnostic group saw the purpose of social work as effecting a healthy personal and social condition in the clientele served, with the specific purpose of the agency not only secondary but also sometimes in a curious way parallel to, detached from, or even in opposition to the purpose of the worker. The functional group saw the purpose of the agency as representing a partial or concrete instance of social work's overall purpose and as giving focus, direction, and content to the worker's practice. They felt that casework method constituted not a form of social treatment of individuals but a method for administering some specific social service with such psychological understanding of and skill in the helping process that the agency service had the best possible chance of being used for individual and social welfare.

Understanding of the Concept of Process

The concept of process was not developed by the diagnostic group, some of whom have referred to social work method as "a repertoire of interventive acts"; presumably acts of the worker. The functional school developed the concept of social casework as a helping *process* through which an agency's service was made available with the principles of social work method having to do with the initiating, sustaining, and terminating of a process in human relationship. This meant that the worker did not attempt to classify a client and select a type of treatment deemed appropriate for that particular kind of client in order to produce an envisioned end—such as maintenance of the status quo in adjustment, return to a former level of adjustment, or achievement of a different level of adjustment—but rather entered into the relationship with avowed lack of knowledge of how it would all turn out, since that answer had not yet been written. Only client and worker together would discover what the client could do with the help offered. The worker's responsibility was for control of his part in the process, not for the achievement of any predetermined end.

The foregoing identifies three areas in which the early functional formulation differed from the then current diagnostic formulation. These differences continue to characterize functional social work today. I should like now to suggest a definition of functional social casework as it presently exists and to identify five principles for the practice of functional social work in all its processes, including the process of social casework, as I have elsewhere developed them.

Definition: Social casework is a method for engaging a client through a relationship process, essentially one to one, in the use of a social service toward his own and the general social welfare.

Five principles for the practice of social work follow.

Principle 1. That diagnosis, or understanding of the phenomenon served, is most effective which is related to the use of some specific service; which is developed, in part, in the course of giving the service, with the engagement and participation of the clientele served; which is recognized as being subject to continuous modification as the phenomenon changes; and which is put out by the worker for the clientele to use, as appropriate, in the course of the service.

Principle 2. The effectiveness of any social work process, primary or secondary, is furthered by the worker's conscious, knowing use of time phases in the process (beginnings, middles, and endings) in order that the particular potential in each time phase may be fully exploited for the other's use.

Principle 3. The use of agency function and function in professional role gives focus, content, and direction to social work processes, assures accountability to society and to the agency, and provides the partialization, the concreteness, the "difference," the "given" which further productive engagement.

Principle 4. A conscious knowing use of structure, as it evolves from and is related to function and process, introduces "form," which furthers the effectiveness of all the social work processes, both primary and secondary.

Principle 5. All social work processes, to be effective, require the use of relationship to engage the other in making and acting on choices or decisions as the core of working toward the accomplishment of a purpose identified as his own, within the purpose of the service being offered.

Although these principles used in concert characterize all social work processes, specifics are involved for each of the primary processes (including, of course, social casework) and for each of the secondary processes. The worker who moves from one process to another must make his own the specific knowledge and skill required, just as he must make his own what is necessary in specific knowledge and skill as he moves from one field of practice to another. However, the more fully and deeply the generic principles of social work practice are grasped, the more readily the social worker can move from one process to another and from one field to another.

Origins of the Functional Approach

The functional theory of the practice of social casework was developed originally at the University of Pennsylvania School of Social Work.[4] The impact of Freudian psychoanalysis on social work theory in the 1920s and 1930s had resulted in the development of diagnostic social work theory as formulated and taught by the faculty of such leading schools as the New York School of Social Work (now part of Columbia University), the University of Chicago School of Social Service Administration, and Smith College School for Social Work. The profound insights developed by Freud, his colleagues, and those who followed him enriched all of social work, just as they revolutionized the practice of psychiatry.

However, it appeared to the functional group that a substantial body of the social work profession, in taking over psychological understanding in the specific form developed by Freud, was influenced by its somewhat mechanistic, deterministic view of man, which saw him for the most part prey to the dark forces of an unconscious and of the harsh restrictive influences of internalized parental dicta in the early years of growth. It was only in the middle 1900s that the

---

4. For a history of the University of Pennsylvania School of Social Work, the site of the development of functional social work theory, see Virginia P. Robinson, "The University of Pennsylvania School of Social Work in Perspective: 1909–1959," *Journal of Social Work Process* 11 (1960).

Freudian group, through its new emphasis on ego psychology, reflected a more optimistic view of man and conceived him to be creator of himself as well as creature.

This latter view of man was first developed for psychotherapy by Otto Rank, a disciple of Freud. The view was later corroborated and developed by a considerable body of writers and scientists in a variety of disciplines, who contributed to the thinking of the functional school of social work from its beginning. Rank served on the faculty of the Pennsylvania School of Social Work and was a dynamic influence in the lives of Taft, Robinson, and the community of social workers in Philadelphia. His contributions to functional social work theory were in such areas as the nature of human growth, the human self—with particular emphasis on the will as a controlling and organizing force—the way psychological help can be given and taken through relationship, the significance of the present experience for releasing growth potential, and the import of "time" and its possibilities for conscious use in the helping processes. His psychological theory was conducive to an appreciation of the psychological value in use of agency function for helping, but he himself never related his theory to this or any aspect of social work practice. Indeed, he is quoted as having replied when someone asked him about the nature of functional social work: "It must be very interesting, but I don't know what it is."

It was Jessie Taft, professor of social case work on the faculty of the Pennsylvania School of Social Work—whose doctorate in psychology had been earned at the University of Chicago where she had studied under Mead and Dewey—who introduced the concept of "use of agency function" as basic in social work helping, an innovation which gave "the Pennsylvania School" its appellation as the "functional school." It was Taft who related the concept of agency function to the *helping process* in social work in her ground-breaking article "The Relation of Function to Process in Social Case Work."[5] Virginia Robinson, longtime associate director of

---

5. Jessie Taft, "The Relation of Function to Process in Social Case Work," *Journal of Social Work Process* 1 (1937):3, reprinted in Virginia P. Robinson, ed., *Jessie Taft, Therapist and Social Work Educator* (Philadelphia: University of Pennsylvania Press, 1962).

the Pennsylvania School of Social Work, first identified in comprehensive yet succinct form the nature of the skill required for functional social casework helping.[6] Robinson also applied functional social work theory to social work education, including the process of fieldwork supervision in social work education.[7] Colleagues of Taft and Robinson and those who followed them, including Aptekar, Dawley, de Schweinitz, Faatz, Faith, Gilpin, Hofstein, Phillips, Pray, Lewis, Smalley, and Wessel, contributed to further development, elaboration, and use of functional theory in practice.

The beginnings of functional theory as developed by Robinson and Taft are evident in the following quotations. Writing in 1930, Virginia Robinson stressed the significance of the worker-client relationship for the casework helping process:

If the history of social case work teaches anything, it teaches this one thing outstandingly that only in this field of the individual's reaction patterns and in the possibility of therapeutic change in these patterns through responsible self-conscious relationships can there be any possibility of a legitimate professional case work field. If case work accepts squarely this responsibility for relationship it has a field for research, for experiment demanding the most untiring scientific accuracy and the most sincere unceasing self discipline.[8]

Jessie Taft added the concept of agency function and of process and explicated their interrelationship in the epochal article to which reference has been made.[9] "There is one area and only one, in which outer and inner, worker and client, agency and social need can come together effectively, only one area that offers to social workers the possibility of development into a profession . . . and that is the area of the

---

6. Virginia P. Robinson, "The Meaning of Skill," *Journal of Social Work Process* 4 (1942).
7. See Virginia P. Robinson, "Training for Skill in Social Casework," *Journal of Social Work Process* 4 (1942), and Virginia P. Robinson, *Supervision in Social Case Work* (Chapel Hill: University of North Carolina Press, 1936) and *The Dynamics of Supervision under Functional Controls* (Philadelphia: University of Pennsylvania Press, 1950).
8. Virginia P. Robinson, *A Changing Psychology in Social Case Work* (Philadelphia: University of Pennsylvania Press, 1930), p. 185.
9. Taft, "Relation of Function to Process."

[social work] helping process itself."[10] And also, "There is no escape . . . from the necessity to establish ourselves not merely on the basis of social need, but on a foundation of professional skill."[11]

In establishing the impossibility of basing the helping process of social casework on an understanding of need alone ("something that can never be known exactly or worked on directly") Taft suggested that

We limit our study of needs to the generally recognized categories of social services as they emerge out of the larger social problems and leave to the individual the freedom as well as the responsibility of testing out his peculiar needs against the relatively stable function of a particular agency. There remains to us a large and comparatively unexplored area for future development, an area in which to learn how to maintain our functions intelligently and skillfully and how to isolate whatever can be isolated from the particular situation in terms of the law, the nature, of the general pattern of the helping process.[12]

In summary, functional theory for the practice of social casework originated in the thinking, teaching, and writing of faculty members of the Pennsylvania School of Social Work in the 1930s, notably in the work of Robinson and Taft. It was further developed for all the functional fields for practice and all the methods or processes in social work practice by them and by others of the faculty, by subsequent faculty, by alumni, and by members of the profession generally.

BEHAVIORAL SCIENCE FOUNDATIONS FOR FUNCTIONAL SOCIAL CASEWORK PRACTICE

Although the development of the psychological base for functional social casework theory owes much to the teachings and influence of Otto Rank, it rests also on what Taft brought out of her study with Mead and Dewey. It has since drawn on a variety of theoretical positions associated with various physical, social, and behavioral sciences. It has drawn also on its

10. Ibid., p. 3.
11. Ibid., p. 5.
12. Ibid., p. 8.

own experiences of what worked in offering psychological help to clients in their use of social services.

A concept of human growth that expresses *purpose* and constitutes a *process* has received increasing emphasis over the last thirty years by writers in the behavioral and natural sciences. A feeling for the power of the thrust that inheres in each fertilized ovum is strikingly conveyed in the writings of the embryologist George W. Corner.[13] The growth of the embryo from one cell to 200 billion cells during a period of nine months, from 15 ten-millionths of a single gram to 3,250 grams staggers the imagination. The orderly course of embryological development and the capacity of the embryo to deal, within its own limits, with unfavorable environmental circumstances in its inexorable move toward realization of its purpose of growth suggest an inner direction, force, and flexibility which can be assumed not to cease at birth but to continue to characterize man's biological and psychological capacity for coping and creating throughout his life.

Dr. Corner's description of embryonic life lays a base for understanding (1) the nature of human growth in its purposiveness and orderly progression; (2) respective roles for the environment and endowment, in their interaction, on the course of growth; and (3) the origin and nature of difference between man and other species, and between man and man.

Corner's feeling for the purpose and struggle which characterize both physical and spiritual growth is conveyed in the following:

How then shall I speak of the spirit, but humbly employing such vision as may be granted to an embryologist? I declare my conviction that the spirit of man, all that makes him man rather than beast and carries him onward with hope and sacrifice comes not as a highborn tenant from afar, but as a latent potentiality of the body. It too is received as a germ, an opportunity, something to develop. The spirit with the body must grow and differentiate, strengthening itself by contact with the world, earning its title to glory by struggle and achievement.[14]

---

13. George Corner, *Ourselves Unborn* (New Haven: Yale University Press, 1944).
14. Ibid., p. 122.

Corner refers to the power of choice and decision and exercise of the will as rooted in man's biology.

We are led . . . by the evidence of comparative anatomy to ponder upon the freedom of the will, or at least freedom of action, which we have because our bodies are versatile, untrammeled by specialization for extreme but particular skill, and capable of any tasks the mind may imagine. . . . The scope of the human mind, the freedom of human decision are bound up inextricably with the generalization of the body.[15]

Edmund Sinnot,[16] writing of the biology of purpose, speaks of living things as seekers and creators and of striving for goals as the essence of all life. He states that in man these goals have risen to heights before undreamed of, and suggests that man can set them even higher at his will. He refers to the organizing, goal-seeking quality in life, of life as regulating, purposeful, ascending, of each human being as "an organized and organizing center, a vortex pulling in matter and energy and knitting them into precise patterns never known before."[17] Sinnot does not deny or minimize the effects of the environment on the life of the organism. Indeed, he writes that the exact character of the organism will depend in some measure on the environment within which it develops. "In all these cases the genetic constitution of the organism is not changed but the way this expresses itself in development is very different depending on the conditions under which development takes place."[18] Sinnot's hypothesis that living organisms move toward definite goals both in their bodily development and in their behavior provides a unified conception not only of man's nature but also of his relation to others and to the universe.

Embryologists, biologists, psychologists, anthropologists, psychiatrists, psychoanalysts, educators, and philosophers are placing increasing emphasis on the place of purpose in life, on the human capacity for choice and decision

15. Ibid., p. 175.
16. Edmund W. Sinnot, *Cell and Psyche* (Chapel Hill: University of North Carolina Press, 1950). Also see idem, *The Biology of the Spirit* (New York: Viking Press, 1961).
17. Sinnot, *Cell and Psyche*, p. 69.
18. Ibid., p. 70.

making, on the power of rationality. Gordon Allport writes:

Up to now the behavioral sciences have not provided us with a picture of man capable of creating or living in a democracy. These sciences have in large part imitated the billiard ball model of physics, now of course outmoded. They have delivered into our hands a psychology of an "empty organism" pushed by drives and molded by environmental circumstances. What is small and partial, what is external and mechanical, what is early, what is peripheral and opportunistic—have received the chief attention of psychological system builders. But the theory of democracy requires also that man possess a measure of rationality, a portion of freedom, a generic conscience, appropriate ideals, and unique value.[19]

Allport concludes that the emerging figure of man appears endowed with a sufficient margin of reason, autonomy, and choice to profit from living in a free society, and he adds, "The portrait however does not discard the darker portion of truth discovered by the youthful psychology of the recent past. The truth stands and it will ever remain the duty of psychology to correct idealistic exuberance."[20]

Maslow's concept of self-actualization, Karen Horney's view of man's inner strivings as positive and of the individual as a continuously growing person, Lecky's development of a theory of unity and consistency of the self as well as contributions of Angyal, Fromm, Goldstein, Rank, and others have been brought together by Clark Moustakas in *The Self: Explorations in Personal Growth*.[21] Moustakas, in his preface, describes his book as stressing the positive healthy growing potentials of the individual, points to the essential quality of intrinsic human nature and its uniqueness, variation, and difference, in presenting the individual self as unified and consistent, as being and becoming. The theoretical contributions of all these writers and of many others constitute the behavioral and natural science underpinnings for functional social work.

19. Gordon W. Allport, *Becoming* (New Haven: Yale University Press, 1955), p. 100.
20. Ibid., p. 101.
21. Clark Moustakas, ed., *The Self* (New York: Harper and Brothers, 1956).

Of particular interest and value for developing the psychological point of view on which functional theory is based is the work of Helen Merrell Lynd,[22] who presents a psychology of potential abundance to replace a psychology based upon the economics of scarcity, which she contends characterized the period when Freudian psychology developed. She writes, in opposition to a "compensating" theory of personality:

Accurately as a theory of compensation accounts for many aspects of personality development, particularly in our contemporary society there are other aspects that cannot be accommodated within it. Human beings . . . have capacities for being spontaneously active and creatively interested in other persons and in the non personal world that find only meager expression in what we call human behavior or human nature in our society. In this perspective, goals, instead of being only specific objects to release tension become expanding purposes in which the whole personality may be involved. Wonder, curiosity, interest, thought, sympathy, trust, love are all seen as characteristic human attributes, not simply as secondary derived aims. Reality becomes something capable of yielding knowledge, interest and fulfillment, instead of being mainly a threat to be coped with. A whole philosophy of society and of history is expressed in the widely current use of the phrase "coping with reality" which implies that society and reality are felt as difficulties or dangers by the individual, something to be warded off, coped with, at great sacrifice adjusted to. A psychology of potential abundance may replace a psychology based upon an economics of scarcity.[23]

In this connection, Lynd's footnote to the foregoing statement is important: "Questioning the concept of reality as something to be coped with does not imply that reality can ever exclude conflict or that conflict is necessarily dysfunctional. It implies only that society and reality can be something other than threats to human beings."[24] Lynd's references to literature, to scientific writings, and to philosophy support and elaborate her thesis and themselves are useful

---

22. Helen Merrell Lynd, *On Shame and the Search for Identity* (New York: Harcourt, Brace and World, 1961).
23. Ibid., p. 141.
24. Ibid.

and used underpinnings for the psychological base of functional social work theory.

To summarize, the functional school of social casework has drawn on the ideas of scientists in diverse fields, philosophers, educators, and professional persons including social workers, who have recognized that man is properly conceived of as the center of his own life, capable of acting upon others as well as being acted upon, creator of himself as well as creature, able to use circumstance and human relationships to achieve his own purposes, including the purpose of the continuous creation of himself. These beliefs do not deny the irrational, the unconscious, the powerful, potentially crippling effects as well as supporting effects of life experiences on the individual, particularly early experiences and relationships within the immediate family. It is recognized as essential that any worker within the field of human relations know the limits imposed on human development by endowment and by circumstance, and the hazards to which every developing human being is subject at every point in his existence from conception forward.

The functional school sees the push toward life, health, and fulfillment as primary in human beings, and the human being as capable throughout his life of modifying both himself and his environment, in accordance with his own changing purposes within the limitations and opportunities of his own capacity and his own environment. This view sees man as capable of using human relationships, including the relationship with a social worker, to find and to strengthen his own purpose for himself and to move toward its realization.

In addition to establishing a base for understanding human nature as expressing purpose, the functional school has developed a base for viewing human growth as process. For social work help to be effective, the individual (or group or community) served must be understood in its uniqueness and difference as well as in the characteristics it shares with others of its kind. The difference of the individual person inheres in part in genetic endowment but also in the fact that the individual is a process, moves in time, and has a series of experiences which affect the self he becomes, just as he is affecting the "outside."

Each individual, each bearer and sharer of the human condition began with the first stirring of life on earth and before that time as part of the mystery of life's origin. He constitutes an expression of life force which is unbroken since life began. More narrowly, he is the product of a multitude of ancestors over thousands of years. Most recently he is the product of what may be thought of as his "immediate ancestors," whose traditions, customs, and characteristics known through living relationship are passed along through family, influencing his development as do the genes he has inherited and the immediate circumstances and relationships which constitute his present environment.

So similar, to the strongest microscope, is each tiny fertilized ovum which constitutes a living human being's beginning as an individual self; yet each is already teeming with both biological and cultural differences. As embryonic life pursues its orderly course, the purpose of creation of a human self is consistently at work and is also idiosyncratically at work, since differences in rate and quality of growth have been noted in fetal life.

The new individual, in some respects a parasitic growth within the mother's body, suspended in fluid, unable to perform independently the functions of respiration, digestion, and circulation, is yet quite unlike the true parasite, for it carries from the moment of conception the tremendous task and potential for creating its own structure, evolving complex differentiated systems of organs until that moment when independent life becomes physiologically possible and eventuates through birth.

The significance of birth in the life of an individual has been variously appreciated. Otto Rank's emphasis on its importance for subsequent psychological development marked his break with certain tenets of established Freudian psychology.[25] Rank emphasized the development of life fear and death fear out of the birth experience and saw all individuals as experiencing and expressing these two fears throughout life in varying and changing degrees: the fear of not living, not experiencing, not realizing potential which

---

25. Otto Rank, *The Trauma of Birth* (London: Paul, Trench, Truber & Co., and Harcourt, Brace, 1929), no translator given.

may be thought of as death fear; and the fear of separation, of independent existence outside the womb, and so of any kind of separation or differentiation as a person, which may be thought of as life fear. In this connection, the central intent of Rankian therapy is to free the individual to use an experience in relationship with the therapist for the "claiming" of his own difference and to leave the relationship for the discovery, affirmation, and furtherance of his capacity for living as a separate but related self.

Jessie Taft wrote:

The two basic needs that form the two poles of the psychological growth process are the need for dependence upon the other, as it is first experienced in the oneness of the uterine relationship, and the opposing need for the development of self dependence as the goal of movement toward adulthood. The two are never divorced in living, and it is on their essential conflict and interaction that we rely for the dynamic that keeps the individual moving to correct the inbalance that exists and must exist at any given moment in his use of himself.[26]

It is not necessary to recapitulate the life cycle through which each individual moves from conception forward. The formulations of Erik Erikson[27] have been found particularly useful in understanding the nature of the psychological crises and opportunities of each of the life periods which constitute the cycle of any individual life. In addition, functional theory draws upon many other writers who have made significant contributions to each of the particular life periods or to various aspects of growth or change within the total life cycle, whether physical, social, intellectual, or emotional.

An understanding of growth as purpose and growth as process suggests the following concepts which have relevance as a psychological base for the development of a theory for functional social work practice, involving as it does the professional use of a relationship between one individual, a so-

---

26. Jessie Taft, "A Conception of the Growth Process Underlying Social Casework Practice," in *Proceedings*, National Conference of Social Work, Atlantic City, 1950, part 2, Social Work in the Current Scene (New York: Columbia University Press, 1950), p. 294.

27. Erik H. Erikson, *Identity and the Life Cycle*, Psychological Issues 1 (New York: International Universities Press, 1959).

cial worker, and other individuals, in whatever configuration, toward an end both individually and socially constructive.

1. The individual is central in his own growth. From conception to death he is actively engaged in the development and use of himself in the direction of realization of his potential as an individual who is part of a larger whole.

2. To this end and in every stage of his life he makes use of his particular innate capacities and his environment, including the human relationships in his environment, both taking in what he needs and can use and putting out what he must in the interest of his growth. He both acts upon his environment and is acted on by it.

3. The nature of this environment is continuously changing throughout every phase of the life cycle, as it moves for the individual from the purely physical chemical environment of the womb to the first relationship to the mother, the immediate and then extended family, the neighborhood, school, community, and the world at its widest, as it is known in full maturity and as it narrows in old age.

4. Each individual brings continuously changing capacities to bear on his continuously changing environment. Here too there is a crescendo of increasing capacity, a peak of capacity (uneven in its several aspects), and a reduction of capacity which ends in death.

5. Each age period, moving often imperceptibly to the next, has its characteristic opportunities and tasks as posed by social expectation, which itself shifts and is not wholly consistent even at a given point in time.

6. The inner development of the individual is characterized by its own purpose to master the tasks posed, not out of compulsion from without but in response to inner readiness and capacity which has resulted in the kind of expression and activity from which the social expectations derive.

7. The environment may influence, retard, divert, and complicate the development of the individual, but he remains in control of his own growth, central in his own development, and capable of continuing development throughout his life's course within the limits of his particular capacities and environmental opportunity at a given point in time.

8. Cultural factors such as social and economic class may affect and color social expectations of an individual and his

expectations of himself, but they do not alter his continuous inner necessity to find a balance between the realization of himself as an individual and as a member of the particular society of which he is a part.

The peculiar genetically determined characteristics of a given individual in interaction with its first environment, the womb, the nature of the birth experience itself and the subsequent environmental circumstances, as well as the changing relationships with the mother (and others), eventuate in each person's formation of an identifiable *pattern* which tends to retain an essential identity and continuity throughout life. At the same time there is abundant evidence that each self is capable of growth within its pattern (How else can we justify education, therapy, social work?).

The individual pattern of any self may be understood in many ways. Functional social work theory views it as a balance of impulse, intellect, feeling and emotion, and will. Will is used here in the sense of an organizing and controlling force. Rank[28] was a theoretical source for the development of an understanding of the will, as was Taft, who equated—or rather substituted—will for the concepts of ego and self and saw it as a source for understanding the nature and character of emotional life.

Impulse, the raw tendency to action in the immediacy of the moment, differs in its strength, frequency, and nature of expression in individuals just as the character of the emotional life differs, and as does the character and nature of the will. So each individual is viewed in functional social work theory as developing his unique gestalt of feeling, impulse, and will—in their respective strengths and nature and in their relative places in the self's expression. And in each self the intellect—the thinking, comprehending, planning capacity—has its unique place and relationship to other aspects of the personality or self.

Because the self of another cannot be known through intellectual assessment alone, since a human compassionate,

---

28. See for example, Otto Rank, *Trauma of Birth;* idem, *Beyond Psychology* (Published privately, 1941; New York: Dover, 1958); idem, *Will Therapy and Truth and Reality,* trans. Jessie Taft (New York: Alfred A. Knopf, 1947).

caring relationship is essential if selves are to open up and become what they may be, the education of functional social workers requires use of the total educational experience for self-development and self-awareness so that the social worker may become the kind of self who can be a helper. The self which is known by a worker at once human, caring, knowledgeable, and skillful is a different self from that diagnosed by one who removes himself in feeling from the relationship in an attempt to be a dispassionate observer and helper. As an adolescent girl once said to her new social worker in referring to a former worker: "She knew all about me but she didn't know me."

The educational preparation of social workers of deepened human dimension calls for the use of literature, fiction, biography, and personal experience as well as material from the behavioral sciences in developing a behavioral foundation for practice. It calls also for a total kind of educational experience which involves the student as a whole feeling-thinking-acting person.

A further scientific base for functional social work helping is found in theory related to process itself. Northrup, Hoffman, Drucker, and Huxley, as well as Rank, Robinson, Taft, Faatz, and Hofstein,[29] are among the writers who have made significant contributions to the nature of process as understood and used in the education of functional social workers. It is appreciated that twentieth-century science, in turning away from the mechanistic-deterministic science of an earlier day and in developing the concepts of relativity, energy, particularity, emergence, and potential, laid the base for the development of a theory of process. Applied to the practice of social work, this theory led to a distinctive concept of social work practice. The essence of functional social work is its recognition of all phenomena served, whether individuals, groups, or communities as processes, marked by a high degree of particularity, possessing integrity and wholeness, and yet characterized by continuous change and embodying a po-

---

29. For an original and penetrating article on the significance of an understanding of *process* for social work, see Saul Hofstein, "The Nature of Process: The Implications for Social Work," *Journal of Social Work Process* 14 (1964).

tential for realization or actualization which can be furthered by the social work process itself.

Such a theory leaves room for the emergence of the unknown, the unpredictable, for "becoming" through the utilization of the immediacy of a continually shifting life situation. It calls for the development of a method which requires the social worker's engagement of the other in a relationship process through which that other may both discover and modify his own wanting and develop new power for satisfying his own wants. Social work in process-based practice is not a method of study of a relatively static object in order that the worker may apply specific techniques to achieve the worker's own preconceived ends for client, group, or community. It is rather a process for entering into a relationship with another or others with mutual and continuous discovery of the nature of the phenomenon being served. It is a process that seeks, from the present situation and from the social work relationship, for change in the course of the service being given, with the intent of providing the best possible opportunity for the other to use his own continuously shifting capacity for achieving his own goals as these goals are appropriate to the purpose which has brought social worker and client together.

Social work practice which is process based requires that the worker control not the phenomenon being served but his own part in the process through applying in the specific instance certain generic social work principles, and other principles congruent with the generic principles but specific to the particular social work method engaged in.

A final underpinning to functional social work practice concerns theory which throws light on the phenomenon of being served. I have already spoken about materials related to an understanding of the individual. Small group theory, as developed by such writers as Olmsted, Bavelas, Homans, Lewin, and Bales, is relevant to the development of an understanding of the nature of the small group, and of the significance of group experience for individual and group development is just as important for social workers who serve individuals through casework as for social group workers. To an understanding of the nature of a community, Roland Warren, Herman Stein, Harold Lewis, Kenneth Pray, and Roland Lippet, among others, have made significant contributions.

Underlying all behavioral and social science theory taught as a foundation for social work practice is material concerned with the nature of stress and the significance of conflict and stress for growth and development. Hans Selye, Rank, Robinson, Taft, and Faatz have all made significant contributions to an understanding of the place of conflict and disequilibrium in human growth. Selye writes:

As I see it, man's ultimate aim is to express himself as fully as possible, according to his own lights. . . . The goal certainly is not to avoid stress. Stress is part of life. It is a natural by-product of all our activities; there is no more justification for avoiding stress than for shunning food, exercise, or love. But, in order to express your self fully, you must first find your optimum stress-level, and then, use your adaptation energy at a rate and in a direction adjusted to the innate structure of your mind and body. The study of stress has shown that complete rest is not good, either for the body as a whole, or even for any organ within the body. Stress, applied in moderation, is necessary for life.[30]

Taft describes growth in terms of personality development as

a stormy painful affair which is not to deny that we want it more than anything else in life. No love relation however fulfilling can outweigh the joy of a new found self, nor can a love relationship compensate entirely for the self development it may hinder . . . the basic need of the individual is not pleasure but more life, to make more and more of the underlying energy accessible for integration, to go with the life process instead of fighting it, to find and use one's own capacity for relationships and for creativity, however slight.[31]

An objection to the familiar conception of homeostasis is that it suggests a maintenance of the status quo as the desideratum and leaves no room for growth development and creativity. Insofar as it refers to a physical status it can be conceived of as the kind of equilibrium which furthers positive health. In the psychological realm, functional theory

30. Hans Selye, *The Stress of Life* (New York: McGraw-Hill Book Co., 1956), pp. 299–300.
31. Taft, "Conception of the Growth Process," p. 336.

regards the individual's thrust as not to "hold the line" but to grow, to develop, to go beyond, however blocked and distorted the attempt may be because of innate lacks, the crippling effect of life experiences, or lacks in the immediate environment.

The effort of the functional social worker in working with individuals, groups, or communities, then, is not to avoid or minimize conflict, to produce a deadly harmony or an "as you were" condition, but to facilitate the full experiencing of conflict which presently exists. It is even to stimulate a "divine discontent" with what presently is, as a base for furthering and strengthening effort to resolve conflict in a way that constitutes growth and forward movement. Sometimes this means intervention and modification of environmental stresses that press too heavily, sometimes help toward reaching a state of physical and mental health conducive to more full and fulfilled living. Inevitably it means taking into account, as nearly as it can be known, the nature of the individual, group, or community being served—including potentials and limits—in order to maximize capacities for finding and following the client's own direction.

THE INITIAL PHASE

I should like to begin discussion of the initial phase of social casework helping within the framework of what I have elsewhere identified as Principle 2—use of time phases (see the first section of this chapter). I shall then refer briefly to how each of the four other principles I have identified for social work helping is applicable to the beginning phase of social casework helping. To restate Principle 2:

The effectiveness of any social work process, primary or secondary, is furthered by the worker's conscious, knowing use of time phases in the process (beginnings, middles, and endings) in order that the particular potential in each time phase may be fully exploited for the other's use.

The understanding of process as characteristic of all life can conduce to the capactiy to go *with* life, to *be* in effect a process, in relation to other processes with affirmation and with exploitation of each present moment for its full and unique value. It is this capacity developed in himself which the social worker seeks to use in furthering like capacity in those he serves. A heightened understanding of time phases as characterizing process makes their use possible in the interest of the clientele served and furthers the clientele's acceptance and utilization of each present and passing moment.

Beginning any venture in which there are elements of the unknown, particularly a venture involving human relationship and within which the one served by another is expected to do something or become something, leads inevitably to feelings of hope, excitement, and the mobilization of energy. At the same time, the new venture evokes fear, uncertainty, and even a "setting of the self against," perhaps to protect a hard-won inner balance and sense of integrity. The particular gestalt of feeling for any individual depends on the character of the individual, his characteristic way of beginning as it has evolved through experience, and the nature and significance of the particular undertaking which is being begun. For the individual, the beginning of life *as* an individual is birth. Each significant new beginning recreates the life fear—the fear of separation, individuation—and the death fear—the fear of not living, not experiencing, not realizing potential. Subsequent beginnings reflect and carry the feel of the common (birth) experience in a generic sense and idiosyncratically as well.

It is the worker's sensitivity to what is involved in a particular beginning, within the context of his understanding of what is true for beginnings in general, that makes it possible for him to lessen the fear and resistance, and exploit the marshaling of energy and use of new life which attend beginnings. This he does by such "techniques" as making the unknown known by being clear about his agency's service, the conditions under which it is available, what can be expected of it, and of him as worker, and what the requirements and expectations of the other are. The known is less feared and more manageable than the unknown. At the same time the worker encourages immediate engagement of the other in expressing hopes, intentions, and fears in respect to what is being offered in the way of service. The more quickly the other gets into action and makes clear to the worker as well as to himself his part and stake in the situation that brings them together, the more readily his life force and energy can be utilized in dealing with a situation rather than in protecting himself against its impact, and against the impact of the one who represents the threat of change. As the other experiences what he wants and what he is like, and learns what the agency in the person of the worker is like and what it expects and requires (stripped of some of his projections of what he wants it to be or fears it is), a working relationship develops which the other is free to use in his own behalf, within the known purpose and intent of the agency or service.

Additional ways of furthering fruitful beginnings include the partialization, or breaking up and breaking down, of what is felt as a total problem or global purpose into something that is small enough to be encompassed to start on as one piece of that problem or purpose. The worker's responsibility is to help the other find a place to take hold, to *begin* with some aspect or part of his problem, need, or intent. Experience in staying with and using the partialized, focused service leads to the development of confidence and competence to cope with other related problems and needs. Nothing is so conducive to frustration and scatter as trying to do everything at once.

Perhaps most essential of all is the worker's sensitivity to what the other is experiencing in beginning and his response to that feeling, *in a way appropriate to the particular situation,* so that the other is freed to move through and beyond feelings which may be impeding his getting started. It cannot be overstressed that it is the worker's appreciation of the general promise and problems in beginnings, and his capacity to exploit this particular beginning for this particular client— *to stay with the beginning and let it be a beginning,* in all its inevitable awkwardness and tentativeness, rather than to rush to try to solve all the problems in the first interview— that embodies skill in this aspect of the social work process. The warm human connection which the worker extends to the client is felt and responded to, and thus facilitates entering the new experience. But love is not enough, and it can be overwhelming if put out too totally or in a way that leaves the other carrying all the "bad" feelings of fear, suspicion, and ingratitude for help extended.

The goal in any beginning is to find a common base for

worker and client to work together toward a common purpose—with the rules of the game known, and its elements broken down into what can be encompassed for immediate engagement. To let a beginning be a beginning, and to *further* its being a good beginning, demands knowledge and disciplined skill in a process that is truly professional.

It will be immediately clear that beginnings in the broad field of social work are of many kinds. A client begins with an agency through a relationship with a worker. Each interview that follows the first one will have its own beginning, middle, and ending until the service is terminated. It is possible to feel and utilize the rhythm of these time phases and to do what is appropriate in respect to beginnings, major and minor, within a process which is under way. This principle (use of time phases) is equally applicable in working with groups and communities, in research, supervision, administration, and teaching, but we are concerned here only with beginnings in social casework.

In speaking about beginnings I must speak also about middles and endings, since the end is implicit in the beginning, and recognition and use of this can further a good beginning.

Middles are more generally conceived as difficult to understand and utilize. Indeed, Taft once disposed of them by saying, in respect to therapy, that there are no middles. Once a patient is thoroughly in, he is seeking and finding the way to get out—to leave, to end. There is application of this truth for social work processes. Yet middles do exist and they have their own character. Social workers in all functional roles have felt the dead level quality of middles, the slump that follows the exhilaration of truly beginning and precedes the getting ready to end and continue on one's own. Middles are characterized by the other's taking increased responsibility for his part in the situation and by a deepening of the relationships involved. How can we keep middles from being flat, stale, unprofitable, or unproductive of movement? Social work method is directed toward helping the other feel and take increased responsibility for his part in the project. The very act of working together and what the worker puts in of professional concern, respect for the integrity of the other, and skillful help, conduce to a deepening of worker-client relationship which is then available for the other's use. There is always opportunity for a new focus within the ongoing experience, as appropriate, if it does not constitute an evasion of what is presently the focus. Workers, whatever their functional roles, have intuitively made use of introduction of the "new" to capture the new life potential of beginnings, to deepen the engagement and relationship, and to make it possible for the other to gain a new sense of accomplishment and power through bringing something to conclusion. In any event, middles need to be understood as time phases in their own right, so the worker can take responsibility for knowing how their particular potential can be fully utilized for deepening of engagement and movement toward more independent functioning.

Endings have their own feeling and quality. Just as beginnings are psychologically imbued with the feelings of birth, so endings are imbued in varying proportion and degree with the feeling of death—of separation. As such, endings may be resisted and feared. When one has had an experience of significance it is hard to end. There is always the question of whether one can survive the ending. Clients may resist and postpone endings even after the relationship has lost its meaning or is to be terminated under the conditions of agency service, as when a mother, the client of a protective agency, is providing care to her child above the "floor" required by the community. Or, endings may be rushed toward prematurely—to prove that "I can get along without you very well"—when the self doubts it.

Yet endings are welcomed too and even invited. Every ending carries within it the feeling of accomplishment, a sense of something lived through and taken into the self; and there is the wish to be free, to try it on one's own, to use the new power and the new self in new situations. Patterns of endings are as diverse as patterns of beginnings, because they are influenced by past ending experiences and evolved ways for dealing with them as well as affected by the nature of the particular ending situation presently faced. What is the significance of what is being left behind and of the new beginning which is to follow? Social workers, both intuitively and knowingly, have done more with beginnings than with endings. The literature speaks of "intake procedures" and "getting started" in various professional situations with varying degrees of skill consciously identified and utilized. Endings, on the other hand, are usually allowed to happen when the client is worn out, "wearied out," and the relationship has lost its meaning. There is room for the use of as much skill in exploiting the value of endings as in exploiting the value of beginnings.

Sometimes the ending is fixed by the situation; for example, the termination of convalescent leave from a hospital for the mentally ill, or a child's graduation, in a school social work situation. Exploitation of any ending involves recognizing that it either is going to occur or *should* occur in the interest of effective service, and helping the other to recognize it, look at it, and capture his own accomplishment within it. This he may be helped to do through his recapitulating the meaning the experience has had for him, assessing his own learning or movement in it, expressing whatever regret, sadness, or fear of going on alone he may have, as well as the wish and readiness he feels for what now looms as a new beginning in other ventures with their promise and hope and opportunity for using what has been learned. To "end" is to experience the new self with its fresh courage, power, and perhaps capacity for relationship, because what has been done in relationship with the worker and others involved in the undertaking is completed.

The use of ending as one aspect of skill in social work process has been much misunderstood. There should never be a practice of setting a rigid and arbitrary time limit at the point of entering on a service as a "technique" unrelated to the needs and requirements of a particular situation or service. When the ending is *in the situation* it can be used with sensitivity and skill, which involves not only technical capacity for dealing helpfully with what is involved in ending for the other, but also the worker's own capacity to let go. *When there is no ending inherent in the situation it can be psychologically helpful to establish one at the point of beginning.* The ending time established will be based on the time usually required for doing something productive in a particular kind of situation. Setting an ending time can alleviate a client's feeling of being trapped in something that may go on forever with his own will and self lost to the control of an outside force. It can serve as an incentive to the control of an outside force. It can serve as an incentive to him to use the present moment productively out of a recognition that the relationship or service is not going to last indefinitely. In developing capacity and courage to enter on something, use it, and let it go, the client develops capacity and confidence in living with all things temporal, and in small degree with the fact of life itself, with its inevitable physical ending.

When an ending is set, on the basis of collective agency experience, it is stated by the worker at the time of the beginning as, "Let's work on this for three months [or six months, or twelve weekly sessions, or whatever] and see where we are. It may be that by that time you will have found what you want to or can find here. If more time is needed, we can talk about it then." Such a method is particularly helpful in marriage and family counseling services, which lack the external form and structure of services that carry their own endings in their function or nature. When there is a time limit in the situation, that fact is referred to and used in the beginning.

In certain situations, "natural" time periods may be used, such as (in school counseling) the school year, or until Christmas vacation. Sometimes a short time period is indicated by the nature of the problem. Time structures may also be used to break up a long process through the establishment of a time period for an application process, followed by a period of continuing service, with a still different time structure for ending the service.

Imagination is needed to develop an appropriate and skillful use of endings, major and minor, within the whole process of social casework service and within individual interviews. The essential thing is that endings be understood as a psychological experience having the potential for another's more sure possession of a more fully developed self which can be owned or affirmed through the very act of ending. As is true for beginnings and middles, both the promise and the problems of endings can be consciously exploited for the value the ending can have for the other's use of service.

In writing of the principle of use of time phases, beginnings, middles, and endings as briefly as must be for this purpose, there is a risk of being superficial. Volumes could be devoted to the nature of beginnings, middles, and endings and their potential for social work exploitation. I am also aware that social workers "have always done that" in the sense of developing intake procedures (one form of utilization of beginnings as a time phase) or helping clients sum up what they have accomplished over a given period of time. What *is* claimed is that when these activities are viewed not as disparate techniques but as ways of relating to and making appropriate professional social work use of "time," a comprehension of its significance as a general principle results. It can lead to the affirmation and imaginative exploitation of the use of "time." as one essential of professional social work skill.

I should now like to refer very briefly to the implications of each of four other principles for the initial phase of the social casework helping process.

Principle 1. Diagnosis. *That diagnosis, or understanding of the phenomenon served, is most effective which is related to the use of some specific service; which is developed, in part, in the course of giving the service, with the engagement and the participation of the clientele served; which is recognized as being subject to continuous modification as the phenomenon changes; and which is put out by the worker for the clientele to use, as appropriate, in the course of the service.*

The worker never begins with a blank mind. He brings his understanding of people in general and his understanding of people of the particular age period, sex, cultural, racial, national, social, or economic group, and condition of mental and physical health and ability represented by the particular client. He has, it is hoped, consulted records and materials available in relation to this client. But with that understanding available to him, he is also prepared to let the client, in fact to *help* the client, reveal himself in the immediacy of the beginning relationship as a highly individual person who will be discovering and understanding himself as he is and as he becomes; just as the worker will be understanding him in the course of their work together. Whatever of the worker's understanding of the client in the initial phase of helping might be helpful to the client in making use of the service offered is shared with him.

The understanding which the worker "puts together" out of his social work and general knowledge and all that is available to him through records and other material is related to the purpose that has brought worker and client together. For the school social worker understanding is focused on what seems to be interfering with a child's effective and full use of school; that is, what is in *him* and in his environment—school, home, and wider community—that interferes. In other words, the purpose of the service being offered helps to give sharpness and focus to the diagnosis or understanding needed for this particular service.

Principle 2. Use of time phases has been discussed.

Principle 3. The use of agency function and function in professional role gives focus, content, and direction to social work processes, assures accountability to society and to the agency, and provides the partialization, the concreteness, the "difference," the "given" which further productive engagement.

In entering on the helping service, the worker is obligated to be not only knowledgeable about, but identified with, his agency's service. He *is* the agency in action. This requires an understanding and responsibility for the particular psychology involved in representing a particular kind of service. It requires also that he understand, take into account, and help the client deal with what is involved in *using* a particular kind of service. It asks that he know and share the conditions of agency service with the client at the outset, and use agency purpose to help the client establish jointly with him a focus for their work together. In other words, the agency service becomes real, known, and partialized as experienced through the relationship with the worker in the initial phase of that relationship. Similarly, the functional role of the social caseworker becomes known as it is experienced by the client as user of social casework service from the initial phase forward.

Principle 4. A conscious knowing use of structure as it evolves from and is related to function and process introduces "form," which furthers the effectiveness of all the social work processes.

In the initial phase, the worker will use the structure of time, clarifying how long the interview will be (approximately), over how long a period service will be available, and how frequently and at what intervals subsequent interviews will be held. As noted earlier, if the nature of the service is not conducive to a structured use of time, the worker will introduce whatever time structure can lend some form to the continuing relationship so that it is not left in an indefinite state that would hold considerable insecurity for the client. The worker will also make use of whatever structure in application forms has been found conducive to the effective and helpful giving of service. He will use the structure of place, indicating where the ensuing encounters are to be, if it can be known. He will make a decision for first and subsequent interviews about the number of people involved; for example, in marriage counseling, whether it is desirable to see both partners in the first interview, together or separately. Finally, he will use agency policy and procedure as structure and present it as "the rules of the game" so that the client may know what he is dealing with. The use of structure in the beginning, as in all phases of the helping process, should be related to the particular service being given, appropriate to it, and designed to further the flow of the helping process, not to deaden it or stop it. For this reason, structure needs to be constantly reviewed to see whether it should be modified in the light of the agency's changing experience with it. However, the use of little or no structure and the failure to capitalize on it as potentially conducive to helpfulness can result in a haphazard, formless series of encounters with less potential for the client's use than otherwise might obtain.

Principle 5. All social work processes, to be effective, require the use of relationship to engage the other in making and acting on choices or decisions as the core of working toward the accomplishment of a purpose identified as his own, within the purpose of the service being offered.

In the initial phase of the helping process, the first task of the worker is to help the client identify his own purpose in using the service, and to clarify with him whether and how that purpose is congruent with what the agency is set up to do. If the purpose might seem to be the agency's or society's in the initial phase (as in protective service, for example), there is recognition of this with the client, together with a question whether the client himself is satisfied with his situation and an offer of help in bringing about the "must" of change as it fits in with what the client himself can discover and claim as his own wish. This principle suggests the importance of immediately engaging the client in considering what the service is and whether he can use it or wants to try, rather than initiating a period of assessment during which the client remains relatively passive. Attention is accordingly focused in the initial phases on Where do you want to go? as well as on How did you get to the spot you are in? although both of these strands will weave back and forth throughout the helping process (i.e., the relation of past to present, understanding to helping). The feel of the first interview will be, Can we do business together? and the mutuality and engagement of the client in active participation will characterize the first interview in order that he may experience what using the agency service is going to be like as a basis for choosing or rejecting it. The goal of the initial phase is to establish whether the client seems to be able to use the agency service through helping him try to use it.

ASSESSMENT OF THE CLIENT IN HIS SITUATION (DIAGNOSIS OR ITS EQUIVALENT)

The first principle generic for social work practice, having its specific application to the practice of social casework, which I have elsewhere stated[32] has to do with the nature of "diagnosis" and the use of diagnosis by the social worker (see Principle 1).

For effective social work service to be given, the phenomenon served must be "understood." But what must be understood? How is that understanding arrived at? How is it used in the giving of service? Functional social work does not see, in the use of the method of social casework, any need to understand the total situation. This is considered both impossible and irrelevant to the particular purpose being discharged. (Similarly, less than exhaustive and exhausting study of a group or community can serve as a base for offering a service, with fuller understanding developing as the phe-

---

32. Smalley, *Theory for Social Work Practice.*

nomenon—individual, group, or community—changes in the course of using or not using the service offered.)

As stated earlier, the worker brings his own understanding —developed, organized, and available most surely through a process of professional education—of the nature of the particular phenomenon with which he is immediately engaged to the beginning of the process. Within these broad categories of phenomena he brings understanding of particular *kinds* of individuals, groups, or communities. Important here in his understanding of an individual, by way of illustration, is his knowledge of the growth process, the characteristics, and the needs of any and all individuals at various points in the life process, the varied ways of dealing with stress, the nature of various degrees of mental retardation, and of the more common physical, psychological, and social illnesses and their more usual meanings to the individual affected and to others in his environment. He brings an understanding of social processes and of the way individuals are affected by and affect the various groups, large and small, of which they have been and are continuously a part. He brings an understanding of socioeconomic and cultural differences and how such differences affect the way any individual life expresses itself. He brings an understanding of the various patterns of individual life expression in a particular gestalt or balance of will, emotion, and impulse.

The caseworker brings, then, a rich understanding of the phenomenon he seeks to serve. As he is engaged in work with different kinds of clients it becomes his responsibility to augment his general knowledge through independent or formal study of the particular kind of persons to whom he is currently offering service. In addition, some of his understanding will derive from records and reports of various kinds available or securable within his own and other agencies and institutions. But he brings also a capacity to let this particular and unique individual discover, reveal, and modify himself in the course of using or failing to use the service offered. So it is that the worker's understanding develops *in part* from what the other brings to, and does with, the service offered. And one aspect of his skill is his engagement of the client in making himself known both to the worker and to himself in the immediacy of the moment.

Such a view of diagnosis recognizes that people do not stay in categories, and that any attempt to place and keep them there, or to plan a specific kind of service or help on the base of a firm diagnosis by category, may deny potential for growth and change and may actually be stultifying and inhibit growth through too arbitrary an expectation of what can be expected from "this kind" of individual. Similarly, the caseworker is encouraged never to let any single characteristic—whether disease, culture, socioeconomic condition, age, or whatever—loom larger than, or obscure, the individual as a whole. The individual remains separate and unique in his own integrity as a person and requires response to that fact.

The point has been made and is here reinforced that the worker brings an understanding of the phenomenon served, the kind of phenomenon and the particular phenomenon, which helps him to be realistic at the same time he is open-minded about what a given individual may do with the service offered. For example, the worker does not approach a mentally retarded person with a communicated (or uncommunicated) expectation that he may want to think about going to college.

Imagination will suggest the way an understanding of any client comes to focus in assessing this person's capacity to use service toward an end that is or can become his own as it relates to the purpose of the particular service being given. The mother who is neglecting or abusing her child discovers no less than does the agency whether she can come to meet the minimal requirements of the community *as a mother*. The boy on probation discovers no less than the probation officer whether he is or can become the kind of boy who can realize his potential in a way that does not violate society's laws. The couple seeking marital counseling discover no less than the worker whether they can or cannot make a go of their marriage.

So in establishing a diagnosis, each individual in a sense "writes his own ticket"—makes his own diagnosis of himself and revises that diagnosis as he in fact becomes different. However, it must be emphasized, the worker brings to the process of diagnosis his understanding of "an individual," and the particular kind of individual served, as well as his own developing understanding of this specific individual.

The understanding out of which the caseworker acts is enriched and accompanied by the client's understanding of himself, in all his particularity, as he grows and changes. This brings us to the final implication of the principle of practice being discussed—the nature and use of diagnosis or assessment in social work practice.

Instead of merely making his judgment on what this individual is "like"—noting it in the record, sharing it with his supervisor, or even using it as a base for his own planned action—the worker states—frankly and freely, with professional caring and relatedness, for the client to use toward the achievement of his own purpose—his own present understanding. This, of course, is done discriminately, with a sense of timing related to the readiness of the other to use constructively what is being shared. The free sharing of understanding within the limits indicated conveys an appreciation of the other as a unique individual and a belief in his capacity to use what is being expressed, and furthers an engagement in the relationship process as well.

A caseworker may say to a client: "You tell me you are a mousy person who can't stand up for her own rights, and yet the way you are with me today, coming late to your appointment and wanting everything pretty much on your own terms, suggests a lot of strength to control." Discrepancies in what the client is saying may also be pointed out, not for the purpose of catching him in a trap, but to help him experience more deeply his own ambivalence as he discovers and develops that part of himself most true to what the self as a whole desires, or can come to desire.

The concept and use of diagnosis which has been developed reflects a belief in the individual as his own center for change, capable of continuous growth and development and of using the outside (including a relationship with the worker) to achieve that growth. It reflects an understanding of the significance of use of the agency function at every step of the helping process and of casework method as skill in the use of a process to affect a process (i.e., an individual).

Diagnosis is developed here within the context of an understanding of method in social work. It is considered a way of engaging in a human relationship process which frees the other to define his own goals for himself as they fall within or coincide with the goals of a specific program being administered, and to work toward their achievement, with the worker's help. In other words, method in social work is viewed not as method for studying or diagnosing the client-system served, but as method for affecting the client-system served. The method for studying and diagnosing in order to affect, *and as a part of the affecting,* has its own characteristics. It finds its place as part of a social work method whose essential quality is to affect, to induce change, to help. Social work method in use leads to social work process, and involves an interaction of study *and* affecting or helping, with each being continuously altered by the other. How is the study, the development of understanding modified by what is happening in the helping? How can the client participate in the study of himself, with more accurate understanding resulting and the process of helping furthered? How can what is newly known and discovered be immediately utilized in the helping? A social work method that requires the social worker's utilization of self in a relationship process with the clientele served, according to defined principles of action and toward a defined social purpose, eschews diagnosis by fixed categories of personality types with treatment related to the particular type, and leaves room instead for the emergence and utilization of the unknown, the unexpected, the newly possible in the course of the helping process, for any and all clients served.

TREATMENT PRINCIPLES AND METHODS

As stated earlier, the functional approach uses the term helping process rather than treatment because it more accurately expresses the concept that the center for change resides in the client, with the worker facilitating what the client can do, rather than that the worker is responsible for "treating" someone who, by implication, is the passive recipient of treatment. The goal of all the helping efforts of the social caseworker is expressed in the definition of social casework which I stated earlier: *Social casework is a method for engaging a client through a relationship process, essentially one to one, in the use of a social service toward his own and the general social welfare.*

This statement defines social casework's goal as discharging the purpose of some social service sponsored, and to some extent controlled, by "society." The purpose of any institutionalized form of social service is only one instance of the overriding purpose of social work, which includes both programs of social service and methods for their administration and actualization through a variety of social work methods, primary and secondary. The overriding purpose of all of social work is, as I see it, the development, modification, and administration of programs of social service which further a progressively constructive relationship between the individual and society. In a society which values dignity and difference, and appreciates the interdependence of its members, social work is an expression of society's concern with the relationship between the individual and society, with recognition of the responsibilities of individual and society to each other in their mutual interest.

The goal of social casework as method, then, is congruent with the goals of the programs of social service it administers. It seeks to release power for improved social functioning. This is done by focusing on this release in relation to some specific problem or purpose (as reflected in a society-supported agency purpose) which has brought worker and client together. Since the whole client is involved in whatever focused area he is engaged in, in using a particular service, it is highly probable that improved social functioning in some aspect of behavior would result in improved social functioning generally.

The use of social casework method is as appropriate for the multiple function agency as for the single function agency. Its task is always to find the focus for working at a particular time within a larger purpose or combination of purposes, all of which may be subsumed under the general purpose of social work.

As suggested earlier, no formal classification scheme is used as a base for engaging in a certain form of social work helping distinctive for a particular "type" of person. However, the distinctive characteristics of each person served, within the several groupings in which he falls—of age, sex, personality pattern, cultural groups, intellectual ability, mental and physical health, and other factors—needs to be appreciated if the social work help is to be as effective as possible. The social casework process operates from the same generic principles that characterize any social work process. Two of these generic principles, as they operate for the social casework process, I have already elaborated in some detail: the process of establishing and using a diagnosis or understanding of the individual served as part of the social work helping, and the use of time phases, beginnings, middles, and endings within the total social casework process. I shall speak briefly about what is involved in the use of the three additional principles which I have elsewhere developed in greater detail[33] as characterizing all social work methods but as having special application for each of the distinctive methods.

Use of agency function (see Principle 3) in the social work processes asks that what the social worker does not only be related to, but also embody and constitute an implementation of the purpose of the social agency within which he is functioning. The "content" of what goes on between the worker and those he serves is determined both by the purpose of the agency that employs him and the purpose of his role within it. His goal is always to realize these purposes (the purpose of the agency and the purpose of his functional role) and to make them come true to the fullest possible extent, in the interest of the supporting society, the agency, and the clientele served. In fact, the first task in the use of agency function is to determine through initiating the process whether the purpose or purposes of those he seeks to serve and the purpose of the agency or institution or service he represents can come together in fruitful engagement toward a common end.

Use of agency function as an integral part of social work skill offers a "difference" to the client or group who may come to an agency full of his own problem, or need, or intent, and full of projection that the agency will or will not be well disposed and helpful to him. The introduction by the worker of who he, as agency, really is and what he can and cannot be and do in relation to the client and his problem or purpose helps the client take account in a fresh and more responsible way of himself as separate from the outside. It

---

33. Ibid. See also the first section of this paper.

also gives him something to struggle with and against, to try to control and to yield to, and so allows him to develop new and more effective ways of dealing with the outside in relating to others, in becoming responsible for his own self and his own will, and, through the experience of ending with the worker and agency, of managing on his own.

Use of agency function requires the use of all the resources of the agency and all the resources of the community. Not only are these resources made available by the worker, but it is part of his skill that they will be made available as appropriate to any need expressed, at a time and in a way that gives them the best possible chance of being used.

Not only does use of agency function introduce a focus, a partialization, a difference which serves as a dynamic in the the worker-client relationship and which the client may and often does use for psychological growth of great depth and pervasiveness, but it assures social responsibility as well. For whatever reason the agency came into existence, as long as an agency continues to exist and to receive public support through tax moneys, voluntary contributions, or both, it can be assumed that it is fulfilling a needed social purpose for which the public is willing to pay. Understandably, the public wants the service for which it is paying carried out with the greatest possible skill and efficiency. Use of agency function or purpose to provide content and give direction to worker activity assures that society is getting what it is asking for and paying for.

It is obvious that agencies outlive their usefulness, that vested interests may keep them going rather than either societal or individual need, and that agency purpose may be vaguely formulated. The effort of the social caseworker, as a part of the total agency operation, working through responsible channels and in appropriate social work ways, should be directed to helping the agency clarify, modify, or even give up purpose (and its own life if indicated). But so long as he is an employee of the agency, he is obligated also to represent and be the agency, and to discharge its purposes in relation to those he serves.

Utilization of agency function as a principle for social work helping may be thought of and implemented in its richness, its potential of breadth and depth, rather than viewed and

offered as a lamentable constriction of help. Lack of imagination and range in any worker can result in a rigid, wooden
hewing to the line that fails to realize agency purpose in its
potential fullness through failure to see the connection and
relevance of the range and depth of content and experiencing
possible in any social work relationship, whatever its focus.
But failure to use this principle consciously and skillfully
as an element in helping for which the worker takes responsibility can result in dispersion of effort, want of purpose
and direction for the worker, vagueness and lack of forward
movement for the clientele, and no assurance to the community that what it supports as purpose is truly being realized.

As was earlier suggested, although use of agency function
is a generic principle in all social work processes and in all
fields of practice, one of its aspects is that each functional
field of practice or service is recognized as having its own
body of knowledge and its own "psychology" which the
worker must make his own and integrate in his helping skill.

No school of social work can prepare any student with all
he needs to know and all the skills he needs to practice with
equal effectiveness in all fields. But it can hope to graduate
him with a general body of knowledge, possessed of a skill
characterized by the use of certain principles of action which
he has developed within some specific field, and with a commitment for continuing personal-professional development
which includes openness to new knowledge and skill as he
moves from one function to another. What is essential is his
recognition that in every field there is something new to be
learned and, in a sense, to become which can improve his
effectiveness in the use of those principles which are generic
for all fields and processes.

The use of what I have elsewhere identified as the "fourth
principle" for social work helping relates to the use of structure as an aspect of casework helping.[34]

Structure or form in social casework helping, as in all the
social work processes, should arise from the process itself and
serve to channel, contain, and make that process effective
toward the realization of some agency function or purpose. I

34. Ibid.

referred earlier to kinds of structure which need to be devised to carry out or facilitate the process. One such structure relates to use of *time*. This refers to setting time periods to accomplish the social work purpose and to develop forms appropriate for use at certain times, such as intake forms, evaluation forms, and termination of service forms. I have already discussed some of what is involved in the use of time and time phases to further process.

Place also gives form to the several work processes. Although a caseworker knows that an interview can be held anywhere—in a car, on a street corner, in the client's own home, as well as in an agency office or building—and that circumstances will suggest the most effective place in the individual instance, he knows too that holding a series of interviews in the same office is conducive to stability, and constitutes a form, a structure which may make the interviews more usable to the client. Indeed when the place of interviewing is changed, backward movement has been known to result. Certainly, as part of helping skill, the fact of change needs to be noted in the interview to aid the client in taking in and encompassing the shift. So an agency conducts its business in a certain building, whether as a storefront operation or a more traditional one. If a move to a new building is contemplated, not only must account be taken of the suitability of the new structure (form) to the undertaking, but a process should be established for moving into and adjusting to the new place.

Place as structure needs not only to hold steady (in the usual instance) but also to be suited to the undertaking, the function to be discharged.

Policy itself serves as structure and gives form to an undertaking. Once policy is established through an orderly process and with the intent of making more effective the carrying out of agency purpose, it gives form to the particular undertaking and avoids the inequity which could result from lack of policy. Policy is designed to assure an operation that always works the same in like situations and that carries the intent of the program in its design. It embodies the comfort and accountability of a form, a structure, on which the community, the worker, and the client can rely. It constitutes a given, a known, something concrete and real which the client can grapple with, something which will hold steady and so facilitate the client's own movement in relation to it.

From the establishment of policy flows the development of procedures or specific methods, ways of implementing policy. Policies require constant scrutiny and evaluation by the caseworker as they are tested in the crucible of actual operation. As agency purposes are modified, policies must be modified to carry the changed purpose. Similarly, procedures need constant evaluation. They may be too many, too few, inoperable for one reason or another, or overelaborate. They may actually impede the process they were designed to further. Policy and procedure constitute pieces of structure available for the caseworker's use as part of the social casework helping skill.

Agency function influences form and gives rise to the development of structure for making a particular kind of service available, as suggested earlier in this section. The configuration of relationships implicit in each of the social work processes, and within the social casework process, constitutes a form which can be used well or poorly as an integral part of the helping skill.

Structure or form of any kind may be used rigidly, woodenly, without appreciation of its potential significance for the conduct of the process it is designed to further or of its relationship to the purpose of the particular undertaking comprehended as a whole. Skill in the development and use of form or structure requires that it be employed in quite another way, with full comprehension of its necessity, with wisdom, and with constant testing and modification of it, in the interest of its effectiveness for making a service available in a helpful way. Too much form can stifle creativity and result in working from the book, with the own self and opportunity for the new and emergent left out or minimized. But too little form or absence of form can waste effort and lead to purposelessness, disorganization, confusion, amorphousness, or outright chaos.

What is suggested here is that acceptance of the use of form and structure as a principle for practice can lead to its imaginative development and productive employment as a required element of social work helping skill.

The final element of skill in the social casework helping process to which I shall refer derives from what I have identified as Principle 5.[35]

All the principles which have been described come to focus in this central and final principle. All are designed to further what is here established as the central, generic core of social work practice in all its processes—the engagement of the other through the use of a relationship process in working toward his own social purpose.

The nature of engagement requires some elaboration here. It characterizes all the processes, and here we are concerned specifically with the process of social casework, from beginning to end. It is as true in beginning, in establishing diagnosis, as in ending. This is not to imply for the process of social casework that everything the caseworker does is in immediate relationship with the person or persons served. The worker may bring about change in the environment, may enlist and utilize community resources in addition to the resources of his own agency, may serve as "advocate" for the client, but everything he does has its focus in releasing the client to use himself and his situation—as it is, as he makes it different, and as the worker makes it different— toward the fullest possible realization of his own individual and social potential, in respect to the problem of immediate concern.

What specifically makes engagement possible? What, in method, accomplishes it? Identifying a purpose, as it inheres in agency purpose, discovering with the other whether it can become his own purpose for himself, whether he can *choose* it as purpose, facilitating the expression of the other's own purpose for himself, clarifying both what the other is saying and asking and what is available in agency and community resource to meet expressed need or intent, questioning to develop further mutual understanding of problems and choices for solution, identifying conflict or ambivalence for the other to resolve, introducing facts or information which may be useful, eliciting and responding to thinking and feeling as appropriate to the situation and the particular phase of the helping process—a whole array of "techniques" is use-

35. Ibid.

ful to further true engagement of the other in working on his problem or intent in relation to a mutually affirmed purpose.

The significance of choosing, of making and acting on decisions for affirmation of and development of capacity for responsible action, is developed with unusual penetration by Faatz in *The Nature of Choice in Casework Process*.[36]

The role of feeling and response to feeling in furthering productive engagement is generally accepted as primary in the practice of social casework. Feeling and thinking occur and are utilized in changing balance in the individual instance. It is through the relationship with the caseworker that the client discovers his own self, his own feeling, his own willing. As he, with the worker's help, takes back some of his projections on the worker and others in his life situation and as he identifies with the worker and the worker's quality as a person, he also makes some of the worker's strength for coping his own. His discovery may sometimes entail very little intellectual assessment of what he is like in theoretical terms, but it always involves an experiencing of what he is like in the situation with the worker for a surer possession of a more developed and more affirmed self. This knowing, experiencing, and possessing the self occur in relation to what he and the worker are working on together in his own life situation, as well as in his relationship to the worker. As he leaves the casework situation it is a new self, a more courageous and able self, within its own pattern, which he takes as it has emerged through working as a whole self on a limited situation or problem. It is this new and whole self which is available for subsequent living, in the variety of situations and relationships he will encounter.

The use of the five principles which have been presented as generic for all social work processes and as they have specific application for the social casework process, and of the various techniques and specifics which find their place in relation to the principles, constitutes the essence of functional social casework helping skill. A whole array of techniques and skills are involved in the imaginative use of the "principles" as a whole and in relation to each other; but "skills"

---

36. Anita Faatz, *The Nature of Choice in Casework Process* (Chapel Hill: University of North Carolina Press, 1953).

are viewed not as discrete entities, a "repertoire of interventive acts," but as integral parts of a process that has unity and wholeness and is directed toward a central purpose which inheres both in the method (social casework) and in the purpose of the agency in which it is being used.

THE TARGET GROUP

The functional approach is applicable to all fields of practice for social work, in dealing with all social problems in relation to which social work has a contribution to make, and to all the social work methods both primary (ordinarily thought of as social casework, social group work, and community organization), which deal with the clientele or client-system directly, and secondary (such as supervision and administration, research, and education for social work).

It may be clarifying at this time to state what functional social work sees as the purpose of all social work effort.

The underlying purpose of all social work effort is viewed as the release of human power in individuals for personal fulfillment and social good, and the release of social power for the creation of the kind of society, social institutions, and social policies which make self-realization most possible for all men. Two values which are primary in such a purpose are respect for the worth and dignity of every individual and concern that he have the opportunity to realize his potential as an individually fulfilled, socially contributive person. This implies a value that society be the kind of society which furthers such self-realization for all men.

Kenneth L. M. Pray identified social work as

a normal constructive social instrument, a necessary part of the structure of a civilized, well-planned society because it is directed to helping individuals meet the problems of their constantly shifting relationships with one another and with the whole society, and with helping the whole society at the same time adjust its demands upon its members and its services to them in accordance with the real needs of the individuals that compose and determine its life.[37]

37. Kenneth L. M. Pray, "The Role of Professional Social Work in the World Today," in *Social Work in a Revolutionary Age* (Philadelphia: University of Pennsylvania Press, 1949), pp. 33–34.

Social work is based on a recognition that in our complex society, with its often conflicting demands and its uneven provision of opportunity for different individuals, there are inevitable stresses as individuals, groups, and whole communities seek to find a meaningful and productive place for themselves within the scheme of things. This is a seeking which can never be finally achieved. Life does not stand still; neither the life of a total society nor the life of any individual, group, or community.

Into a world characterized by continuous change in the relationship between man and his society, and by continuous change in each of the parts of that relationship, comes social work. The central concern of social work is that the relationship be progressively productive for the individuals who make up society, through promoting their well-being and providing opportunity for their realization of potential, and for society as a whole through the continuous development of the values, customs, and institutions which further such well-being and self-realization for all its people.

Karl de Schweinitz brought clarity into the often confused picture of social work—as differentiated from the social services and from social welfare—through formulating the following definitions in the course of teaching a class in the history of social work:

Social Welfare: The well being of people everywhere in their personal daily lives, in particular the fullest possible opportunity for spiritual expression and satisfying human relationships at home and abroad, for health, education, pleasant housing, interesting employment, recreation, cultural development, social security, and an income adequate to these and other essentials.

The Social Services: The instrumentalities through which men translate into action their sense of obligation to contribute to the well being of others and to the development of those phases of social welfare which contribute to that well being.

Social Work: The body of knowledge, skill, and ethics professionally employed in the administration of the social services and in the development of programs for social welfare.[38]

A concept of social work as the professional administration and development of social services limits its purview to no

---

38. Karl de Schweinitz, as quoted by Smalley in *Theory for Social Work Practice,* pp. 3–4.

one kind of person, to no one class or group, to no one category of social problem, and to the use of no one method in work with individuals, groups, or communities.

In summary, social work is characterized by its special concern with man's social relationships and opportunities, in essence with the relationship between man and his society, and by its responsibility for the furthering of a relationship that will be progressively productive for both. It is characterized, furthermore, by its responsibility to operate from its own defined values and to employ its distinctive body of knowledge and its distinctive methods for practice, or operating skills, as they are continuously developed by the profession for the most effective discharge of its purpose, however microscopically represented in a specific program of social service.

It is the program of service which society not only supports, in its own interest as well as in the interest of the clientele served, but also controls; both through financial contribution and through the direction given by boards of directors as representatives of society's stake in the operation of a particular program. It has been well said that social agencies are the *agents* of society. Professional social workers are employed to administer programs of social service because the administration of such programs constitutes the particular purpose of social work as a profession and because the knowledge and skill specific to social work is required for the most effective operation of social service programs. Social workers have a responsibility to contribute their professional wisdom and to give informed leadership to the shaping and changing of social service programs, to community patterns of social service programs, and to social policy as it relates to the development and operation of programs of social service. But their primary task remains the provision of a service which society, or groups of persons representing the interest and stake of society, has identified as important, and which society supports. The general direction of the program or service, whether it continues to exist at all, and if so in what form, will be determined by its source of support: the public. From the "functional" point of view, if social workers cut themselves off from society and see the agency or program whose services they are administering as somehow a hindrance to what they, as social workers, really want to do, are prepared to do, and should be doing, they may well be denying the essential nature of their profession and failing to realize the richness of the contribution they alone, as a profession, can and are responsible to make.

Social work constitutes a single profession then, first of all through its unifying values and its unifying purpose, however diverse its programs. An equally compelling requirement if it is to constitute a single profession is a unifying method, or professional skill for realization of purpose. My own point of view is that the generic principles to which reference has been made earlier in this chapter characterize all social work methods, and within them each method develops its own specific character and requirements. All social work methods, including the method of social casework, may be used in any and all fields for social work practice.

The present trend to prepare social workers in a generic social work method or to prepare workers for use of more than one method seems to me to ignore the complexities and the differences of the several methods. However, it does point up the necessity for all social workers to be conversant with both the generic principles which characterize all methods and some of their specific requirements in knowledge and skill. It can lead to an individual worker's greater facility in using a variety of methods or moving from method to method without denial of the differences in the method being used.

Individual social agencies are increasingly using more than one method for the "delivery" of their services. Here I should like to speak specifically about the greater use of work with groups by many agencies which have previously used social casework as not only the primary but almost the exclusive delivery form. This places an obligation on the agency (not on the individual worker) to determine how both processes shall be employed by a given agency, in what kinds of situations, and for what kinds of clients. Social work departments of mental hospitals and child placing institutions, to name but two categories of service agencies, have long used work with groups as one form of administering their programs. As both forms (work with individuals and work with groups) are used increasingly, both agency and worker are responsible for furthering the individual worker's capacity to use both processes—a responsibility made easier by changing trends in social work education, which is now preparing for more flexibility in use of social work method.

To conclude this section on the target group for social work practice, the social casework method is viewed, as here developed, as being equally applicable to all kinds of clients, in their infinite variety, and to all·fields for practice appropriate for social work. Its use for a particular kind of client or within any specific field for practice will require adaptation and specific knowledge and skill which the worker is obligated to develop on the base of his preparation as a social worker.

UNRESOLVED PROBLEMS: A DISCUSSION OF THE MAJOR THEORETICAL PROBLEMS AND ISSUES

The following seem to me to be most significant issues for social casework today, or rather for social work as a profession as it considers the method of social casework which has long constituted and which continues to constitute the methodological practice form for the great majority of its practitioners. I shall state the issues as questions.

1. *How may a concept of the essential purpose and nature of social casework be related to professional, and wider, appreciation of its significance?*

Does the profession's current emphasis on social reform, social action, social planning, social welfare organization and administration (in the executive sense) need to result in a downgrading and even repudiation of social casework as a significant activity for social work and social workers? Might this tendency be lessened if social casework were generally conceived as a method for the achievement of social work purpose through the realization of some social agency purpose rather than as a form of psychosocial treatment of individuals? It is understandable that in a time of great and rapid social change, a revolutionary time, the fate of the "individual" is sometimes viewed as relatively unimportant, certainly as secondary to sweeping reforms destined to benefit some great body of individuals. However, might the place and significance of the social caseworker on the present social scene gain greater understanding and acceptance both within and outside the profession if, in addition to the role or function clarification suggested above, there could be increased emphasis on the social caseworker's role in evaluating social welfare programs for their effectiveness and in contributing to changing social policy and social welfare organization on the basis of firsthand experience with the way present social welfare organizations are affecting the individuals served *in addition to* continued emphasis on his responsibility to administer the programs which presently exist?

2. *What are some implications, for the profession and the society it serves, of a conception of social casework as a social work method in its own right for which preparation is given within formal programs of professional education as against a conception of "generic social work method"?*

It is possible to identify social casework as one distinctive method in social work, operating from generic principles which characterize all social work methods, both primary and secondary, and from values and broad purposes which activate all social workers, while yet retaining distinctive attributes as method requiring some distinctive knowledge and skill. This issue has obvious bearing on programs of social work education. If the "generic social work method" concept is accepted as preferable, is it educationally possible to prepare social workers who are equally proficient in working with individuals, small groups, and communities? If not, is it nonetheless preferable to sacrifice depth in method skill for range and flexibility in method skill? I have suggested both in this chapter and elsewhere in greater detail[39] one frame of reference for identification of specific method within a generic method context. Should and could others be developed from other ideological bases?

Should all method concentration in social work education be abandoned in favor of some other form of concentration, such as social problem area? What would be the gains? Might there be losses for the social work profession and so for the society it serves in letting go of what is required to produce social workers skilled in social work method, whether generic, multiple, or specific? Will social welfare programs achieve as fully as they might the purposes for which they are designed if there is a watering down or dilution of the professional skill necessary to get the services to the client with maximum helpfulness? Will the abandonment of social casework as

39. Smalley, *Theory for Social Work Practice.*

one possible method concentration (or social group work as one possible method concentration) result in the loss of two highly developed bodies of social work method knowledge and skill having unique as well as generic characteristics?

3. *What are the "social value" implications, not only for social work but for society, of weakening or failing to continue to develop social casework as one distinctive methodological form for social work practice?*

Social casework, in its very nature (i.e., in its focus on the individual or the "case"), expresses a valuing of the individual in his difference and a belief in his capacity to use help extended through a human relationship to solve problems in a self-fulfilling, socially constructive way. A present tendency on the part of many social workers is to view individuals and groups as "victims," helpless in themselves, needing "advocates" and radicaly changed social conditions *before* anything can or should be expected of them in the way of responsible, productive behavior. Can this attitude go so far that social work as a profession may contribute to the weakening of individual initiative, responsibility, and power for self-realization in socially constructive ways? Is it possible that social work may have a significant role to play in keeping alive and furthering the profession's and society's appreciation of the individuality of the person and of his power for self-realization *at the same time* that it takes an increasingly vigorous part in working toward the improvement of social conditions and the increasing of social opportunity for disadvantaged individuals and groups?

4. *What is the import, for the continuing development of social casework as one form of social work method skill, of what is commonly identified as the "manpower problem" in social work?*

From the manpower problem derive two related "thrusts": the profession's assumption of responsibility for all workers in the welfare field regardless of educational preparation, and the breaking up of the social caseworker's function into a series of tasks, some of which are identified as appropriate for the professional and some for the paraprofessional worker, plus the identification of kinds of clients or situations appropriate for paraprofessional service. There has followed an increasing blurring of the outlines of what constitutes a professional social worker, whether defined by

education or by competence. May the unitary nature of the
social casework helping process be lost through conceiving it
either as something simple enough for anybody to do, or as
consisting of a series of discrete tasks, some of which can be
"farmed out"—a practice which tends to wipe out the place
of sustained human relationship in process eventuation?
What are sound ways for utilizing persons with less than full
professional education for social work within the social welfare complex without risking loss of the contributions which
only the professional social worker is prepared to make, both
to the clientele and to society as a whole, through method
knowledge and method skill used to implement social work
values and purpose?

Bibliography

Allen, Frederick. *Positive Aspects of Child Psychiatry*. New York:
  W. W. Norton Co., 1963.
Faatz, Anita. *The Nature of Choice in Casework Process*. Chapel
  Hill: University of North Carolina Press, 1953.
Hofstein, Saul. "The Nature of Process: Implications for Social
  Work." *Journal of Social Work Process* 14 (1964).
Lynd, Helen Merrell. *Shame and the Search for Identity*. New
  York: Harcourt, Brace and World, 1961.
Moustakas, Clark, ed. *The Self*. New York: Harper and Brothers,
  1956.
Pray, Kenneth L. M. *Social Work in a Revolutionary Age*. Phila-
  delphia: University of Pennsylvania Press, 1949.
Rank, Otto. *Will Therapy and Truth and Reality*. Translated by
  Jessie Taft. New York: Alfred A. Knopf, 1947.
Robinson, Virginia P., ed. *Jessie Taft, Therapist and Social Work
  Educator*. Philadelphia: University of Pennsylvania Press, 1962.
Robinson, Virginia P., ed. "Training for Skill in Social Case
  Work." *Journal of Social Work Process* 4 (1942).
Robinson, Virginia P. *The Dynamics of Supervision under Func-
  tional Controls*. Philadelphia: University of Pennsylvania Press,
  1950.
Smalley, Ruth E. *Theory for Social Work Practice*. New York: Co-
  lumbia University Press, 1967.
All volumes of *Journal of Social Work Process*. Philadelphia: University of Pennsylvania Press, published 1937–42 and 1953–69,
  for formulations of theory and use of theory in practice, in a
  variety of fields for practice.

4 | The Problem-solving Model in Social Casework

Helen Harris Perlman

INTRODUCTION

When *Social Casework: A Problem-solving Process* was first published, I assigned it for a seminar I was leading at Berkeley. But it could not be found in the university bookstore. Then someone's sharp eye discovered it, standing lonely among the alien texts on calculus and trigonometry, in the section on mathematics.

I tell you this story now, twelve years later, because there still persists among some social workers the notion that "problem-solving" means some intellectual, totally logical, rational process by which a problem is attacked, brought to heel, and tidily resolved, with a Q.E.D. stamped on its neatly packaged bottom. So I must begin in what may be considered a negative way, by saying first what problem-solving as a social casework process is *not*.

Problem-solving as a casework process is not a manipulation of people or objects or circumstances to bring them from disorganization to order, from dilemma to resolution. Problem-solving is not a series of strategies by which a "fixer" or arranger moves by the laws of logic and abstract reasoning from some difficulty to its dissolution. Problem-solving is not a game by which the person who knows its rules guides and controls the person who is in trouble and moves him into a marked-out goal called "home" or "cure" or "there, now." It is none of these.

The problem-solving process in casework is, first of all, a *process*, which is to say *it is a forward moving course of transactions between active agents*. In casework those active agents are the caseworker and his client and the peopled and circumstanced life-space in which they are involved. The problem—which is to say the difficulty that is in the center of concern at any given time—is felt by, carried by, and experienced by the help-seeking person. That person, with his subjective reading of and reaction to his problem(s) must also be his own problem-solver. The problem cannot be dealt with except through him, with him, and by involvement of his powers.

Those powers, present or absent in varying degrees, are

Helen Harris Perlman is Samuel Deutsch Professor, School of Social Service Administration, University of Chicago.

motive, affective, perceptive, cognitive, adaptive powers. In short, they are the functions we group together and conceptualize as "the ego." When the complex operations embodied in that tiny word "ego" are recognized and understood they may clearly be seen to be the personality's problem-solving operations. This was what Freud repeatedly implied in his tentative explorations of his ego concept, and it is what the ego psychologists who followed him have made explicit. From the moment of birth to the moment of death every human being is involved in continual problem-solving, both conscious and unconscious, in order to maintain his stability-in-movement, or to retrieve stability-in-movement, or to achieve it at some higher level. That process of ego functioning by which a person perceives inner or outer reality, reads its meaning, and variously adapts, defends, protects, copes, accommodates, retreats, renounces, compromises, chooses, grapples, and engages himself with his reality—that process is the way by which a person deals with his encountered problems, whether those problems are in the nature of pleasure to be gained or un-pleasure to be avoided. It is sometimes unconscious, sometimes preconscious, sometimes fully in consciousness.

It was in my clinical casework observations of the ways human beings "just naturally" tried to deal with their needs and wants, and in my further explorations and observations as a teacher of how human beings think and learn, that I came suddenly to see a synthesis that I was ashamed I had not seen long before. It was there bold and clear. It was that we think and learn, feel and react, adapt and cope as the expression and exercise of the ego's usual problem-solving processes. Poor thinking, poor learning, blurred perception, inappropriate or inept coping are the symptoms of some functional failures or inadequacies or blocking. Good thinking and good learning resulting in good adaptive behavior are the symptoms of accrued competence in the exercise of conflict-free ego capacities. Philosophers of education and of mental processes—and I was particularly familiar with John Dewey's thought—had simply put what was for me a "discovery" into other terms within another frame of reference. The emphasis in the educational framework was, of course, upon cognitive forces; the emphasis in the psychoanalytic framework was upon affective forces. Within both frameworks are to be found the conception of the human being as endowed with dynamic capacities for feeling, thinking, and acting in response to pleasurable or unpleasurable stimuli, to threat or to promise. In the writings of both Dewey (and his followers) and Freud (and his) is to be found this major thesis: that living is a problem-solving process, and further, by implication, that both education and therapy have as their purpose the furtherance of better rather than worse, systematic rather than disordered modes by which this process may be enhanced and facilitated.

I am reminded now of what Freud said to his skeptical audience in his lecture "The Dissection of the Psychical Personality."

In ego psychology it will be difficult to escape what is universally known; it will rather be a question of new ways of looking at things and new ways of arranging them than of new discoveries [sic].[1]

In this new way of looking at things I saw the immediate and powerful connection between the person's normal problem-solving drives and the strategies of the ego, and between these and the potentially systematized and professionally controlled problem-solving efforts of a helping process such as casework. The latter, I saw, were the responsible and skilled means by which frail or dwarfed or distorted ego capacities might be empowered or reformed or restored to effectiveness.[2]

---

1. Sigmund Freud, New Introductory Lectures on Psychoanalysis, trans. and ed. James Strachey (New York: W. W. Norton & Co., 1964).
2. In Helen Harris Perlman, "The Basic Structure of the Casework Process," Social Service Review 27 (September 1953):308–15.
I first set forth this view of normal ego functions in their relation to casework's problem-solving process. I glimpsed there "a rather interesting parallel to the normal problem-solving processes of the ego." Later, in 1957, I proposed that "human life [is] itself a problem-solving process. . . . [It] is the work in which every human being engages from the moment of birth to that of death. . . . [The] major, common kinds of ego operation . . . are involved in all human problem-solving efforts" (Helen Harris Perlman, Social Casework: A Problem-solving Process [Chicago: University of Chicago Press, 1957], pp. 53–54). In 1961, Dr. Bernard Bandler proposed that "life with its processes and successful methods of solving problems and resolving conflicts, is our model for psychotherapy" ("The Concept of Ego-Supportive Psychotherapy," in Ego-Oriented Casework, ed. Howard J. Parad and Roger R. Miller [New York: Family Service Association of America, 1963]).

My subsequent development of the problem-solving model for casework was not in any sense a fabricated construction into which a caseworker and a client were set and told, in effect, "Look, if you want to be scientific or artistic—whichever you value—you must fit your actions into this mode." Rather the model suggested, "This is the way a person's conscious efforts to cope with a problem usually operate when they are *more* rather than *less* successful, when they are more adaptive than maladaptive, more apt than inept." Then it said, "These operations are transferable into a professional process that helps people when their own coping efforts fail them." Thus problem-solving as a process of exercise of ego coping powers became a casework process.

THE CHARACTERISTIC ELEMENTS IN PROBLEM-SOLVING CASEWORK

Social casework is one of the helping modes within the human welfare profession of social work. Its aim, congruent with all social work, is to raise and undergird the level of human competence and satisfaction in daily living, in the ongoing person-to-person and person-to-task transactions involved in social functioning. In its ethical precepts, its value commitments, its sources of sanction, casework is at one with its parent-body, social work; so for this paper these will be taken for granted. The distinguishing mark of casework as a helping mode in social work is that it takes as its unit of attention and concern the individual instance, a person or a family. The person (or family) considered to be a prospective user of help via the casework process is one who is experiencing some problem in his relationships with one or more other persons, or in his satisfactory performance of one or more role tasks. Some aspect(s) of his social comfort, relationships, or functioning are problematic for him. At this moment in time and circumstance his own usual problem-solving means are, for whatever reasons, inadequate, inappropriate, or inaccessible to him. So he turns to a social agency for material, psychological, or social help in coping with his problem.

The implicit assumption is that the person's inability to cope with his problem on his own is due to some deficit in or absence of one or a combination of the following problem-solving means: the *motivation* to work on the problem in appropriate ways; the *capacity* to work on the problem in appropriate ways; the *opportunity*, whether of ways or means, to meet or mitigate the problem. (This assumption will be examined in more detail later because it is a central one in the problem-solving model. Here it will only be noted that it is different from the unspoken but tacit assumption that has at times governed some other forms of casework practice, which is that the person seeking help is "sick," or has a "weak ego," or that the presence of what is for him at this time an insurmountable problem is the consequence of personality malfunctioning.)

On the basis of this central assumption, the casework process consists of calculated actions on the helper's part:

1. to release, to energize, and to give direction to the client's motivation for change. This can be said more technically: the problem-solving process aims to minimize disabling anxiety and fears and to provide such support and safety as encourages a lowering of constricting ego defenses, a heightening of reward expectation, and thus, a freeing of ego energies for investment in the task at hand.

2. to release and then to exercise repeatedly the client's mental, emotional, and action capacities for coping with the problem or with himself in connection with it. This can be said another way: the problem-solving process aims to release and exercise the ego's functions of perception, feeling, cognition, comprehension, selection, judgment, choice, and action as they are required to deal with the problem under consideration.

3. to find and make accessible to the client such aids and resources as are necessary to the solution or mitigation of the problem. This can be said another way: the problem-solving process aims to make accessible those means in the external environment which are essential conditions and instruments for satisfying and satisfactory role performance.

Within this broad (and rough) outline a considerable diversity of emphasis and operations may exist. The problem-solving model, like any other, is one way of selecting certain perspectives and of shaping action to them. Problem-solving is, I propose, a model for the translation of ego psychology into action principles.

The usual active elements in the problem-solving model are these: a *person* beset by a *problem* seeks help with that problem from a *place* (either a social agency or some other social institution) and is proffered such help by a professional social worker who uses a *process* which simultaneously engages and enhances the person's own problem-solving functions, and supplements the person's own problem-solving resources.

As a process, problem-solving, whether in casework or in the normal course of living, consists of several operations. These may or may not occur in the order in which linear logic must set them down; they may rather occur simultaneously, or in unlogical sequence. But any conscious effort to move from quandary to resolution must involve these modes of interior or external action.

1. The problem must be identified by the person—that is to say, be recognized, named, and placed in the center of attention.

2. The person's subjective experience of the problem must be identified—that is, how he feels it, how he sees it, how he interprets it, what it does to him and what he does to affect it—to cause, exacerbate, avoid, or deal with it.

3. The facts of the problem's causes and effects and its import and influence upon the person-in-his-life-space must be identified and examined.

4. The search for possible means and modes of solution must be initiated and considered, and alternatives must be weighed and tried out in the exchange of ideas and reactions that precede action.

5. Some choice or decision must be made as a result of thinking through and feeling through what behaviors or material means seem most likely to affect the problem or the person's relation to it.

6. Action taken on the basis of these considerations will test out the validity and the workability of the decision. Then some ensuing steps may be considered to reinforce and broaden the opening-wedge effort; or, if it has not proved workable or useful, alternative perspectives and actions may need to be the subject of discussion and change and decision.[3]

Two further factors enter in, variable but omnipresent.

---

3. For full exposition of this model see Perlman, *Social Casework: A Problem-solving Process,* especially index pages under "Problem-solving.

Without them the problem-solving model would be largely a model of a cognitive, conscious, and rational process. With them the problem-solving model is charged with the energies and directions of emotional needs and gratification-seeking. One is the factor of relationship. This will be dealt with separately because of its vital importance. Here, though, it must be mentioned at once, because relationship is the bond that vitalizes, warms, and sustains the work between helper and helped. Without it problem-solving would be a process of cool reason only; with it, the process is infused with the emotional gratification and support that make the game worth the candle.

The second vital variable that determines the nature and outcome of casework's problem-solving efforts is the involvement and effect of the help-seeker's "significant others"— the persons and social circumstances within the help-seeker's problematic network. Their transactions with the help-seeker may be for good or for evil, toward constructive or destructive results. Therefore, the caseworker who seeks to help a person cope with some problematic aspect of his interpersonal or task relationships must not only be aware of these "others," persons or objects, with which the client is engaged, but must often actively involve and deal with such "others" in the attempt to influence them. Unless the caseworker does so the help-seeker's motivation, capacity, or resources for coping with his problem may be consistently subject to outside influences over which the helper has no control.

This is generally accepted in casework. But its special relevance to the problem-solving model may be seen further on, when the help-seeker or client, who may or may not have a personality difficulty, is seen and treated as a member of a role system, and when the problem, whatever its manifold past causes, is seen and treated as a problem-to-be-solved in a current transactional exchange.

TARGET GROUP AND GOALS

There is no special "target group"[4] of persons or problems en-

4. I use this term with some aversion. It suggests to me a stationary set at which something is aimed and to which something is done. However, I yield to current usage and take it to mean the center of attention and concern.

visioned in the problem-solving model. Treatment of environmental problems is not distinguished from treatment of psychological problems, because it is always the *person* who is being helped in relation to what he finds stressful or emotionally unsupportable. Whether his is a chronic or a recent problem, whether his deficits are of material resources and services or of psychic energy or of emotional balance, the same process holds, although of course the content that is dealt with, the emphases repeated, and the length of contact will differ by diagnostic decisions. Even if the identified problem is largely intrapsychic its manifestations or the test of its import will be seen and known in the client's person-to-person or person-to-task transactions. It is in these that he will find the gratifications that say "problem modified" or "problem managed" or, unhappily, "problem unyielding." Thus, what the person sees, wants, feels, thinks, and does in his response to his identified problem and to the now present provisions of compassionate support and guided consideration and services that the caseworker offers are the constant content of problem-solving work, no matter what the problem.

Before one can assess whether a model is good or bad, more or less useful, one must ask and answer the questions, To what ends is it to be used? What is its aim? What are its goals?

The generalized goal of casework is that of all social work: to help people achieve socially constructive and individually satisfying lives. But there has been something illusory about that goal, as there is likely to be about most idealized formulations. The illusion it bred was that some steady state of being (unassailable equilibrium, contentment, or happiness) can be achieved and sustained. Thus in the past (and still today in some places) caseworkers labored endlessly, though with growing malaise, to try to bring their clients to some state of "cure" of their problems or to some point where the client could say "There now, I'm fixed!" and the caseworker could say "He is free of problems."

What actually happened was that cases seemed to close themselves, often in the midst of turmoil. Clients dropped out of treatment, or if the client and caseworker came to a joint agreement on termination (and the infrequency of this is suggested by the difficulty in finding case records that will show it) there was often a reluctant release by the caseworker with some uneasy feeling that he had somehow not come up to his ideal goal.

The problem-solving model stands firmly upon the recognition that life is an ongoing, problem-encountering, problem-solving process. Every life holds its crucial phases and its crisis events. Every day holds its choices and decisions to be made, some trivial and some heavy with significance. Every person thus is involved every day, in greater or lesser degree of consciousness and competence, in recognizing and coping with his problems, in the form of questions to be answered or decisions to be made.

The problem-solving process of casework is for helping individual persons (families) to cope with or resolve some difficulty that they are currently finding insurmountable, in ways that will maximize their conscious effort and competence. The by-product of these conscious uses of ego functions toward more competent coping with self and problems is learning a way by which tomorrow's (or next year's) difficulties and decisions may be dealt with. One must admit, in honesty, that this is a *hoped-for* by-product. The probability of its occurrence depends on a number of factors, among which are reinforcement rewards and repetition of the problem-solving exercises—multiple factors that cannot be discussed here. This hoped-for by-product may be said to be one goal in the problem-solving model—the goal of equipping a person with a way of coping that may serve him for the new problems he will inevitably encounter as long as he is alive.

The primary goal of the problem-solving model, however, is to help a person cope as effectively as possible with such problems in carrying social tasks and relationships which he now perceives, feels as stressful, and finds insuperable without outside help. The rationale for this modest goal is severalfold.

1. This is what the applicant for casework help wants; it is what he applies for. He does not typically say "Change me" or "Help me with my neurotic [or deviant or inappropriate] reactions and behavior." With a few exceptions (so notable, perhaps, that they have become unconsciously multiplied in caseworker's minds) the applicants to social agencies, as intake studies show, want help with self-management or other-

management in some currently experienced relationship or task.[5] That the client's identified problem may be reformulated during the course of help; that it may be found to require intrapsychic exploration and psychotherapeutic treatment; that it may be the end product of a whole chain of other problems—these possibilities lie in any case. The plain fact is, however, that one must start where the applicant is; and if and when he has been led to see and feel his problem differently and is motivated to tackle it in those new perspectives, his goals become expandable. They can always be stretched. Goal is an unfolding concept.

2. Help with perceived and felt problems within as short a time as possible is, quite naturally, what most applicants want.[6] Like goals, treatment time can always be extended when the client sees and feels the need for it.

3. A short-term goal, aimed for within time limits, serves for both caseworker and client to mobilize their energy and efforts. This has been amply supported both in practice observations and recent research.[7] The achievement of a short-term, partialized goal, when it "pays off" in the self-sense of accomplishment or by the helper's approval, is the "success" which infuses hope into the next steps forward.

4. Particularly in work with those who today are central to social work's concern—the economically and educationally deprived, the hard-to-reach, the nonintrospective, long-and-chronically deprived persons, the crisis-prone and crisis-

5. At this writing another study adds factual evidence of the client's conception of the purpose of casework help. Julianna T. Schmidt ("The Use of Purpose in Casework Practice," *Social Work* 14 [January 1969]: 77–84) finds that "almost one-half [of the caseworkers in six family service agencies] ranked such aims . . . as insight, self-identity or self-confidence as most important. [But] only one-third of the clients agreed that such objectives were of top priority; the balance cited improvements in their interpersonal relationship, role functioning or related social goals as most important."

6. "Both agencies and clinics [in this study] tended to overestimate the anticipated number of interviews." Howard J. Parad, "A Study of Crisis-Oriented Planned Short-Term Treatment," *Social Casework* 59 (June 1968):346–55.

7. The values for clients in short-term goals are demonstrated clearly in the recently published research of William J. Reid and Ann W. Shyne, *Brief and Extended Casework* (New York: Columbia University Press, 1969).

ridden—a nearby, reachable, easily imagined goal is the only one that has reality. And though the goal may be as material as getting and using money aid, or as practical as gaining reentry into school for the dropout, the rudimentary steps of problem-solving may be involved and taken by client and caseworker.

5. When one or several short-term partialized "goals" are achieved (part of the problem solved, or mitigated, or felt with less anxiousness and more confidence), and when the client is made aware of how his problem-solving efforts contributed to these outcomes, then the twofold goal of the problem-solving model may be said to have been achieved. The means and ends are one.[8]

The Initial Phase

The aim of the initial phase "may be said to be this: to engage this client with his problems and his will to do something about it in a working relationship with this agency, its intentions and special means of helpfulness."[9] This aim may have to be reworked and reconsidered between caseworker and client several times during the ongoing of giving and taking help. Whenever a new problem or some shift of concern is introduced, the question to be posed and discussed is whether and how the client wants to grapple with it. So in the long course of any case there may occur new beginnings—reinitiations, so to speak. In any ongoing case there is always involved the person and some identified problem in process of help-using or help-resisting. The particular perspectives of the problem-solving model on these *perpetual* elements, whether in the initial phase or in the ongoing phase, require the further explanation which follows.

---

8. For exposition of this point of view see Perlman, *Social Casework: A Problem-solving Process,* pp. 198–203.

9. Perlman, *Social Casework: A Problem-solving Process,* p. 113. Later I recognized that particularly with the involuntary applicant the beginning problem-to-be-worked is to help him undertake the role of client; that is, to want to employ the agency's services, to move from role of "applicant" to that of "client." See Helen Harris Perlman, "Intake and Some Role Considerations," *Social Casework* 41 (April 1960):171–77, and its poscript in *Persona: Social Role and Personality* (Chicago: University of Chicago Press, 1968), pp. 172–76,

THE PERSON

The person is viewed as a product of his inherited and constitutional makeup in continuous transaction with potent persons and forces in his life experience. He is thus a product of his past. But in no sense is he viewed as a finished product. He is seen, rather, as a product-in-process of *becoming*—becoming more, less, better, or worse than he was. This conception of the person-in-process is based upon commonly observed changes in adults during their adulthood, sometimes changes that have been consciously induced and sometimes those that have been unconsciously motivated and propelled. It is based, further, upon personal accounts of dramatic or gradual changes of feeling, self-regard, opinions, and modes of behavior under conditions of potent stimuli, and upon recently emerging research which finds that growth of aspects of intellectual competence extend into adulthood and that behavioral changes are responsive both to cultural expectations and to changes in values and in life perspectives.[10] There is no claim here that the basic pattern of personality is subject to full reorganization or radical alteration. Rather there is the view that certain surfaces and aspects of the personality, exposed to powerful stimuli at crucial times, may undergo modification and shifts which result in personal change.

These powerful stimuli and crucial times occur within the common vital life roles of all adults. Within any present-day encounter an adult may experience another person or a new situation in ways that drive deep into personality organization. Emotions roused in this day's encounter may be as vital, as shaking, as moving and as deep as those roused in the past. The person's reaction to them may be unconsciously compelled repetition. Or, depending on many intrapsychic and external factors, the response may be different, even

10. For full discussion of these views see chapters 1 and 2 in Perlman, *Persona*. For studies on some aspects of growth in adulthood see Nancy Bayley and M. H. Oden, "The Maintenance of Intellectual Ability in Gifted Adults," *Journal of Gerontology* 10 (January 1955):91–107; Bernice Neugarten, "Personality Changes during the Adult Years," in *Psychological Backgrounds of Adult Education,* ed. Raymond D. Kuhlen (Chicago: Center for Study of Liberal Education for Adults, 1963).

quite new. The crucial moment is a moment of potential new learning.

In short, the personality is seen as an open system, continuously (but to varying degrees) responsive to "input" and "feedback" from outside itself, especially responsive at points of high need in emotionally invested roles. The cruciality of help-needing, help-seeking, help-getting may have great powers for changes in feeling, thought, and action and for new learning. Thus the therapeutic encounter in casework is viewed as an existential experience.

The person seeks this encounter not because he wants such an experience, but because of some breakdown or impairment in one or more of his emotionally invested roles. So he must be viewed not just as himself but as himself as part of a role network, a two-or-more-some, in which what he feels, thinks, and does is in large part called forth and responsive to what "the other" does in relation to him. He is a person-in-transaction. He cannot be assessed, then, except as he is seen in this transactional field, with its dynamic realities of expectation and acts.

Yet the person-becoming-within-a-role network brings what he *is* to the life space within which he is viewed and helped. What he *is* has undergone some reconsideration in recent years by theorists and researchers on the human personality. One of these new perspectives, consonant with ego psychology (and thereby also consonant with the problem-solving model), is Robert White's concept of "effectance drive" and "competence motivation."[11] White postulates that there is innate in man the push to extend himself, to use his powers in order to be an active "cause" of happenings, to seek pleasure not merely in release of tension but in freely sought experiences that test and reward his competence. His theory is consonant with that of the neo-Freudian ego psychologists who posit the ego's autonomous existence from birth, and claim that many ego functions are "conflict-free,"

---

11. Robert W. White, "Competence and the Psychosocial Stages of Development," Nebraska Symposium on Motivation (Lincoln: University of Nebraska Press, 1960); "Motivation Reconsidered: The Concept of Competence," *Psychological Review* 66 (September 1959); *Ego and Reality in Psychoanalytic Theory*, Psychological Issues, 3 (New York: International Universities Press, 1963).

which is to say they are available and ready for use without having to be hammered out in the forge of conflict-resolution.

The "drive for effectance," or "mastery," may, of course be blocked by punitive life experiences or dwarfed by poverty of stimuli and opportunities, and it may be utilized in self-destructive or socially unacceptable ways. Or it may be nascent, waiting to be freed, channeled, engaged in more effective forms of coping. Its significance as a perspective in the problem-solving model is twofold. First, it adds a dimension to our concept of personality to which we have given little attention in the past: the potential presence of push for greater competence, for the expansion of the sense of self. This is in some contrast with the more pessimistic view that conflict resolution must precede coping efforts. It is not hard to see how the steps involved in problem-solving, when they yield some small sense of competence and mastery, may give this drive considerable reinforcement.

Still another perspective about the person differentiates the problem-solving model from that of more traditional casework. There is, to be sure, the recognition that at any moment in time a person is a living "whole," a biological-psychological-social system. But this recognition is a very different matter from the assumption that the person must either be diagnosed or be dealt with "whole." Within the problem-solving model the caseworker does not set out to either *diagnose* the person wholly nor *treat* him wholly. (Of the diagnostic problem of "the person as a whole" more will be said later.) Moreover, there is a very great difference between *viewing* whole and *doing* whole, between the ability to perceive and infer and assess a great number of variables and their configurations and the ability to control and deal with all these variables. It is in line with the primary condition for the ego's problem-solving—whether that ego is the client's or the caseworker's—that for purposes of *action* some partialization should take place. "Partialization" means centering of attention on revelant and selected parts of what is presented to view.

The organismic view of man is a way of sensitizing us to the infinite complexities within the biopsychosocial system that is the human person. But it may lead to paralysis of helping action unless it is cut to size—unless we are bold enough to say, "For purposes of helping this person I will focus and concentrate not on what he is whole, but on what he is being and becoming at this time, in this space, in relation to this designated problem-to-be-worked."

The fact is that no person can be known whole—even those with whom we live in intimate and continuous contact. (This is one of the wonders and delights of the human being that makes studying him so infinitely interesting and capturing him so elusive.) A person is "knowable" and "understandable" to himself and to another only in the context of a given set of circumstances—within the boundaries of a given situation or life space, in transaction with given forces. He may put "all of himself" into such a situation. Or he may put in only some parts of himself.

We know from everyday experience that certain social roles and particular circumstances call some aspects and dimensions of our personality into dominance and subordinate others. In a gathering of physical scientists I feel inept, even stupid; in a gathering of social workers I feel adequate. In the former I am reduced to silence or withdrawal or, at best, tentative queries for information. In the latter I may have to be forced to be silent, or I may be foursquare in the middle of argument and discussion. What *happens* to me as a result of either experience may, indeed, permeate beyond the specific situation into a prolonged memory, and its effects may affect other temporarily subordinated aspects of the personality. But what would be predominant in my awareness, in my efforts and in the responses of others in the interchange would be not the totality of me, but some appropriately selected aspects or dimensions of my personality, seen and read within a given life space and social set. The person, in short, is conceived of as whole and complete[12] but the problem-solving model of treatment requires that those aspects of his personality and behavior be plumbed and dealt with in their specific relation to the problem with which he wants or needs help.

One further perspective on the person as seen in the problem-solving model is this: the person is taken to be *more*

---

12. Herman Hesse writes in his novel *Steppenwolf*, "The self is made up of a bundle of selves. . . . As a body everyone is single, as a soul never."

than his personality disturbance or his psychosocial problems. This "more" consists of his motivation and capacities
for engaging himself in working in some new way on his
problems. This "more" inheres in the concept, also, of his
effectance drive and in the existential idea that an experience
of intensity and immediacy may call forth unanticipated,
"unknown" dimensions of the personality. It is a thought
that keeps us professionally curious and sensitively aware of
the possibilities in each human being we reach out to.

THE PROBLEM

The problem-solving model is, by definition, based upon
the presence of, and the naming and identification between,
a help-seeker and a helper of a problem for which help is
being either sought or proffered. For a situation to be problematic for the help-seeker, he must have subjective discomfort about it. (In instances of the hard-to-reach person, who
does not voluntarily seek help or who resists it, discomfort
may be denied or otherwise defended against; but his discomfort may be roused and felt, acutely, by the intrusion of
the social worker who upsets his precarious equilibrium.)
The problem named and identified need not be *the* problem,
either by being the basic causative agent in the person's difficulty or by being of major importance. It is simply a problem
in the help-seeker's current life situation which disturbs or
hurts him in some way, and of which he would like to be rid.
It is, thus, any problem that is currently alive (and therefore
accessible), that is emotionally disturbing to its victim (or
creator), and that the help-seeker is motivated to get rid of
(at best) or to mitigate (at least). Because it is bounded by
time—*now*—because he can put his finger on it and call it
by name, and because it is accepted by the helper as a reasonable matter of concern, the help-seeker feels some hope of its
amenability to his effort. It is not too big for an ego already
under a double stress—the stress of encountering trouble and
of having no adequate means by which to cope with it.

This is a rather different view from some other approaches
in casework which encourage the applicant for help to ex-
patiate on his problem in the beginning, to explore it in its
historical aspect as well as its emotional impacts, to view its
connectedness with many other aspects of his life, or to view

it as a manifestation of his personality needs. Such exploration may yield a richly tapestried fabric of understanding for the helper. But it holds the danger of the increase of anxiety for the problem-carrier, because his problem grows bigger and more complex in all directions. It holds the further danger of diffusion as boundaries are loosened between past-present, he-me, yearning-needing.

Here I am talking about the initial steps in the identification of any problem to be focused upon for help. In the ongoing work with almost any problem there may surely be called forth considerations of its history, its course of development, the ways it affects other persons and circumstances or is affected by them, the connection between it and the creator-victim or victim-creator who "has it," and so forth. Moreover, the initially presented problem may often shift, either through the help-seeker's own direction or as a result of the helper's guidance, to other more vital or more crucial—or simply more workable—problems. The important concept for problem-solving, however, is that at any given phase in the helping process the *problem in work* must early be defined and held clear before the eyes of both help-seeker and helper, between client and caseworker; that it be circumscribed enough so that an already overwhelmed ego need not retreat from it; that it be current and accessible enough so that the client's effort to cope with it in some new ways, learned within the casework interviews, has some chance of making a dent in it or in his feeling about it.

"The problem" in the problem-solving model is usually taken to be some difficulty in person-to-person or person-to-task relationships. It is usually focused on as a problem in today's social functioning. I first formulated this idea in 1953 when I was trying to find the particular professional domain of social casework.[13] Since then several studies have supported the assumption that persons who choose to go to

---

13. "The problem which a client brings to a social agency is perceived by him to be a problem in his social adjustment"; "it makes itself known to him as he plays out his social roles and engages in his social tasks"; "the person in interaction with some problematic aspects of his social reality is the focus of the social caseworker's concerns." Helen Harris Perlman, "Social Components of Casework Practice," in *The Social Welfare Forum, 1953* (New York: Columbia University Press, 1953), pp. 124–36.

social agencies, rather than to psychiatrists or to clinics, themselves tend to place and interpret their problems as being within their social role transactions.[14] Today there is overwhelming evidence that among the now visible poor there is a tendency to place the problem, whatever its nature, on forces impinging upon the person from outside himself.

In brief, it is only the small proportion of "ideal" clients, those who are cast in the image of psychiatric "patients," who say in effect, "I am the hurt but also the hurter. I want help with my internal malaise [or sickness] and its consequences." Yet, even for these introspective, psychologically sophisticated, verbally competent clients "the problem" is manifested in some area of his present social transactions. So it must be identified and spoken of and examined in terms of the daily social transactions in which it plays itself out as well as in terms of its subjective contents. This focus provides the stuff that reality is made of.

Further, today's problem is viewed not only as the end effect of a sequence of preceding events and conditions but also as a live *cause* of emerging problems. Like the person himself, his problem is not merely the product of the past. Because it is making itself felt now, in transactions with other persons and objects, experienced as stress within the person's physical, psychological, and social systems, it is an active factor in shaping the next hours and days of the person's life. Today is tomorrow's past history. What we encounter from outside us today is internalized by tomorrow. And, by the same token, a problem coped with today—or set

---

14. Thus Ripple found, in two private family welfare agencies, that out of 351 statements by applicants of the nature of the problem with which they wanted help, 289 (well over three-fourths) defined the problem as lying outside themselves or in interrelationships between themselves and other persons (Lilian Ripple and Ernestina Alexander, "Motivation, Capacity, and Opportunity as Related to the Use of Casework Service: Nature of the Client's Problem," *Social Service Review* 30 [March 1956]: 38–54). A recent more general study supports in greater numbers and range the claim that most people tend to define and "read" their problems in social functioning terms. Of over two thousand "representative Americans," 83 percent reported that when they had sought help for problems they defined them as difficulties between themselves and other persons or circumstances (Gerald Gurin, Joseph Veroff, and Sheila Feld, *Americans View Their Mental Health: A Nationwide Interview Study* [New York: Basic Books, 1960]).

on the way to resolution—raises the person's level of hope-fulness in regard to his chances of coping and being satisfied. These old saws explain why helping a person identify and center on some problem that he feels, sees, and experiences in its present immediacy may cut into the problem's vicious spiral and offer him incentive to invest further problem-solving effort.

One more perspective on "problem" as seen in the problem-solving model is, again, the idea of partialization and focus. The idea of partialization is simply cutting a dilemma down to size. The more beset the ego the narrower its capacity for coping. Thus some carved-out piece of what is often felt as an overwhelming larger problem is less threat-ening to the person who has it; it feels more manageable to him. Within that piece it is usually possible to find a minia-ture representation of the whole. The person is in it—his feelings, his thinking, his action tendencies and outputs; the significant associated persons and circumstances are to be found and elicited in any part of the problem; and as the per-son finds himself able to cope or even to plan what he may do in small part, his capacity for considering the relation of the small to the larger piece expands.

THE PLACE

The problem-solving model takes account, in every instance, of the place—the particular organization or agency—which utilizes casework as a mode of helping people with their problems. It notes that the purpose of a given agency will determine its built-in resources and its community linkages. It notes, further, that an agency's purposes define its func-tions, services, and the areas of social concern it considers to be within its purview. But because all casework models op-erate within these conditions and understandings (with the notable exception of what may occur in private practice) the "place" as part of the problem-solving model will be given no further space here.

RELATIONSHIP

Now the person with the problem is at the place where help is promised and proffered. What happens?

As in any attempt to describe a human interchange, the ensuing effort to describe relationship within the problem-solving process must fail to some extent. Verbal-linear communication says "first this, then that, and so, sequentially, onward." Living experience on the other hand says "now, at once, simultaneously, at several levels of awareness, I-me, they-you, now-then"; experiencing does not, in short, follow the laws of logic. (And in this, probably, lie some of the reasons learners in casework and in other forms of interpersonal helping find it hard to put together the cool reasonableness of the theory they read and the visceral "sunbursts" they feel in their actual encounters with people in trouble.) With this recognition, here are a few notes on relationship.

No matter what the theoretical model by which one human being attempts to be of help to another, the most potent and dynamic power for influence lies in relationship. The human drive and need for social connectedness and social recognition (to at least one "other") are lifelong movers and shapers of the personality. These are what any "meaningful" or "potent" relationship contains: caring and respect, love (in one of its many faces) and social exchange and affirmation.[15] The need for these peculiarly human forms of nourishment is intensified at times of helplessness, vulnerability, and stress. So it may be expected that a person who finds himself resourceless and empty-handed in the face of a problem will need and want connection with someone who combines caring for him with (imputed) social power and authority to help him. (There are, of course, persons in need who have lost the trust in other human beings that makes relationship possible. This can only be noted here, not dealt with.)

The potency of relationship probably explains why people have been helped to move from despair to hope, from mental chaos to rational order, from conflict to equanimity by radically diverse methods. The creators and disciples of various schools of psychological influence may fight bitter battles to

---

15. For "love" in its complex meanings and its therapeutic dynamics see Perlman, *Persona*, pp. 17–22, 225; for social connectedness as need, pp. 23–27, 225. See also Perlman, *Social Casework: A Problem-solving Process*, pp. 67–70 on love and authority; pp. 72–74 on therapeutic values.

establish the "truth" of their theories, and point here to the orthodoxy and there to the heresy, and teach and argue the merits of one philosophic stance or one body of techniques over the other. But when the tumult and the dust of battle die down there remains at base within every school of thought the dynamically charged mystery of the relationship of love and power offered by the helping person to the other, and hungrily fastened onto, believed in, and incorporated by the needful one. Beneath all therapies and modes of benign psychological influence lie the stirring and securing nurture of empathy and the warm acceptance and caring that emanate from a helper who seems secure, genuine, real, and empowered by knowledge or social sanction.[16]

"Relationship" as used here embraces all relationships between caseworker and client. Whatever the problem to be dealt with, a helping relationship in casework combines caring, concern, acceptance, and expectation of the client-person with understanding and know-how and social sanction. These expressed and demonstrated attitudes and helping powers may be experienced, in varying degree, as serving-healing even in only a one-time encounter.

Relationship is the continuous context within which problem-solving takes place. It is, at the same time, the emerging product of mutual problem-solving efforts; and simultaneously it is the catalytic agent in the under-levels of the personality of unconscious shifts and changes in the sense of trust, the sense of self-worth, the sense of security, and the sense of linkage with other human beings.

Within the problem-solving approach it is relationship that warms the intelligence, sustains the spirit, and carries the person forward in what would otherwise be a cool, rational process. It is what differentiates problem-solving in casework from problem-solving as a purely intellectual process. Its rewards of nurture and steadfastness and recognition make it possible to bear the frustrations and compromises that problem-work involves, since there are few life

16. In his most recent book, *The Therapeutic Relationship and Its Impact: A Study of Psychotherapy with Schizophrenics* (Madison: University of Wisconsin Press, 1967), Carl Rogers identifies the vital "set" of factors that characterizes an influential therapeutic relationship as the "necessary and sufficient conditions of therapeutic personality change."

situations that yield easily to problem-solving efforts and fewer still that may be completely "solved." Moreover, relationship developed offers the sense of oneness or identification of client with caseworker. In this there inheres the chance to "borrow strength," to learn by both imitation and unconscious incorporation.

But now, one must ask, if relationship is such a potent force for human change, why should one bother with problem-solving processes at all? Why not bank on the benign powers of person-to-person influence to release the client's own potential for coping, supplemented as necessary with some material aids or environmental modifications? The reasons follow for the use and repeated rehearsals of the problem-solving mode in casework within the context of even the best of relationships.

No applicant comes to a social agency asking for a relationship. He does not say "I want love"—or "I want social affirmation," although his problem in interpersonal relationships may reveal such needs. He comes, as has been said, to get help with some tangibly identified problem in his social transactions. He hopes that the person who is charged with giving him such help will be competent, will be authorized, and will lend himself with concerned attentions to his needs. If he is in the painful throes of conflict, anxiety, or despair, he hopes that the helper will, beyond acceptance, be understandingly compassionate with him. Relationship, varying in intensity by the particular complex of persons and problems, leaps into being spontaneously when emotionally charged material is shared between help-seeker and helper, expressed by the one, received by the other. In simplified terms one may say that the applicant comes to talk about his problem; *how* it is talked about is both the input and the outgrowth of relationship.

Second, problems encountered in daily social functioning often need interventions and provisions of many sorts outside of what a relationship can provide. This is one of the major differences between social casework's problem-solving modes and those of many other kinds of therapeutic effort. In the latter—in, for example, nondirective therapy or psychoanalysis or the various forms of counseling that proliferate today—the "interventions" and "provisions" are almost exclusively those of psychological influence of helper upon helped. Casework as a process within social work holds within its purview and responsibility those significant "others" (persons) and those significant circumstances (conditions and things) that may need to be involved and used if the client is to be able to cope with them. So in many—perhaps most— instances of help by the casework process, problem-solving may involve actions in addition to psychological influences within a therapeutic relationship.

But most important, the use and exercise of the problem-solving mode within the casework relationship rests its case for validity upon the fact that it exercises the client-person's ego functions in ways that are assumed to free and strengthen them. Problem-solving, when consciously undertaken, educates a person in the use of his cognitive, motile, decision-making capacities. He becomes aware of a way to control impulses and to become his own decision-maker rather than the victim of his previously unrecognized drives. If he is able to learn and incorporate this mode (and such incorporation will depend heavily upon relationship rewards), he will have acquired a means by which to cope more competently with problems of everyday living on his own.

Now I must say what this process of exercise of the ego's problem-solving functions consists of.

PROCESS

The process[17] of engaging a person in problem-solving activity must be based upon a conception of the ways human beings tend to operate "just naturally"; then one must identify those factors that undermine or distort usual adaptations and coping. The problem-solving process, based upon ego psychology, views ego functions as roughly fourfold:

Perception of internal, subjective wants and needs; perception of external and relevant reality demands and opportunities; integration-mediation operations between the two sets of perception towards selection and choosing of means for gratification by the

---

17. What follows has been set forth in greater detail in Perlman, *Social Casework: A Problem-solving Process*. See especially chap. 5, pp. 53–63, and chap. 7, pp. 84–101.

"reality principle"; planning and/or management of conscious, voluntary behavior.[18]

In persons with "weak" or underdeveloped egos, starved on inadequate relationship or developmental experiences, any one of these functions alone or in combination may be inadequate to the life tasks they encounter. In persons with emotional or cognitive disturbances, whether as part of a disease process or as the product of excessive stress, these functions may be disturbed or undermined. Caseworkers typically deal with persons whose ego functions either are underdeveloped or are under the handicapping stresses of excess anxiety, conflict, or unmet life needs. So, to the provision of necessary aids and the necessary conditions by which psychological footing is to be regained or secured must be added the support and leading out and exercise of ego functions toward strengthening them and thus the person's sense of himself as "coper."

The first step in the problem-solving process (whether at the point of first exchange between applicant and caseworker or at any point in the ongoing work where a new problem or a different face of an old one is placed under consideration) is the clear identification of that problem. What is it that hurts, threatens, or frustrates the person? What does he want to change or have changed or get rid of? The detailed drawing from the applicant of his perception of the problem, its present (or near present) causes and consequences, and its radius of influence, and the questions and comments put in by the caseworker for clarification are all in the service of increasing the applicant's (or client's) *perception of the objective problem.*

Weaving in and out of this identification and clarification of the problem, simultaneous with it, sometimes central, sometimes peripheral, is the expression and clarification of the emotions, the feelings, the subjective reactions of the problem-carrier to his dilemma. This serves several purposes:

---

18. These paraphrase the categories of ego operations proposed by Franz Alexander in his essay "Development of the Fundamental Concepts of Psychoanalysis," in *The Impact of Freudian Psychiatry,* ed. Franz Alexander and Helen Ross (Chicago: University of Chicago Press, Phoenix Books, 1961).

the release of pent-up feeling; the establishment of a relation-ship bond as emotion is expressed and received; and the in-creased and clarified perception by both client and case-worker of the *person's subjective involvement* in the problem —his experience of the reality.

But this is not yet all. The kinds of help or solutions avail-able (or absent), the conditions under which that help may be had (or forfeited), may present the applicant with a new problem: that of taking and using help as it is defined by the helper. And this may require considerable clarification so that he can perceive and take in both cognitively and emo-tionally this sometimes inexorable and often frustrating reality. So the identification and clarification of his problem and his expectations of the help he wants must now be sup-plemented by the identification and clarification of the actualities and possibilities available to him. We cannot as-sume, just because he has a problem and wants help with it, that he wants and accepts the particular kinds of help that the social agency proffers, or that he has faced the probable compromises that realistic solution almost always requires. If the help-seeker is really to be a participant in work on his problem rather than simply a trustful client dependent upon the wisdom and good intentions of his helper, he must know, clarify, and subjectively react to at least the beginning con-ditions and possibilities of what "help" is and will involve. His first conscious decision-making, his first "self-determina-tion," then, is his choice and agreement to take the chance that this person in this place will proffer him the best avail-able aids by which to cope with his problem. This is the point where he moves from the role of applicant to that of client— the point of "contract."[19]

One can see that this beginning and recurrent identifica-tion and clarification of the problem-to-be-worked at any given time in its emotional and cognitive aspects for the person involved and the subsequent clarification of realistic expectations in the help-giving and help-using roles (of case-worker and client) is in full consonance with good ego func-tioning and with good problem-solving. It is an aspect of

19. For explication of this point see Perlman, "Intake and Some Role Considerations," with some additions reprinted as chapter 7 in *Persona*.

casework practice that, I believe, has been given too little attention and even less understanding. Some anxious quest to be "scientific," as if this were a value to be desired in and of itself, has enthroned "study" of the client and his situation as preliminary to his involvement in problem-solving.[20]

I suggest that there is a severalfold fallacy here that has been perpetuated over the years. One aspect of it is the questionable assumption that if one is "scientific" one is ipso facto helpful. This is certainly open to question in a field of practice where the most potent forces upon which we draw—relationship, empathy, trust, competence, and motivation, for example, remain as yet insufficiently plumbed and understood.

I will not enter here into that tedious identity problem of casework about whether it is "an art or a science." In the nineteenth century the logician William Jevons clarified the interrelatedness of these two forms of human operation. "A science teaches us to know and an art to do." "To know," to understand the nature and meaning of the material with which one is "to do" is absolutely essential. But what has been lost sight of in much of traditional casework practice is that the material to be "known" is not simply "what is the matter" and "how it got that way" (the usual focus for "study") but also *How does the client see it, feel it, read it, and interpret it and himself as part of it?* and always, further, *What does he want* and *expect* and *how does he react to the reality of what lies ahead?* In short, the study lens has not always been focused effectively to catch the essential dynamic material.

Another question within the "study process" is the purpose for which a case is being carried: Is it for studying or for helping? Both cannot be achieved in equal measure, nor is the latter the inevitable outcome of the former. Cases *need* to be studied, far more than we have done, in every aspect of their contents, but perhaps especially in the dynamic

20. Thus in a recent article, "Social Study: Past and Future," *Social Casework* 49 (July 1968):403–9, Carel Germain supports "the study process" as the first step in the study-diagnosis-treatment sequence in the "conviction that study continues to be an essential element in a scientifically based practice." "Indeed," she goes on to say, "the spirit of scientific inquiry on which study rests is more than ever necessary."

transactions between helper and helped. The necessity for swift and effective help-giving and engagement of the client may have to preclude meticulous study. We may have to help before we know more than the rudimentary outlines of the person-in-a-situation. This has clearly been recognized in crisis treatment and in short-term treatment too. Moreover, the client's responses and reactions to the new and different supports and stimuli put in by the caseworker are among the most telling data to be observed, "studied," and assessed. They do not tell, it is true, what his problem is made up of; this we will come to know. But they tell what his problem-solving powers (or resistances and incapacities) are—and this is the stuff with which we deal.

It is important that we differentiate our scientific purposes from our therapeutic purposes. Freud differentiated these when he stated firmly and clearly that his method, psychoanalysis, was for research purposes; he did not put it forward as a therapy, although for many understandable reasons it had therapeutic by-products. Perhaps caseworkers have tended to blur the distinction between what is good for their own state of knowledge and what is good for their client.

Perhaps too there has been some anxious need to know everything before doing anything. The exploration of an applicant's presenting problem over a number of sessions has tended to place him in the position of a raconteur, a teller of his story, with the implication that if and when it is all told the solution somehow will be revealed. The power for that revelation has seemed to lie not in the teller, but in the person "studying" the situation. The nature of the solution-process and the relation between the "study" and the applicant's realistic or illusory expectations have tended to be inexplicit. Thus the applicant can only "choose" or "decide" to trust and hope. His sense of his own problem-coping powers and responsibilities is not exercised by his being largely a narrator and expresser of his problems; indeed they may be lessened as he deposits more and more data into the lap of his compassionate listener.

To put the difference in a nutshell, the problem-solving process starts at once, from the first moment, with treating the person. He is not "treated" for his problem, because this is yet to be known—studied and diagnosed and assessed. The person is treated (in the sense of being "dealt with") for the purpose of helping him to reveal himself to himself and to the caseworker in his currently recognized trouble—in his feelings about it, in the wishes and hopes he brings for its resolution, and in his reactions to what he finds are the present possibilities. The help that is given is to enable the person to want and use the available helping ways and means. Then, when the *person* has been fully attended to, the *problem* (and the person's involvements in it) can begin to be unfolded and examined.

A second aspect of the problem-solving process (I do not say "step" or "phase," since these imply a logical sequence which, as has been said, does not always occur in the spontaneity of action) is the exercise of the selective, integrating, mediating, judging, and assessing functions of the ego. More simply, it is the *thinking about the facts.* What "facts"? They now include not only the facts of person-problem-life situation involvement, of recent cause and current consequence, but also the facts of the person's coping efforts, of his involvement both as victim of and actor upon the problem, and also the facts of what the person wants and how much he wants it and his conceptions of and reactions to alternative opportunities or ways of coping that the caseworker will open for his consideration. The caseworker will, of course, have gleaned a considerably larger body of facts and impressions from observations of the client as he has been heard and watched. From these the caseworker will have made some diagnosis of the client's apparent motivation and capacities as a problem-solver. What the caseworker proposes, comments upon, questions, or lets pass is based upon his evolving understanding of the needs and powers of this-person-in-this-problem-situation.

Between the caseworker and his client, however, a kind of diagnosis will be taking place. That is their joint agreement on what seems to be the trouble. The caseworker may not be in full agreement or he may even assess the situation very differently from the client, and the problem-to-be-worked may become that of helping the client move from *his* interpretation of the problem to that of the caseworker. So the joint agreement is subject to change on one part or the other. But some such agreement is essential if the caseworker is to start where the client is in order to lead him out to where in the caseworker's professional judgment he needs to be.

Beyond the temporary agreement on what the problem seems to be made up of, the mutual diagnostic process involves helping the client repeatedly see himself as both affecting and affected by the problem. At the risk, again, of oversimplifying, one may say that the caseworker helps his client to move from "I have a problem," to "Yes, I am emotionally involved in it," to "Yes, my feelings about it make me act in ways that affect the problem or my adequacy in coping with it," to "Yes, I am an actor in that problem—a factor in its being," to "Potentially I am a power in coping with it." This may occur in one interview. More frequently it will take many interviews—for this is a long way to go!

So the client is led to express, to explain, to speculate, to suppose, to see relationships, to consider ways and means, to consider reasons and resources—in brief, he is rehearsed in the internal work of problem-solving, in what Piaget calls "interiorized action." This internal thinking-work is the differentiating mark of a person's operation by the reality principle rather than by the so-called pleasure, or impulse-driven principle.

Because I cannot say it better now than I have before, I presume to quote myself:

In this work of thinking through, the ego takes responsibility, so to speak, for the exercise of its consciously controlled functions. As a person turns over in his mind considerations of relationships (as among cause and effect, action and reaction, act and consequences), as he concentrates on some aspects of a problem and excludes others, as he makes connections and isolates differences, as he conjures up the images of people and situations and anticipates thair actuality and his behavior in relation to them, as he expresses and views his feelings in the light of reason, as he measures his striving against his reality—as he does all these things he is exercising his adaptive capacities in preparation for adaptation in action.[21]

This work must be continuous and repeated in every phase

21. Perlman, *Social Casework: A Problem-solving Process*, p. 92.

of a helping or therapeutic process. It need scarcely be said again that the empathy and security in the flow and flux of the relationship give this work both its impetus and its reward.

The client rises from his chair in the caseworker's office (or the caseworker does so in the client's home) and something must yet happen to carry forward the problem-solving work. This something may be further thinking or rumination on the part of the client. Better still, it may be some small action he is to take in the light of some conscious decision to deal with himself or his situation in some small but different way. Such action, usually tentative, a tryout, involves ego functions of voluntary control and self-management. Because such trial actions are usually charged with emotion (they are motivated by discomfort, and hope, and determination, and feelings for the helper—all of these, in complex) they are experienced as self-powered. If they are rewarded by success (good response on the part of others, or even the negative response of "nothing lost" but a "good try"), they tend to accrue to the person's sense that he has the power to make things happen, that by his action something has been affected. This ties in closely with the "drive for effectance," or the sense (described by Lois Barclay Murphy in her study of young children) that "I *am* because I *do*."[22] It meets the need to experience oneself as a "cause" of some effect. When these "effects" are experienced as "good" there ensues, ego psychologists propose, an enhanced sense of self-esteem and confidence.

Actions do indeed speak louder than words. That is why the third aspect of the problem-solving model is a preparation of the client by rehearsal, by consideration of all his "buts," and "what ifs"—and other anticipated actions and reactions—to enable him to carry into some action (or to desist from habitual actions, as the case may be) some choice and decision about what he will do in some part of his problem. Sometimes those choices and decisions seem to occur by "spontaneous combustion," the result, probably, of unconscious ego integrations that are responsive to certain stimuli

---

22. Lois Barclay Murphy, *The Widening World of Childhood* (New York: Basic Books, 1962), p. 373.

or inputs. The use of the problem-solving model of casework aims to provide the stimulation and inputs for the person's conscious choice—his self-determination, so to speak[23]—of the behavior that it is anticipated will eventuate in his more gratifying and adequate coping.

To this "opportunity" must be added, in many instances, the work of changing and modifying the behavior of the other persons involved in the problem's network, or the life conditions which create or bear upon the problem. For these latter there may be needed and used many material supports or organized services. Such supports and services are not without their difficulties. The caseworker who uses the problem-solving method is aware that help and service under certain conditions may be hard to stomach. So the person's use of such help or service may become the problem-to-be-worked for a time. Meanwhile, with his left hand, so to speak, the caseworker may be at work upon the resource or aid itself to make it more accessible and acceptable to the client, or he may need to work simultaneously with the attitudes and behaviors of the other persons involved in the problematic role network.

I have said nothing yet about techniques. Perhaps all that needs to be said is that in the skilled use of such words, affects, and actions that aim to exert psychological influence there is no mode that is not potentially useful in the problem-solving method. Sustainment, "ventilation," exploration, clarification, confrontation, interpretation, reflective discussion, reinforcement—name all the ways by which we have over the years denoted casework's techniques (and those of other educative-therapeutic endeavors too), and one will find them used and useable within the process of problem-solving. Current research seems to find that casework's armamentarium of treatment techniques is fairly limited.[24] Perhaps further

<hr/>

23. For discussion of self-determination in its relation to ego-processes see Helen Harris Perlman, "Self-Determination, Reality or Illusion?" *Social Service Review* 39 (December 1965):410–21; and *Values in Social Work,* monograph 60 (New York: National Association of Social Workers, 1967).

24. Recent studies of interviewing content confirm this. The work of Florence Hollis in attempting to devise and study typologies of casework treatment reveals the high incidence in the usage of only a few

study of the helping actions of caseworkers will reveal that factors of degree and frequency and discriminative choice of our identified action techniques are the telling variables.

Increasingly recognized as a potent factor by those who are studying therapeutic techniques is the "style" of the individual therapist or helper.[25] Ideally this "style"—this spontaneous, honest expression of the self in the role of professional helper—flows out from the caseworker's real concern and respect for his client, out of his being unafraid, either of the person or his problem, and out of his deep wish to be of maximal help. In the professional encounter, style is consciously managed by the helper's clarity of purpose in every instance and by his diagnostic appraisal of the nature of the material with which he is working. Style—the helper's ways of relating, of drawing out feelings, of responding empathically, of stimulating and guiding thought, of accrediting and affirming, of presenting reality—is utilized not in a free-form, any-sort-of-dialogue-goes-as-long-as-it's-lively way. Rather, it is contained within the structure provided by both the purpose and the process of problem-solving. Such structure, it has seemed to me, offers the security of content and direction which then frees the caseworker to use himself fully in the interest of his client.

In sum, the process of problem-solving aims in varying (and modest) degree to offer the help-seeker a sustaining and stimulating emotional experience of connection with a concerned and respectful helper; a clarified perception and understanding of his problem and himself as actor in it; the

techniques—"description-ventilation and reflection on the here and now," for instance ("A Profile of Early Interviews in Marital Counseling," *Social Casework* 49 [January 1968]:35–43). Her classification of techniques assumes "that treatment consists of a blend of relatively few procedures" (Explorations in the Development of a Typology of Casework Treatment," *Social Casework* 48 [June 1967]:335–41). Research by Reid and Shyne, reported in *Brief and Extended Casework*, reveals that in studying taped interviews "it proved difficult to obtain clear differentiation in practice between the modifying pattern, which was to be directed at increasing the client's self-understanding, and the supportive pattern. . . . A content analysis . . . indicated that differences in casework technique between these two patterns were generally in expected directions but were neither sizable nor stable."

25. See Edward J. Mullen, "Differences in Worker Style in Casework," *Social Casework* 50 (June 1969):347–53.

repeated exercise of his drives and capacities to cope more competently; the provision of means of meeting material deficits or of enriched opportunities; and in strengthening emotional and action linkages between the person and the people and prospects in his own social network through whom he can find his ongoing fulfillment.

DIAGNOSIS

The placement of the section on diagnosis here, *after* treatment, has, I must hurry to say, no symbolic significance. It is occasioned, again, by the difficulty of explaining one process, treatment, that has simultaneity by means of another process, writing, that has only linear sequence.

Diagnosis, like treatment, begins with the first glance between the help-giver and the help-seeker. Consciously or not, the caseworker makes some spontaneous judgment of what the person he is about to talk with "is like." The more experienced and knowledgeable the caseworker, the more likely he is to recognize "the nature of the material" with which he is to work. (This is why diagnostic acuity and sophistication cannot be *taught;* it can only be *learned* by meticulous observations of the repeated attributes and qualities of certain types or categories of problem or personality.)

But the inexperienced caseworker *can* be taught the frameworks within which the diagnostic content of social casework can best be identified, and the areas for his concentrated observation and conclusions. Those areas will shift as problems-to-be-worked shift their intensity and relevance; so at different times in a case one or another aspect of person-in-relation-to-his-problem will be under diagnostic scrutiny. Diagnosis is, then, an ongoing process throughout the life of a case. Ongoing diagnosis designs—or should design—ongoing treatment. But in the inevitable circularity of cause-effect, effect-cause, it is treatment itself that brings out and reveals most of what the caseworker needs to know about his client as a person-with-a-problem-in-pursuit-of-a-solution.

The thought-modes of diagnosis are those of any effort to identify and explain the nature of a given problem, to appraise it within a framework of particular interest or intentions, and to use that appraisal as a predictive guide to action.

But the *content* of diagnosis, those facts and forces that are
placed in the spotlight for examination at any given time and
in any given case, must be specified and particularized by
the "what for" of the effort. "Diagnosis for *what?*" is the
question that must be answered plainly and explicitly before
any worker, whether craftsman, artist, healer, educator, or
scientist can identify what it is he wishes to know and understand about the material he intends to influence. Whether
that "material" is a human being in trouble or some object,
the purpose and conditions of what is to ensue determine
what parts of that material will be evoked, scrutinized for
examination, and appraised.[26] (Of course, any "diagnosti-
cian" may, by virtue of his talents and experience, see and
understand far more than his purpose calls for. But such insights are not necessarily relevant to his specific professional
purpose in a given case.) Thus the problem brought for solution, the function and program of the place to which it is
brought, the goal and outcome sought and judged feasible,
all predetermine what factors are to be subject to scrutiny
and analysis in order to plan appropriate treatment.

Within these considerations, the diagnostic content of the
problem-solving model is in line with the model's purpose.
Briefly it may be said to include these variables: (1) the specification of the problem-to-be-worked (at any given time), its
objective and subjective stresses, its precipitating causes, and
its current spirals of causes-effects, effects-causes; (2) the person seeking help, assessed especially in relation to his motivation and capacity for using help to resolve his difficulty,
and the forces within or outside him which thwart or disturb
his optimal level of problem-solving; (3) the resources and
opportunities within the person's own command or those
which must be mobilized for him in order to fill realistic
deficits or to aid him in coping.

Because it is in diagnosis of the person that the problem-
solving model departs most notably from the traditional psychosocial model, this difference needs to be explained here.

Problem-solving diagnosis does not focus upon the biopsychosocial organization of the total personality, because it

---

26. Dealt with in more detail in Perlman, *Social Casework: A Problem-
solving Process,* especially pp. 164–69.

does not aim at total personality change or reorganization. As has been indicated, it postulates that certain *aspects* or *dimensions* of personality become super- or subordinate in relation to certain roles or crucial stresses and that these may be affected helpfully toward desired or necessary changes in behavior, or in the attitudes and convictions that govern behavior. When "understanding the total person" is set as the goal, the diagnostic inquiry, perforce, becomes endless; it invites a broadside, buckshot form of study, diffused and confusing by its very lack of focus. Or, alternately, it proves so Herculean a task as to send most caseworkers into diagnostic collapse. It is no wonder then that a recent writer, editing a book titled *Differential Diagnosis and Treatment in Social Work* finds "divergence between our value commitment to the importance of diagnosis and the reality of our practice." And finds, moreover, a "reluctance to diagnose."[27]

The content of diagnosis of the person in problem-solving has two major focuses, often overlapping. The one is the beginning, ongoing, and continuous appraisal and reappraisal of the person's motivation, capacity, and opportunity to put himself into working on the problem at hand. The other is the finding and assessment of what factors and forces deter or thwart his motivation or his capacity or his opportunity. Those factors and forces may lie in his past life experience and its impress on him, or they may lie in his present situation; they may emanate from the significant other persons in the client's life, past or present, or in the immediate relationship between him and the caseworker; they may reside in his physical, emotional, and intellectual makeup, in their deficits or sickness or strengths; they may lie in the actual lack or failure of social means and resources by which the

---

27. Francis J. Turner, *Differential Diagnosis and Treatment in Social Work* (New York: Free Press, 1968), p. 12. Mr. Turner remains, however, a firm proponent of *total* diagnosis. "It is assumed that all treatment must be geared to the whole person and not to particular parts of that person" (p. 16). Yet, he says, "Time and time again, records of social workers are examined, without being able to locate within them a place where a diagnosis was formulated" (p. 12). I believe the explanation is apparent: what the ego finds too hard to do it must defend against. Or, to use a principle from another psychological system: behavior (making a diagnosis) that is not rewarded (by providing treatment guidelines) tends to become extinct.

problem either is created or is amenable to change. In short, the diagnosis in the problem-solving model focuses *first* upon what the person wants and how much he wants it (motivation)—in relation to the problem-to-be-worked; upon what capacities the person has (or has not) or can develop (or cannot) by which to cope with the problem-to-be-worked; upon what means there are (or are not) in the client's own environment and in the aids and services the caseworker has on tap—by which the problem-to-be-worked can be affected. Simultaneously it seeks to discern why, for what reasons, the person's motivation or capacity or opportunity is inadequate to enable him to cope.[28] As has been said, the diagnostic focus will change as the problem changes or, often, as the problem is reinterpreted by the caseworker and his client together.

One frequent cause of the person's inability to cope is that, despite his conscious motivation, some inner deficit or disturbance makes it impossible for him to feel or think or act in the ways he would if he could. Some intrapsychic sickness or malfunction now is a factor to be reckoned with. The extent to which a so-called clinical diagnosis by the caseworker is useful remains a question of difference not only among caseworkers but among psychiatrists too. Arguments about the value or worthlessness of clinical categories of diagnosis still flare among psychiatrists, between those who work hard to develop and elaborate classification systems and those who see such systems as useful more for epidemiological purposes than as guides to individual treatment. Recent research reveals that there is very little agreement among psychiatrists in their categorization of individual mental illness or dysfunctioning.[29] One psychiatrist's schizophrenia may be an-

---

28. For elaboration see Perlman, *Social Casework: A Problem-solving Process*, pp. 55–58, 164–69, 180, 183–203. See also, for definitions of motivation, capacity, and opportunity, Lilian Ripple, Ernestina Alexander, and Bernice W. Polemis, *Motivation, Capacity, and Opportunity: Studies in Casework Theory and Practice,* Social Service Monographs, 2d ser., no. 3 (Chicago: School of Social Service Administration, University of Chicago, 1964), chap. 3.
29. See, for example, William A. Hunt, Cecil L. Wittson, and Edna B. Hunt, "A Theoretical and Practical Analysis of the Diagnostic Process," in *Current Problems in Psychiatric Diagnosis,* ed. Paul Hoch and Joseph Zubin (New York: Grune & Stratton, 1953). Also see Hans Strupp and Joan V. Williams, "Some Determinants of Clinical Evaluations of Dif-

other psychiatrist's anxiety hysteria. Further, whether in psychiatric or social casework treatment, it is often hard to discern any direct connection between the clinical (and etiological) diagnosis and what is done thereafter in treatment; the clinical diagnosis and all the developmental factors that seem to explain it have not, somehow, provided the design for social casework's action.

But when there is intrapsychic disturbance or sickness its identification is essential. In problem-solving as in other forms of casework it will suggest certain expectable behaviors that are characteristic of the disease and will predict certain limitations of change or outcome. (The symptoms may, of course, also signal the need for psychiatric consultation, diagnosis, or treatment.) With the clinical disorder classified, there still remains the problem of what the caseworker is to do. Typically caseworkers do not treat neurotic or psychotic (pre- or present or post-) conditions. They treat *people who have such conditions.* The people who have them are not the same as their sickness. One "schizophrenic" person may have a different problem in his social functioning than another one, even if his "social functioning" is confined by the walls of a locked ward; one "compulsive neurotic" has greater motivation for help than another. In short, the work with psychically disturbed people by caseworkers is usually with that margin of the person that is still involved with trying to cope with some segment of his life situation. So, again, his motivation and capacity and opportunity to work on that problem become central to problem-solving diagnosis.

Moreover, recent work with persons in traumatic or crisis situations reveals that "persons with a variety of clinical diagnoses tend to act in similar ways under the impact of a particular situational provocation."[30] Thus, that "situational provocation" needs examination and assessment.

Since most of the problems brought for casework help are

ferent Psychiatrists," *Archives of General Psychiatry* 2 (April 1960): 434–40.
30. Lucille Austin in her foreword to *Crisis Intervention,* ed. Howard J. Parad (New York: Family Service Association of America, 1965), p. xiii. Mrs. Austin comments further: "The client's cry for help, the nature of the disruptive forces in his current life situation, and the range of his successful and unsuccessful coping methods must be given priority."

problems of interpersonal or person-to-situational crisis or stress, the second major diagnostic focus in the problem-solving model is upon the persons in the problematic role network. The questions to be answered are, What is the nature of the role dysfunction or breakdown? And why are the persons involved unable to cope with it? The probability is that some deficits (of material or psychological means), some disturbances (of personality or circumstantial factors), or some discrepancies (in role definitions and expectations)— any one or in combination—can be identified and centered for treatment efforts.[31] Treatment, then, is "designed" within the boundaries of a diagnostic focus upon persons endeavoring to regain equilibrium in some aspect of their current social functioning or to gain it at a more gratifying level.

There is a seeming paradox when one speaks of diagnosis-treatment sequence. Actually, treatment *produces* diagnosis. It is the personal-situational *response* to the casework input that reveals not only what is the trouble but, more important, what person-situation powers may be utilized in problem-solving. If one sets out to diagnose a *problem* (marital discord, school failure, identity diffusion, or whatever) it can be pinned, known, understood, and categorized, all in advance of a treatment proposal. But if, as in the problem-solving model, one sets out first to diagnose a *person* as problem-victim or creator, but now also as *potential problem-solver,* he must not only be viewed as cause or creature of his besetting difficulties but must be considered in his wish and capacity to do something about it. This is why the problem-solving model puts its first diagnostic lens upon the person who is to be involved in the problem-solving process. Certain stimuli and supports must come from the caseworker at once—a kind of "treatment"—to give this person the security and then the small-part impetus to relate to the caseworker, to express himself, to begin to consider what is the matter and what he wants. In this small sample of the casework process the client reveals a small sample of his capacity to relate, to act, and to react with appropriate responsiveness. From this there ensue steps into a wider area for consideration.

---

31. For elaboration of this see chapter 9, "Role and Help to Troubled Adults," in Perlman, *Persona,* especially pp. 198–216.

That diagnosis is produced by treatment was wryly put forward by Freud. "Our diagnoses are very often made only after the event," he wrote. "They resemble the Scottish King's test for identifying witches. . . . This king declared that he was in possession of an infallible method of recognizing a witch. He had the women stewed in a cauldron of boiling water and then tasted the broth. Afterwards he was able to say: 'That was a witch' or 'No, that was not one.' "[32]

One further note on the diagnostic "stance" in the problem-solving model. It is in regard to the concept of causality. Traditional, linear causal analysis—"this cause produces that effect"—has not taken into account such causal phenomena as present aspiration, present goals, new behavior in response to new stimuli, or the idea of "symptom as cause" or "treatment as cause." Causation in the problem-solving model is seen as a spiral phenomenon. Its symbol is the loop, not the line.

THEORETICAL BASES AND LINKAGES

Shaped as I am by the problem-solving mode I have had to say as explicitly as I could what something *is* or purports to *be* before I could turn to how it got that way. Now, at last, I move to identify the theory sources which have been drawn upon largely or in part as the "foundation" or undergirding of problem-solving in casework.

As has been stated, the basic dynamic theory is that of ego psychology. Ego psychology is still in fertile growth, still fluid, and increasingly being put to the tests of precise observation and innovative research; so the growing margin of understanding of human coping (problem-solving) and of the conditions under which it is best actualized (or worst constricted) provides a lively pulsing conceptual base for casework's helping modes. The concepts of Erikson[33] and White[34] have particularly contributed to the bent of the problem-

---

32. "Explanations, Applications and Orientations," in Freud, *Introductory Lectures on Psychoanalysis*.

33. Erik Erikson, *Identity and the Life Cycle*, Psychological Issues, 1 (New York: International Universities Press, 1959).

34. Robert W. White, "Competence and the Psychosocial Stages of Development," in *Ego and Reality in Psychoanalytic Theory*.

solving model—Erikson because he has made a brilliant and
believable fabric by weaving together the psychodynamics of
Freud (father and daughter both) with the dynamics of
sociocultural forces, and White because of his lucid propositions of "effectance motivation," by which he adds the person's drive to be "cause" (and explorer and problem-solver)
to the libidinal and aggressive drives postulated by Freud,
and because he affirms and extends the post-Freudian ego
psychologists' postulates of an autonomous ego and its
conflict-free energies.

Few great theorists (except perhaps Freud) have been more
widely misquoted and misinterpreted, by both friends and
enemies, than John Dewey. From the rich burgeoning of
Dewey's thoughts I drew two main supports for the problem-
solving model. One was his analysis and structuring of re-
flective-thinking processes, his examination of the ego's
cognitive functioning (though he did not use these latter
terms). The other was his propositions about the person as
an active agent, not simply as a responder to stimuli but as
an actor always involved in attempting to deal with some
problem-induced stress or to achieve some goal within a
dynamic social structure.

Dewey's concepts of the individual as developing through
his active engagement in social transactions in pursuit of
problem-solution or goal-in-view and the concepts underlying the problem-solving model seemed (to me) to be in
full congruence.[35]

A vital social science concept that, to my mind, has immediate connection with problem-solving in social work is that of
social role. My interest in role began with my recognition that
most problems brought to social caseworkers are problems in
role transactions. This is what "social functioning" implies:
the individual is in some status and action vis-à-vis one or
some other persons or objects. Role transactions, then, are the
special arena for social casework's operations. The concept of
role expanded for me when I came to see that role was the

---

35. See John Dewey, "The Natural History of Thinking," in *Essays in
Experimental Logic* (Chicago: University of Chicago Press, 1917); "Anal-
ysis of Reflective Thinking," in *How We Think*, rev. ed. (New York:
D. C. Health & Co., 1933); and *Art as Experience* (New York: Putnam &
Sons, 1934).

vehicle by which an individual expressed his personality in action; further, that it related closely to his self-concept and sense of identity. The exercise of ego functions takes place, always, within some social role-set, in the effort to solve some role problem. Thus parts of the role concept attached themselves (as if drawn magnetically) to my concept of social casework's problem-solving, affecting its focus and purpose.[36]

The triangular framework of motivation, capacity, and opportunity is a framework within which an individual's wanting, being able, and having provisions by which to cope with his identified problems in role functioning may be assessed. Thus it is a construct of particular usefulness to caseworkers. It was first formulated by Charlotte Towle; under her leadership it was developed by the casework and research faculty of the University of Chicago and was refined and fashioned into a research instrument by Lilian Ripple.[37] Its salience in the problem-solving model's diagnosis has already been dealt with.

There remains now the necessity to identify the sources of the ideas and notions that fashion the actions of the helping process itself and that may one day be integrated as "action theory." These, understandably, have been more native to casework and other psychotherapeutic endeavors than to the behavioral "sciences." I note them here both out of my sense of debt to contributors to the problem-solving model and for any reader who takes pleasure in identifying sources.

"Relationship"—its powers and management—has been a dynamic since time immemorial in any endeavors by one person to influence another. All forms of social casework depend upon it centrally. It hardly needs saying that Freud's revelations and insights on transference (and countertransference)

---

36. See Perlman, *Persona*, for my efforts at integration, and especially pp. 321–32 for references on role concept.
37. Charlotte Towle, "Casework Methods of Helping the Client to Make Maximum Use of His Capacities and Resources," *Social Service Review* 22 (December 1948):469–79, reprinted in *Proceedings of the National Conference on Social Work, 1949* (New York: Columbia University Press, 1949); and in *Helping: Charlotte Towle on Social Work and Social Casework*, ed. Helen Harris Perlman (Chicago: University of Chicago Press, 1969). Helen Harris Perlman, "The Client's Treatability," *Social Work* 1 (October 1956):32–40. Ripple, Alexander, and Polemis, *Motivation, Capacity, and Opportunity*.

opened vistas and depths of understanding of these lifelong
need and emotion freighted bonds. All responsible helpers
draw nurture from Freud's explorations and discoveries relevant to relationship. In casework practice the "functional
school," it seems to me, probed and banked on the potency
of relationship most consistently and cogently. Beyond Robinson's recognition[38] of the moving powers in relationship,
"Rankian" psychology was permeated with a belief in the potential power of the immediate encounter between a helper
and a help-seeker, in the releasing and stirring forces of experiencing the self-and-other in some heightened awareness.
Thus, through relationship (accompanied by other conscious
uses of the helper's self and agency) it was postulated that
dormant personality strengths or motives might be released
and utilized. The likeness between this conviction and that
of existentialism is manifest (though, to my knowledge, Rank
never identified himself with this philosophy). This belief
in the potential potency of the present moment as it is experienced in a genuine, self-other-aware relationship is probably not subject to empirical testing. The further probability
is that it will be rejected or embraced, as the case may be,
according to a helper's individual experience or style. The
relevance here is that this concept of relationship, combined
with that of the powers within immediate experience, has in
part fashioned the focus and operations in the problem-
solving model.

One further comment in line with this: Jessie Taft's[39] emphasis upon the developing self as a consequence of transaction with a significant other (the caseworker) within a
specified social set (the agency) has never been satisfactorily
explained to me by her allegiance to Rankian psychology.
Only recently I found what are possibly the pre-Rankian
sources of Jessie Taft's working philosophy. In 1913 she

---

38. Virginia Robinson's *A Changing Psychology in Social Casework*
(Chapel Hill: University of North Carolina Press, 1930) pointed up the
therapeutic powers of relationship and was, in its time, a milestone contribution to casework.
39. For those who have entered social casework only recently it should be
stated that Jessie Taft and Virginia Robinson were the founders of the
"Rankian" or "functional" school of social work at the University of
Pennsylvania.

earned her Ph.D. in social science at the University of Chicago. John Dewey had left Chicago only a few years before, but his thinking continued to exert a powerful influence upon sociology and social psychology there for many years thereafter. W. I. Thomas and G. H. Mead, both social psychologists and sociologists, were leading thinkers in the subject matter Jessie Taft studied. Their ideas of the "definition of the situation" as determining behavior, of "emergent properties" of personality, of "social becoming" as a product of interaction between the person and his social reality—these must have been in the very air Jessie Taft breathed during her studentship at the university.

Some further "functional" concepts which fit and therefore blended into the problem-solving model were the principle of partialization; assessment of the current transactions between client and caseworker as having priority over etiological diagnosis of the problem; the limits upon goals imposed by time and place and the defined situation. Many of these have by now become so completed digested into all forms of good casework practice that they are scarcely identifiable as "different" anymore.[40]

In current casework practice the problem-solving model will be found to overlap or be consonant with several other theoretical constructs that are in the forefront of interest. These constructs are of several orders—those concerned with modes of casework action and those concerned with dynamics of sociopersonal change. I will touch on them only briefly.

The Crisis Intervention Model
In one of the clearest presentations of the "theoretical underpinnings" of the crisis concept, Rapoport repeatedly refers to "problem-solving mechanisms" (of the ego).[41] The treatment

---

40. In 1949, when the battles between "diagnostic" and "functional" schools still raged high (especially in the east), I tentatively put forward a statement affirming their commonalities. See Helen Harris Perlman, "The Parable of the Workers of the Field," *Social Service Review* 23 (March 1949):21–24.

41. Lydia Rapoport, "The State of Crisis: Some Theoretical Considerations," *Social Service Review* 36 (June 1962):211–17. Reprinted in *Crisis Intervention,* ed. Howard J. Parad (New York: Family Service Association of America, 1965).

conditions put forward to facilitate "problem-solving during a state of crisis" are (1) clarification and formulation of the problem; (2) expansion and management of feelings, facilitated by "explicit acceptance by the helping person of the disordered affect, the irrational attitudes or negation responses"; (3) the use of both interpersonal and institutional resources, since, it is postulated, the person in crisis is most susceptible to the influence of significant others. Rapoport asserts the compatibility between "crisis theory" and "general role-transition states, and social network." If I understand it correctly, its closest psychodynamic and action parallel is those formulations contained in the problem-solving model.

Short-Term Treatment Model

Close on the heels of the crisis concept is the revived interest in short-term treatment or brief therapy. (The history of the vicissitudes of this treatment idea and its forms both in casework and psychoanalytic circles is worth tracing if one is to learn not to repeat the foibles of a professional past!)[42] A number of factors contributed to the revival of interest in the short-term treatment mode: the reported successes of crisis treatment combined with the stern realities of the excessive cost of long-time treatment effort, the excess of service demand over casework manpower and, perhaps most shaking, the repeated research evidence that in most psychiatric clinics and family service agencies, the client/patients themselves tended to drop out of planned long-term treatment.

Of most cogency is the recently completed study comparing treatment outcomes in short-term and open-ended treatment efforts on similar groups of cases.[43] With middle-class, middle-income, voluntary clients as their study sample (in short, with "ideal" clients) the researchers found that short-term treatment of interpersonal problems yielded more progress than long-continued service, and that the progress was equally durable. The explanation for these outcomes bears on prominent aspects of the problem-solving mode. Specifically: the

---

42. For a brief noting of the major contributors to short-term treatment concepts see Howard J. Parad and Libbie L. Parad, "A Study of Crisis-Oriented Planned Short-Term Treatment: Part I," *Social Casework* 49 (June 1968): 346–55.

43. Reid and Shyne, *Brief and Extended Casework.*

happier outcomes in planned short-term treatment were judged to be related to clear identification of the problem-to-be-worked; to partialization of that problem; to realistically circumscribed and limited goals; to the focus upon the problems of current interpersonal transactions rather than upon intrapsychic malaise. The researchers add, "Evidence has been provided that the greatest changes in client functioning may occur relatively early in treatment." This is consistent with the notions of crisis theorists and is also consistent with the problem-solving model, which begins with the problem as perceived, felt, and understood by the person in its immediate, "now" dimensions, and which aims not at total amelioration of the stresses and tensions in interpersonal functioning but at setting in motion ways of more satisfactorily coping with them.

"Hard-to-Reach" Treatment Model

In sharp contrast with the client group for which long-term treatment has traditionally been thought feasible is that large group of persons who, within the past ten years or so, have become uncomfortably visible to social workers, and whose needs—economic, educational, social, and motivational—are multiple and massive. Social work in all its forms has resolutely turned to face and to find its place within this disadvantaged, deficit-suffering population. When individual families or persons have applied or been sent to social agencies for necessary material aids or guidance, casework has been the helping process of choice. But, as the literature of both casework and accompanying social science research attests, there are many special problems in the so-called culture of the poor that require some radical revisions of the traditional casework mode. These are problems of differences in communication capacities, in capacities for impulse control, in the valuing of action versus talk, in the need for immediate rather than postponed reward, in the frequent distrust of relationship and therefore the incapacity to sustain it—and so on. The exploration of the problem in depth or breadth, the expectation that symbols of speech can substitute for action, the introspective considerations that are the product of both trust and relative freedom from external threats, the willingness and capacity to postpone this day's gratification for some later, confidently hoped for reward—all these are not typically to be found among the hard-to-reach or hard-to-hold client.

Several aspects of the problem-solving model (with modifications shaped to individual diagnosis) are particularly useful, it seems to me, for work with these often unwilling and alienated persons. They were tested and found useful in one of the pioneer projects in working with the hard-to-reach—the Saint Paul Family-Centered Project.[44] Specifically, these emphases in the problem-solving model proved useful: the readiness of the caseworker to give concerned attention to the "now problem" as defined and felt by the client; the treatment-diagnostic effort to draw out and heighten his motivation and to relate to "what he wants"; the focusing upon small sectors of what were usually multiple and diffuse problems; the clear definition of possible choices of action on the client's (or worker's) part; the exercise of the client's decision-making and "stock-taking" capacities within the (usually narrow) limits of his reality; and the aiming for short-term goals with their small but accessible rewards. All this, of course, was buttressed by the continuous reward of the caseworker's relationship of concern and consistent recognition and support. That personality pathologies—disorganization and deficits—were "causes" of many of the sociopathological conditions in these hard-to-reach families was often clear. But each had some present and pressuring problem. If they did not themselves feel it as crucial, it was made so by the intrusion of the community's representative, the caseworker. So the problem of social malfunctioning had to be faced and defined and coped with, even though it might have been a derivative of chronic psychosocial maladaptation. As that clear and present problem was faced, was considered for its harmful effects, and was viewed against potential solutions, and as the persons involved in it made and embarked on decisions to try to cope with it, they were involved in the experience of coping in adaptive ways. What was repeatedly demonstrated here and in numerous other efforts with multideficit families is the necessity for small rewards swiftly

---

44. See Alice Overton et al., *Casework Notebook Family-Centered Project* (St. Paul: Community Chest and Councils, 1957).

realized if there is to be continued problem-solving effort. The problem-solving model's concepts of focus, problem-identification, and partialization, and its goal of finding some immediate rewards within the client's current transactions, enhance the limited motivations and capacities that often characterize the client who, for whatever reasons, is hard-to-reach or hard to engage in using agency help.

A Glimpse Ahead

Now at the growing edge of social work there emerge several new theories that, in part because of their promise of "scientism," will probably affect the shape of things to come in casework practice. I touch on one, and that only tentatively, because I have as yet only limited understanding of it —but it seems to me to promise vital connectedness with the problem-solving model. It is system theory.

One of the postulates of system theory is that the personality is an open system; that the person is formed, developed, "becoming" through his continuous transaction with social realities. This concept of personality as "becoming," as perpetually interpenetrated by and interpenetrating social experience, is, as has been said, basic to the problem-solving model, which posits all living as a problem-solving process, posits process as the very condition for growth, and posits that the casework encounter can be a transactional experience of moment in the changing adaptation of a human being.[45]

Since a system is, by definition, characterized by some degree of connection among its parts, it is postulated that change in one part of the system will affect some other parts. This has its parallel in the problem-solving model in that it is held that "partialization," by focus upon an identified problem, has validity on the assumption that the amelioration of stress in one aspect of living will have a permeation effect upon some other aspects (or parts of the "personality system") and that resumption of balance or increased compe-

---

45. It is interesting to note the frequency with which the name of John Dewey, G. H. Mead, and W. J. Thomas, as "social interactionists" or "symbolic interactionists," are invoked today by social scientists working on systems theory.

tence in one aspect of the life situation will increase the person's sense of potential or actual mastery in some other aspects.

Still on the borders of system theory, since a "social system" exists when two (or more) persons interact, the concept of role—which is a definition of interlocking functions—must of necessity be central. Here it can only be noted that the focus upon deficiencies, disparities, or disturbances in everyday social relationships, which the problem-solving model takes as its main field of intervention, is a focus upon the individual in his social transactions shaped by the role requirements and expectations within his role system.

One further note: "inputs and feedback" in open systems are held to be not linear, but circular. The traditional view of the sequential chain of causes which has permeated so much of casework's diagnostic thinking must consider those "causes" which are emergent, which are spontaneously generated in current transactions, and those "effects" which become "inputs" and thus new causes. Diagnosis in the problem-solving model focuses its viewing lens sharply upon the emergence of motivations and capacities for coping which treatment inputs call forth.

Finally, among these new glimpses and fragments, I am intrigued by the recent statements of a well-known physicist who is currently the director of a mental health research center. As a physical scientist in some recent explorations into the physiology of human perception and its relation to the sensory-motor "decision-system," John Platt writes, "Operationally there is no past for a decision-system except what is stored there in the present instance . . . all time is present together in this Now . . . remembering and planning is now. All time and space that is *operationally real to us and actionable* is present to us here and now."[46]

The problem-solving model is, in essence, a theoretical structure by which the caseworker and client together can "seize the day," can use Now, and make it liveable.

---

46. John Platt, "The Two Faces of Perception," in *Changing Perspectives on Man,* ed. Ben Rothblatt (Chicago: University of Chicago Press, 1968).

Bibliography

Dewey, John. *Art as Experience.* New York: Putnam and Sons, 1934.

―――. "Analysis of Reflective Thinking." In *How We Think,* rev. ed. New York: D. C. Heath and Co., 1933.

Erikson, Erik. *Identity and the Life Cycle,* Psychological Issues, 1. New York: International Universities Press, 1959.

Perlman, Helen Harris. *Social Casework: A Problem-solving Process.* Chicago: University of Chicago Press, 1957.

―――. *Persona: Social Role and Personality.* Chicago: University of Chicago Press, 1968. See especially chapters 1, 2, 7, and 9.

Reid, William J., and Shyne, Ann W. *Brief and Extended Casework.* New York: Columbia University Press, 1969.

Ripple, Lilian; Alexander, Ernestina; and Polemis, Bernice W. *Motivation, Capacity, and Opportunity: Studies in Casework Theory and Practice.* Social Service Monographs, 2d ser., no. 3. Chicago: School of Social Service Administration, University of Chicago, 1964. See especially chapter 3.

Simon, Bernece K. *Relationship between Theory and Practice in Social Casework.* Social Work Practice in Medical Care and Rehabilitation Settings, monograph 4. New York: National Association of Social Workers, 1960.

Towle, Charlotte. "Casework Methods of Helping the Client to Make Maximum Use of His Capacities and Resources," "Some Aspects of Modern Casework," and "New Developments in Social Casework." In *Helping: Charlotte Towle on Social Work and Social Casework,* edited by Helen Harris Perlman. Chicago: University of Chicago Press, 1969.

White, Robert W. *Ego and Reality in Psychoanalytic Theory.* Psychological Issues, 3, monograph 11. New York: International Universities Press, 1963.

5 | Behavioral Modification and Casework

Edwin J. Thomas

INTRODUCTION

The emerging knowledge and practice of behavioral modification are relevant to casework simply because caseworkers are also intimately involved in the business of modifying behavior. Much of what most caseworkers do as treatment or intervention is intended to change or stabilize some aspect of the behavior of clients or of others involved in the social worker's professional activity. All of what any caseworker might do has the potential to change or maintain the behavior of clients or others. Furthermore, it is difficult to contest the assertion that caseworkers actually change some aspects of their client's behavior even if some of the changes are not intentional or indicative of successful modification.

Social work has just recently begun to give serious attention to the contributions behavioral methods may make to direct practice. Schools of social work are beginning to teach subjects relating to behavioral modification; institutes on this subject appear to be held in increasing numbers; publications presenting aspects of the behavioral approach have now been prepared for social workers;[1] selected social work prac-

Edwin J. Thomas is professor of social work and psychology, School of Social Work, University of Michigan, Ann Arbor.

Preparation of this manuscript was facilitated by a grant to the author from the Social and Rehabilitation Administration, Department of Health and Education and Welfare (grant SRS-CRD 425-8-286), for the purpose of conducting research on the utilization and appraisal of sociobehavioral techniques in social welfare.

1. For example, see Derek Jehu, *Learning Theory and Social Work* (London: Routledge and Kegan Paul, 1967); Edwin J. Thomas, "Selected Sociobehavioral Techniques and Principles: An Approach to Interpersonal Helping," *Social Work* 13 (January 1968):12–26; Edwin J. Thomas and Esther Goodman, eds., *Socio-behavioral Theory and Interpersonal Helping in Social Work: Lectures and Institute Proceedings* (Ann Arbor, Mich.: Campus Publishers, 1965); Edwin J. Thomas, ed., *The Sociobehavioral Approach and Applications to Social Work* (New York: Council on Social Work Education, 1967); Michael Picardie, "Counter-Conditioning and Assertive Training in Social Work Practice," *Case Conference* 14 (December 1967):292–96; Michael Picardie, "Learning Theory and Casework," *Social Work* (U.K.) 24 (January 1967):10–15; Donald J. Mueller, ed., "Applications of Behavior Theory to Social Welfare," mimeographed (University of Wisconsin-Milwaukee School of Social Welfare, 1967); and Robert D. Carter and Richard B. Stuart, "Behavior Modification Theory and Practice: A Reply," *Social Work* 15

titioners are starting to apply behavioral methods; and research is being conducted on behavioral methods applicable to direct social work practice. The challenge to casework is that the technology of behavioral modification is growing at a more rapid rate than is the effort to assimilate and adapt its contributions in casework.

GENERAL CHARACTERISTICS OF THE APPROACH

A Brief Historical Background

The basic research on learning and conditioning that undergirds most contemporary behavioral methods may be traced back directly to about the turn of the century, at which time seminal experiments were conducted by such researchers as Thorndike and Pavlov. There have been over fifty years of research bearing upon the principles of learning and conditioning. Important portions of the research antedate the more recent advent of behavioral therapy proper. Aside from a few seminal demonstrations and an occasional proponent such as Watson, behavioral therapy cannot be said to have made its entry into the therapeutic marketplace until the decade of the 1950s and, at least in this country, the movement did not appear to get started rapidly or directly. However, enough was then known about learning and conditioning to provide the foundation for rapid developments in several related directions. Many of the so-called schools of contemporary behavioral therapy started or were developed during the last twenty to twenty-five years.

A few of these earlier developments deserve brief mention. During the early 1950s writers such as Dollard and Miller,[2] Mowrer,[3] and Shoben[4] addressed the relationship between

(January 1970):37–50. A number of additional contributions are in preparation.

2. J. Dollard and N. E. Miller, *Personality and Psychotherapy* (New York: McGraw-Hill, 1950).

3. O. H. Mowrer, ed., *Learning Theory and Personality Dynamics* (New York: Ronald Press, 1950); and O. H. Mowrer, ed., *Psychotherapy: Theory and Research* (New York: Ronald Press, 1953).

4. E. J. Shoben, "Psychotherapy as a Problem in Learning Theory," *Psychological Bulletin* 46 (1949):366–92; and E. J. Shoben, "Psycho-

particular learning processes and psychoanalytic theory, personality development, and psychotherapeutic process. (Incidentally, these are precisely the questions many dynamically trained caseworkers raise today after their first exposure to learning theory and behavioral modification.) Writings such as these are still timely for those who are curious about such linkages and conceptual interrelationships.

As useful as they were, such interpretations and explications had no discernible impact upon the therapeutic practice of the 1950s. More germane were the behavioral research and clinical practice of this period.[5] Skinner's research and point of view have been singularly influential.[6] Skinner and his followers, especially Lindsley, Ayllon, Goldiamond, Ferster, Azrin, and Premack, conducted basic research in operant behavior, much of which had therapeutic implications. Ayllon was among those who did pioneering and now classic demonstrations of behavioral modification practice in mental hospitals (one of the areas he examined more recently was that of the token economy).[7] Wolpe's research into and practice of systematic desensitization laid the foundation for what is probably the most widely practiced behavioral therapy and one of the most vigorously researched areas of behavioral therapy.[8] It was during the 1950s that the effectiveness of conventional psychotherapy came under attack and Eysenck

therapy and the Learning Process," in Mowrer, *Psychotherapy: Theory and Research*.

5. For example, the empirical work of Mowrer on a behavioral approach to bedwetting was probably much more influential in practice than his theoretical views, as penetrating and wise as they were. See, for example, O. H. Mowrer, "Enuresis: A Method for Its Study and Treatment," in Mowrer, *Learning Theory and Personality Dynamics*, pp. 340–417.

6. Although Skinner's basic scientific research was most influential among psychologists, his other writings have perhaps done more to influence the viewpoints of those interested in applied work. For example, see B. F. Skinner, *Science and Human Behavior* (New York: Macmillan Co., 1953); and B. F. Skinner, *Walden Two* (New York: Macmillan Co., 1948).

7. For example, see Teodoro Ayllon and Jack Michael, "The Psychiatric Nurse as a Behavioral Engineer," *Journal of the Experimental Analysis of Behavior* 2 (1959):323–34.

8. A basic report by Joseph Wolpe, *Psychotherapy by Reciprocal Inhibition* (Stanford, Calif.: Stanford University Press, 1958).

was among the more vocal and persuasive of the critics.[9] Although his own research and theory are controversial even among behaviorists, his appeals for a therapy based upon scientific principles of learning have been heeded.[10] Eysenck also helped to familiarize therapists with Pavlovian conditioning, as did the practice writings of Salter[11] and the more basic researches of investigators such as as Gantt.[12]

Behavioral modification and therapy may be said to have become competitors in the therapeutic marketplace in the 1960s. There is now a relatively vigorous and rapidly growing group of practitioners and researchers in the area of behavioral modification, and there are emerging professional associations[13] and several important journals devoted exclusively to practice and research in behavioral therapy and modification (among the most important of these are *Behaviour Research and Therapy* and the *Journal of Applied Behavior Analysis*). All areas of interpersonal helping have now had exposure to developments in behavioral therapy and modification.

Some Common Emphases in the Behavorial Approach

The details and diversity of behavioral approaches cannot possibly be reviewed here. However, some of the common themes in the approach, along with some elements of the rationale can be characterized.

The first common theme is a focus upon observable responses. Contrary to the accusations of some critics, this is

---

9. For example, see Hans J. Eysenck, "The Effects of Psychotherapy: An Evaluation," *Journal of Consulting Psychology* 16 (October 1952):319–23.
10. For example, see Hans J. Eysenck, "Learning Theory and Behaviour Therapy," *Journal of Mental Science* 105 (1959):61–75.
11. A. Salter, *Conditioned Reflex Therapy* (New York: Creative Age Press, 1950).
12. For example, see W. Horsley Gantt, "The Conditional Reflex Function as an Aid in the Study of the Psychiatric Patient," in *Relation of Psychological Tests to Psychiatry*, ed. P. H. Hoch and J. Zubin (New York: Grune and Stratton, 1950), pp. 165–89.
13. For example, there is the Association for Advancement of the Behavioral Therapies: Group for the Clinical Application of the Principles of Behavior Modification. Also, the clinical psychology division of the American Psychological Association has a subdivision concerned with the experimental foundations of clinical psychology.

not a narrow conception of human activity. Actually, this idea is very generic. All behavior is pertinent—"thoughts," "affect," as well as motor action—providing that it is discernible through the senses of the observer and can be reliably denoted. Although no dubious, hypothetical inner psychic states are postulated, this conception of behavior does not deny that there are inner physiological, neural, and biological processes of mind nor that many of these may be made objective and observable through scientific measurement. By focusing steadfastly upon observable responses there is less chance of making incorrect inferences about behavior and of attempting to take action with respect to factors that are essentially not identifiable, accessible, or manipulatable.

A second theme is a focus upon more fundamental classes of behavior. A great deal of research in experimental psychology and in biology during the past half-century has revealed that there are at least two rather different classes of behavior.[14] The first, called operant behavior, involves the striated muscles and the skeletal system. Much but not all of what is ordinarily construed as voluntary behavior is illustrative. Walking, talking, and much of what we call thinking are examples. The second class of behavior, called respondent, implicates mainly the glands and smooth muscles. Much but not all of what is called involuntary behavior is illustrative. Respondent behaviors most often dealt with in casework are anxiety and the responses of sexual arousal.

Research indicates that in general different principles of

---

14. Although there are other classes of behavior, such as the instinctual, the differences between operant and respondent behavior are well established and the principles for these two realms of behavior are different. For a good discussion of these matters, see Thom Verhave, "An Introduction to the Experimental Analysis of Behavior," in *The Experimental Analysis of Behavior: Selected Readings*, ed. Thom Verhave (New York: Appleton-Century-Crofts, 1966), pp. 1–47. It is essential to acknowledge that despite the importance of the differences between the operant and respondent realms of behavior, there would appear to be at least some interrelationships. For more details see H. D. Kimmel, "Instrumental Conditioning of Autonomically Mediated Behavior," *Psychological Bulletin* 67 (May 1967):337–46; and Robert A. Rescorla and Richard L. Solomon, "Two-Process Learning Theory: Relationships between Pavlovian Conditioning and Instrumental Learning," *Psychological Review* 74 (May 1967):151–83.

behavior operate for each class of behavior. Operant behavior is controlled mainly by its consequences in the environment, whereas respondent behavior is controlled mainly by the eliciting stimuli which antedate the responses.[15] The principles relating to operant behavior do not apply in general to respondent behavior[16] and, likewise, the principles of respondent conditioning do not apply to operant behavior. As I shall attempt to indicate at a later point, these principles provide important guidelines for the modification of behavior.

From this point of view, symptoms are observable responses of an individual that are labeled as deviant or problematic. No hypothetical or as yet unspecified "psychic disease" or underlying condition is presumed. Most behaviorists allege that symptoms are no different from other responses in that (1) the behavior falls predominantly into the respondent or the operant realm, (2) it was learned through processes of conditioning, (3) it obeys the same laws of learning and conditioning as does so-called normal behavior, and (4) it is amenable to modification through the careful application of what is known about learning and modification. However, this does not mean that a so-called symptom is unrelated to other behaviors, including some that will necessarily occur more commonly if the symptom behavior is reduced,[17] or that it was acquired under ordinary or benign environmental conditions.

---

15. For a succinct summary of the principles of operant conditioning, see Verhave, "An Introduction to the Experimental Analysis of Behavior." More detailed views on specialized subjects in operant behavior are to be found in Werner K. Honig, ed., *Operant Behavior: Areas of Research and Application* (New York: Appleton-Century-Crofts, 1966). Among the basic secondary sources here are Fred S. Keller and William N. Schoenfeld, *Principles of Psychology: A Systematic Text in the Science of Behavior* (New York: Appleton-Century-Crofts, 1950); Skinner, *Science and Human Behavior*; Honig, *Operant Behavior*; and Arthur W. Staats and Carolyn K. Staats, *Complex Human Behavior: A Systematic Extension of Learning Principles* (New York: Holt, Rinehart and Winston, 1964).For more elementary statements see, for example, Fred S. Keller, *Learning: Reinforcement Theory* (New York: Random House, 1954), and the beginning lectures for social workers on this subject by Edwin J. Thomas in Thomas and Goodman, *Sociobehavioral Theory and Interpersonal Helping.*

16. Thomas, "Selected Sociobehavioral Techniques and Principles."

17. The reader who believes in the dynamic doctrine of symptom

Without denying the importance of the initial developmental conditions or intervening learning experiences, a strong emphasis is placed upon the role that may be played by contemporary sustaining conditions. This is another theme among behaviorists. These sustaining conditions are the immediate stimulus antecedents for the problematic responses in question as well as the stimuli that occur immediately following the behavior. Often referred to as controlling conditions, these immediate antecedents and consequences of problem behavior serve as the focuses of assessment and as potential points for intervention. In behavior that is largely respondent, the focus is upon the stimuli conditioned to elicit the problem responses. For example, the stimuli in the child's environment that trigger the onset of phobic responses would constitute the antedating, sustaining conditions for the phobia. Among the consequences of particular interest to the behaviorist would be those that are either reinforcing or punishing. In the case of a school-phobic child, failure to go to school might be accomplished by operants that result in their reinforcement by the mother.

This focus upon alteration of either the immediate antecedents or consequences of problem behavior is still another common theme among the modifiers of behavior. As we shall see when modification techniques are discussed, most of them involve specific procedures by which antedating stimuli may be altered or the consequences of problem behavior may be rearranged.

Instead of purporting to work on global and general objectives, most behaviorists endeavor to modify very specific behaviors. The behavioral objectives are essentially efforts to achieve the acquisition of behavior, or its strengthening, maintenance, weakening, or elimination.

Behaviorists also tend to share preferences for the nature

---

substitution would do well to find evidence for it in scientifically reputable inquiries. I have not yet found any studies that support the doctrine. Also, a number of behaviorally oriented studies have sought to discover whether behaviors change so as to merit the judgment of symptom substitution and I have not yet located any evidence for the alleged substitution. For a recent study that expressly examined this problem, see Bruce L. Baker, "Symptom Treatment and Symptom Substitution in Enuresis," *Journal of Abnormal Psychology* 74 (February 1969):42–49.

and quality of evidence. Observation is favored over intro-spection, measurement over imprecise reckoning, firsthand empirical knowledge over speculation and theory, and single-organism research designs over uncontrolled case studies or cross-sectional studies of aggregates of subjects. These prefer-ences permeate most of the researches upon which behavioral knowledge is based as well as the methods of assessment and modification employed in practice.

Variant Emphases

Brief mention should be made of the so-called specialized behavioral schools active in the therapeutic marketplace.

1. *The operant.* This is a dominant group in this country and includes those who emphasize "reinforcement therapy" as well as practitioners who make use of many operant techniques.
2. *The respondent.* Most exemplary here perhaps are the behavioral therapists who rely most on the principles and techniques of Pavlovian conditioning.
3. *The personalistic.* Behaviorally oriented personality theorists who practice behavioral theory which is in-formed by personality assessments and theory are illus-trative here.
4. *The specialized technique.* Practitioners who employ mainly one behavioral technique, such as systematic desensitization, are exemplary.
5. *The eclectic.* This is perhaps the largest group and in-includes those who employ particular blends of tech-niques. There are at least three noteworthy types of eclectic practitioner.
   a. *The behavioral eclectic* uses many different be-havioral techniques. The extreme here would be the general behavioral practitioner, analogous in breadth to his medical counterpart.
   b. *The broad spectrum eclectic* uses selected behavioral techniques along with more conventional thera-peutic approaches. (Most caseworkers today who identify themselves as behaviorally oriented are, in my experience, broad spectrum eclectics.)
   c. *The sociobehavioral eclectic* uses techniques derived from behavioral therapy, behavioral modification,

social psychology, other areas of behavioral science, and from practice, providing that the techniques have empirical support and can be made operational for purposes of achieving change. This approach, as I have stated elsewhere,[18] is the one that I believe has the most promise for the field of social work, for it embraces contributions to direct service, meeting selected criteria, for all relevant behavioral science disciplines and from practice in social work as well as in other helping professions.

BEHAVORIAL SCIENCE FOUNDATIONS

A review of knowledge is impossible here, but the significant classes of information may be delineated, along with some of the contributions which knowledge in these classes makes.

The first class of information consists of studies of the effectiveness of psychotherapy and of behavioral methods of achieving change. The results of such researches support two related conclusions: that conventional therapies have not been demonstrated to be particularly effective, and that behaviorally oriented approaches have generally been found to be superior to conventional methods or to untreated controls.[19] One must acknowledge that there are important de-

---

18. Edwin J. Thomas, "The Socio-behavioral Approach: Illustrations and Analysis," in Thomas, *Socio-behavioral Approach and Applications to Social Work*, pp. 1–15.

19. For psychotherapy, see, for example, Eysenck, "Effects of Psychotherapy"; for a more recent and detailed review, see Hans J. Eysenck and Stanley Rachman, *The Causes and Cures of Neurosis* (San Diego: Robert R. Knapp, 1965), pp. 242–67; and for reviews of evaluative studies in family services, see Scott Briar, "Family Services," in *Five Fields of Social Service: Reviews of Research*, ed. Henry S. Maas (New York: National Association of Social Workers, 1966), pp. 16–21; an important evaluative study in social work having a control group design is in Henry J. Meyer, Edgar F. Borgatta, and Wyatt C. Jones, *Girls at Vocational High: An Experiment in Social Work Intervention* (New York: Russell Sage Foundation, 1965). Also note such studies as Gordon L. Paul, *Insight vs. Desensitization: An Experiment in Anxiety Reduction* (Stanford, Calif.: Stanford University Press, 1966); Peter J. Lang and A. David Lazovik, "Experimental Desensitization of a Phobia," *Journal of Abnormal and Social Psychology* 66 (June 1963):519–25; and Arnold A.

tails and exceptions and considerable research remains to be done. Not all conventional therapies have been shown to be unequivocally ineffective, and there are noteworthy variations in the efficacy of those behavioral methods that have been carefully studied.[20] I have no doubt that had the conventional therapies been demonstrated to be more effective in earlier evaluative studies, the contemporary emphasis upon behavioral methods would have been retarded. It turned out, however, that at the very time researchers and practitioners were attending to the essentially depressing results of the evaluations of more conventional therapies, the studies of the efficacy of behavioral methods were indicating greater success.[21]

The second important class of information consists of the more basic scientific research on the processes and principles of learning. We are speaking of the studies made of respondent (or classical Pavlovian) conditioning as well as the inquiries into operant (or instrumental) conditioning. Growing out of these thousands of experiments is considerable information concerning the conditions under which classical conditioning will be effective and the variables influencing

---

Lazarus, "Group Therapy of Phobic Disorders by Systematic Desensitization," *Journal of Abnormal and Social Psychology* 63 (November 1961): 504–10.

20. For some differences in effectiveness of behavioral approaches, see, for example, John M. Grossberg, "Behavior Therapy: A Review," *Psychological Bulletin* 62 (August 1964):73–88; and Carolin S. Keutzer, Edward Lichtenstein, and Hayden L. Mees, "Modification of Smoking Behavior: A Review," *Psychological Bulletin* 70 (December 1968):520–33.

21. Despite the newness of the behavioral approach, I judge that there is presently more research concerning the efficacy of the various behavioral techniques than there is for the conventional techniques. Evaluations have been made of the use of behavioral methods for nearly every clinical and problem category and, for many of these areas, there are contemporary reviews to which the reader may turn for details. For example, see Robert Leff, "Behavior Modification and the Psychoses of Childhood: A Review," *Psychological Bulletin* 69 (June 1968): 396–409; M. P. Feldman, "Aversion Therapy for Sexual Deviations: A Critical Review," *Psychological Bulletin* 65 (February 1966): 65–79; S. Rachman, "Systematic Desensitization," *Psychological Bulletin* 67 (February 1967): 93–103; and James P. Flanders, "A Review of Research on Imitative Behavior," *Psychological Bulletin* 69 (May 1968): 316–37.

operant conditioning.[22] Two main principles emerge from these researches.

The first might be called the *principle for operant behavior*. This principle asserts that behavior in the operant realm is controlled by its consequences. Following the emission of a response in the operant realm, reinforcing or punishing stimuli may be applied, withheld, or removed. If one has information concerning whether the particular stimulus is reinforcing or aversive, whether it has been applied, withheld, or removed, and the schedule with which these operations are engaged in, it then becomes possible on the basis of prior research to anticipate what the probable consequences will be. The various operant techniques of behavioral modification are essentially names for operations that accompany demonstrably different consequences for operant behavior.

Another main principle is the *principle for respondent behavior*. This principle asserts that behavior in the respondent realm is controlled by the stimuli which immediately antedate the responses. Such stimuli are typically conditioned elicitors of respondents or otherwise neutral stimuli that may be paired with unconditioned stimuli so as to become conditioned eliciting stimuli.

A third class of information undergirding behavioral methods consists of research on the particular techniques of modification. There are now studies of this type relating to almost every specialized technique in behavioral modification. Principles based upon such work have been crucial to the techniques involved. Consider, for example, Wolpe's principle as it relates to systematic desensitization:

If a response antagonistic to anxiety can be made to occur in the presence of anxiety-provoking stimuli so that it is accompanied by a complete or partial suppression of the anxiety responses, the bond between the stimuli and the anxiety responses will be weakened.[23]

Scores of investigations have been conducted to examine the

---

22. For example, see William F. Prokasy, ed., *Classical Conditioning: A Symposium* (New York: Appleton-Century-Crofts, 1965); and Werner K. Honig, ed., *Operant Behavior: Areas of Research and Application* (New York: Appleton-Century-Crofts, 1966).
23. Wolpe, *Psychotherapy by Reciprocal Inhibition,* p. 71.

procedures as well as the behavioral factors which relate to the efficacy of systematic desensitization. Thus, inquiries have been conducted into the role played by subject relaxation, the arrangement of anxiety-evoking stimuli, the comparative effects of placebo and the expectation of improvement, and the part played by extinction, among others.[24] Refinements in technique and clarifications in the understanding of systematic desensitization have resulted from these inquiries despite the fact that much more research is needed to understand further the most efficient procedure as well as the basic underlying behavioral mechanism. It is research precisely of this type that will increasingly be the foundation for the continuing development of procedure and understanding of behavioral methods.

The value and influence of such studies into specific behavioral modification techniques may be illustrated with selected developments in research on the token economy. In a token economy, participants may engage in a variety of desired behaviors each of which "pays" the participant in tokens that may be exchanged for a large range of reinforcers. Despite a large amount of research indicating the efficacy of generalized secondary reinforcers in the control of behavior, the basic inquiry into the efficacy of token methods was not reported until 1965.[25] In 1968 Atthowe and Krasner reported that some twenty-two separate institutions had such programs in various stages of operation with chronic mental patients.[26] During this same year, a basic report was published concerning the principles of token economies, the volume entitled *The Token Economy* by Ayllon and Azrin.[27]

---

24. For a review, see Rachman, "Systematic Desensitization." An example of the research referred to here is Eileen Gambrill, "Effectiveness of the Counterconditioning Procedure in Eliminating Avoidance Behavior," *Behaviour Research and Therapy* 5 (November 1967):263–75.

25. T. Ayllon and N. H. Azrin, "The Measurement and Reinforcement of Behavior of Psychotics," *Journal of the Experimental Analysis of Behavior* 8 (November 1965):357–83.

26. John M. Atthowe, Jr., and Leonard Krasner, "Preliminary Report on the Application of Contingent Reinforcement Procedures (Token Economy) on a 'Chronic' Psychiatric Ward," *Journal of Abnormal Psychology* 73 (February 1968):37–43.

27. Teodoro Ayllon and Nathan H. Azrin, *The Token Economy: A Mo-*

In 1969 Paul reported that "at the time of this writing, no negative reports have appeared concerning the effectiveness of token-economy programs."[28] Principles of token economies are currently being employed in token or point systems not only in a variety of closed institutional contexts but in families and schools as well.

A fourth important class of information that supports the use of behavioral methods is the so-called clinical demonstration. In addition to the inquiries referred to above, hundreds of clinical demonstrations have now been reported.[29] Unlike case studies with which most of us are familiar, these inquiries generally have much stronger designs. This is typically found in the use of before and after measurements; even more powerful are designs using a systematic step-by-step introduction of a series of modifications, and techniques of reversal and reinstatement. Baselines and monitoring are generally employed throughout. These are among the reasons that such clinical demonstrations generally yield more precise and valid information than did the earlier case studies. But even so, many demonstrations are not designed to reveal which of the elements of the intervention is operating to produce the results. Still, practitioners and researchers can learn much from these demonstrations, for many are imaginative and ground-breaking and provide important suggestions for the proper procedures one might employ for assessment and monitoring.

INITIAL PROCEDURAL DETAILS

The caseworker who endeavors to employ behavioral methods in his practice will inevitably encounter problems commonly met in other forms of therapy. Among these are what might be called initial procedural details.

---

tivational System for Therapy and Rehabilitation (New York: Appleton-Century-Crofts, 1968).

28. Gordon L. Paul, "Chronic Mental Patient: Current Status—Future Directions," Psychological Bulletin 71 (February 1969):89.

29. An influential collection of papers, most of which are clinical demonstrations, is Leonard P. Ullmann and Leonard Krasner, eds., Case Studies in Behavior Modification (New York: Holt, Rinehart and Winston, 1965).

Early Decisions

Who is to be involved, when to meet, and where are among the early decisions to be made. Few generalizations here apply uniquely to the behavioral approach, but in open settings there appear to be some emerging tendencies. Whenever possible, relevant agents and mediators whose behavior significantly influences or can affect the client are involved early in the modification effort. Contacts are generally held more frequently and are sometimes longer than fifty minutes per week. Home observation and intervention are strongly favored, where these options are afforded. Agency constraints and function enter here as in other approaches and, perhaps most germane of all, the particular behavioral procedure to be employed has a major guiding influence.

Initial Socialization

Most behavioral practitioners explain the procedures of their modification regimen and, increasingly, there are those who attempt to teach the principles upon which the modification is based. There are some behavioral practitioners who believe that it is as important in the long run for the client to be taught the principles of behavioral analysis and modification as it is to achieve particular changes for given contracted problems.

The Contract

Where it is possible to make a contract, most behavioral practitioners make explicit what is to be worked on. Some even employ written contracts as well as verbal agreements. An explicit contract serves to focus the attention of all parties upon the particular problem to be dealt with and provides better ethical protection for the client than a general, implicit agreement or no agreement at all.

Commitment

Still another early matter is the client's commitment to cooperate fully in the modification regimen. There are many who believe that this commitment should be strongly emphasized in order to encourage client compliance with the requisites of assessment and modification and, thereby, to increase the likelihood of achieving success.

There is no particular unanimity in the approaches of behaviorally oriented practitioners to the initial procedural details discussed above. One reason for this is that the behavioral modification techniques suitable for given problems often call for highly specialized approaches, and much more work needs to be done on the appropriate principles and procedures for behavioral practice in fields such as social welfare.

REQUISITES FOR ACHIEVING MODIFICATION

The literature on behavioral modification makes little or no reference to "relationship," and this can be disconcerting to caseworkers who have been taught that relationship is the basis upon which most beneficial changes in therapy may be achieved. Notions of relationship are too vague, nonspecific, and diverse to appeal to the behavioral modifier. The mystery, intrigue, near reverence and, to use Peterson's words,[30] "sentimental sham" associated with conceptions of relationship confuse more than clarify. However, one must hasten to say that behaviorally oriented practitioners are no less open, friendly, civil, or humane than their nonbehavioral counterparts. Behavioral modifiers have been most interested in the specific techniques of modification that serve to promote the modification or maintenance of behavior. Indeed, many of these behavioral techniques may specify behaviors that are the referents of some component concepts of relationship (e.g., compare reinforcement with "support").

In my own analysis of the writings of relationship I have discovered scores of definitions, and in order to obtain some understanding of the problem from a behavioral viewpoint, I found it useful to employ the behavioral method of analyzing the apparent referents of the concepts. When this is done, referents may be found for what presumably occurs (or should occur) before treatment, during treatment, and afterward; and for all these phases there are referents that pertain to the behavior of the helper, to the behavior of the client, or to interactions of the behavior of the helper and client. (There are nine cells here, for those who like paradigms.) To

---

30. Donald R. Peterson, *The Clinical Study of Social Behavior* (New York: Appleton-Century-Crofts, 1968), p. 127.

the extent that the writings assert what in fact occurs, such assertions are empirical questions and subject to study. There is now an extensive literature pertaining to these matters and it includes such factors as the therapist variables affecting patient response (e.g., empathy), the reinforcing capabilities of persons who are liked, ways to control your eyes in order to increase the probability that someone will like you, how best to sit in your chair when interviewing, and interviewing style, to name a few.[31] If pronouncements concerning such matters are to be made as principles or prescriptions for practice, they should be based upon a thorough review and appraisal of relevant studies. As important as such a review would be to an understanding of relationship phenomena, it has not yet been made. But even so, such an appraisal will not obviate the need for knowledge about specific modification techniques.

One important problem remains, and this is more logical than empirical. It is the question of what are some of the necessary conditions for achieving behavioral modification. If a behavioral analysis is applied to the requisites for achieving modification, one can identify five distinguishable features. Three of these pertain to both the worker and the client (or clients).

1. It is necessary to maintain sensory contact among all parties. This may be accomplished by face-to-face exposure, by telephone, by visual media such as movies, television, or reading matter, or by tactile means, as is illustrated by braille or skin communication. (It is increasingly not farfetched to imagine intercranial brain stimulation as a potential means for achieving sensory contact.) Without sensory contact through some medium, natural influences cannot be exercised.

---

31. To illustrate the importance of findings relating to one feature, posture and position, see Albert Mehrabian, "Significance of Posture and Position in the Communication of Attitude and Status Relationships," *Psychological Bulletin* 71 (May 1969):359–73. There are analogous reviews and many studies of other behavioral factors in relationship. For a more general behavioral analysis of phenomena frequently associated with relationship, see Israel Goldiamond and Jarl E. Dyrud, "Some Applications and Implications of Behavior Analysis for Psychotherapy," in *Research in Psychotherapy,* ed. John M. Schlien, III (Washington, D.C.: American Psychological Association, 1968).

2. All parties must engage, at least to some extent, in attending responses with respect to the stimuli conveyed through the sensory medium. That is, it is necessary to look, to hear, to feel, as appropriate for the medium. In a word, messages must be received; stimuli must have an impact.

3. There should be habituation of all parties so that there is familiarization with the human and nonhuman stimuli of the situation. This is required to reduce competing response tendencies, such as those that can occur when a person is first exposed to strange stimuli. Habituation simply increases the likelihood that the crucial stimuli to which responses are desired may be effective.

In addition, there are two other requisites that apply almost exclusively to the worker.

4. The worker must maintain conventional, culturally patterned civility. By this is meant that the worker generally is courteous, friendly, and open with clients and others in the modification effort. Our cultural background and context require such civility.

5. The worker must maintain access to manipulatable and potentially potent controlling conditions. Such controlling conditions consist of factors that alter the consequences of behavior, such as reinforcers or punishers, or of access to factors which control the evocation of behavior, such as eliciting stimuli or discriminative stimuli. This is perhaps the most significant feature of all, for if the worker does not have access to manipulatable and potentially potent controlling conditions he cannot hope to achieve the modification required.

ASSESSMENT

Conceptions, procedures, and techniques continue to develop apace. Even among the procedures already developed, there are variations that make it impossible to identify a single orthodoxy. Nonetheless, there are some common themes in the emerging behavioral approaches to assessment, and those relevant to casework are highlighted here.

Common Focuses

In all behavioral approaches to assessment there is a common emphasis upon behavioral specification. Such specification takes several forms and is applied to many types of information. Only the more common focuses will be mentioned here. Methods and techniques are discussed subsequently.

Specification applies, first, to problem identification. This entails not only an agreement concerning the nature of the problem to be worked on but also the identification of the particular behaviors that serve to define the problem for the client. The heart of the specification task is to obtain information concerning the particular behaviors that control the words the client uses to define and label the problem. Clients, like most of us, use concepts differently, and most clients have not been trained to be sufficiently concrete and denotative concerning their own or others' behavior. Hence, no label or problem definition can be taken at face value; no abstraction can substitute for the event it refers to.

Baselines are also commonly specified to determine the frequency or magnitude of problem behavior before intervention. Without knowing the "level" of behavior before intervention, it is not possible to determine the extent to which modification is successful. Some baselines can be obtained in a relatively short period of time providing that the problem behaviors occur very frequently (e.g., stuttering). Others, such as some drinking patterns or sexual practices, might require a considerably longer period of time. Frequent and nonvariable behaviors generally allow for short baselines (a day or two) whereas infrequent and variable behaviors call for long baselines (weeks or even months). Needless to say, extremely infrequent behaviors or behaviors requiring immediate crisis intervention are not ordinarily subject to being baselined.

Specification also applies to the conditions associated with the emission of the problem behavior. Most relevant here are the particular stimulus antecedents and consequences attending the problem behavior. There is somewhat less uniformity among behavioral practitioners in obtaining such data on associated conditions; some practitioners focus predominantly on stimulus antecedents, especially for respondent behavior, and others focus mainly on consequences, as in the operant approaches. In my experience, it is desirable to obtain both the antecedents and the consequences for any problem and to do so with a record of time for the occurrence of the particular problem behavior, for the stimulus antecedents as well as for the consequences.

Still another common practice in assessment is to monitor the frequency or magnitude of problem behavior during intervention as well as following it. This information serves to indicate whether the modification regimen is functioning as intended.

Methods of Assessment

Methods of assessment are largely either experimental or naturalistic. The most commonly employed method of assessment is nonexperimental in that before modification proper, no interventions of any type are used and no experimental design is imposed upon the collection of data. The objective is to obtain valid specimens of behavior in the situations in which the behavior normally occurs. The observation of the behavior of children and parents in the home under ordinary life conditions is essentially a naturalistic method.

Experimental methods of assessment systematically vary either the antecedents or the consequences of problem behavior in order to learn more precisely what the controlling conditions are. For example, if physiological and subjective reports of anxiety were to be obtained for a client's response to a series of stimuli which were potentially anxiety-evoking, the capability of the stimuli to evoke anxiety might be discerned. In any case, this method would generally yield better information than would self-reports alone, without such experimental stimulus presentation. Quasi-experimental methods are sometimes appropriate also. For example, clients can be observed in different life situations, strategically arranged, and variations of behavior may thereby be disclosed.

Techniques of Assessment

The observation of behavior in its natural life situation, such as in the school, home, or neighborhood or on the job, is perhaps one of the most important techniques that caseworkers may use in assessment. Many more behaviors could be observed in vivo that are presently examined in this way in casework. But some behaviors, such as sex, are ordinarily not subject to caseworker observation and for these other techniques of assessment must be employed.

Client descriptions of his own behavior are also widely used among behavioral modifiers. Such self-reports are ordinarily used in the interview and also to collect data systematically. Among the ways in which the behaviorally oriented caseworker may make self-reports more systematic are the following: to specify precisely the events to be recorded; to make charts or forms upon which events are to be recorded; to specify the time of recording (ordinarily, soon after the event has occurred); to check the adequacy of the recording and to provide corrective feedback, if necessary; and, where possible, to corroborate the accuracy of the recording. Although there are of course individual differences in the reliability and validity of self-reported data, the experience my colleagues and I have had so far in this area has been most encouraging.

Electrical and mechanical devices are extensively used in behavioral modification and many such devices will no doubt have some use in casework practice. It is already clear, for example, that simple counters, stopwatches, ordinary timepieces, and tape recorders have a variety of uses in the assessment of problems commonly encountered. The technology for sound and visual monitoring is already available, and it is not inconceivable that many facets of behavior may soon be monitored through telemeters. For example, Schwitzgebel has developed a belt that delinquents may wear that contains sending (auditory and tactile) and receiving equipment such that, by radio telemetry, continuous monitoring and two-way communication may be maintained for given geographical locations of the delinquents.[32] Electromechanical devices promise ultimately to yield automatic, unobtrusive assessment for selected behaviors.

What a Problem Is

The concept of problem is employed by professionals and

32. Robert L. Schwitzgebel, "Survey of Electromechanical Devices for Behavior Modification," *Psychological Bulletin* 70 (December 1968): 444–59.

laymen alike to identify and label selected behaviors or conditions. The concept implies atypicality or deviance and is generally evoked when the behaviors or conditions to which it refers are somehow aversive to those who apply the label, and the implication is that the behavior or conditions should ideally be modified or at least be different.

Most behavioral modifiers distinguish clearly between the definitional processes and the phenomena that control the discriminations relating thereto. That is, label and referent are distinguished. No problem can be said to exist unless there is at least minimal consensus among those in the defining community. In voluntary contacts, such minimal consensus generally consists of the concurrence of client and professional that a given behavior could be worked on as a problem. In nonvoluntary relationships, where the active consent of the client would not ordinarily be obtained for reasons such as legal constraints on voluntarism, some minimal agreement among the professionals who have legitimate authority is ordinarily all that is required. (Wherever possible, however, client consent should be obtained.)[33] If the client is the only one who defines something as a problem, the focus of modification may be upon the alteration of his definition. Departures from consensus, if great, generally result in no action to change the behavior of a given person but, rather, frequently lead to efforts to change the definitions of others, if anything is done at all.

The properties of responses that tend to control the evocation of problem labels consist largely of whether the response occurs in surfeit or deficit, by some normative criterion. Consider, for example, the following: excessive fear in the presence of common stimuli in contrast to a lack of fear in the presence of objectively dangerous stimuli; passivity versus activity; impotence versus satyriasis; frigidity versus nymphomania; working too little versus working too much. Responses of which there is deficit generally call for endeavors to establish or strengthen them; and responses of which there

---

33. The ethical obligations of the behaviorally oriented caseworker are the same as those of all professional social workers. The problems and dilemmas of ethics, especially in nonvoluntary contexts, are likewise shared by all social workers.

is surfeit generally call for modification techniques placing emphasis upon weakening or elimination.[34]

When responses are labeled as problematic, there is generally the implicit or explicit identification of whether these responses fall predominantly in the operant or respondent realms, or in both. Behaviors falling predominantly in the operant realm direct the practitioner toward one set of techniques, where those falling predominantly in the respondent realm direct him toward a different set.

The stimulus conditions attending the particular responses may also control the use of the problem label. For example, the so-called dependence of a child may involve not only an apparent surfeit of approach behaviors to parents or others, but the particular reinforcing behavior of the mother. More generally, controlling conditions that often cause the behaviorally oriented practitioner to identify something as a problem fall essentially into three main classes. There may be deficits in the *discriminative cues,* such as lack of stimulus control or the presence of controlling stimuli which evoke problem responses; the *eliciting stimuli* may be incapable of evoking desired respondents, or there may be eliciting stimuli that evoke problem respondents; the *consequences of behavior* may involve reinforcing stimuli that sustain problem behaviors or the inadequacy of reinforcing stimuli for sustaining prosocial behaviors and, likewise, there may be punishers that suppress desirable behaviors or reinforce negatively the occurrence of undesirable behaviors.

TECHNIQUES OF MODIFICATION

As much is known about the techniques of modification as about anything else in the field of behavior modification.

---

34. Response cost is a somewhat different criterion and is sometimes evoked to define a problem. For example, a given response can occur at a frequency or magnitude within a given normative range but incur so much effort, anxiety, or time to produce that it is too costly for the individual. Still another criterion sometimes evoked among behavioral modifiers is the appropriateness of the response, especially as this applies to discriminative responses. However, that which is referred to as inappropriate may ordinarily be seen as either a response surfeit or a response deficit.

Although many of the techniques have now had frequent use and there is increasing concurrence concerning the principles upon which they are based, techniques are still being evolved and basic research on behavioral modification is continuing. There is no agreed-upon framework or taxonomy for the techniques of modification, although there is increasing agreement concerning what the specific techniques are, what procedures may be employed to implement them, and some of their particular uses. Although there will probably not be a standard taxonomy of techniques for some time, the existing and emerging techniques may be systematized more than they have been without violating the essentially empirical approach of the field of behavioral modification and without denying the inevitable relevance of ongoing and future research. A provisional framework for ordering many existing techniques is presented so as to (1) provide the relationship of the techniques to principles of modification, (2) show the interrelationships of techniques, and (3) relate the techniques to specific classes of problems commonly met in casework.[35]

Objectives of Modification

After a contract has been established to work on a problem and assessment has been completed, specific responses will have been identified as those which occur in surfeit or deficit. It is mainly this information that serves to specify the objectives of modification. For example, behaviors that occur in deficit may be in the repertoire, and if so, techniques to strengthen the responses are called for. If the deficit responses are not in the repertoire they must be established, and for this purpose techniques pertaining to response acquisition are applicable. In contrast, responses that occur in surfeit call for either weakening or elimination. Techniques pertaining to response maintenance are generally applied for responses that are weak and subject to countervailing influences.

But first, before presenting this framework, let us consider the objectives of modification.

Operant-related Techniques

We identify techniques here as being operant if they per-

---

35. This framework was initially proposed and developed in Thomas, "Selected Sociobehavioral Techniques and Principles."

tain to the alteration of behavior predominantly in the operant realm and involve different operations and consequences for the responses in question. For a more complete statement of this framework and for more details on the operant techniques, the reader is referred elsewhere.[36] These techniques are given in more detail than the others to follow, because the operant-related techniques are currently those that are clearly relevant to casework practice.[37]

Positive Reinforcement
Condition: An established operant response.

Operation: The presentation of a stimulus following the emission of the response.

Functional consequence: An increase in the future rate of responding.

Example: Saying "good" to a mental patient who has just made his bed, with the consequence that the patient makes his bed more frequently in the future.

Main uses: To strengthen or maintain behavior.

Negative Reinforcement
Condition: An established operant response.

Operation: The removal of an aversive stimulus following the emission of a response.

Functional consequence: The increase in the future rate of responding.

Example: An increase in self-feeding behavior of fastidious mental patients who had been unwilling to feed themselves but who found it aversive to have nurses systematically and apparently inadvertently spill food on them in the course of spoon-feeding.

Main uses: To strengthen or maintain responding.

---

36. Thomas, ibid.

37. The characteristics of a technique employed here derive in part from the desiderata Millenson developed to explicate behavioral phenomena. Thus, our conception of condition corresponds to Millenson's given, our view of operation to Millenson's procedure, and our category of functional consequence to Millenson's process and result. Also, we have added the category of main uses. See J. R. Millenson, *Principles of Behavioral Analysis* (New York: Macmillan Co., 1967), pp. 41, 77.

Extinction

Condition: An operant response sustained by positive reinforcement.

Operation: The withholding of the reinforcer when the response is emitted.

Functional consequence: A reduction in the rate of responding.

Example: The reduction and elimination of tantrum behavior, established before as operant responses and sustained by parental attention, as a consequence of the withholding of parental attention.

Main uses: To weaken or eliminate a response.

Differential Reinforcement

Condition: Two operant responses, one of which is defined as problematic and the other of which is designated as prosocial.

Operation: The presentation of a stimulus following the emission of the prosocial response and the withholding of reinforcement for the emission of the problem response.

Functional consequence: An increase in responding of the prosocial response and a decrease for the problem response.

Example: The use of the caseworker's attending responses and saying "good" when the client gives concrete details concerning a contemporary problem, with a consequent increase in such client responses; and the use of inattention and no verbal reinforcement when the client discusses remote and nonspecific materials, with a consequent reduction of such responding.

Main uses: To strengthen or maintain prosocial responses and to eliminate or to weaken problem responses.

Response Shaping

Condition: A low probability of responding in the desirable operant response class.

Operation: The presentation of stimuli following the emission of responses which approximate successively the desired responses combined with the withholding of reinforcement for responses that do not approximate the desired terminal behaviors.

Functional consequence: An increase in the rate of responses which approximate the desired terminal behavior and, ultimately, an appropriate level of responding in a new response class.

Example: The reinforcement of sensible talk of a psychotic who has been mute for many years, beginning with the reinforcement of mouth movements, then sounds, utterances of words, sentences, and finally the reinforcement of sensible talk combined with no reinforcement for psychotic talk.

Main uses: To establish new classes of operant responses in the repertoire.

Punishment

Condition: An established operant response.

Operation: Following the emission of a response, the presentation of an aversive stimulus.

Functional consequence: A reduction in the rate of responding, either large or small, permanent or temporary.

Example: Saying "that's incorrect" when a child makes an ungrammatical statement, with a consequent reduction in the rate of such ungrammatical statements.

Main uses: To weaken or eliminate responses.

Respondent-Related Techniques

The techniques included here generally involve problems pertaining largely to respondent behavior and conditioning procedures particularly suitable to the alteration of respondent behavior. Readers interested in more details about these techniques are encouraged to consult the references given in each as well as generally appropriate services listed in the bibliography.

Classical Conditioning

The conditioning of previously neutral responses to serve as eliciting stimuli for respondent behavior is generally referred to as Pavlovian, or classical, conditioning. As mentioned before, respondent behavior concerns mainly the operation of the smooth muscles and the glands.

There are essentially two main uses of classical conditioning in the context of behavioral modification. The first concerns the conditioning of previously neutral cues so that they serve as eliciting stimuli for prosocial respondents. Thus the respondents associated with the reflex action of bowel evacuation may be classically conditioned to neutral cues.[38] Chronically constipated individuals have been trained so that when they evacuate, cues of mild electrical stimulation are associated with evacuation and, eventually, other cues such as the time of day (e.g., the morning just after arising) become capable of eliciting the nonvoluntary aspects of evacuation.

The second main use of classical conditioning involves the conditioning of previously neutral cues to serve as eliciting stimuli for anxiety and related emotional reactions. This has generally been called aversive conditioning. This type of conditioning is illustrated in the use of shock with alcoholic patients to condition aversively the sight and odor of alcohol.[39]

Systematic Desensitization

The objective of systematic desensitization is to counter-condition anxiety responses with incompatible prosocial responses.[40] Responses incompatible with anxiety, such as relaxation, aggressive assertion, and sexual arousal, are made to occur in the presence of anxiety-evoking stimuli. The incompatible responses, such as profound relaxation, are trained to occur upon cue from the helper. The anxiety-evoking stimuli are those particular conditions, events, or persons that the client reports make him anxious to varying degrees. Such stimuli related to a particular anxiety are grouped (e.g., fear of snakes) and, for each group, the stimuli

38. C. Quarti and J. Renaud, "A New Treatment of Constipation by Conditioning: A Preliminary Report," in *Conditioning Techniques in Clinical Practice and Research,* ed. Cyril M. Franks (New York: Springer, 1964), pp. 219–27.
39. See, for example, Cyril M. Franks, "Alcohol, Alcoholism and Conditioning: A Review of the Literature and Some Theoretical Considerations," in *Behaviour Therapy and the Neuroses,* ed. Hans J. Eysenck (New York: Pergamon Press, 1960), pp. 278–302.
40. Wolpe, *Psychotherapy by Reciprocal Inhibition;* a more recent statement is in Joseph Wolpe and Arnold A. Lazarus, *Behavior Therapy Techniques: A Guide to the Treatment of Neuroses* (New York: Pergamon Press, 1966).

are ordered by the helper, on the basis of information provided by the client, in terms of their ability to evoke that anxiety state. The procedure of desensitization evokes the incompatible prosocial response, such as relaxation, along with the imagination of particular anxiety-evoking stimuli, beginning with the stimuli associated with the smallest amounts of anxiety and proceeding, step by step and successively, to the more anxiety-evoking stimuli. Thus, for each anxiety-evoking stimulus, the incompatible response is made to occur before the stimulus is presented. When the incompatible prosocial response has been made to occur finally in the presence of the stimuli which previously evoked the maximum degree of anxiety, but which now no longer produce any anxiety, this treatment regimen is completed.

Flooding

One form of this technique has been called "implosive" therapy and consists essentially of presenting cues maximally associated with anxiety for relatively long periods of time, so that large amounts of anxiety are experienced at first in the full presence of these cues. With prolonged presentation of the stimuli along with the elicitation, at first, of intense anxiety, the continued presentation presumably eventually leads to a successive reduction in the ability of such cues to elicit anxiety. If the client were afraid of snakes, for example, all stimuli associated with snakes would be evoked together and for a long period of time. By this procedure, the anxiety-evoking cues have been found, in some studies, to lose their capacity to evoke anxiety more rapidly than some alternative procedures.[41] However, much more research is needed to demonstrate the efficacy of this particular technique.

Complex Techniques

Techniques are designated as complex when more than one

---

41. For early empirical reports in support of this statement, see Robert A. Hogan and John H. Kirchner, "Preliminary Report of the Extinction of Learned Fears via Short-Term Implosive Therapy," *Journal of Abnormal Psychology* 72 (April 1967): 106–10; for evidence indicating the comparative ineffectiveness of flooding, see also Stanley Rachman, "Studies in Desensitization: II. Flooding," *Behaviour Research and Therapy* 4 (March 1966):1–7.

operant technique is involved or, more commonly, when both operant and respondent features are entailed. The techniques considered here also almost always involve at least two behavioral objectives. Behavioral rehearsal, for example, is typically employed to reduce problematic responses and to increase alternative prosocial responding. The complexity of the techniques to be mentioned here does not mean that the operations and the consequences cannot be explicated with some accuracy. The complexity, however, has generally meant that there has been incomplete understanding of the essential, active behavioral factors. Much more research is needed on this problem and such inquiry is ongoing for most of the complex techniques.

All the complex techniques given below may be employed, under proper conditions, in casework practice. However, the last five (verbal instructions, behavioral rehearsal, rule making, model presentation, and position structuring) would generally be more widely applicable than the first three, listed immediately below.

Negative Practice

This procedure consists of inducing an individual to engage in performing a problematic operant for exceedingly long periods of time so that, through fatigue and the aversiveness associated with prolonged, constant repetition, the cues associated with performing the undesirable behavior become conditioned aversively—thereby making much less the future probability of the problematic response.[42]

Satiation

This technique consists of the presentation of a reinforcer on a periodic, noncontingent basis, in relationship to problematic behavior associated with the seeking of that reinforcer, until the stimuli associated with the reinforcer have become aversively conditioned.[43]

---

42. For example, see G. F. J. Lehner, "Negative Practice as a Therapeutic Technique," in Eysenck, *Behaviour Therapy and the Neuroses*, pp. 194–206.
43. For a practice example, see Teodoro Ayllon, "Intensive Treatment of Psychotic Behavior by Stimulus Satiation and Food Reinforcement," in Ullmann and Krasner, *Case Studies in Behavior Modification*, pp.

Stimulus Shaping ("Fading")

Stimulus shaping is a means by which externally presented stimuli conditioned to produce desirable responses may be gradually eliminated (faded), so that the behavior in question becomes autonomous, or merged into different stimuli, so that the responses are controlled by an entirely different set of stimuli from those originally presented.[44] For example, if a parental reminder, after a given period of television viewing, signaled the time for the child to go to bed, and whenever the parents' requests were given, the child in fact went to bed, the bedtime reminder could be faded by gradually reducing length, intensity, and explicitness so that other stimuli (e.g., the advertisement presented at about that time, and other time-related stimuli) took on the ability to control going to bed at the appointed hour.

Verbal Instructions

Directions and advice given to individuals that serve as discriminative stimuli constitute the occasions for which compliance may be met with reinforcement. If verbal instructions are given properly and the responses required are already available in the repertoire, they may achieve relatively complete stimulus control over the behavior in question.[45] "Be-

---

77–84; for a comparative research study on the effectiveness of satiation and other behavior-reductive procedures, see W. C. Holz, N. H. Azrin, and T. Ayllon, "Elimination of Behavior of Mental Patients by Response-Produced Extinction," *Journal of the Experimental Analysis of Behavior* 6 (1963):407–12.

44. A recent experimental study is reported by Murray Sidman and Lawrence T. Stoddard, "The Effectiveness of Fading in Programming a Simultaneous Form Discrimination for Retarded Children," *Journal of the Experimental Analysis of Behavior* 10 (January 1967):3–17.

45. An example of the explication of selected features of verbal instructions is in J. Stacy Adams and A. Kimball Romney, "A Functional Analysis of Authority," *Psychological Review* 66 (July 1959):234–51; also, see Staats and Staats, *Complex Human Behavior*, pp. 185–99, 321–24. For a sociobehavioral procedure that draws heavily on verbal instructions, see Edwin J. Thomas, "Instigative Behavioral Modification with a Multiproblem Family" (paper presented at the Conference on "Progress in Behavior Modification: Programs and Results," sponsored by the Youth Development Center, University of Hawaii, Honolulu, 29 January 1969).

havioral assignments" are accomplished in large measure through the use of verbal instructions.

Behavioral Rehearsal (Role Playing)
Through practicing behavior under the guidance of a helper, one may establish and strengthen desirable behaviors while, in some cases, also weakening undesirable elements of the response repertoire. Behavioral rehearsal consists of response emission, generally in the operant realm, under descriminative control of instructions of another person and of the reinforcing contingencies mediated by that person, by the client himself, and by any others who may be present.[46]

Rule Making
This technique consists of making a rule to govern behavior and establishing the reinforcing contingencies for compliance and, if suitable, the punishing contingencies for noncompliance.[47]

Model Presentation
Actual or symbolic models may be presented as exemplars of desired behavior and, under proper conditions, serve to bring about the acquisition of new behavior or to strengthen or weaken existing behavior.[48]

Position Structuring
This technique is defined by the proper arrangement of the

---

46. For selected examples and procedures, see Raymond Corsini and Samuel Cardone, *Roleplaying in Psychotherapy: A Manual* (Chicago: Aldine, 1966).

47. For a procedure and rationale useful for parents, see Judith M. Smith and Donald E. P. Smith, *Child Management: A Program for Parents* (Ann Arbor, Mich.: Ann Arbor Publishers, 1966); for theoretical factors relating to prescriptive phenomena, see Edwin J. Thomas and Bruce J. Biddle, "Basic Concepts for Classifying the Phenomena of Role," in *Role Theory: Concepts and Research*, ed. Bruce J. Biddle and Edwin J. Thomas (New York: Wiley, 1966), pp. 26–28.

48. For one explication of aspects of imitation, see Albert Bandura, "Vicarious Processes: A Case of No-Trial Learning," in *Advances in Experimental Social Psychology*, ed. Leonard Berkowitz (New York: Academic Press, 1966), 2:3–48.

system of prescriptions and sanctions (reinforcements for compliance and possibly punishments for noncompliance) for a social position, so that the behavior of the person engaging in the role is systematically modified or stabilized.[49]

The behavioral techniques reviewed here are not completely comprehensive,[50] but in general they include the main techniques in use today.

Selection of a Technique

Given the availability of this relatively large battery of techniques, a crucial question is the bases for selecting one technique over another. There are at least three classes of criteria that serve to narrow the range of relevant techniques.

The first involves the main area of behavior—operant, respondent, or a combination—into which the behavioral difficulty predominantly falls. The so-called operant techniques are of course generally applicable to behavioral difficulties involving operant behavior; the respondent techniques are generally most relevant to behavioral problems falling into the respondent realm; and the complex techniques typically apply to problems involving clear operant and respondent features and, in some cases, multiple objectives.

The second class of selection criteria relates to the behavioral objectives of intervention. If the objective is to achieve acquisition, then response shaping, classical conditioning employed to cue prosocial reflex behavior, behavioral rehearsal, rule making, model presentation, stimulus shaping, and verbal instructions are among the available alternatives.

If the objective is to strengthen already existing behavior,

---

49. For an example of position change for the "ding up," see William Crain, "The Chronic 'Mess-Up' and His Changing Character," *Federal Probation* 28 (June 1964):50–56; for a discussion of role factors that one would have to consider in changing a deviant position see, for example, Edwin J. Thomas, "Role Problems of Offenders and Correctional Workers," *Crime and Delinquency* 12 (October 1966):354–65; for a discussion of role modification and adjustment, see Henry S. Maas, *Building Social Work Theory with Social Science Tools: The Concept of Role,* Special Report no. 41 (Los Angeles: Welfare Planning Council, Los Angeles Region, 1954).

50. For example, stimulus change, physical force, and deprivation are among other candidates that might have been mentioned.

then positive reinforcement, classical conditioning, behavioral rehearsal, rule making, model presentation, position structuring, stimulus shaping, and verbal instructions are among the available techniques. Systematic desensitization and differential reinforcement very often have behavior strengthening as an important secondary objective. In general, it is from this same group of techniques that one selects specific approaches to maintain behavior.

The practitioner has available a large group of techniques if his objective is to reduce behavior by weakening or eliminating it. I am speaking particularly of extinction, punishment, classical conditioning employed as aversive conditioning, systematic desensitization, flooding, satiation, and negative practice. Rule making, model presentation, position structuring, stimulus shaping, and verbal instructions may also be employed to reduce behavior. Differential reinforcement has behavior reduction as one of its two conditions, and behavioral rehearsal may also be used to reduce problematic behavior as well as to establish behavior.

The third class of criteria concerns the effectiveness of alternative techniques for handling the same behavioral problem. Thus if one wishes to reduce anxiety, one may employ systematic desensitization or flooding, among other techniques. Much more is known about systematic desensitization, and for that reason it is favored over flooding. Some research is being done on these comparisons,[51] but much more needs to be conducted before judgments about differential effectiveness may be entertained.

EMERGING HELPER ROLES

There are many possible helper roles that may entail the use of behavioral techniques, and already it is apparent that specialists and generalists are emerging. It is most probable that caseworkers who adopt behavioral methods will ultimately become specialists in those procedures and techniques most useful in modifyfing the behavior of clients in particular welfare settings.

In addition, there are several functions that cut across the

---

51. For example, see Lazarus, "Group Therapy of Phobic Disorders."

techniques of modification, and some of these appear to be particularly relevant to casework. One is that of the *direct modifier,* by which is meant that the caseworker is himself the agent of modification. Thus, the caseworker might go into the home and use a technique such as positive reinforcement to strengthen selected parental behaviors relating to child management. Another role is that of the caseworker as *behavioral instigator.* Instead of directly acting on controlling conditions for the behavior to be modified, the instigator arranges the conditions, perhaps through instructions or behavioral assignments, so that others are enabled to engage in the direct modification. Giving behavioral assignments to a parent in the agency concerning how he might increase desirable behaviors of the children by using behavioral methods would be illustrative, as would the introduction of a point system for reinforcers in the home or the programming of a token economy for classroom management. Behavioral instigation, if engaged in properly, appears to be much more effective than one might expect, and this type of modification is particularly useful when the caseworker cannot or should not act as a direct modifier. Still another role is that of the *teacher* of behavioral methods to clients. Parents, related professionals, and paraprofessionals are among those who may be taught. This is likely to become an important role function for caseworkers, especially as the technology develops further into methods by which self-modification programs may be taught.

UNSOLVED PROBLEMS

There are many unsolved problems in basic behavioral knowledge and in the field of behavioral modification proper, and if research continues at its present rate we may anticipate a relatively rapid reduction of uncertainty and proliferation of ideas and practices to which social workers should attend. The main unsolved problems for casework, in my view, involves how best to make use of the contributions of behavioral modification. The following are among the problems casework researchers, scholars, and practitioners may work toward solving.

1. There is as yet no coherent set of principles and pro-

cedures for a behaviorally oriented casework. The principles and procedures of such an approach must be informed at the very least by the knowledge and practice of behavioral modification and by the several functions beyond behavioral alteration itself that are served in the agency and program contexts of casework practice. My colleagues and I are presently engaged in the development of one set of policies and procedures applicable to the practice of behaviorally oriented casework in open welfare settings.[52] The task is not easy and no doubt several alternative approaches will have to be developed for trial and appraisal in the next few years.

2. The particular methods and techniques of behavioral assessment most useful in casework need to be developed and used.

3. The techniques of modification most appropriate for caseworkers need to be distinguished, applied, and evaluated.

4. The evolution and creation of appropriate role types for a behaviorally oriented casework are needed. This is important because we must avoid rejecting behavioral methods out of hand, accepting some indiscriminatingly, or adopting everything so as to become miniature behavioral therapists.

5. The agencies and programs of casework today are compatible with or actually designed in relationship to an existing casework technology that is essentially nonbehavioral. A behaviorally informed and oriented casework may well require different organizational structures and suggest alternative program objectives. It is highly unlikely that an intelligent and well-conceived behaviorally oriented casework could function unfettered without some alterations of the existing agencies and programs.

6. Alternative divisions of labor are suggested by a behaviorally oriented casework. It is already clear that the

52. For an early report, see Edwin J. Thomas, Eileen Gambrill, and Robert D. Carter, "Progress Report and Plans for Further Work: Utilization and Appraisal of Socio-behavioral Techniques in Social Welfare—Pilot Phase," mimeographed (Ann Arbor, Michigan, 1969).

functions of behavioral assessment and modification may be divided diversely among professionals, technicians, paraprofessionals, and clients. The many alternative assignments of assessment and modification need to be explored even more boldly than they have been in behaviorally oriented practice.

Bibliography

Ayllon, Teodoro, and Azrin, Nathan H. *The Token Economy: A Motivational System for Therapy and Rehabilitation.* New York: Appleton-Century-Crofts, 1969.

Eysenck, Hans J., ed. *Behavior Therapy and the Neuroses.* New York: Pergamon Press, 1960.

Franks, Cyril M., ed. *Conditioning Techniques in Clinical Practice and Research.* New York: Springer, 1964.

Honig, Werner K., ed. *Operant Behavior: Areas of Research and Application.* New York: Appleton-Century-Crofts, 1966.

Jehu, Derek. *Learning Theory and Social Work.* London: Routledge and Kegan Paul, 1967.

Millenson, J. R. *Principles of Behavioral Analysis.* New York: Macmillan Co., 1967.

Thomas, Edwin J. "Selected Sociobehavioral Techniques and Principles: An Approach to Interpersonal Helping." *Social Work* 13 (January 1968):12–26.

Thomas, Edwin J., ed. *The Socio-behavioral Approach and Applications to Social Work.* New York: Council on Social Work Education, 1967.

Ullmann, Leonard P., and Krasner, Leonard, eds. *Case Studies in Behavior Modification.* New York: Hole, Rinehart and Winston, 1965.

Wolpe, Joseph. *Psychotherapy by Reciprocal Inhibition.* Stanford, Calif.: Stanford University Press, 1958.

Wolpe, Joseph, and Lazarus, Arnold A. *Behavior Therapy Techniques.* New York: Pergamon Press, 1967.

6 | Theory and Practice of Family Therapy

Frances H. Scherz

FRAME OF REFERENCE

By principle, personal existence in a psychological sense is inseparable from relationships. This statement, expressed in innumerable ways in the broad spectrum of the behavioral sciences, is the essence of the human condition, and for people in trouble is the human dilemma. It synthesizes the knowledge and belief that the human's existence and growth, his behavior, is conditioned by interaction between himself and his environment; that he is inseparably a biological-psychological-social entity. It encapsulates the well-documented belief that the bases of becoming a social being, like others yet uniquely different, are laid down in the family.

Despite the ever changing forms and functions of the family, no adequate substitute has been found for the primary task of socializing the human, for initiating and nurturing him in the two main tasks of life—loving and working. The recent unprecedentedly rapid changes in society brought about by developments in technology, instant communication, challenges to education, inner-city unrest, reactions to war, have affected and altered the forms and functions of the family and must be taken into account because they profoundly affect the human's developmental ability to live productively in the world. But his basic capacities to adapt to and change the world derive from his family biological and cultural heritage. His ability to plan for the future, to act without acting out, to trust in himself and in others without fearing loss of self-esteem and loss of self-identity, his ability to develop self and group identity, is learned first in the family relationship system. The family teaches him to love, to think reflectively, to be self-responsible, to perform necessary social roles. The family provides nurturant care, status, and incentives for its members. The human's self-worth and the behavior that expresses it are directly related to the family's view of itself, heavily conditioned by society's view of the family. The individual is perceived as a product of his innate inheritance, his family influences, and society's measure of him and his family.

Casework from its inception has recognized the importance

Frances H. Scherz is director of casework, Jewish Family and Community Service, Chicago.

of the family to the individual's development and functioning. It always has been, to an extent, family-focused when
working with an individual, taking into account his current
and past family relationships. Family interviews have been
a feature from the time casework was promulgated as a
method. But for many years, until the middle 1950s, the primary casework approach was to and with the individual.

It is difficult to know and assess all the forces that operated
in the initiation of family therapy as an approach that has
distinct differences from work with the individual. The forces
that were tentative in the 1950s have steadily gained impetus
until now it can be said that family therapy has, in many
social work settings as well as in psychiatry, achieved the
status of a therapeutic model. Although there are some differences in underlying theories and many differences in the use
of techniques, there is general agreement among those who
accept family therapy as a therapeutic model that unless
there are specific contraindications, the family should be the
unit of attention for casework exploration and treatment.

Perhaps enough experience with treatment of individuals,
its successes, shortcomings, and failures—fed by the ever
pressing need for effective means of working with troubled
people—led to experimentation with other models, such as
group, milieu, and family therapy. Certainly it became clear
in many instances of individual treatment that anticipated
goals fell short because of interfering relationship forces
within the family; for example, the husband who influenced
his wife to resist self-change or to leave treatment because he
feared what change might do to the marital relationship, or
the parents who unconsciously sabotaged a child's treatment
because they feared loss of control over him. The well-known
tenacity of the schizophrenic process did not, in many individuals, yield to treatment of the patient alone until the family was brought into direct therapeutic interaction with him.

Developments in ego psychology, notably the work of
Hartmann[1] and Erikson,[2] who extended the views of adapta-

1. Heinz Hartmann, *Ego Psychology and the Problem of Adaptation*
(New York: International Universities Press, 1958).
2. Erik Erikson, *Identity and the Life Cycle, Psychological Issues*, 1 (New
York: International Universities Press, 1959), pp. 1–171.

tion and identity as including the individual's potential for contributing to the modification of existing environments and the creation of new ones, bringing into clearer perspective such dynamic elements of the environment as role, class, and family structure; Sullivan's[3] theories on the meaning and use of interpersonal relationships in treatment; Parson's[4] contributions on family, socialization, and the interaction process; Jackson's[5] work on communication, and new insights from small group dynamics theory, have had and are having an impact on casework's movement toward family therapy. The work of the Mental Research Institute group under Don Jackson brought new dimensions to treatment through theories about the family as a system within the larger social systems. These and other contributions added to the store of knowledge from psychoanalytic theory. Gradually they are being welded into a conceptual framework of family developmental theory and family therapy.

How a case is approached, the techniques used, and the plans of strategy for intervention depend on a frame of reference. The frame of reference in this paper is the approach to the family as the unit of investigation and treatment. Many of the theoretical assumptions that underlie this approach are held by other investigators in the field of family development and family therapy; but the application of these theories in method and technique, described in this paper, is not the same by all who practice family therapy.

A major theoretical assumption is that the family is a system, here defined as two or more units relating to each other in such a way that if there is a change in one it affects the other and the reaction of the second in turn affects the first. The family is viewed as a regularly interacting, interdependent system forming a unified whole, transacting life events among its members under the influence of related forces. It is

---

3. Harry Stack Sullivan, *The Interpersonal Theory of Psychiatry* (New York: W. W. Norton and Co., 1953).

4. Talcott Parsons and Robert F. Bales, *Family Socialization and Interaction Process* (Glencoe, Ill.: Free Press, 1955).

5. Don D. Jackson, "Family Interaction, Family Homeostasis and Some Implications for Conjoint Family Psychotherapy," in *Science and Psychoanalysis*, vol. 2, ed. by Jules H. Masserman (New York: Grune and Stratton, 1959), pp. 122–41.

an open-ended system, as members enter and leave during the family's life cycle; it is a unique system influenced by unique biological, cultural, and social forces, with its own recognizable role formations, patterns of behavior and communication, patterns of emotional reactivity, coping patterns, values, and ways of relating to the larger social community, all adding up to a unique family life style. Each family is unique in the way it manages the instinctive impulses and drives of its members, in its permissions and taboos of behavioral expression, in its conscious and unconscious agreements about the rules it lives by, in the coalitions and collusions formed by the family and its subgroups, in its secrets and myths, and in the ways these are reflected in life outside the family.

Each family develops conscious and unconscious rules to encompass the growth needs of its members and to regulate patterns of interaction for the purpose of providing avenues for solution of growth conflicts, for buttressing of crucial defenses against anxiety, for social direction of its members, and for stable maintenance of the family. Although the families of origin influence the establishment of rules, the new family is different from its individual origins. Intrapsychic and conscious reorganization of motivation, perception, expression, defense, and behavior take place in the individuals forming a new family in order to take cognizance of and accommodate to the partner and later the children. The patterns of conflict and resolution of life tasks emerge from the establishment and changes in rules during the family life cycle.

The family, then, is a gestalt, because it is a total which is larger than the sum of its parts. Each person is an integrated but different part of a total family unit. The family is a highly complicated network of forces expressed in complicated relationships. Just as the individual has a life of his own, influenced by his unique biopsychosocial developmental tasks, the family has a life of its own, expressed in its relationship systems, an overall family system, and subsystems, such as marriage, parenthood, and siblings. These systems, lived out in innumerable interactions and transactions, develop a life of their own in the sense that certain relationship behavior-affect patterns become autonomous and repetitive

despite individual differences. Family behavior-affect patterns become integrated in the individual and, therefore,
cannot be divided into separate individual pieces if they are
to be understood. Because these family patterns are unconsciously integrated and therefore largely outside the conscious awareness of the family and its members, and because
they need to be understood if the individual and family are
to be assessed as correctly as possible for treatment strategy,
direct observation of family processes and relationships is
necessary. The original individual sources of the relationship
systems often are long forgotten and obscure, but repetitive,
predictable, stable patterns seriously influencing the management of individual and family life tasks can be observed, for
example, in the use of trigger words and actions which start
off a customary interchange, follow a set rhythm, and result in definable effects. The usual course and outcome of
husband-wife quarrels is a commonplace illustration.

Although caseworkers are accustomed to drawing inferences about causal factors and connections from clues in the
current and past life of an individual and are accustomed
to drawing inferences about family relationships from an
individual's description, it is, I believe, reasonable to assume
that significant short cuts and greater accuracy in the study
phase can be obtained when direct observation of the family
processes influencing individual behavior is undertaken. The
observation of the specific *processes* of the relationship systems tends to obviate one of the major difficulties in individual treatment; that is, translation of individual change to
family change that the person must make. For example, although individual change through treatment often effects
positive change in the family, this does not occur always as a
matter of course. The relationship patterns often persist stub-
bornly. They can tend to vitiate the change in the individual. It is not uncommon, following individual treatment, for
treatment of the relationship itself to be necessary to support
and maximize individual and family change. In the family
interviews the individual feelings, the meanings and effects
of behavior, the hurts and tenderness, are experienced directly. The gaps betweeen behavior and felt understanding
among the members are more likely to be exposed and nar-
rowed in a shorter period of time. Family-focused treatment

is often undertaken via work with an individual, but family therapy, because it is concerned largely with effecting change in the relationship systems for all, requires direct intervention into the system itself. Thus, the total family is the unit of study and frequently of treatment.

In order to understand the different aspects of the relationship systems, one theory now gaining acceptance is that the marital relationship system heavily influences the management of individual and family developmental tasks and that to understand the problems of the individual and family it is necessary to understand the nature of the marriage.[6] The theoretical assumption is that in most marriages, apart from the usual conscious reasons for selection of mates, the unconscious reasons represent residual or active neurotic conflicts for which a solution is sought in the partner. Each partner seeks in the other something that is lacking or is a defect in himself, or hopes that his anxieties and defenses will be buttressed. He seeks, and often finds, someone who has similar needs and conflicts. Marital partners tend to reflect the same level of maturity. Their needs are the same but may be expressed differently as, for example, in the living out of a rescue fantasy when the man rescues the woman who looks for a rescuer. When the basic needs intermesh so that both partners are constructively satisfied and personal conflicts are allayed or modified, thereby freeing productive energy for life tasks, the marriage is stabilized along lines that permit reasonable development of children. In such marriages, the parents can permit sufficient differences in each other while at the same time maintaining the kind of parental coalition that provides the children with the appropriate freedoms and the necessary restrictions for growth.

In disturbed marriages the needs often intermesh but are not met to the constructive satisfaction of the partners; so the individual conflicts continue to exist actively throughout the marriage or become active at stress points in the life cycle. The partners continue to seek resolution of their own conflicts by projecting them on each other. In the search for per-

---

6. Charles H. Kramer, *Psychoanalytically Oriented Family Therapy: Ten Year Evolution in a Private Child Psychiatry Practice* (Oak Park, Ill.: Kramer Foundation, 1968).

sonal comfort, the marriage tends to become stabilized in a
conflictful manner. A marital relationship system develops
that is one of mutual projection, characterized by repetitive,
circular, predictable transactions. In many disturbed marriages one can discern the development of the projection system arising from similar personality structures, similar levels
of ego integration, similar needs and conflicts, and similar
defenses that may be overtly expressed in like or dissimilar
behavior—the two sides of a coin. As the marital projection
system stabilizes into marriage equilibrium, the nature of its
behavior-affect expression becomes self-perpetuating, developing a life of its own in which the original individual
sources may be unknown or forgotten.

The nature of the marital equilibrium affects all family
members, but in different ways and to different degrees. In
many disturbed marriages, when children arrive, the parents
turn to them for resolution of those conflicts that have not
been resolved individually or met satisfactorily in the marriage. The children, dependent for survival on the parents,
enter actively into the marital projection system, often becoming symptomatic of the expression of their own and the
parents' conflicts, and a family projection relationship system
develops and becomes stabilized. Although children differ in
relation to their unique developmental drives and patterns,
their place in the family and what they represent to the parents at different times influences their development. None
seem to escape entirely the influences of the marital and
family projection system. It is common, for example, for a
"well" child to become "sick" when the "sick" child gives up
his symptoms or to find that a "good" child, in contrast to the
"bad" one, pays a subtle high cost for his part in maintaining
the marital and family equilibrium.

This general description of what occurs in the development of a family projection system should be qualified. In
some disturbed marriages the marital conflict is not only
open but is largely contained in the marriage, and the couple's parenting function is relatively unimpaired. The children, although suffering from the effects of marital strife,
may not be drawn in a serious measure into the parents'
marital projection system and may not become symptomatic.
In other disturbed marriages, the partners repress or deny

the marital conflict, view the marriage as compatible and satisfactory, and present a united front of harmony, but characteristically have a disturbed child or children through whom the hidden marital difficulty is funneled. These children are frequently symptomatic. In many marriages that end in di vorce, the degree of disturbance in the children represents the degree to which the marital projection system included them and the degree to which the parent they live with continues to seek for resolution of his marital and personal conflicts via the children.

In any event, children in all families are affected developmentally by the nature of the marital equilibrium because they introject the parents as models, guides, and educators. The evolution of a personality system, then, is linked to social process in the family. Children are active participants in the stabilization and change in the marriage and family equilibrium. By their symptoms they express their own and family conflicts, and often their symptoms—the "cry for help"—are the instruments that impel the parents to seek help and that begin to force change in the marital and family stabilization. Parents commonly push for change in the disturbed child but at the same time unconsciously fear that his change will disrupt the marital equilibrium. The child may want relief from the symptoms but resists change because he senses that the underlying message from his parents is not to change lest the marital and family stabilization be threatened or destroyed. This is the concept of the double-bind factor in personality development; that is, the use of negative injunctions, of conflicting messages that underlie exhortation to positive growth and change. The effects of double-bind messages are seen in many families in which communications about rules of behavior are contradictory, explicitly and implicitly; in which family members have difficulty in learning to distinguish between behavior and feelings or to integrate them appropriately, and in which there is confusion in the establishment and management of individual and family roles. The parental negative injunctions underlying the demand for positive change, along with projections on the child of responsibility for the trouble, can interfere seriously with his development. Family stabilization, achieved at the expense of a designated symptom or problem bearer, whether child or marital partner, although often fixed, is paradoxically precarious and impedes constructive and flexible resolution of life tasks. To understand the nature and degree of individual disturbance, then, it is necessary to understand the marital system as well as the total family relationship systems. These systems, not too susceptible to verbal description, are best understood as the family demonstrates their meanings, affects, and effects directly.

A second major theoretical assumption is that family developmental tasks parallel individual developmental tasks. The same developmental tasks that the individual must master, such as self-control and self-responsibility, intimacy and distance, separateness and dependence, individuation and interdependence, must be mastered by the family if both are to achieve maximum self-realization. Just as the individual meets each task in developmental sequences that overlap but also have transitional stress points, the family has parallel and also different sequential tasks and stress points. The stress points contain the potential for crises out of which can come constructive resolution, stultifying regression, or chronic difficulties. Each normal transitional stress point requires change in the nature of marital equilibrium, in conscious management of tasks and roles, and in changes in the nature of object relationships. Each change in these aspects is a challenge toward the next developmental step for individual and family, but also carries with it a normal sense of loss accompanied by mourning and temporary ego regression, followed by integration of the loss and forward movement. There is always inner individual conflict between the wish to struggle to meet the forthcoming task and the wish to remain status quo. This is true for the family also. Thus, individual homeostasis is intermeshed with family homeostasis. For the family the stress points seem to cluster in the first period of marriage when the task is the making of the marriage,[7] the major features being the final relinquishment of infantile ties to the parents and the acceptance of a new kind of closeness and a new kind of acceptance of difference; the

7. Rhona Rapoport, "Normal Crisis, Family Structure and Mental Health," *Family Process* 2 (March 1963):45.

coming of the first child with the requirement for change in the marital equilibrium, that is, in division of responsibility and in the beginning coalition of the marital pair as parents; the final breaking of the physical and psychological symbiosis between mother and child when the latter develops independent motility, thereby creating a clash between the child's autonomous strivings and the parents' concept of themselves as "good" parents; the entry of the child into school with its pulls into the outer world, accompanied by a sense of parental loss; adolescence, with its severe identity crisis accompanied by the middle years' identity crisis of the parents; the children's departure from home for good, leaving the parents to face the need for a drastic change in their relationship to each other; the experience of becoming grandparents, a totally new and different role; and finally old age with its losses of meaningful figures, physical changes, work losses, and new adaptation requirements.

Each developmental phase and stress point within a family requires new identifications, alliances, role transitions, and family rules. Each new task requires that the marital partners support each other constructively against undue regression that could interfere with the mastery of individual and family developmental tasks. The transitional stresses can become acutely critical or chronically dysfunctional if previous family life tasks have not been mastered. Crises may develop if the new tasks arouse past individual conflicts that now become unmanageable; or if the family structure is altered by such accidents as death, divorce, or serious illness, or if social difficulties such as economic stress, upward or downward, are paramount at the same time that new tasks emerge.

Each stage of individual and family development is intermeshed in new, repetitive, and overlapping tasks that require a continual balance between stabilization and change in the family structure. The continuing and changing tasks in the marriage need to mesh with the growth tasks of children. Individual separateness and connectedness to the family, reflected in closeness and distance, is a life-long problem-solving process. At each stage the task to be mastered requires family support, tolerance for temporary regression, and permission to mourn the losses occasioned by object relationship changes. Roles must be maintained, modified, and changed to meet the demands of the tasks.

The two major theoretical assumptions about the family and marital systems, as well as the meaning of family development, are the base of family therapy and have led to the following concepts that influence practice:

1. Whenever one member of a family is in trouble, all are in trouble. The symptoms in an individual serve to balance forces within the family as well as his own intrapsychic forces. Understanding the meaning of the individual symptoms requires understanding what they represent for him and for the family for purposes of treatment planning. Thus, symptoms do not in and of themselves determine the nature of treatment. A phobic symptom in a child, for example, may lead to his treatment, to treatment of the family unit, to combined, concurrent treatment of the parents and child, or to treatment of the parents. Certainly a symptom offers clues for exploration. But the degree to which a symptom develops a life of its own in the individual's own system, that is, the degree to which it is embedded and ego syntonic or ego alien; the degree to which the individual and family cling to the symptom in order to maintain family equilibrium; the degree to which the relationship systems can be changed so that the symptom loses its value and reason for being, or later becomes amenable to individual treatment because the change in family relationships gives true permission for individual change, are the intermeshing guiding clues to initial treatment strategy and to possible changes in the strategy. To carry this further, the nature and degree of individual pathology, as with the nature of the symptom, does not dictate the specific treatment approach. Rather, the extent to which cause and effect of the pathology lie in the family transactions and, therefore, in the family system, and the extent to which the family can at a given time permit entry into the system, are clues to differential treatment approaches. These concepts are based on the theory that all in the family have a share in the forces of stabilization and forces of change. Because the motivational determinants of one

person's actions lie not only in his but also in another's self-delineation needs, all in the family are producers, collaborators, gainers, and victims in the family relationship systems.

2. The nature of family structure, that is, identifications, object relationships, collusions, alliances, and roles, are significant indexes of family functioning and are causative in individual development. When there is room for age appropriate identifications; when there is reasonable establishment of appropriate object relationships and flexibility in this occasioned by the inevitable changes in family structure; when alliances are phase appropriate and when roles are established and adequately discharged, individual developmental needs are met reasonably and family tasks reasonably encompassed. In understanding the nature of family structure it is significant that it provides a base for the concept of how roles are established and discharged. Although it is not possible within the confines of this chapter to consider in detail each factor of family structure elements, some brief exposition can be made. Each factor is understood to be meshed with the others and all require changes during the family life cycle. Parental models, introjected by children and expressed behaviorally through role performance, are the basis for the development of individual identifications and differences. The parents' image and use of themselves as individuals, as husband and wife, as parents, and as workers outside the home, influence the child's image of himself and of them as he identifies in part or wholly with both or either. The productive coalition of the marital pair in the parenting role enables the child to maintain sufficient distance from and closeness to the parents while he is struggling with impulses, drives and ego tasks.[8] The parents' capacity to change the nature and strength of their object relationships to each other and as parents during the child's various developmental phases enables him to separate emotionally for the en-

---

8. Ivan Boszormenyi-Nagy and James L. Framo, ed., *Intensive Family Therapy* (New York: Hoeber Medical Division, Harper and Row, 1965).

compassing of his new tasks while continuing as an integral part of the family. Appropriate alliance with the part of the same sex in the various phases of his development promotes sound role identification with the parent while establishing his own role differences. A theory underlying the concept of family structure is that roles are assigned and accepted in the light of family dynamics. Thus, the assignment of roles in the family not only arises from the needs for individual impulse discharge and self-delineation but also from the family's needs, including the preparation of the individual for his roles in society.[9] The resolution of such individual tasks as the development of trust, self-esteem, self-control, and intimacy evolves from the nature of family structure as expressed in role establishment and performance.

In disturbed families, behavioral difficulties, symptoms, or delays in personal development indicate faulty family structure that is expressed in poor role performance. Unhealthy collusions among the family members, inadequate parental coalition, distorted object relationships, problems in physical separation and emotional separateness, and in individual autonomy and family interdependence, emerge clearly in family interviews. Some roles are assigned out of parental needs for passive mastery by delegating unwarranted responsibilities to children or by having them act out unresolved parental wishes, fears, and conflicts. Role reversals and confusions in the parents tend to blur the generational boundaries between parents and children and the maintenance of generational dynamic equilibrium so necessary for good ego development of children. And the acceptance of pathological role assignments breeds crippling anger and guilt in the recipients. Rigidity in parental role discharge tends to make the parents unable to alter the nature of their object relationships in the children's various developmental stages and difficulties in emotional separation for all are likely to en-

9. John P. Spiegel, "The Resolution of Role Conflict within the Family," *Psychiatry* 20 (February 1957):1–16.

sue. Inability to tolerate the need for individual differences within role expectations tends toward the creation of a family whose members are fused together in what Bowen calls "the mass undifferentiated ego family."[10]

3. Communication in the family is the channel through which the rules and roles, the processes of identification and differentiation, the management of tasks, conflicts, and resolutions—in short, the business of life—is conducted. Communication always exists. It can be clear or distorted, verbal or behavioral, conflict free or conflict laden. Messages may be consonant in manifest, latent, and unconscious content, and in their discharge be either constructive or destructive. Messages may express one thing manifestly but convey a different meaning by preconscious and unconscious intent—the double-bind message. Every interaction and transaction expressed in communication is reciprocal in nature, and in every communication the person is affected by the actions in the communications of others and they, in turn, are affected.

Families develop their own communication styles out of their family culture, their social milieu, and the unique permissions and taboos that serve the family equilibrium. Secrets, myths, special looks and touches, and special use of words trigger responses that are part of the family communication style and become integrated into the character of the individual members. Attitudes, feelings, values, biases, and prejudices that evolve in the family become so built in that they are often outside individual conscious awareness and can be perceived and understood better when observed in family interaction. Families tend to develop stable, predictable patterns of communication. It is not uncommon to find in disturbed families communication that is stable but sterile in that words are divorced from feelings; communication that is discharged characteristically through impulsive action; or the inability to

10. Murray Bowen, "The Family as the Unit of Study and Treatment," *American Journal of Orthopsychiatry* 31 (January 1961):40–60.

"hear" correctly the communication of others or to hear them only in the light of personal needs. With the present rapidity of change in family functions and roles in our society, there is need for more open, explicit communication than in previous periods when family roles were more implicitly structured and understood. This creates a need for more direct, clear communication in the family. There is specifically the need for communication that maintains generational boundaries between parents and children in a society that has difficulty in managing this. Family therapy relies on understanding the communication patterns in the family and in intervening in those that are currently dysfunctional in the family system.

These major theories, concepts, and assumptions provide the bases for the family therapy model presented here. Family therapy, in this frame of reference, can be described as a treatment approach designed to modify or change those elements of the family relationship system that are interfering with the management of the life tasks of the family and its members.[11] The overall approach holds that any family may be able to engage in family therapy at any given time in its life history. The modifying factors of this broad statement will be described later. In family therapy the individual is no longer the major or sole point of reference. Although family therapy takes into account the qualities and needs of the individual, it does this in a special way, through understanding his qualities, and works with them through the established interactional systems in the family. By principle, family therapy requires that at least two members of the family be engaged regularly in treatment. But this principle does not rule out various concurrent treatment combinations, such as marital pair and individual spouse, total family unit, or an individual. Nor does the principle rule out shifts in treatment, such as from family-focused work with an individual to family therapy or vice versa, from family unit to marital pair, or from marital pair to individual.

By family unit is meant all persons who are, in a major

11. Nathan Ackerman, *The Psychodynamics of Family Life* (New York: Basic Books, 1958).

sense, emotionally involved in the current dysfunctional family situation. This may incude all members of the household nuclear family, extended family members in or outside the home, divorced spouses, and so forth.

Family therapy is a clinical approach in that it is based on assessment of the unique family relationship systems and their conscious and unconscious implications for the individual members. Because it is concerned with understanding what the individuals bring to the family system and its problem and what their own needs are, it relies on psychoanalytic personality theory in a special way. That is, the approach views the individual not solely as an individual but also as part of a system. Therefore, "adding up" the individuals does not lead to an assessment of the family system. The system itself must be understood. Family therapy is a behavior-affect approach in that it focuses on the what, how, when, and why of intermeshing behavior-affect systems in the family, on the specific interactions and transactions in the current dysfunctional relationship systems, on how and why the individual members participate in and are affected by the systems, and on how manifest, latent, and unconscious feelings in communication create behavioral effects that interfere with life tasks. Family therapy is a group approach in that it deals with more than one family member at a time and utilizes understanding and techniques from small group dynamics. But it does so recognizing that the family is a unique group, with members who are bound to each other in special enduring relationship programs. Technically, family therapy operates by a three-pronged approach: (1) content or data; (2) process of interaction and transaction; and (3) family structure—the rules, roles, identifications, alliances, and collusions, as evidenced in the communication patterns of the family in relation to individual and family life cycle stage and the task at hand.

THE INITIAL PHASE

In the initial phase the approach is to the family, regardless of presenting request, complaint, or symptomatology. Whether the first interview is with the family unit, the marital pair, or an individual depends on the problem as it is presented (usually on the telephone), on the management of resistance that may occur about who is to be included in the first interview, and on the style of the worker. Worker style may lead to seeing the parents first to assess motivation and to deal with resistance to involvement, and to establish parental responsibility for change. Some workers prefer seeing the total family first in order to engage all and to manage possible counteridentification tendencies. Characteristically, when the complaint is about the marriage, the marital pair is seen first, and when the complaint is about a child the total family is seen. But in any event, the intent is to see the whole family together as soon as possible.

The overall purpose of early family unit interviews is to understand the place of the problem for the family as a whole and for individual members. Family unit interviews also are held to avoid, as much as possible, the development of individual transference phenomena and to minimize the worker's possible overidentification with an individual or marital pair. Early family unit interviews tend to develop a therapeutic alliance with all the family members, thereby lessening the problem of dealing with individual resistance to involvement in the present and future.

By therapeutic alliance is meant the establishment of trust; trust on the part of the family that the worker wishes to help and trust on the part of the worker that the family wants help. The establishment of a therapeutic alliance contains the ingredients of emotional and intellectual involvement by family and worker, of mutual respect, and of acceptance of different responsibilities in the therapeutic task. The therapeutic alliance is largely unspoken and develops from the process between family and worker. It is different from a treatment contract in that the latter is a conscious agreement between family and worker to work in certain ways toward certain goals. The treatment contract is ineffective unless preceded by a therapeutic alliance.

The specific purposes of the family unit interviews are: (1) to demonstrate the mutuality of what the family members are doing and saying in relation to the presenting complaint so that they can become aware of the existence of a family problem; (2) to demonstrate how the reverberations of feelings echo and reecho in immediate behavior-affect manifestations; (3) to demonstrate the family's use of circular, repetitive dysfunctional themes, (4) to defocus the family's emphasis on the designated problem bearer by demonstrating that the conflicts are intrafamilial even when the family places them elsewhere, as in school or work, and thus to arrive with the family at an identification of the dysfunctional themes and issues that indicate or preclude further exploration and treatment; (5) to develop a family therapeutic alliance; and (6) to show why the therapy may need to involve all, different pairs, or individuals at different times.

Characteristically, the initial phase includes interviews with the marital pair. Because the marital relationship has its own unique responsibilities, intimacy, and communication modes, and because it is viewed as having crucial significance in the etiology and maintenance of family and individual health and pathology, it is essential that the nature of the current relationship be understood. In most instances, this is best achieved by seeing the marital pair. It is difficult to understand and to demonstrate the effects on the partner of the circulatory nature of communication when only one spouse is seen. Much about marital interaction may emerge in family unit interviews, but the added advantage in seeing the marital pair is that their responsibility for change can be underscored, hidden marital conflict may emerge more quickly and directly, and a therapeutic alliance with the adults, an essential if change is to occur, can be established. There may be valid private matters that cannot, or should not, be exposed in the presence of children. Children frequently expose the conflicts in the family more readily than the parents, but they need permission from the parents to change before they can risk themselves in ongoing interaction in the therapy.

Interviews with individual members, sibling pairs, relatives in groups or alone, or significant others, may be held in the initial phase. For example, it may be necessary to see how an individual functions apart from the family. Or content that is hinted at and that it seems advisable to explore further may dictate seeing an individual or subgroup. Resistance that is not amenable to one kind of interview may indicate the need for another kind. Some picture in depth of an individual or the marriage may be required. These decisions lie with the worker. When other than family unit interviews are included, the worker must stipulate to the family that content from these interviews may be brought into the family interviews at the worker's discretion; otherwise, he may become a collusive partner to a secret that is influential in the family's dysfunction and that then binds them and him in treatment. The nature and emotional meaning of the secret affords clues to how and with whom it is to be dealt with. When a family member is absent from an interview planned to include him, his absence, unless realistic, is considered as evidence of family resistance and becomes a focus of discussion.

The content of these interviews includes the complaint, why and how the family arrived at a decision to apply now, what efforts were made to deal with the difficulty, how the various members view and react to the complaint, what they see as disturbing problems, how the family lives in day-to-day matters, and what avenues of pleasure exist or existed in the past. The clues furnished by the request, and why it was made now, lead the worker to collect the facts and feelings relevant to the problem. Salient features, that is, those that are emphatic or repetitive, afford clues to the data to be sought and reveal themes that are used later in more specific and partialized consideration in treatment. Historical data is selectively obtained as it appears to be relevant to the problem and to those participating in the interviews.

The focus and techniques are on the "here and now" of the interpersonal interactions and transactions as they are evidenced and experienced in the interviews. Resistance to engagement, often expressed by one family member, is dealt with as an expression of his and the family's resistance. The worker deemphasizes the complaints about the "sick" member by balancing the complaints, showing the reciprocity of behavior and the family attitudes expressed in the behavior and its effects, by not permitting scapegoating of the "sick" for too long, and by not permitting undue hostile ventilation or withdrawal. Efforts are made to elicit participation by all and to gain the permission of the adults for the children's participation.

Conscious and preconscious verbal and nonverbal communications that show distortions, confusions, and collusions in role perceptions and performance are demonstrated by the worker for his understanding and to stimulate the observing ego capacity of the family members. The significant parallels between individual and family tasks and problems are made known to stimulate family involvement. The worker identifies the repetitive themes in behavior that are operative in the problem by showing the family the derivatives of its projections in behavior and feelings, by clarifying misperceptions, and by demonstrating how to experience—that is, how to observe and feel, because both are needed in balance. The intent, in the latter, is to show how what an individual feels internally is used interpersonally. Such affects as loss of control, hostility, guilt, use of words or attitudes to obscure feelings, and violent feelings underlying surface affect are brought to awareness and limited or encouraged by the worker. The worker supports all by refusing to accept individual blame or responsibility. *Setting in motion and encouraging the family to observe the process of its feelings and its fears about them is the core of exploration and treatment.* The major problem in therapeutic management in this phase is not obtaining data or content about the difficulties as the family sees them. Rather, it is opening channels of communication about the feelings attached to the content. The intent of family therapy is to help the family members to expose, face, and alter the interfering feelings as honestly and directly as possible. This process is begun in exploration and remains the vital overriding theme in treatment. When and to what degree these process techniques are used depends on the worker's assessment of clues pointing to strengths, needs for defenses, and vulnerability at the time.

A particularly useful technique in the first interview is focus on the event that triggered the application. Obtaining the content and process of the trigger often serves to engage the perceptions and feeling reactions of all, makes it more possible to move in quickly to demonstrate the reciprocity in the problem, and leads to significant data about precipitants that may lie in past events.

ASSESSMENT

The avenues for assessment—content, process, and family

structure—are discharged through the use of the various types of interviews and incorporate the frame of reference. The following outline is suggested as a guide for exploration and assessment.

1. *Content*

   Identification of the family: the household members, their ages and relationship to each other; work and school data; economic status; religious affiliations; significant others outside the family, such as extended family, physicians, teachers. Presenting complaint and request: reason for application, trigger, and precipitants; nature of complaints, about whom or what, and their onset and duration; differing and similar perceptions and reactions by the family members to the complaint; and the efforts made to evaluate and deal with the problem by the family.

2. *Family Structure and Processes*

   a. Division of responsibilities in relation to age-space roles and their affects; family patterns of living in day-to-day operations.

   b. Patterns of identification and role discharge: role appropriateness in relation to alliances, collusions, generational boundaries; reciprocal relationships in the various family systems related to current individual and family developmental stage; role relationships with extended family and other significant figures.

   c. Nature and level of object relationships: degree of individuation in the family—that is, how family members use each other for expression of needs and satisfactions; how much permission exists for growth needs of individual members, for self-delineation needs, for age-appropriate dependence, separateness, and interdependence.

   d. Handling of feelings in the family: capacity, tolerance, and control of affects in such areas as intimacy, aggression, sexuality, anxiety and regressions, secrets, and myths; permissions and taboos in the expression of needs and affects.

   e. Capacity for reality perception: capacity for observation of the self and others; the nature and use of family defenses and resistances.

   f. Patterns of conflict and resolution: decision making
in the family, handling of stress, processes of solution
resulting in family cohesion, fragmentation or collapse, in scapegoating and collusions.

   g. Value transmissions: cultural and social influences,
management of moral, ethical and religious points of
view, social aspirations and goals, how the family sees
itself in relation to society and how society views it.

   h. Communication patterns: cultural influences, style
in relation to verbal and nonverbal communication,
purposes and effects of communication, such as double-level messages, permissions and taboos, defense
and attack; clarity and fusion of language in its
meaning and unconscious intent.

  3. *Family History*
Relevant data about the problem, such as history of
the marriage, child development; significant events and
changes in family structure in roles and object relationships occasioned by growth needs, losses, or illnesses;
relevant data to explain or reinforce content about the
stabilization of the family, its capacity to manage stress,
its repetitious patterns of family functioning and dysfunction, and its adaptation to social requirements.

  4. *Individuals*
Behavior, symptoms, health, adaptations, and difficulties in the family and the outside world. Selected retro-
spective data to illuminate the problems and adaptation.

  5. *Energy Available for Working on the Problem*
Strength and vulnerability in relation to age, health,
preoccupations with personal concerns, ability, and willingness to work on the problem as a family or in other
ways. Specifics to include fears and anxieties about the
marital equilibrium, family wishes and fears about intimacy and separateness, and ability to tolerate exposure of feelings in family therapy.

  This schematic guide for assessment is, like all guides, sterile unless the process by which the data is obtained engages
people emotionally. Any guide that attempts to be inclusive
and specific should also be viewed as partialized in use, in the
sense that few situations require the full range of inclusive-

ness and specificity. Selection of pertinent data should be related to what is needed at a given time.

The worker always lets people know why the data is sought and when possible makes connections between the content and process. The focus is maintained on the interaction, what it is, what its intended effects represent in adaptation and dysfunction, and sometimes, during exploration, on the underlying motives of the problem. Whether there is more or less emphasis on content or process will depend on the nature of complaints and symptoms, and on the family's style of communication. Thus, specifics of content may be highly significant in families that present complex, convoluted psychological family structures and in which language communication is subtle and involved. With these families, the sequence in which content is given, its nature, and how content relates to the processes of interaction need to be closely observed. In other families, the verbal content is less significant than the interaction process. These families are often behaviorally oriented, the verbal content is static, and affect lies predominately in action with each other rather than in content. Some families show severe gaps between cognition, behavior, and feeling, and dealing with the relationship of process and content in detail is significant in order to effect a bridge.

The content, process, and understanding of family structure should lead to formulation of a treatment plan, its goal, and specific methodology. It should answer questions about: (1) the placement of the current problem—that is, whether it is predominately situated in the interpersonal systems, in the total family or in parts of it, outside the family, or in an individual whose difficulties would continue regardless of family situation; (2) why the existing stabilization is no longer functional or possible to maintain; (3) what energies and vulnerabilities exist that promote or modify possible treatment approaches in relation to who in the family is to be directly involved at a particular time; (4) what strategies can be employed in immediate and long-range goals. For example, a long-range goal may be individual treatment or work with the marital pair, but until certain aspects of the family relationship system are worked with, treatment of the marital pair or individual cannot be permitted by the family. Whatever the goal, family and worker need to be in agreement.

Assessment should lead to a mutually agreed upon treatment contract that includes the ingredients of the therapeutic alliance, the family members to be engaged, the use of therapeutic time, and tentative goals.

TREATMENT PRINCIPLES AND METHODS

As described previously, family therapy seeks to modify or change those aspects in the family relationship system that, although stabilized, are for some reason no longer functional or satisfying and hence are interfering with the management of life tasks. Treatment goals may include help for a time-limited period of upset, a crisis, when the usual coping capacity is limited, anxiety is high, and accessibility to help is good; they may encompass long-term help in modifying or changing maladaptive roles in the family, or in establishing appropriate roles where none or few exist; or in helping to effect individuation in families whose members are symbiotically tied to each other. The approach may be short term in effecting separateness or separation during critical transitional individual and family developmental phases or longer term in dealing with developmental difficulties that reside in neurotic or characterological family interaction. The goals may include help in establishing a new marriage, whether it is the first or a remarriage, or to enable a fragmented but existing family to become more cohesive.

Immediate and long-range goals include, characteristically, helping the family members to become better attuned to each others' needs, to "hear" what the others are saying and what they mean, to overcome fears about expressing honest feelings, to learn how to communicate more directly and clearly, and to learn different ways of behaving and feeling.

By principle, family therapy emphasizes the here-and-now of family interaction as the arena of treatment intervention. Its main focus is on the disjunction between the individuals and their familial system. It is particularized in the sense that it focuses on particular themes of dysfunction in the family situation and does not attempt to deal with all the problems in the family. The specifics within the family approach, such as work with family unit, marital pairs, and other combinations concurrently, are based on choice of immediate salient need themes, on energy and vulnerability, and on encompassable goals. Although the salient need themes are partialized, there is constant awareness of the whole, and specific treatment methodology is changed as salient needs and goals are singled out and reached. For example, the major dysfunctional theme may be that any expression of aggressive and negative feelings will annihilate the family. The family's salient need to inhibit these feelings may lead to a decision of family unit treatment, unless there are overriding problems of anxiety—of vulnerability in specific individuals—or unless the family is unable to muster the energy required for this type of treatment.

Family therapy is task oriented in relation to problems in the current life situation. It does not lend itself, therefore, to the usual clinical nomenclature that has been designed for well-defined individual emotional disorders, and a new classification scheme needs to be developed to specify the currently vague descriptions of sociopsychological family process. Because family therapy is task oriented and is essentially experimental in nature, and because the worker uses immediate clues to intervene early in the process, the study phase can be called exploratory treatment.

The therapeutic emphasis is on preserving and enhancing those elements in the family stabilization that are adaptive and intervening in those elements that are dysfunctional by dealing with immediate life processes. The large goal is the development or increase of social competence in coping with life situations. In that sense, the worker supports and fosters adaptive capacities in the family relationship systems and relies less on working with individual cause and effect pathology. The focus throughout family therapy remains on the interactions and transactions, their evidences, intents, and effects. An individual family member may and often does make connections to his own past that are useful, and the worker may encourage consideration of similarities and differences from past experiences in the present, but these are always related to the interactional sphere. If clues point to the need to pursue past experiences in depth with an individual, they become a new theme and require a shift in treatment approach.

Because the initial and exploration phases merge with

treatment—although specific treatment direction may not yet be possible—the demonstration techniques described previously, as well as other techniques, may continue in planned treatment. The worker may begin to educate or reeducate the family in communication patterns by offering his own communications as a model, by showing how projections distort and confuse communication, by pointing out the use of double-level communication and double-bind messages. He may actively demonstrate and teach the need and use of controls against deleterious behavior. He encourages the development of appropriate roles in decision making and emphasizes the establishment and maintenance of appropriate generational equilibrium. He discourages regression and dependence on him by encouraging family responsibility for working on the problems. The worker often suggests "homework" about issues and behavior to be worked on between the therapeutic sessions. He deals with resistances to change, with fears of feelings, and with fears of destruction of the family and marriage by helping the family expose and examine hidden feelings and immobilizing secrets. He deals with transference reactions, when addressed to him by individuals, not only by relating these to the individual but also by redirecting them to the family interaction. The treatment emphasis is always on getting the family to observe and deal with its own processes, the relationship between behavior and feelings.

Because transference reactions occur largely between the family members and because interpretations about behavior and affects are made in interpersonal terms, the worker can be more direct in dealing with the use of inappropriate defenses, can move toward exposure of disabling family secrets and myths earlier than in individual treatment, and can more quickly show the nature and meaning of dysfunctional alliances and collusions. He is in a better position than the individual-therapist to support generational boundaries, to help expose tender feelings, to underline existing and latent strengths, and to be insistent about the need for change, because responsibility is placed on all, commensurate with age-space roles in the family.

The use of all or selected techniques is applicable depending on the family's communication style and its unique strengths and vulnerabilities. Shifts in the membership of those in direct treatment are made as salient needs alter and treatment goals are achieved. Interviews with individuals or other combinations of family members may be interspersed occasionally or periodically by the worker's decision, or when validly requested by the family members. If, in the worker's judgment, both members of the marital pair should be seen consistently, he may refuse to hold an interview when this is not adhered to by the expected participants. Home visits are common during exploration to gain a view of family dynamics and physical life style that is unobtainable in the office. Treatment may be undertaken in the home when young children cannot tolerate the confines of an office or when the family, for cultural or personal reasons, cannot make use of the agency setting. Treatment interviews may also be held in the home when the worker believes it is necessary to give active demonstrations in household management or child care.

Most of the techniques used in one-to-one treatment, such as guidance, advice, education, and reflection, are used in family therapy, with the difference that they are always directed to the interactional process. Suggestions, clarifications, and interpretations may be directed to an individual, but only in the interest of the total group. Individual reflection and introspection are not pursued unless they have value for the group and will elicit their participation or further their understanding of the individual's needs.

When treatment continues beyond symptomatic relief or crisis resolution, other techniques may assume greater proportion and significance. There is likely to be less dealing with the what, how, and effects of interpersonal behavior and more interpretation of underlying motives. There probably will be less directive activity by the worker and more encouragement to the family to examine with each other the processes of behavior in relation to underlying motives. There may be more interpretation of the meaning of individual conflicts to the person and the family. As individual motives are explored in their effects on family process, one or another family member may take the spotlight for some time. Interpretation of resistance and transference phenomena often become the main technique as the family moves into more difficult and painful exposure of motives.

It is common that symptoms become intensified or move from one individual to another, and the family needs to be made aware of this as it struggles with resistance to change. When families place the problem on a child it is difficult to engage them in family unit treatment until the parents recognize and can tolerate treatment of the marriage. In long-term family therapy, as in individual treatment, symptoms and conflicts may recur when termination is at hand.

Some families seek symptomatic relief only, others want to understand and work on the meaning of behavior and its related feelings; some move from family unit to marital to individual treatment as salient needs are met and redefined. Families in which there has been considerable individual treatment that has been useful but has not sufficiently served to alter the relationship systems may need to work on this aspect as a family unit.

The Role of the Worker

Family therapy requires a high degree of professional knowledge and skill. In this approach the rapid gathering of relevant facts, the identification of salient need themes in the presenting request, the awareness of interaction, the ability to communicate with all in the family regardless of age, individual defensive postures, and behavior, and the capacity to form therapeutic alliances with all in the family and to distinguish between the different nature of the establishment of the therapeutic alliance with the marital pair and children, require not only a new knowledge base that includes the systems with their characteristics and linkages but also a new ingredient, that of identification with all, to the usual self-awareness and control of counteridentifications. The worker who earlier made direct use of himself in intervention in one-to-one treatment may require a new measure of professional security about uncertainty of understanding and possibility of error.

Workers need to learn to consistently view the family members as involved in a relationship system and not primarily as individuals. This is difficult. It is, for example, far easier to fall into treating an individual with the family group present than to hold to focus on the group.

As in all treatment, the course is not smooth and constant. In family therapy there are new and different pitfalls for the worker. The family characteristically resists change by attempting to suck the worker into its dysfunctional system or by keeping him out of it in innumerable ways. The family may try to make him an arbiter, to choose sides, to engage in internecine fights or withdrawals in such ways that he is not able to enter the system, or they may present a helpless front so that he may feel impelled to offer advice that militates against the establishment of valid role responsibilities. The family may provoke him into identifying with one or another or gang up on him in a united front of resistance. These tactics are not entirely escapable. The worker probably will fall into some of these resistance traps from time to time because of the intensity of the experience for him, as well as for the family. His recognition of these resistance maneuvers and of his entrapment in them enables him to disengage himself so that treatment movement can take place. It is important during the early phases of exploration and treatment that the worker not take sides with individual members, but when the therapeutic alliance is established firmly, he may be able to do this appropriately. The worker must be prepared for behavior, for expressions of feelings and attitudes, for fears, anxieties, and values that are alien to his culture and perhaps personally distasteful to him. These are hard to tolerate because they are discharged openly in his presence. If his ambivalent or negative feelings are communicated overtly or covertly to the family, they may tend to increase or inappropriately inhibit the disturbing behavior. If his fear is sensed by them, they may find it impossible to expose their own fears. This is not to say that he will not express disapproval with some families—those who need to reduce inappropriate behavior quickly before anything else can be undertaken in the treatment need explicit disavowal of destructive behavior.

The range of techniques and the worker's use of himself is wide. Each worker develops his own style in the implementation of the theories and techniques cited above. Whether one or two workers should be engaged with a family is an open question and practice presently seems to be related largely to agency settings. In hospitals and clinics, where the team approach is used, two therapists are likely to be engaged routinely. In family and child placing agencies, where one worker is traditional, it is more common for this to continue. Although there are as yet no clear criteria, a certain rationale currently is advanced for each. Those who espouse the use of two therapists feel that much of the family interaction may be missed by one worker, or that his own identification difficulties may interfere with his understanding and intervention. Also, one worker may represent one model to the family while the other represents another, as in cases where the salient need is the establishment of male and female roles in the marriage. It may be possible for two workers to differ openly and yet convey to the family that differences are not necessarily destructive. Two workers can take sides more openly when this is appropriate. On the other hand, when one worker is engaged with the family there is less possibility of the development of multiple transference and countertransference reactions. Two workers may have similar blocks or lacks in self-awareness and may thereby compound gaps in understanding. When two workers are used a very high degree of collaboration and communication is necessary, as well as professional respect for each other's competence and difference, which is not always easy to achieve.

There are occasions when the use of two workers is indicated on a diagnostic basis. Certain cases may require, from the outset, separate workers for different members in the family; for example, when the salient need theme is the fostering of male and female identification. Or when the members cannot share one worker because of excessive fears, narcissistic blows, or dependency needs, and individual treatment is first undertaken. In such instances, if and when family therapy becomes possible, both workers need to be involved or the family shifted to a new worker because of the development of strong transferences. In some cases in family therapy, a member may need strong advocacy against the assaults of the rest of the family. This is too difficult for one worker to encompass and two workers may be involved from the outset. Some families are so large that one worker cannot be sufficiently alert to the interaction.

Indications for Family Therapy

The attempt here is to describe the conditions for family therapy. Family therapy, comprising the family unit or some segment of it, in various combinations concurrently or sequentially, is applicable to all families but not necessarily at all times in the life cycle. In general, the condition is that the family have, emotionally, some sense of being or wishing to be a family. To participate in family unit therapy, the family needs to begin with or develop some recognition of the problem as concerning the family and to have or develop some wish, ability, and tolerance for working on the problem as a family. The salient need and current task should be identified and assessed in terms of whether it primarily represents difficulty in family interpersonal relationships or in individual preoccupation with self-needs. If the former, focus on the manifest conflicts among the family members is the first methodological approach.

When the salient need is for urgent, rapid restoration or change in family structure in crises brought about by situational life difficulties, such as loss of a member, illness, or work changes; in changes in object relationships necessitated by maturational tasks; in role transition crises imposing new ego tasks; or in crises brought about by anniversary reactions to old conflicts, the family can more often be dealt with effectively as a unit because these crises tend to reverberate strongly in the total family.[12] For example, in a mourning process with its regression and integration features, the family members can ventilate feelings and lend support to each other, and thus restore and increase coping capacity.[13] Transitional identity crises, as in adolescence, having to do with control or management of impulses aroused in the adolescent and parents, with accompanying inhibitions or acting out of aggressive, dependent, and sexual impulses in the adolescent, arouse similar residual conflicts in the parents that more often lend themselves to treatment of all together because of the interlocking forces in the conflict. When, in

---

12. Howard Parad, ed., *Crisis Intervention: Selected Readings* (New York: Family Service Association of America, 1965).
13. Erich Lindemann, "Symptomatology and Management of Acute Grief," *American Journal of Psychiatry* 101 (September 1944):101–41.

earlier phases of development, there is derivative behavior
of oedipal content, because the child so strongly needs the
parents' permission to deal with these inhibitions to growth,
family treatment may be the choice unless the family cannot
tolerate the anxiety engendered. Thus, in a specific sense,
learning inhibitions are fit content for family therapy.

Family therapy often has much to offer when the family
members present interlocking chronically disturbed functioning that points to serious family and individual characterological defects or delays in ego development. These
families, frequently described as chaotic in psychological
functioning, often show marked inadequate social competence. They may show a range of personal and family
psychodynamics from severe acting-out, antisocial behavior
to psychotic functioning in some or all aspects of life management. Often these families are action-oriented, with little
capacity for reflection. There is little tolerance for frustration
of impulses or anxiety, and projection on individual members or the outside world is likely to be extreme. Because
they have little capacity for viewing themselves introspec-
tively, they can better learn to "see," understand, and change
behavior when it can be demonstrated as a family interactional process. The family that is tied in a symbiotic system often cannot tolerate treatment of individual members.
It is as though the family possesses a common ego and the
treatment of an individual is too threatening for all. The
chief task in family therapy is to help the members establish
some sense of self-identity by focusing on the right to be
different through sorting out, establishing, and promoting
role differences.

Delays and defects in ego development occasioned by
rigidities in object relationships, in problems of emotional
separateness, by infantilization of children or inhibition of
aggressive and sexual needs, are grist for the mill of family
therapy. The "identified patient" in these situations often
feels little or no pain himself and is not likely to change
until the family system changes and either forces him to
change for the better or to develop symptoms that are disturbing to him. The sufferer from disabling and anxiety-
provoking neurotic symptoms may, if the symptoms are not
intransigent, benefit from family therapy in which he is given

permission to give up responsibility for carrying the family's burden. Whether delays, defects, and neurotic difficulties in development can be dealt with adequately in family therapy is open to question. In some instances it may be sufficient; in others, family therapy may be a forerunner to individual treatment.

It is now, to some extent, accepted that when a child is in trouble and may at some point benefit from individual treatment, family therapy of the parents or of parents and children together is often the treatment of choice. The concept is that until changes in the system are made, the child is not likely to have permission to use personal treatment effectively. Aged members of a family, enfeebled to the point of requiring protective care but still able to participate in treatment, fare better, on the whole, when their adult children are involved with them in family treatment. Old conflicts in adult children, rearoused by current parental failure, for example, can lead to inadequate planning, unless they work on the problem with the aged member.

The specific treatment approach, whether to the family as a unit or to some combination of family members, will depend on the nature and degree of *mutual reverberation* in the systems; that is, who is involved in the current emotional dysfunction in the family, for what purposes, and to what extent. It will depend on how reverberation and salient need mesh. It will depend on the nature of *content;* for example, intimate marital sexual details, money management, or other private concerns of the adults are, for the most part, best dealt with by the parents together or singly, particularly when children are young and could not tolerate such exposure, or when there are adolescents whose age-phase sexual instability might be increased by parental seductive sexual revelations and behavior. Content in this sense becomes related to intergenerational factors. It will depend on the specific current *vulnerability* revealed by content and process, such as the degree of personal narcissistic and dependency needs, blows to self-esteem, preoccupation with work, or illness; on the degree of need for emotional distance in the marital pair; on the nature of fears of loss of control; and on the nature of problems of separateness and individuation. It will also depend on the *energy* available to work on the problem, such as the degree of emotional depletion or physical illness in a family member. The immediate *goals* are also a factor in the treatment decision. Resolution of a crisis; the making or cementing of a new or fragmented family; the establishment, reinforcement, or change in roles; and ambivalence in closeness and distance, and in separateess and interdependence, may well take goal priority over other evidences of personal pathology and lead to family therapy as the first treatment choice.

Contraindications to Family Therapy

The factors mentioned previously—mutual reverberation, salient need, content, process, vulnerability, and energy—may preclude family therapy at a given time or throughout the life of the case.

When the marriage is no longer a marriage, that is, when emotional energy is mainly directed to other extrafamily relationship or to divorce, family unit therapy is not the treatment of choice. When one family member is heavily involved in treatment elsewhere, family unit therapy may not be possible. Older adolescents and young adults who are mainly preoccupied with disengagement from the family and with personal concerns relating to the world outside the family require individual treatment. Adult children of aged parents often require treatment of their conflicts before the aged parent can be brought in.

Hostile attacks, impenetrable by the worker, on other family members, consistent withdrawal by a family member, or refusal by one parent to engage in treatment render family unit therapy ineffective. Overwhelming personal narcissistic needs or persistent holding to masochistic responsibility for the problem by a marital partner do not permit family therapy. Needs for basic emotional distance, without concomitant (albeit ambivalent) wishes for closeness, may preclude family engagement. Severe blows to self-esteem, emotional depletion or physical illness, or the need to hold to an interfering secret may require individual treatment as the sole method or as a forerunner of family therapy. A united family front of sustained resistance may make it impossible to engage in family therapy.

The one-parent family poses special treatment problems.

This family may or may not lend itself to family therapy. The mother or father who is preoccupied with problems about work or finding a new mate or resolving personal difficulties often needs individual treatment. Overriding seductive aspects in a relationship between a parent and an adolescent are likely to preclude family unit therapy. The special needs of the one-parent family to establish new generational boundaries and new ways of coping, particularly when children are in adolescence, may also point to individual treatment or combined family and individual therapy.

For the worker there are also special problems in one-parent families. He is likely to be regarded by the family as a substitute parent or spouse and to be drawn into the family system in a way that makes family unit therapy ineffective. His own counteridentifications are likely to be increased and distorted so that he may find himself enmeshed in the family system unproductively or destructively.

Combined Family and Individual Treatment
Combined, concurrent forms of family treatment, such as parents together and child separately, are common. They are likely to be undertaken when the marital pair need and can work on their relationship together and can permit individual treatment of a child or adolescent who has his own personal problems. This combination is often undertaken when parents require help with establishing or reinforcing generational boundaries and an adolescent requires delineation of his own responsibility for his actions.

The intensity of conflict between aged parents and adult children who cannot tolerate total family exposure of hostile feelings may lead to combined concurrent treatment.

Older adolescents or young adults struggling with both emancipation from the family and personal problems of relatedness to the larger world may require treatment as part of the family as well as individually. Younger adolescents struggling with dependency conflicts as part of the family system, as well as with private longings, fears, and fantasies in sexual and peer relationship aspects, may need to be seen with the family as well as alone. Some family members may be eliminated from family therapy when the current salient need has been assessed as lying mainly with other members or when they are too young to participate in the treatment.

Group therapy is also being used in combination with family therapy. Only limited examples can be given here. When overriding inhibiting fears and anxieties hinder or delay movement in family therapy, group therapy may be less charged. When emotional distance in the marital pair is basic to their existence, group therapy may be more tolerable while at the same time family therapy deals with less laden emotional content. Adolescents may work on peer relationship problems in group therapy while other conflicts are dealt with in family therapy. As indicated earlier, sequential shifts in treatment methodology are undertaken in the light of changes in salient need, vulnerability and energy, and changes in goals.

THE TARGET GROUP

In this frame of reference there is no family, by virtue of nature of social problem, nature of symptomatology and pathology, economic status and communication style, that cannot be viewed as potentially accessible to family therapy. Nor does agency setting or field of practice influence the possibility of employing this treatment model.

There are undoubtedly adaptations and modifications that relate to field of practice and agency setting. Although the intent of this paper is to present theories and practice considerations that are broadly based, the author's experience in the family field influences some of the practice techniques and the use of illustrations. However, evidence is accumulating that similar practice techniques are usable in child guidance clinics and psychiatric and medical outpatient clinics. In these settings the essential practice problem lies in the modification of the "identified patient" concept. It is difficult but not impossible for family and worker to move toward family exploration and treatment at the same time that the patient's personal needs are met. Indeed, in many instances focus on the family will eliminate or modify the problems that helped to create the identified patient, particularly in emotional illness or in the emotional aspects of physical illness. Also, it is well known that the complex, often conflicted feelings that arise in the family when a member is ill may interfere with his recovery unless family feelings are dealt with. Chronic illness, emotional and physical, whether the patient is in or outside a hospital, and chronic disabilities in brain-damaged or retarded children create problems for the total family. The anxiety, guilt, and hostility of the family members; the unexpressed fears; the displacement of feelings, affect all in life tasks. When these can be exposed and dealt with as a family problem, the "sick" member and the others are likely to benefit.

The decisions about who, in a multidiscipline setting, is to treat the family may pose problems. In the traditional structure of the child guidance clinic, for example, the use of the social worker for evaluation and work with parents and the psychiatrist for evaluation and work with the child may need to be modified in terms of the complexity of the case and related to specific knowledge and specific skills. It may be more productive for one or both to see the family as a unit before proceeding to diversified exploration and treatment planning. It is easier to make these shifts, with less transference difficulty, when the whole family has been engaged initially and becomes knowledgeable about the reasons for the treatment decisions.

Modifications and adaptations are perhaps more complicated in the child placing field. The family therapy approach requires certain changes in the present institutionalized features of these agencies. For example, as more becomes known about the meaning, strength, and tenacity of family relationships to the individual child, it becomes clearer that when a child is placed in a foster home, he should be helped to become, as much as possible, an integrated member of that household at the same time that he remains a member of his original family. If he is to establish and develop the capacity to make appropriate object relationships, he should not remain an outsider. This means that the child and the foster family members need to be worked with together as a unit; it means that the natural parents, when available, not only need continuing work as parents but must be encouraged to maintain active contact with the child and the foster parents. Family treatment, then, may include both families as a unit, or the foster parents and child as a unit and natural parents and child as a unit. Complex though this is, and difficult as it is to deal with competitive and other elements, the approach may enhance child and family developmental management by reducing interfering fantasies about desertion, abandonment, or idealization through helping the foster child and his family to work on the current reality relationship problems. When it is planned for the child to return to the natural parents and he must suffer the pangs of separation from the foster parents, his integration into the foster home is of great value because it profoundly affects his ability to develop the capacity for object relationships, a matter of primary significance in personality development.

Similar adaptations can be made in residential group settings. Adaptations can include working directly with parents and child when visits are made, treating the family in his home when the child visits, or bringing other children in the family for visits with him, during which family interviews are held. Again, the dispelling of fantasies by all and focus on current interpersonal conflicts promotes the enabling of developmental tasks for the individual and family. The same adaptations can be followed for aged family members who require care outside the home. Aged people are likely to fare better and to deteriorate less when there is continuing good interaction with their families. And the handling of the guilt of the adult children over the placement, when worked out in family interaction, is likely to result in healthier engagement with their parents.

The patient in a hospital may be too ill physically or emotionally to engage in family therapy. Severe psychotic depressions or hallucinations or critical physical illness may preclude this treatment approach. But when patients are recovering or in reality contact, they can be involved directly with the family. Experience attests that when, in mental hospitals, the family can be engaged with the patient in family therapy, his status as the identified patient may alter significantly for the better; the family's fears, angers, and misperceptions about his illness may abate or disappear; planning for aftercare may be sounder, recovery hastened, and recidivism lessened. The key is that the concern of all is recognized and dealt with in family interaction. Even when the hospital is distant from the family and visits are necessarily few, some time of the visit can be used for therapeutic sessions with the available family members and patient together. This is already under way in some veterans' regional hospitals.

There is beginning experimentation with greater freedom of visiting by families to jail inmates and of home visits by the inmate. Perhaps such experimentation can also lead to the use of family interviews at those times. Similarly, it is now being recognized that in programs such as Headstart and other preschool settings, work with the family permits the child to use the program more effectively, and his gains are more likely to be sustained.

UNSOLVED PROBLEMS

Many unsolved problems remain. Although there is significant agreement about the values of family therapy and the meaning of family relationships for individual development and functioning, there is lack of agreement about some of the theoretical constructs, methods, and goals. These differences require further clarification and conceptualization, practice testing and validation.

Some investigators are primarily concerned with the family as a currently operating system and tend to negate the influences of past individual life experience. For example, some tend to view the individual solely as a member of the family, believing that motivations for behavior arising from the families of origin cannot be known, understood, or assessed in relation to the current life situation. The psychoanalytic theory of personality is less significant for them; change in current behavior is the goal of treatment, and methodology is more likely to be directed toward the total family at all times. Learning theory, behavior theory, role theory, and communication theory are the primary targets of conceptualization and practice use.

At another extreme are the proponents of family therapy in the specific interests of a family member. They tend to concentrate on the individual and on an examination of his underlying personal motives for behavior, using the family as a backdrop or screen to furnish information or to validate their interference in the life of the individual. Group process is less significant; there is greater reliance on psychoanalytic theory and methodology, and the goal is less related to family than to individual homeostatic change. Outward behavior manifestations are less likely to be dealt with in an interactional process; behavior is seen more as the result of individual motives, although influenced by family.

These illustrations of extreme differences in theoretical approach show some of the problems still to be dealt with.

Knowledge about the intricacies and dimensions of the family relationship system is far from complete. It is likely that the projective system described in this paper is only one aspect of a variety of systems in the family system. The complicated dynamics of the family system in relation to their subsystems are still not defined. Also, much work needs to be done to understand the meaning and influence of other social systems on the family relationship system. This requires examination of roles, norms, and values of other social systems. Also required is greater knowledge than is currently possessed about behavior norms, values, and roles in different families. Perhaps this is to be achieved by the development of a classification scheme based on problems of family living rather than on emotional or social disorders. The specific tasks in the family life cycle and a range of behavioral norms within them need clearer and more refined delineation. The intermediate steps between underlying unconscious motives and manifest behavior in an individual or in the family as a unit are unknown.

The problem of how to integrate theories of psychoanalytic personality development, small group process, learning, role, behavior, communication, and systems theory into a usable entity that leads to a holistic theory is enormous. It may be that the placing of system theory in the foreground of investigation will enable ultimate integration of these theories and will provide for the degrees of emphasis that the various theories should have within the whole.

Whether there should be attempts to develop a classification of family types suitable for family therapy is open to question. Classification schemes based on types tend to become static and ultimately meaningless because they cannot allow for the infinite variations that exist. They may do injustice to families by a kind of stereotyping that tends to limit the therapist's scope of intervention. This chapter attempts to describe the usability of the family therapy model by relating the choice of method to the dynamics in the family. The effort is as yet rudimentary. Is it possible to pursue this approach by more careful investigation of the different and various dynamics in the family system and build some classification scheme on this base? Would it then be possible to relate these dynamics to a delineation of the variety of problems of living? Germain[14] suggests the possibility of conceptualizing disturbances in the life situation in such terms as life crises and role transitions. Investigation along these lines may provide a view of life about the individual and family that is not one of distinct health and pathology but rather of function and dysfunction on a continuum specifically related to current life situations.

It is possible that such a view of family life might lead to broadening the scope of work to include an endeavor that is not necessarily therapeutic in intent but rather is based on enhancing family life. This kind of help could be extended to families who are not in difficulty but who are "normally" struggling with "normal" problems in role transitions, and who, by gaining some better knowledge and means of dealing with them, could move more readily and easily into the management of new life tasks. This possible expansion of service requires understanding of the "normal" family life cycle and its tasks in the specific ways that Rhona and Robert Rapaport, among others, have been investigating.

Within these large questions are other related ones. What are the specific goals of family therapy? Are they to be detailed only in terms of family functioning with the idea that the individual members will benefit sufficiently? Should the goals be formulated only in relation to change in the current life situation in terms of social competence or should they include inner change in the individual? How is change to be defined and evaluated? Is change evaluated as modification or alteration of dysfunctional behavior, as amelioration of the presenting problem, easing of stress, relief from symptoms, resolution of interfering conflicts? Should the concept of dealing with the current salient needs be in the foreground as the change goal alone, or is there a professional

---

14. Carel B. Germain, "Social Study: Past and Future," *Social Casework* 49 (July 1968):403–9.

obligation to open up and pursue other attendant or different needs and conflicts? Some of these questions exist for all casework approaches and certainly are not clarified for family therapy.

Differences in methodological approach and techniques require further clarification. Does a system approach mean that the family unit is always the direct focus of treatment? Some practitioners define family unit to exclude children under age nine, others under age four, on the grounds that the verbal communication required in the process is not adequate at these ages. The approach in this chapter, because it includes, along with family system approach, theories from the psychoanalytic framework, attempts to focus also on individual members as well as on subsystems in the family group and, therefore, does not hold to the total family unit as the only direct treatment focus. Also, the framework suggested here considers the needs of individual development and of subgroups in relation to content as well as process within the therapeutic approach. Thus, certain content is considered to be private; for example, the sexual fantasies and longings of the adolescent, the oedipal fantasies of a younger child that might overwhelm him if exposed to family light, or the unique properties that belong to the marital pair or to the life of an individual member. This point of view influences methodological approach. Some practitioners hold that all content should be available for exposure in the total family.

Techniques for knowing how to deal with the total family system are still rudimentary. As yet there is greater knowledge and skill about helping an individual or marital pair. How to translate salient need into dynamic theme into therapeutic task with a whole family in a way that is understandable to them all is very difficult. Family transference reactions are only grossly understood and require more knowledge and refinement. Much needs to be done about identifying different family communication patterns and styles. The traditional reliance on verbal communication in the therapeutic process is not adequate to meet the styles of different families. Nor are we, as yet, comfortable in knowing how to link verbal and nonverbal communication.

Finally there is the problem of how to prepare practitioners for the family therapy model. Do the existing frames of reference provide sufficient conceptualized structure so that theories and methodology can be taught in the schools of social work? Is this model considered to be generically significant for casework and, therefore, to be incorporated in the school curriculum, or is it to be considered a special model that pertains only to specific agency settings and fields of practice and, therefore, to be learned by in-service training in agencies? Is it necessary to teach methods of helping individuals as a forerunner to other methods or can all go hand in hand? Because family therapy relies on group process, how do teaching and learning relate to the traditional methods divisions in social work? Some students are being exposed to family therapy in fieldwork without consideration of it in the classroom. Some schools of social work have incorporated family development into human growth and development and methods courses, and have elective courses in family therapy.

The point of view expressed in this paper is that despite the number and gravity of unresolved problems in theory, method and technique, family therapy will continue to develop as a primary helping model in casework practice.

Bibliography

Ackerman, Nathan. *The Psychodynamics of Family Life.* New York: Basic Books, 1958.

Bowen, Murray. "The Family as the Unit of Study and Treatment." *American Journal of Orthopsychiatry* 31 (January 1960): 40–60.

Boszormenyi-Nagy, Ivan, and Framo, James L., ed. *Intensive Family Therapy.* New York: Hoeber Medical Division, Harper and Row, 1965.

Caplan, Gerald. *Principles of Preventive Psychiatry.* New York: Basic Books, 1964.

Erikson, Erik. *Identity and the Life Cycle.* Psychological Issues, 1. New York: International Universities Press, 1959.

Germain, Carel B. "Social Study: Past and Future." *Social Casework* 49 (July 1968).

Hartman, Heinz. "Psychoanalysis and Developmental Psychiatry." In *Psychoanalytic Study of the Child,* edited by R. Eissler et al., 5:7–17. New York: International Universities Press, 1950.

Jackson, Don D. "Family Interaction, Family Homeostasis and Some Implications for Conjoint Family Psychotherapy." In *Indi-*

vidual and Familial Dynamics, vol. 2 of *Science and Psychoanalysis,* edited by J. Masserman. New York: Grune & Stratton, 1959.

Kramer, Charles H. *Psychoanalytically Oriented Family Therapy: Ten Year Evolution in a Private Child Psychiatry Practice.* Oak Park, Ill.: Kramer Foundation, 1968.

Lidz, Theodore. *The Family and Human Adaptation.* New York: International Universities Press, 1963.

Lindemann, Erich. "Symptomatology and Management of Acute Grief." *American Journal of Psychiatry* 101 (September 1944): 101–41.

Parad, Howard, ed. *Crisis Intervention.* New York: Family Service Association of America, 1965.

Parsons, Talcott, and Bales, Robert F. *Family Socialization and Interaction Process.* Glencoe, Illinois: Free Press, 1955.

Rapoport, Rhona. "Normal Crisis, Family Structure and Mental Health." *Family Process* 2 (March 1963):68–80.

Spiegel, John P. "The Resolution of Role Conflict within the Family." *Psychiatry* 20 (February 1957).

7 | Crisis Intervention as a Mode of Brief Treatment

Lydia Rapoport

CHARACTERISTICS OF THE THEORY

Crisis theory, and its application in brief casework treatment, has rapidly gained sizable attention and interest in the last decade. Crisis theory is not as yet a well formulated or holistic theory which has systematically validated propositions. It probably is premature to dignify it with the term "theory." At best, and pragmatically, it exists as a framework for viewing individuals and families in situations of urgency and stress, and as an approach it leads to the generation of useful practice principles applicable to both clinical work and modes of primary prevention in mental health work. There is no one articulated school of thought with its own disciples, although sizable recognition is given to the seminal work, both research and applied, of Erich Lindemann and Gerald Caplan and their colleagues at Harvard and the Wellesley Human Relations Service. There are increasing numbers of workers in both social work practice and the mental health field who make use of some central notions that are general guidelines to action. The parameters of crisis theory have not been spelled out, and thus the theoretical framework needs to remain open-ended. There is a growing body of literature in social work and in allied fields of social and clinical psychiatry, social and clinical psychology, and in physiological research. Unfortunately, as is characteristic of social work theory, we do not consistently build on the available contribution of our own and allied fields.

Crisis theory as it is emerging is not radically new. It is essentially eclectic in nature, and has come to represent a new synthesis. This feature may be one factor in its general attractiveness and acceptability among practitioners. It incorporates a good deal of familiar and accepted knowledge and clinical notions as well as relevant principles and techniques geared toward behavioral and personality change. The theoretical framework thus far developed perhaps brings so-called conventional casework theory more into line with the actualities of much of casework practice. For many practitioners who have familiarized themselves with crisis theory, it has provided a rationale, an underpinning, and a conceptual

Lydia Rapoport is professor of social welfare, School of Social Welfare, University of California, Berkeley.

frame of reference which has been useful in structuring and guiding a sizable portion of their practice. For some workers, integration of crisis theory in practice has required considerable philosophical and theoretical reorientation. For others, less firmly or consciously grounded in other theoretical perspectives, it has filled a theoretical vacuum.

Because of the propensity of social workers to latch on enthusiastically to new ideas and even fads, probably out of a sense of frustration and need for approaches that work with better "payoff," there is the danger of uncritical and undifferentiated usage and application as a new panacea. We need more and better systematic and experimental applications of this approach in order to achieve a better developed model. At this point in time, the intellectual work required to specify answers as to when, where, and with whom this approach is a method of choice has not been done. These and other issues are discussed in the last section of this chapter.

ORIGINS OF THE APPROACH

Crisis-oriented brief treatment had an interesting beginning from the point of view of the development and convergence of different ideas and separate endeavors over both time and space. The convergence of different concerns was aided by certain catalytic forces centered largely in the burgeoning community mental health movement. The two major areas of convergence were in the fusion of concepts of crisis and concepts of brief treatment.

Concepts of crisis have been developing mainly in studies of population groups or communities confronted with states of disaster or extreme situations. Most of these studies by social scientists gave a description and analysis of the event and its impact from a social-psychological perspective. Some of these studies focused on people confronted by natural disasters such as floods and tornadoes and on extreme situations such as war and concentration camps. There have also been field observations and clinical studies of individuals under stress ranging from extreme life threatening experiences to less catastrophic stresses such as threats of surgery, polio epidemics, or reactions to burns. The prototypical research that generated many new developments was the often cited study

of the disaster of the Cocoanut Grove fire in Boston by Lindemann.[1] This study investigated the impact of death and loss
on individuals and families and examined the experience
of bereavement. The leads in this classic study lay fallow
and were not picked up until some years later when the
field of social psychiatry developed. Social psychiatrists, with
other researchers, then brought a perspective to these studies
that elicited some bridging concepts from the more macro-
scopic events and their meaning in individual and family
functioning or breakdown. This perspective generated principles applicable to modes of intervention and prevention.
For example, Caplan's early work of crisis intervention in
Israel grew out of the experience of mental health work with
large population groups of immigrant children in institutions during the postwar period. This work sharpened the
recognition of the impact of a crisis on a child's life and on
the caretakers and institutional setting. It also discovered a
potential for remedial action within the crisis situation.[2]
This early work also gave rise to subsequent technical developments which led to the formulation of mental health
consultation as a distinct methodology and as an indirect
method of intervention in the mental health field.

Concepts of, and references to, brief treatment or brief
services have been available in the literature for many
decades. In casework, "brief" was linked with service that was
understood to be concrete or specific in nature, such as providing resources or referral elsewhere. It was distinctive from
psychological approaches which were traditionally conceptualized as needing to be long term. This dichotomy, and
the high prestige and value attached to the long term psychotherapeutic model, prevented the field from examining the
potentialities of brief intervention. However, there were cues
in the literature all along and other trends awaited to be
exploited. Contributions of early theoreticians such as Bertha

1. Erich Lindemann, "Symptomatology and Management of Acute
Grief," *American Journal of Psychiatry* 101 (September 1944). Also in
Crisis Intervention: Selected Readings, ed. Howard J. Parad (New York:
Family Service Association of America, 1965), pp. 7–21.
2. Jona Michael Rosenfeld and Gerald Caplan, "Techniques of Staff
Consultation in an Immigrant Children's Organization," *American
Journal of Orthopsychiatry* 24 (January 1954):42–62.

Reynolds,[3] the theories of the functional school, and later Helen Perlman's concept of "focus" in problem-solving,[4] highly developed brief service practices by such specialized agencies as Travelers Aid,[5] numerous studies on the vicissitudes of both the waiting list[6] and the actual length of contacts with clients—even highly motivated clients in voluntary counseling agencies—all raised serious question regarding the model of the ideal casework client and the ideal casework procedure. Further investigation of casework "dropouts" in follow-up studies revealed the astonishing information that numerous clients felt helped by the brief contact and claimed improved personal and social circumstances. Nevertheless, many professionals remained skeptical about such reports, since they conceptualized "dropouts" as a failure to engage clients in long term casework and because the brief contact had not been purposeful or by plan.

Outside the social casework field, in psychoanalysis and psychoanalytic psychotherapy, there were attempts to reexamine the classical model. Alexander and French's book *Psychoanalytic Therapy*[7] was an early landmark in departing from the psychoanalytic model. Their concept of brief treatment, however, was seen in relation to a long term classical psychoanalysis, and brief treatment as they described it would be considered long term by present-day practice. Worthy of note in this context was the observation made by Malan in *A Study of Brief Psychotherapy*, that in psychoanalysis "the most easily identified tendency, manifested re-

3. Bertha Capen Reynolds, "An Experiment in Short-Contact Interviewing," *Smith College Studies in Social Work* 3 (September 1932): 1–101.

4. Helen Harris Perlman, *Social Casework: A Problem-solving Process* (Chicago: University of Chicago Press, 1957).

5. Ruth Chaskel, "Assertive Casework in a Short-Term Situation," in *Casework Papers 1961* (New York: Family Service Association of America, 1961). Also in *Crisis Intervention: Selected Readings,* ed. Howard J. Parad, pp. 237–47 (New York: Family Service Association of America, 1965).

6. Helen Harris Perlman, "Some Notes on the Waiting List," *Social Casework* 45 (1963):200–205. Also in Parad, *Crisis Intervention: Selected Readings,* pp. 193–201.

7. Franz Alexander and Thomas M. French, *Psychoanalytic Therapy: Principles and Application* (New York: Ronald Press, 1946).

peatedly as each new advance was made, has been towards an increase in the length of therapy. Thus anyone who tries to develop a technique of brief psychotherapy is trying to reverse an evolutionary process impelled by powerful forces." He noted further that early analyses were achieving therapeutic results with much briefer time, by being more active and ignoring manifestations of both resistance and transference. This, of course, was labeled later as primitive.[8]

Many pressures and forces operated as catalysts in the reexamination of our social work practice and theoretical models: the impelling commitment to serve greater numbers and more population groups, more diverse as to social class, ethnicity, and personality structure; the hopeless and widening gap between needs and manpower resources; research studies which questioned the efficacy of results of conventional treatment modes; pressures for new service structures, service delivery systems and modalities of intervention; expectations that the profession realign the proportion of effort in remedial work to a greater effort in basic provision and modes of prevention. Similar exigencies and pressures have also characterized the mental health field. Therefore it was propitious that there was reactivation of interest in brief methods of casework treatment at a time when a conceptual orientation was available that could put brief treatment efforts into the context of crisis theory. The blending of these two frameworks opened up new perspectives and possibilities in brief treatment work, which, although widely practiced previously, had been used not by conscious intent but largely by default.

BEHAVIORAL SCIENCE FOUNDATIONS

As implied earlier, crisis theory represents a synthesis of a wide spectrum of concepts, empirical observations, and clinical insights drawn from the behavioral and social sciences as well as from several practice fields. Rather than listing each concept and identifying its origins and original usage and specific adaptation, this section identifies the range of sources

---

8. David H. Malan, *A Study of Brief Psychotherapy* (London: Tavistock Publication; Springfield, Ill.: Charles C. Thomas, 1963), p. 6.

from which crisis theory is drawn and describes, in essence, the central concepts and core notions of crisis theory as it has developed.

Crisis theory, insofar as it requires an understanding of the individual, needs to be anchored in personality theory. Psychoanalytic theory, first as it developed as a theory of the neuroses and in its later evolution into a theory of personality with its explication of personality structure and development of psychopathology, seems still to serve as a most useful base because of the comprehensiveness of the phenomena described. Of particular relevance is the developmental psychology of Erikson with its explication of biopsychosocial maturational stages and potential for crises and the relevant psychosocial tasks required for subsequent maturation and growth.[9] All developments in ego psychology are of great significance in crisis theory. Ego psychology has moved from an explication of the dynamics of defense mechanisms[10] to questions of synthesis, adaptation, and coping.[11] The ego, viewed as either endowed with neutralized energy or endowed with intrinsic energies of its own as an autonomous force, and its complex functions of exploration, manipulation, motility, language, perceptual and cognitive functions, and reality appraisal and testing directed to adaptation, coping, and mastery, becomes a pivotal concept in dealing with the important issue of effectiveness.[12]

Stress theory contributes fundamental concepts to crisis theory, and indeed, the terms are often used interchangeably in some of the literature.[13] The term "stress" is used to denote three different sets of phenomena: (1) it is equated with the noxious stimulating condition, the stressful event or situ-

9. Erik Erikson, "Growth and Crisis of the Healthy Personality," *Personality in Nature, Society and Culture,* ed. Clyde Kluckhohn, Henry A. Murray, and David M. Schneider, 2d ed. rev. (New York: Alfred A. Knopf, 1953), pp. 185–225.
10. Anna Freud, *The Ego and the Mechanisms of Defense* (New York: International Universities Press, 1946).
11. Heinz Hartman, *Ego Psychology and the Problem of Adaptation* (New York: International Universities Press, 1958).
12. Robert White, *Ego and Reality in Psychoanalytic Theory* (New York: International Universities Press, 1963).
13. Richard Lazarus, *Psychological Stress and the Coping Process* (New York: McGraw-Hill, 1966).

ation, sometimes referred to as "stressor"; (2) it is used to refer to the state of the individual who responds to the stressful event, and thus we talk of the client who responds with feelings or symptoms of stress; (3) more often, stress refers to the relation of the stressful stimulus, the individual's reaction to it, and the events to which it leads.[14]

Stress conditions can be disruptive and cause serious disturbances in biological, psychological, and social functioning with disturbed affects, motor and behavioral reactions, changes in cognitive functioning and physiological changes. Stress is generally conceived of as a powerful pressure which greatly taxes the adaptive resources of the biological or psychological system. It is considered to be a noxious stimulating condition, one which has pathogenic potential. The term "stress" has its origins in engineering, where its consequences are conceptualized as "strain." The concept has been adapted in physiological research, where the homeostatic model is a central concept.[15] It has been further adapted for use in the psychological realm, where a "steady-state condition" is posited but can be less readily specified.

A vocal critic of the use of the concept of stress in mental health states, "Of all the metaphors the human behavioral sciences have borrowed from their sister sciences and from literature, none has been more in the need of habitation and name than the concept of stress. Yet in the past its metaphorical habitation has mostly been in the house of hardship, retardation, insult, and affliction, and its name has been synonymous with noxiousness. . . . Stress as the grand metaphor of life and living has found little if any place in a philosophy or psychology of normal development and health."[16]

In the homeostatic model, the potentiality for change, either maladaptive or adaptive and progressive, is thought to reside in the energy that becomes available for change in the fluid personality state which ensues as a result of the dis-

14. Lydia Rapoport, "The State of Crisis: Some Theoretical Considerations," *Social Service Review* 36 (June 1962):211–17. Also in Parad, *Crisis Intervention: Selected Readings*, pp. 22–31.

15. Hans Selye, *The Stress of Life* (New York: McGraw-Hill, 1956).

16. Eli M. Bower, "The Modification, Mediation, and Utilization of Stress during the School Years," *American Journal of Orthopsychiatry* 34 (July 1964):667–68.

equilibrium. This concept is somewhat at variance with some thinking in ego psychology. One view is that ego functions which are neurosis free *themselves direct and facilitate the adaptational shift* rather than the energy itself shifting. It has been pointed out that "conceptualizations are needed to account for the dramatic shifts that are regularly observed to occur in life . . . spontaneous shifts in personality style during the growth process, particularly during adolescence, sudden improvements in psychotherapeutic patients, transference itself, and the formation and disappearance of symptoms. Stage theories, such as Piaget's or Erikson's, are based upon the assumption that clear shifts such as restructuring or reorganization do occur."[17]

Other relevant and enriching sources for crisis theory are learning theories concerned with cognitive processes and functioning.[18] The sources here are widely diverse and reach back into both clinical and academic psychology from child psychology, the developmental work of Piaget, to the work of ethologists. Motivation, competence, and modeling in social learning theory all seem to deal with more complex formulations, and are therefore more readily useful to the clinician than earlier work of academic learning theorists. The renewed interest in operant or instrumental conditioning is also of interest. It should also be noted that the interpersonal process in psychotherapy is being reconceptualized by some as a form of modification which takes place through learning. Alexander dealt with the psychotherapeutic transactional process in terms of learning theory, emphasizing the role of cognitive insights as a means of breaking up neurotic patterns, the concepts of reward and punishment, and the influence of repetitive experiences.[19]

Crisis theory concepts are applicable not only to the individual but also to the family matrix and probably, with some

---

17. Norma Haan, "A Tripartite Model of Ego Functioning: Values and Clinical Research Applications," *Journal of Nervous and Mental Disease* 148 (January 1969):26. ,
18. Jerome Bruner, *Studies in Cognitive Growth* (New York: John Wiley and Sons, 1966).
19. Franz Alexander, "Psychoanalytic Contributions to Short-Term Psychotherapy," in *Short-Term Psychotherapy*, ed. Lewis Wolberg, pp. 84–126 (New York: Grune & Stratton, 1965).

modification, to larger social systems as well. Many studies have examined the vicissitudes of family life under the impact of crisis.[20] The research in, and concepts of, family structure, interaction and functioning are of immediate relevance in dealing with the family unit in crisis. Social role theory has an important place in the analysis of family roles,[21] since impairment of social role functioning is usually one consequence of the state of crisis. Furthermore, the concept of role transition and the vicissitudes of role changes throughout the life cycle are considered to be one dimension of stress that may precipitate a state of crisis in an individual or in a family unit.

Another important frame of reference in crisis theory and its application is derived from the public health model of practice. The concept of prevention is central and is conceived of as a continuum of action classified as (1) health promotion; (2) specific protection; (3) case finding, early diagnosis, and treatment; (4) disability limitation; and (5) rehabilitation.[22] The first two categories are in the nature of primary prevention; early diagnosis and treatment are secondary prevention, and disability limitation and rehabilitation are tertiary. In general, most public health activities are directed at designated groups in the community which are considered, on the basis of epidemiological study, to be populations-at-risk. The public health framework can, therefore, be applied for crisis intervention on a primary preventive level for those crises that can be identified and anticipated for a designated, vulnerable population, and the secondary prevention level can be used for brief clinical intervention of crises that are identified through early casefinding.

The public health approach represents a modification of what is usually referred to as the medical model. There is a good deal of current criticism of the medical model insofar

---

20. Reuben Hill, "Generic Features of Families under Stress," *Social Casework* 39 (1958). Also in Parad, *Crisis Intervention: Selected Readings*, pp. 32–52.

21. John Spiegel, "The Resolution of Role Conflict within the Family," *Psychiatry* 20 (1957):1–16. Also in *The Family*, ed. Norman W. Bell and Ezra F. Vogel (Glencoe, Ill.: Free Press, 1960), pp. 361–81.

22. Hugh R. Leavell and Edwin G. Clark, *Preventive Medicine for the Doctor and His Community* (New York: McGraw-Hill, 1958).

as it has been co-opted in social work, but there is little clarity as to what is meant. There is no one medical model, but there are various patternings and constructs, some of which are more appropriate to social work formulations than others. For example, David Kaplan developed the concept of the "acute situational disorder."[23] This represents one type of medical model in which crises are conceptualized as akin to acute infectious disease states which are usually self-limiting and which may occur in a healthy person or may be superimposed on long term chronic disease states. Crisis intervention would be limited to the alleviation of the acute, reactive state without attempting to deal with the underlying, chronic pathology.

Some of the basic concepts in crisis theory will now be delineated briefly. A crisis may be defined as "an upset in a steady state." This definition rests on the postulate that an individual strives to maintain a state of equilibrium through a constant series of adaptive maneuvers and characteristic problem-solving activities through which basic need fulfillment takes place. Throughout the life span many situations occur which lead to sudden discontinuities by which the homeostatic state is disturbed and which result in a state of disequilibrium. The individual may possess adequate adaptive or equilibrating mechanisms. However, in a state of crisis, by definition, it is postulated that the habitual problem-solving activities are not adequate to the task for a rapid reestablishment of equilibrium. The hazardous events or stress factors that precipitate the crisis require a solution that is novel to the individual in relation to his previous life experience and usual and normal repertoire of problem-solving mechanisms.

The hazardous events pose a problem in the current life situation. Because they also may contain a threat to current instinctual needs, they are likely to be linked with old threats to instinctual needs and may reactivate and trigger off unresolved or partially resolved unconscious conflicts. This linkage may serve as an additional burden in the present crisis and may contribute to the overloading of affect. It has

23. David Kaplan, "A Concept of Acute Situational Disorders," *Social Work* 7 (April 1962):15–23.

been observed in crisis work that old problems which are linked symbolically to the present may be stimulated and may emerge into consciousness spontaneously or can be uncovered and dealt with relatively easily in brief therapeutic work. Thus the crisis with its mobilization of energy may operate as a "second chance" in correcting earlier distortions and maladaptations.

Three interrelated factors produce a state of crisis: (1) one or a series of hazardous events which pose some threat; (2) a threat to current or past instinctual needs which are symbolically linked to earlier threats that result in vulnerability or conflict; and (3) an inability to respond with adequate coping mechanisms.

A hazardous event can be experienced by the individual as either a threat, a loss, or a challenge. A threat may be directed to instinctual needs or to an individual's sense of integrity or autonomy. A loss may be that of a person or an experience of acute deprivation. A challenge may be to survival, growth, mastery, or self-expression. Each of these states has a major characteristic affect. Threat carries with it high anxiety. Loss is experienced with affect of depression or mourning. Challenge is accompanied by some anxiety but carries with it an important ingredient of hope, release of energy for problem-solving, and expectation of mastery.

Other characteristics of the crisis state, such as the phases of upset during the crisis, phases of problem-solving attempts (both adaptive and maladaptive), and the tasks required for mastery are discussed in the section on diagnosis. Here the state of crisis is conceptualized as a time-limited phenomenon. The individual or family does manage in due time to achieve some solution to the crisis. It may be resolved and a state of equilibrium is once again achieved. The outcome, however, may be variable. Thus, from a mental health point of view, the new state of equilibrium may be the same as or worse or better than that achieved before the crisis. The outcome itself is dependent on numerous variables. Current adaptive capacities and favorable environmental factors are of key importance. Less important in influencing outcome is the nature of the prior personality structure or psychopathology. Most important of all is the need to accomplish certain specific psychological tasks and certain related problem-solving activities. This is discussed in more detail subsequently.

ASSESSMENT OF THE CLIENT IN HIS SITUATION

Crisis intervention work requires some important modifications in both the concept and the method of diagnosis as developed in conventional casework. Traditionally, diagnosis in casework consists of a psychosocial description which may be blended with a clinical diagnosis based on psychiatric nosology. There is a further blending of both a dynamic and a genetic formulation. The genetic orientation is concerned with origins and causes and is less relevant in crisis-oriented brief treatment. It may be hard to relinquish this view if one is schooled in a developmental psychology of personality structure and functioning. Traditionally, we have been taught to formulate explanations of causal phenomena by way of reference to origins. "Why" is answered by "how one got that way." This kind of diagnosis is an incomplete formulation. According to one psychiatrist, "genetic accounts can be enlightening but all too frequently they 'explain away' without really explaining."[24] In a similar vein, Bandler states that "everything genetic in the client's personality is not operative in his current dysfunction. The past is not only silent, much of it may also be quiescent. What is genetically determined in the formation of the personality is not necessarily dynamically relevant."[25]

What is most relevant in crisis-oriented brief treatment is a way of diagnosing acute situational stress and a way of classifying hazardous events and people's reactions to them. We also need understanding of the process of personality functioning; that is, how ego processes function in transaction with the external milieu and the internal state. Our

24. John MacLeod, "Some Criteria for the Modification of Treatment Arrangements," in *Ego-Oriented Casework*, ed. Howard J. Parad, pp. 165–76 (New York: Family Service Association of America, 1965). The specific statement quoted was from an earlier version of the paper which was presented in the Monday Night Lecture Series, Smith College School for Social Work, Northampton, Mass., 17 July 1961.
25. Bernard Bandler, "The Concept of Ego-Supportive Psychotherapy," in Parad, *Ego-Oriented Casework*, p. 41.

usual attempt to appraise ego functioning often is no more than an inventory of ego strengths and the specification of the existence and the strength of certain traits without accounting for the person's appraisal of his situation and the restructuring and adaptations he is making. Here we lack the necessary conceptualizations to formulate the interaction of these factors.

It is my belief that some appraisal of basic personality structure and identification of basic defenses as well as habitual adaptive patterns is relevant and important in crisis intervention in order to be able to designate more sharply both the appropriate goals and the techniques for intervention. It does make a difference whether one is dealing with a person in crisis for whom the crisis has laid bare an underlying psychotic personality or whether the current state of disorganization occurs in a person whose habitual capacity for coping and mastery are adequate to his life goals. The goals in either situation may be largely restorative, but such differential knowledge leads to differential thinking and management in regard to reality possibilities. Such a clinical appraisal is not necessary for crisis intervention which may be developed by community caretakers as part of primary prevention efforts beamed at a designated population-at-risk.

The ability to identify personality structure, defenses, and adaptive patterns has usually been based on a systematic investigation—history taking with its vertical and horizontal exploration—with a chronological scanning of development, emotional and social functioning, manifestations of psychopathology, and consideration of both genetic and dynamic factors. Crisis-oriented brief treatment does not lend itself to such a systematic inventory and may not even lend itself to the task of selected history taking, largely because of the crucial factors of time and the need to intervene quickly. Some of the literature on brief treatment still stresses the need for a social and psychological history.[26] These brief treatment methods, however, are not conceptualized as being part of a crisis-oriented approach.

If insights into personality structure, defense, and adapta-

26. Lewis Wolberg, *Short-Term Psychotherapy* (New York: Grune & Stratton, 1965).

tion are important in addition to understanding the state of acute upset, and if the appropriateness of history taking is questioned, what then becomes the source of information and data for diagnosis in brief treatment? Here, there is a strong case for the experienced and skilled clinician who can generate and test hypotheses quickly on the basis of clinical experience, knowledge of personality organization, and the ability to appraise the significance of the client's behavior in reference to himself, his problem, and the social worker, and to the beginning interaction that is generated in the interview. In addition to overt and conscious communication as a source of information, the worker is alert to marginal clues that may be revealed, and focuses especially on preconscious communication and patterns of behavior that may yield insight about the subjective meaning of the precipitating stresses and the special areas of vulnerability which led to the state of crisis.[27] A major, initial diagnostic task is to develop quickly some working hypotheses about the nature of the crisis, the relevant precipitating stress or stresses, the general adaptive capacity of the individual and reasons for present impairment or inability to cope, as well as the extent and degree of his dysfunction. The next step is to appraise his potentialities for adaptive responses and the availability of salient internal, intrafamilial, and community resources that can be mobilized quickly in order to restore some sense of equilibrium.

Another source of knowledge and data which is highly relevant in crisis intervention is research findings concerning the typical or modal responses of people in crisis. This knowledge offers short cuts to generalized insights and understanding of how people behave and try to cope in a crisis situation, and provides a map or an inventory of likely behaviors and responses. A clinician armed with such knowledge is enabled to explore such clinical data for verification, testing, or discarding where irrelevant.

First, characteristic signs are present when an individual is in a state of crisis. The emotional signs are high anxiety, tension, shame, hostility, guilt, depression, and so on. The

---

27. Mary A. Sarvis, Sally Dewees, and Ruth F. Johnson, "A Concept of Ego-Oriented Psychotherapy," *Psychiatry* 22 (August 1959):277–87.

state of upset is also characterized by cognitive confusion wherein the individual is bewildered and literally does not know how to grasp and understand what has been happening to him, how to evaluate reality, or how to anticipate, formulate, and evaluate the possible outcome of the crisis and the possibilities for problem-solving. In extreme states of anxiety, in addition to cognitive confusion, there may also be perceptual confusion in the spatial, temporal, or interpersonal sphere.

Second, there are typical phases that characterize the period of upset. In the initial phase there is a rise in tension in response to the initial impact of stress which may result in a peak of anxiety with a concomitant feeling of great helplessness. During this phase, habitual problem-solving mechanisms are called forth. If the first effort fails, there will be an increase in the level of tension with an increase in feeling upset and ineffective. This state may then call forth "emergency problem-solving mechanisms."[28] Three things are likely to happen: (1) the problem may actually be solved; (2) there may be a redefinition of the problem or a reorganization of expectations and goals in order to achieve need-satisfaction in line with reality possibilities; (3) the problem may be avoided through need resignation and relinquishment of goals. If the problem cannot be solved in any of these ways a state of more major disorganization may ensue.

Third, there is general knowledge of patterns of adaptive and maladaptive coping. Maladaptive coping behavior may take the form of disorganized activities which represent attempts to discharge inner tension rather than solving reality problems. An individual may deal with the hazardous events and his feelings about them with magical thinking or excessive fantasy, avoidance, or denial. He may respond with regressive forms of behavior, with somatization or, in extreme situations, with withdrawal from reality. Coping patterns that are essentially adaptive in nature may be described as follows: the activity of the individual or family is task-oriented; the problem is broken down into component parts, and efforts are made to solve each aspect; the "mental work"

28. Gerald Caplan, *Principles of Preventive Psychiatry* (New York: Basic Books, 1964), pp. 26–55.

is directed toward correcting the cognitive perceptions involving the prediction of consequences and the anticipation of outcomes through cognitive restructuring. Mental work may also entail "rehearsal for reality" and preparation for anticipated activity or affect. The individual or family may seek out new models for identification and for the development of new interpersonal skills as part of problem-solving, particularly in crises involving role transition. In general, the pattern of responses for an individual or family necessary for healthy crisis resolution may be described as follows: (1) correct cognitive perception of the situation, which is enhanced by seeking new knowledge and by keeping the problem in the forefront of consciousness; (2) management of affect through awareness of feelings and appropriate verbalization leading toward tension discharge and mastery; and (3) development of patterns of seeking and using help with actual tasks and feelings by using interpersonal and institutional resources.[29]

A fourth area of knowledge that is becoming available is most fruitful for developing diagnostic understanding and for defining implications for treatment. It should be made a priority area for further research in crisis intervention. This knowledge is concerned with the identification of the specific problem-solving tasks that need to be accomplished to achieve a healthy resolution of a specific crisis. For instance, in regard to the problem of bereavement, Lindemann notes that the duration of the grief reaction seems to be dependent on the success with which a person does his "grief work." A normal course of grief reaction begins when the bereaved: (1) starts to emancipate himself from the bondage of the deceased; (2) makes a readjustment to the environment in which the deceased is missing; and (3) forms new relationships and patterns of interaction that bring rewards and satisfactions.[30]

In regard to the problem of the birth of a premature baby in a family, the specific psychological tasks and problem-solving activities necessary for positive crisis resolution have

29. Gerald Caplan, "Patterns of Response to the Crisis of Prematurity: A Preliminary Approach" (Unpublished paper).

30. Lindemann, "Symptomatology and Management of Acute Grief."

been identified by David Kaplan[31] and are cited in detail as follows.

Phase 1. Mother and infant are in the hospital after delivery. During this critical period the mother is faced with the following psychological tasks: She has to acknowledge that the infant's life is threatened and that survival in the early postnatal period may be uncertain. She has to acknowledge a sense of disappointment and even failure at having been unable to carry a baby to full term. In order to accomplish these psychological tasks, she must prepare for possible loss of the baby with some anticipatory grief reaction such as sadness or depression. Denial of the real threat or too early an optimism and cheerfulness are considered risks from a mental health point of view. Since a sense of guilt and self-blame is frequently aroused, the mother must be able to deal actively with such feelings in order to reduce their intensity and possible later negative effects.

Phase 2. The mother is at home; the infant remains in a hospital nursery for premature babies. The psychological tasks require the development of some hope that the infant will survive and will be home soon, and recognition that a premature infant needs special care but that eventually the needs and characteristics of the infant will be those of a normal child in regard to weight and other developmental factors. The problem-solving activities require that the mother take an active interest in the details of the progress of the baby while it is in the nursery and that she prepare for its needs.

Phase 3. The infant is now at home. The chief psychological task is the establishment of a tender and nurturing relationship between mother and infant, which has been prevented from developing by the premature birth and in some instances by long separation. The problem-solving tasks require the assumption of the nurturing role, attention and sensitivity to special needs, and (in some instances) coping realistically with congenital abnormalities frequently found in prematures.

---

31. David Kaplan and Edward Mason, "Maternal Reaction to Premature Birth Viewed as an Acute Emotional Disorder," *American Journal of Orthopsychiatry* 30 (July 1960). Also in Parad, *Crisis Intervention: Selected Readings*, pp. 118–28.

Certain patterns have been identified which are considered maladaptive and which prognosticate a poor outcome to the crisis of prematurity. For example, some mothers deny heavily the threat to life and the implications of maternal failure. Some fail to respond with hope to indications that the infant will survive. Some have no interest in the details of the baby's development and may refuse to visit or be active in securing information about the baby's growth.

Another example of the delineation of problem-solving tasks was developed by Rhona Rapoport in her study of a normal crisis: the status and role transition involved in getting married. She identifies three tasks salient in intrapersonal preparation for marriage: (1) Making oneself ready to take over the role of husband or wife; (2) disengaging (or altering the form of engagement of) oneself from especially close relationships that compete or interfere with commitment to the new marital relationship; (3) accommodating patterns of gratification of premarital life to patterns of the newly formed couple (marital) relationship.

The tasks involved in the couple's interpersonal preparation for marriage are: (1) establishing a couple identity; (2) developing a mutually satisfactory sexual adjustment for the engagement period; (3) reaching a mutually satisfactory system of communication between the pair and with relatives and friends; (4) developing a mutually satisfactory pattern of decision-making; and (5) planning specifically for the wedding, honeymoon, and early months of marriage.[32]

Such a detailed specification of tasks both helps in identifying where the individual has failed in appropriate coping and offers a framework for intervention. Emphasis on the need for coping and the successful management of psychological tasks helps to clarify the earlier statement that the outcome of a crisis is not necessarily contingent on the underlying personality structure and psychopathology of the individual. These problem-solving tasks have to be undertaken regardless of the underlying personality structure and patterns. The tasks can be taught and developed, and the capac-

---

32. Rhona Rapoport, "Normal Crises, Family Structure and Mental Health," *Family Process* 1 (1963). Also in Parad, *Crisis Intervention: Selected Readings*, pp. 75–87.

ity to deal with them can be strengthened. Of course, the ease and readiness with which people respond, achieve, or fail to accomplish them is related to general personality and ego attributes and capacities, but not exclusively. Other important factors are the nature of the interpersonal and institutional supports that undergird and sustain such efforts.

Specification of coping tasks is also useful for predictive purposes in intervention. It is the kind of knowledge that can be taught to professionals who are not clinically trained, such as nurses and clergy who work with people in a variety of crisis situations. Further research is needed to identify the relevant specific psychological tasks in many other kinds of crisis situations such as accident, disability, unwed pregnancy, or mental illness in the family.

Another area of knowledge and conceptualization that is also of help in rapid diagnostic assessment is the beginning of a classification scheme of hazardous events which offers directions for locating sources of stress. At this point the scheme is one-dimensional and is not linked with the possible reaction patterns of people who go into a state of crisis. What we need is a crisis state typology which combines both factors.

The classification of hazardous events can be conceptualized as follows. The first categorization is along the dimension of whether the hazardous events are largely anticipated or unanticipated. Under *anticipated crises* (which are often overlooked as they are considered to be natural) are the developmental crises identified by Erikson. They have a biological underpinning but also have psychological and social components. Examples are the oedipal period in childhood, identity development in adolescence, beginning parenthood, the climacteric, and senescence. A second category of anticipated crises, related to biological maturation, concerns transition points related to shifts in status and role: school entry, whether at the elementary or college level; entry into the labor market or military services; promotion; engagement and marriage; departure of children from the home; loss of job, demotion or retirement; moving to a new community, and so forth.

Under *unanticipated crises,* sometimes called accidental or adventitious circumstances, there are three subcategories: (1) loss or threat of loss—such as separation owing to death or hospitalization, desertion, or divorce; or threats to well-being such as illness, accident, or disability; (2) accession or the introduction of an unprepared-for member into the social network, such as a premature child or an infant with congenital defects; return from prison or military service; or an aged parent joining the family; and (3) community disruptions or natural disasters such as floods, tornadoes, or fires; sociopolitical upheavals such as war, displacement of population, or riots; economic disasters such as depressions, bank failures, or factory foreclosures; and ecological changes such as urban renewal or school bussing.[33]

It might be noted that by giving emphasis to anticipated or "natural" crises, of both a biological and a role transition nature, the potential is developed for building in supportive services at various entry points to facilitate the transition and to sensitize caretakers and institutions to the mental health implications of such entries. This would have the character of primary prevention. The popular assumption that an event or experience is natural denies the potential for stress inherent in experiences such as childbirth[34] or entry into military service. The unanticipated crises are generally not subject to prevention and control, so that the clinician and others have the responsibility of dealing with the casualities of such crises. However, some events, such as urban renewal or school bussing, can be prepared for to some extent through explicit attention to the concerns and anxieties of the population to be affected.

THE INITIAL PHASE

It is almost impossible to describe the initial phase in crisis-oriented brief treatment, since it cannot readily be isolated from the total process. Some brief treatment consists of only one interview, although four to six interviews are more typical. Some brief services build in opportunities for as many

---

33. Naomi Golan, "When Is a Case in Crisis." *Social Casework* 50 (July 1969):389–94.
34. Grete Bibring et al., "A Study of the Psychological Processes in Pregnancy and of the Earliest Mother-Child Relationship," in *Psychoanalytic Study of the Child* (New York: International Universities Press, 1961), 16:9–72.

as a dozen interviews. This discussion will confine itself, therefore, to the initial interview, which is of special significance in all treatment approaches. In brief treatment, however, the initial interview assumes extra significance because of the condensed time dimension. There is, so to speak, no margin for correcting error or neglect.

Certain basic assumptions of crisis theory which influence the nature of the initial interview need to be made explicit. A state of crisis is conceptualized as a time-limited process during which there is a peak in the state of upset. There are no clear indications of how long this state persists. No doubt it varies with individual vulnerabilities and patterns of response. Caplan suggests that six weeks is a usual time limit.[35] It is clear that the acute phase of a crisis does not go on indefinitely because the individual or family system pushes toward reestablishing itself and achieving some new kind of equilibrium. This equilibrium, however, may be in the direction of greater pathology. The important point is that the natural history of the crisis, with its built-in time limits, requires that intervention take place during this period if one wishes to influence the outcome briefly or economically. It has also been noted that the person or family in crisis is more susceptible to the influence of "significant others" in the environment. Moreover, the degree of activity of the helping person does not have to be high. A little help, rationally directed and purposefully focused at a strategic time, is more effective than more extensive help given at a period of less emotional accessibility.

The principle that emerges from the foregoing discussion is that in order to help people in a state of crisis, social workers must have rapid access to them; and, more to the point, clients must have rapid and ready access to helping persons. This then requires a structure in agencies and services that can meet requests for help within a few days, or at most a week, from the time of the request. It presupposes open intake and no waiting list. It presupposes further that there will be continuity in contact with a worker, with no separation of application interviews from treatment. It also presup-

35. Gerald Caplan, from discussions at seminars at School of Public Health, Howard University.

poses that there will not be a formal period of study or diagnosis. In conventional casework theory, emphasis has often
been given to the principle that diagnosis and treatment go
hand in hand. In crisis-oriented treatment, this principle
must be operationalized in fact.

As in all initial interviews, the primary task for the worker
is the development of a tentative diagnosis, or working hypotheses of the presenting problem. The primary need of
the client is to experience in the first interview a considerable reduction in disabling tension and anxiety. One way in
which this is achieved, which may be specific to the brief
treatment approach, is by the worker's sharing tentative hypotheses and structuring a picture of the operating dynamics
in language that makes sense to the client. This enables the
client to get a manageable cognitive grasp of his situation,
and usually leads to a lowering of anxiety, trust in the worker's competence, and a feeling of being understood.

Another need of the client in the initial interview is to acquire some hope of improvement in his situation and of
mastering tasks which previously appeared hopeless. This
imperative leads to the consideration of two factors: the element of hope and therapeutic enthusiasm. Both are necessary attributes of the climate that needs to be generated in
the initial interview as well as throughout the treatment
process. The importance of these factors has been identified
through empirical observation and some experimental work,
but they do not often receive systematic attention because
they lack a scientific aura or rigor and thus tend to embar-
rass us. The absence of hope, or hopelessness, was noted
as characterizing individuals and families suffering from
chronic deprivation which operated as a barrier to motivation and change.[36] Hope has been observed as an ingredient
of therapy or as an attribute of the therapist in experimental
studies by Jerome Frank and his colleagues. They state that
"there has been a unifying thread to suggest that aspects of
the therapeutic situation which arouse and strengthen the
patient's hope of relief are positively correlated with short-
term improvement in a significant proportion of patients. . . .

---

36. Kermit Wiltse, "The Hopeless Family," *Social Work* 3 (October
1958):12–22.

Although a placebo can have such an effect, the essential ingredient in therapy is the ability to convey the therapist's ability to help."[37]

The factor of therapeutic enthusiasm or optimism was commented on by Malan citing an observation of Balint: "The therapist's enthusiasm has a direct bearing on the process and outcome of therapy since it brings with it a corresponding heightened excitement in the patient with the result that repressed feelings come easily to the surface and are experienced with an intensity and completeness so that the further 'working through' process may not be necessary."[38] Grinker also comments on this phenomenon but expresses a contrary point of view. "It has been said that the results from therapy of any type are proportional to the therapist's enthusiasm for his method. This does not insure more than temporary effect . . . the young therapist's over enthusiastic missionary concept of *self* as a curative agent may become a serious liability."[39] We are not necessarily talking about partisan enthusiasm for method per se, but quality of intensity and investment in the client. Here we have another relevant observation made by many social work educators in regard to the performance of social work students who are frequently successful with clients beyond the level expected from their knowledge and skill. Factors of enthusiasm, therapeutic optimism, intensity of commitment, and investment have been noted but have not been examined systematically to discover what therapeutic potentials are embedded in them and how they can be used more effectively and purposefully.

Qualities of hope and enthusiasm are cited, therefore, as ingredients of a climate that needs to be developed by the worker to instill a sense of hope and confidence in the client. These observations suggest that the worker needs to play an active role in the encounter both in terms of creating a climate and in being firmly in command of the management of treatment. The need for a more active approach in brief

37. Jerome Frank, "The Role of Hope in Psychotherapy," *International Journal of Psychiatry* 5 (May 1968):394.
38. Malan, *A Study of Brief Psychotherapy*, p. 13.
39. Roy Grinker, *Psychiatric Social Work: A Transactional Casebook* (New York: Basic Books, 1963), p. 311.

treatment seems to be one of the few areas in which there is considerable consensus in the brief treatment literature.

Notions of investment, commitment, and enthusiasm suggest another concept that is increasingly noted in the literature on psychotherapy of many different schools of thought—the requirement of authenticity in the relationship. It may very well be that the increased concern with authenticity is in part a reaction to the widespread psychoanalytic model of relationship which advocated the neutrality of the therapist and a value-free stance. Such a relationship, although conceived of as being instrumental in purpose, upon examination has been found to be largely a myth.

The whole matter of relationship needs examination in crisis-oriented brief treatment. The concept of relationship in casework is central. We are accustomed to thinking that the positive relationship is the chief tool, if not the dynamic force, in treatment. Implicit in this view is the notion that it takes time to develop "a meaningful relationship" and that one cannot treat without it. Relationship is a rather fuzzy concept since we cannot state with clarity what aspect of relationship, what kind, what symbolic value, what degree of intensity, and so on are essential ingredients of treatment. The pertinent question is whether there are components of relationship that can be identified and can be maximized for use in brief treatment. For example, the worker's authority of competence and expertness may be used more powerfully to capitalize on the client's readiness to trust and relate out of feelings of confusion, helplessness, and anxiety. Such an approach may serve even a deeply suspicious client who, in a crisis, longs for protection. Perhaps the component of "attachment" in relationship is less crucial than the degree of involvement, however brief. Attachment is less necessary, since treatment does not depend on a "corrective emotional experience" (which is the essence of Alexander's earlier concept of brief treatment) or on the "working through" process. Brief treatment depends instead more on cognitive restructuring and unlinking the present context from past concerns.

In regard to the goals of the initial interview the following might be postulated. Engagement of the client is an important objective. This is affirmed in the general literature on casework, but is mostly dealt with in terms of strengthening the client's motivation for longer range goals or of working on a restructured definition of the problem. In brief treatment, engagement refers to immediate problem-solving in relation to mutually defined and agreed upon goals. The determination of goals to be worked on depends on the worker's assessment of what might be called "the useful next step,"[40] a shorthand designation of what in the client's internal or external state can readily be altered which would result in an immediate lowering of anxiety. The most useful or necessary next step may be some form of environmental provision, protection, or modification. Or the useful step may consist of the clarification of the nature and meaning of the precipitating stresses. There have been interesting studies showing that the detailed exploration and understanding of the precipitating stress and its specific meaning is often in itself of such great therapeutic value that no further help may be needed.[41] In this instance, the clarification gives the client a cognitive grasp of the relevant factors in his situation leading to intellectual mastery. This may be a first step in later emotional mastery and may open up a new perspective on appropriate problem-solving steps.

The process of exploration and definition of mutually agreed upon goals in the initial interview should eventuate in what is sometimes referred to as a contract. In the contract there is a spelling out of mutual expectations to avoid confusion or unrealistic expectations which are grounded in fantasy or magical wishes. This step also reduces the proclivity toward a regressive transference. The need for greater clarity in defining mutual expectations and goals has been identified in numerous studies of client dropouts. These studies identify the disparities in both perspective and expectation between worker and client. Social class and cultural factors which produce different styles of problem-solving and conceptualization have led to barriers between workers and clients. One source of lack of congruence that has been identified is the worker's reliance on psychodynamic concepts in

40. Sarvis, Dewees, and Johnson, "A Concept of Ego-Oriented Psychotherapy," p. 287.
41. Betty L. Kalis et al., "Precipitating Stress as a Focus in Psychotherapy," *Archives of General Psychiatry* 5 (September 1961):219–26.

explaining behavior and lack of attention to cognitive elements, which are also instrumental in affecting behavior.[42]
In one experiment on long term therapy, role induction
interviews were conducted to help patients develop appropriate expectations for treatment and therefore behave as
"good patients." This procedure significantly improved the
results of subsequent treatment.[43] All this points to the importance of the need for clarity of expectations.

Another crucial initial goal which remains a focal point
throughout the brief treatment process is the reestablishment
in the client of a sense of autonomy. This needs to be started
in the initial interview so that the client can experience being
able to again take charge of himself in regard to both life circumstances and feelings. The area in which this might take
place may have to be minor, or have largely symbolic significance, but nonetheless is vital in the reestablishment of a
sense of mastery. One example is the case of a man in his early
forties with a known history of instability and periodic active
mental illness who again came for clinic treatment at a point
of crisis when his work situation, a main stabilizing force in
his life, became drastically altered. Symbolically the alteration in the nature of his job represented a threat to his
concept of integrity and autonomy. The worker quickly perceived that the main issue was the fear of loss of control.
Thus, in the second interview she deliberately came without
a watch and put the client in charge of keeping time. This
was a beginning step, actual and mostly symbolic, in his re-
assumption of control and the enlargement of his sense of
autonomy.

Thus far, factors such as the mobilization of hope, engagement, reduction of anxiety, reestablishment of a sense of
autonomy, and the establishment of a contract as goals pertinent in the initial interview have been discussed. These
goals are facilitated by the flexible and appropriate use of
both structure and time. Here, as in other aspects of this
work, a good deal can be learned from the functional school

42. John E. Mayer and Noel Timms, "Clash in Perspective between
Worker and Client," *Social Casework* 50 (January 1969):32–40.
43. Rudolf Hoen-Saric et al., "Systematic Preparation of Patients for
Psychotherapy: Effects of Therapy Behavior and Outcome," *Journal of
Psychiatry*, Research volume 2, 1964, pp. 267–81.

of casework. Time can be used to provide both the structure which provides a framework and boundaries for problem-solving, and limits. This is reassuring to a person whose ego is deteriorating and is in itself ego-restorative. The setting of time limits can operate as leverage and as pressure for both client and worker to get on with the problem-solving task. It can relieve the client of his anxiety about becoming dependent upon the treatment situation and serve as counter-force against the client's self-concept of being emotionally "sick" or incompetent. Time limits can also be used, along with other techniques, to prevent tendencies toward the development of a regressive transference, which is to be avoided at all costs in brief treatment.

The actual manipulation of time lends itself to various approaches and innovations. In many brief treatment services, the length of time available for problem-solving may be set arbitrarily for administrative reasons and be made known to clients in advance. This gives the worker some external controls and makes it easier not to slide into long term relationships. However, it may introduce certain aspects of inflexibility. Another approach, which has not been sufficiently experimented with, is to encourage the client to specify how much time he thinks he needs in order to work on his problems. He should be able to set both the length of time and the frequency of the encounter. I refer to this as a "self-demand schedule." The opportunity to do this is another means of strengthening the sense of autonomy referred to earlier. In order for a worker to be comfortable with this approach he must have enough faith and be sufficiently free of anxiety to be able to accept the client's time schedule. The administrative structure must be flexible enough to permit the scheduling of interviews at other than once a week intervals. There is nothing magic about weekly appointments: they may fit our patterns of working but not necessarily the client's immediate needs. The client may need three appointments in a row, or one each day for a week, in certain emergency conditions. The general experience seems to be that when the client is given a choice he tends to commit himself to a series of interviews well within half a dozen. This would seem to be the "staying power," or perhaps working power, of many individuals. When the agreed-upon time limit has been reached and there is both the indication of need and the willingness to continue working on problems, in some services referral then becomes automatic. In others, where there are no administratively set cutoff points, more interviews might be structured. In that case, it is desirable to renegotiate the contract, to spell out the next series of goals and to again set a limit for further work. Such use of time limits also gives a framework to evaluate what has been achieved and to measure growth.

TREATMENT PRINCIPLES AND METHODS

There is as yet no well-developed treatment methodology in crisis-oriented brief treatment, any more than there is in any other casework approach. Many prevailing principles and techniques are relevant and useful but need to be reordered in keeping with a shift in emphasis. New ones have yet to be devised. It is important to emphasize, however, that crisis-oriented brief treatment is not a short version of long term treatment, although it is apt to be so unless the work is guided by conscious knowledge and application. If the conscious orientation and requisite techniques are absent, most likely the work is a failure and unproductive. This observation has been borne out in a study by Reid, who notes that "short term treatment suggests that this type of service has a distinct methodology of its own—that clients are being given a different kind of treatment from what they receive in continued service, rather than simply less treatment."[44]

The basic treatment model in crisis-oriented brief treatment should be the life model as suggested by Bandler.[45] The trajectory of the life span with its natural processes of growth, development, and eventual decline is the arena for experimentation, learning, and mastery in regard to need satisfaction and problem-solving. The natural, progressive tendencies in human development are strong forces and prevail over the regressive tendencies, barring serious obstacles and obstructions. These natural growth tendencies then be-

---

44. William Reid, "Characteristics of Casework Intervention," *Welfare in Review* 5 (October 1967):18.
45. Bandler, "Ego-Supportive Psychotherapy."

come our chief therapeutic ally. This concept challenges that aspect of the medical model which frames maladaptation and problems in living in terms of illness. Crisis theory explicitly refrains from defining or equating the state of crisis with an illness. Indeed, the crisis state, in contrast to the concept of stress, is viewed as having a growth-promoting potential if favorable factors are operating.

In keeping with this view, we need to abandon the concept of cure and shift to the concept of restoration and enhancement of functioning. The term cure evokes the surgical model of medicine, with removal or excision as a goal. It is a static concept which does not fit many conditions of physical disease. For example, in states of acute infectious disease there is an acute flare-up in an organism previously in a state of health or some state of relative equilibrium, followed by a diminution of acute symptoms and a return to the previous state of functioning. This model of acute infectious disease, referred to earlier, is more akin to the life model with its fluctuations of stress and adaptation. Jerome Frank supports the notion that the customary medical notion of cure may not be entirely appropriate for psychotherapy.

It is quite proper to judge the effectiveness of a remedy for leukemia or cancer in terms of five or ten year results. However, this is only appropriate when the patient's state of illness or health does not depend on a continuous interaction process between him and his environment. It would be highly ambitious to hope to achieve a five year cure for the common cold, for example. The virus and bacteria that cause this condition are always present in some kind of balance with the host. Either a temporary increase in the virulence of the bacteria or a reduction of the host's powers of resistance can upset the balance at any time and the patient will get a cold. The discovery of a way of producing permanent immunity to colds would indeed be a medical triumph. In the meanwhile, most of us would be more than content if we had a remedy that reduced the duration of each cold from, let us say, a week to an hour, and we would regard such a remedy as indeed valuable.

He states further that "the chances of finding therapeutic methods that will confer permanent and total immunity to life stresses are remote."[46]

---

46. Frank, "Hope in Psychotherapy," p. 386.

This discussion points to the need in brief treatment for a genuine acceptance of limited goals. This seems to be hard for many practitioners both on the basis of their understanding and recognition that there are indeed many areas of conflict and pathology in the person and on the basis of their therapeutic ambitions, generally framed in terms of impatience with symptom relief and interest in personality trait modification. What facilitates acceptance of the concept of limited goals (in addition to the hard realities of lack of resources and the inappropriateness of a long term approach for most of our clients) is increasing evidence that even minor modifications in functioning, values, or attitudes may serve as a nucleus for other more profound transformations in the environment, in interpersonal relations, and even in intrapsychic functioning. Improvement can become self-perpetuating, particularly if there are favorable rewards and responses. From the designation of limited goals flows the corollary notion of the application of a focused and segmental approach with conscious and deliberate attention to what will be dealt with and what will be ignored.

The general goal of crisis-oriented brief treatment can be formulated in a way similar to the more global kinds of formulations that usually characterize casework treatment efforts. Basically, crisis-oriented brief treatment is an ego-supportive method. But from one point of view, all forms of therapy are ego-supportive. To cite Bandler again, "We are most obviously supportive [in] those moments of crisis in which the ego is overwhelmed. . . . Every effort is made to maintain the ego and to forestall further disruption."[47] The goals and measures used in this instance are essentially ego-conservative or ego-restitutive, concerned with the maintenance of defenses and repression of instinctual impulse seeking discharge. In other circumstances of crisis, the goal can become ego-progressive, directed toward progressive forces and the growth of the personality. Specifically, this involves attention to new modes of adaptation and strengthening latent coping mechanisms and on developing new ones.

This formulation is consonant with many others, particularly that of Frances Scherz in her paper "An Appraisal of

47. Bandler, "Ego-Supportive Psychotherapy," p. 28.

Treatment Objectives in Casework Practice." She differentiates between the objectives of helping people feel better, cure, and problem-solving. She views treatment objectives as involving (1) delineation of coping; (2) understanding the here and now and life stresses; (3) description of developmental tasks; and (4) provision of skills for problem-solving. She concludes, "Whether the specific treatment goal is related only to the immediate task or to removal of obstacles to further development will depend on the specific assessment of what is most economical, what is safe to undertake, and what can be tolerated in treatment."[48]

The dichotomous formulation of conservation or progression, similar to the FSAA framework of maintaining and modifying measures,[49] although it yields a sort of theoretical simplicity and tidiness, does violence to the richness and complexity of clinical experience. In actual practice, modes of intervention do not fall into these categories. In most instances, both modes and the cluster of techniques that largely characterize each mode are used in crisis and noncrisis treatment situations. The inability to work within this framework is noted in the research study of Reid, in which modifying or supportive measures were to be used in accordance with the requirements of the research design. He concludes that the division of casework into dichotomies as "modifying" versus "supportive" artificially splits apart interlocking sets of techniques. "These techniques may be better seen as constituting the core of the casework method rather than as representing different methods of casework."[50]

The goals of crisis-oriented brief treatment can be more narrowly specified as follows: (1) relief of symptoms; (2) restoration to the optimal level of functioning that existed before the present crisis; (3) understanding of the relevant precipitating events that contributed to the state of disequilibrium; (4) identification of remediable measures that can be taken by the client or family or that are available through community resources.

---

48. Francis Scherz, "An Appraisal of Treatment Objectives in Casework Practice," *Social Work Practice*, 1962, p. 160.
49. Family Service Association of America, *Scope and Methods of the Family Service Agency* (New York: The Association, 1953).
50. Reid, "Characteristics of Casework Intervention," p. 18.

These are the minimum goals that should be achieved as part of crisis resolution. In addition, where the personality and social situation are favorable, and the opportunity presents itself or can be created, work can be done to: (1) recognize the current stresses and their origins in past life experiences and conflicts; (2) initiate new modes of perceiving, thinking, and feeling and develop new adaptive and coping responses that will be useful beyond the immediate crisis resolution.

Crisis brief treatment is primarily present-oriented, with a strong focus on the "here and now." One of the first tasks is to elucidate and identify the precipitating stresses that led to the state of crisis. The specific accompanying affects are accepted and identified as natural and understandable in keeping with the stressful events. Here the purpose is to lower tension, anxiety, and guilt. The purpose of clarifying the precipitating events and subsequent affects is to help the client achieve a cognitive grasp and mastery of his situation by describing, defining, and reordering recent experiences. There is further exploration of adaptive models of coping that have been useful in the past and that can be reaffirmed or may be extended or modified in the present context as ways of handling conflicts or finding solutions. Similarly, there is exploration of defense mechanisms in order to strengthen those with adaptive utility or to develop new ones.

Where the content lends itself to it, and where the opportunity presents itself, there is selective focus on the past insofar as present stressful events reactivate old preconscious or unconscious conflicts or traumas. Without engaging in actual exploration of past events and their ramified meanings, it is possible to unlink the present stressful events from past traumatic events so that they may be perceived and felt as discrete experiences without the added burden of old unresolved needs or feelings. The kind of material which is necessary to make this linkage diagnostically and then to engage in the unlinking process often comes out surprisingly readily when the person is in a state of crisis. At such times the usual defenses are weakened, and the person is less guarded against the revelation of such pertinent information, which ordinarily is repressed or suppressed.

A brief clinical vignette may illustrate this important process. A fifteen-year-old Negro boy recently moved into a newly integrated neighborhood and school. He was a poor student and a serious behavior problem, making many supposedly unprovoked attacks on other children. On the occasion of one such aggressive attack, the school felt helpless and frightened and called the police, who put the boy in handcuffs. He became more violent and threatening, at which point they took him to the local psychiatric ward. His disturbances, outbursts, and threats of more violence increased and there he was put in restraints. He was given a psychiatric diagnosis of schizophrenia, paranoid type. He was subsequently seen for brief outpatient psychiatric treatment. He was handled in a remarkably skillful manner with a rapid lowering of anxiety so that he soon became quite rational. There were no clinical signs that he was psychotic. In about the fourth interview, almost in the nature of a free-associative expression, he recalled an experience at age six (which he misdated to age nine) when he had been hospitalized. He did not know what had been done to him. As a matter of fact he had gone in for a hernia repair and at the same time had been circumcised and had his tonsils and adenoids removed. The event, for which he had not been prepared and which he had not been helped to digest, had been experienced by him as a major body assault. All his subsequent defensive mechanisms were geared to making himself invulnerable and strong, against basic castration anxiety. The recent events had been experienced by him as another assault where he was reduced to total helplessness. The worker was able to unlink the present events from the past trauma, to help him digest both experiences, and to affirm his current capacity to handle himself in keeping with his age and role, showing him he was no longer helpless. Through anticipatory guidance and some role rehearsal he was helped to handle the next stressful situation (a court hearing) with minimum stress or distortion.

In addition to the focus on the present and selected past event when relevant, there is also a heavy emphasis on a future orientation in anticipating needs and tasks that require active coping. The enhancement of coping patterns is achieved by a process that has decided educational components, such as anticipatory guidance, rehearsal for future reality, learning new social and interpersonal skills, and enlarging the capacity for anticipatory thinking and prediction. In some instances, the educational process may be less verbal and be based more on identification. Here, the worker may consciously offer himself actively as a model for identification and encourage the rehearsal of behavior and attitudes in regard to new roles.

The role of the worker, as touched on previously, requires an active and directive stance. The relationship is built not over time through elements of attachment and transference, but on elements of authority based on expertness and competence. It is important for the worker to be more of a real person than a neutral reflector or moderator, and to communicate actively both concern and authenticity. The worker takes advantage of the client's readiness to trust out of a feeling of confusion, helplessness, or anxiety. He also takes advantage of the regressive impulse and longing, without, however, permitting any regressive behavior to develop which would be inimical to short term goals and the specific goals of quickly reestablishing and enhancing self-esteem and a sense of autonomy and self-direction.

The requirement of being active and directive restores the role of advice-giving to an important and useful technique. Giving advice has become almost taboo for both historical and theoretical reasons. Workers have often withheld information and advice on the misguided judgment that the client's problems were based only on unconscious conflicts rather than on a simple lack of information and knowledge. It is true that in unsophisticated hands advice-giving can be abused. However, it can be used in a potent way, especially if its dynamic meaning can be anticipated by taking into account the client's unconscious needs and impulses. Furthermore, in keeping with a more educational approach, it is possible to use the client's greater accessibility and readiness for influence by taking advantage of the "teachable moment."[51] By the same token, crisis casework treatment can

---

51. Helen Harris Perlman, "And Gladly Teach," *Journal of Education for Social Work* 3 (Spring 1967):41–50.

take on the character of the life-space interview since it is conducted during a time when the client is still actively experiencing the effects of stress.

In sum then, from a technical point of view, crisis brief treatment makes use of all the principles and techniques which have been developed in casework methodology that are relevant and useful. However, there is a reordering of, and greater emphasis on, some techniques. The approach is more active, directive, and authoritative. Time limits are used for a framework, to push toward problem-solving and to avoid regression. The client's capacity for autonomous action and decision is maximized. Treatment is highly focused and segmental, and problems to be worked are partialized. Emphasis is on the engagement of the perceptual and cognitive functions of the ego, especially on cognitive restructuring and mastery. The initial task is lowering tension and anxiety through reassurance, but more important is the redefinition and delimiting of the problem and the focus on rapid mastery of some segment of the life experience. There is restoration of old defenses that were previously adequate and adaptive. There is prevention of regressive behavior and transference. Clarification and interpretation are geared to present feelings and current conflicts, and the present stress is unlinked from past unresolved conflicts where possible. Self-understanding or insight is not a goal in itself. Often insight is no more than hindsight and remains unintegrated unless supported by action and behavioral change.[52] In brief treatment the goal is foresight—the enhancement of anticipatory awareness to be used in problem-solving. Focus is on adaptive patterns and ways of handling conflicts and finding solutions. There is a strengthening of coping mechanisms and the development of new social and interpersonal skills through imparting knowledge, advice, anticipatory guidance, and rehearsal for reality, as well as providing new models for identification. There is emphasis on the enlargement of the capacity for prediction and control. There is, of course, mobilization of relevant resources not only for meet-

52. Allen Wheelis, "The Place of Action in Personality Change," *Psychiatry* 13 (May 1950):135–48.

ing basic needs but also for the opportunity to exercise adaptive capabilities.

Termination in crisis-oriented brief treatment is an important function, if not a phase. It is remarkable that there is almost no discussion of termination as a process in the conventional casework literature in comparison with the emphasis given to diagnosis and the early phases of treatment.[53] Only the functional school has given explicit attention to this phase and process and has made it an intrinsic dynamic aspect of the total treatment process. In brief treatment, termination needs to be dealt with explicitly. Depending on how the brief treatment is structured to begin with, and in keeping with the model suggested earlier of a "self-demand" schedule for the client, termination is discussed and initiated in the initial interview. In other words, the ending process is anticipated, if not actually predetermined.

Termination obviously is intrinsically linked with the formulation of specific goals. It takes place when a specifically defined goal has been reached. That may or may not be easily determined. One of the impediments to early termination is the tendency to label certain rapid improvements as "flights into health." This label bespeaks the clinician's mistrust of the natural recuperative powers of people. In actual fact, although it is sometimes difficult, it is possible to distinguish flight into health from genuine changes that are supported by alteration in feeling states and behavior. Another concept, perhaps more useful, is that termination can be achieved when the client *begins* to find solutions to his problems. This means that we do not expect him to work through all his problems, or even those parts of the problem that have been identified for focus. When the client begins to perceive new directions for solutions and new modes of coping, even when they have not been firmly or consistently established, termination can be instituted.

"Letting go" is not easy for social workers, particularly if the client's adaptation is still shaky. But the cost of continuing must also be borne in mind. In one of Alexander's

---

53. C. Knight Aldrich, "Impact of Community Psychiatry on Casework and Psychotherapy," *Smith College Studies in Social Work* 32 (February 1968):102–15.

last papers he stated, "Psychotherapeutic treatment must aim to bring the patient to the point where his natural growth can be resumed. Treatment beyond this point—or infantilization—interferes with the natural growth potential and tempts the patient's ego to take the easy path of continuing dependency on parental figures. This dependency is exactly what the therapy tries to overcome."[54] In another paper he speaks of the need to trust the natural recuperative powers of the human personality, which are largely underestimated by psychotherapists. There is a tendency toward overtreatment. He speaks of an early approach in analysis—of planned interrupted treatment called "fractioned analysis"—which has gone into oblivion.[55]

It is easier to "let go" if one operates on the assumption that there will be, within the life span of all persons, periods of adaptive and maladaptive functioning associated with life circumstances. Thus, professional intervention may be necessary at various times in the life cycle. In order to respond to such a view of man, agencies must have an "open door" policy[56] that invites clients to return for further work when they need it. Acceptance of a life model of problem-solving and a door that is really open makes it easier for clients to return without a sense of shame or failure. This view also helps workers. At present, many caseworkers feel a sense of guilt and failure if clients return for more help. We tend to view this negatively; we expect that a problem solved should stay solved for all times. Reapplication for service should be viewed positively. Experience has shown that clients who return after a brief period of help need even briefer help the second time. They may return because of similar stress; yet the crisis is often less intense. They may use a second period of help to consolidate previous gains. In other instances, the need for help the second time may be entirely unrelated to the first situation, and should be dealt with in accordance with current need.

54. Franz Alexander, "Psychoanalysis and the Human Condition," in *Psychoanalysis and the Human Situation,* ed. Jessie Marmorston and Edward Stainbrook, p. 82 (New York: Vantage Press, 1964).

55. Franz Alexander, in Wolberg, *Short-Term Psychotherapy,* p. 91.

56. Esther Schour and Jennie Zetland, "The Open Door: A Point of View," *Social Service Review* 29 (September 1955):285–92.

THE TARGET GROUP

The question, For whom is crisis brief treatment the method of choice? is difficult to answer. From one point of view all people can benefit from brief and focused intervention, particularly in times of stress. At such times, brief treatment offers what has been referred to "as the useful next step." But to suggest that brief treatment is useful for everyone, particularly as a beginning step, is begging the question. We should distrust any approach that is offered either as a panacea or as an undifferentiated approach. More important, failure to identify the specificity of a concept or the differential application of an approach leads to an excessive elasticity of a concept and causes both the concept and the application to lose their essential utility.

Thus this question turns us back to the basic definition of a crisis. Despite various attempts at theoretical definition and description, the fact remains that practitioners find it difficult to identify when an individual or family is in a state of crisis. The tendency is to equate a crisis with an obvious, dramatic state of emergency such as a suicidal attempt. The inability of practitioners to define a crisis or to identify the relevant precipitating stresses is noted in a study by Parad and Parad.[57]

One approach to the question is to ask, When is a "crisis" not a crisis? The most obvious exceptions are those numerous types of clients who frequent many social agencies—public welfare, corrections, and particularly protective services, and who live in a chronic state of crisis. For them being in a state of crisis is a life style. The overt manifestations of the upset—sense of urgency, disordered affects, disorganized behavior, and ineffective coping—appear to be similar to those of other people in a state of crisis. Nevertheless, deeper examination suggests that for such individuals and families the crises, in addition to the external hazardous events all are heir to, tend to be largely self-generated. Here we deal with people who have severe and chronic ego depletion and ego

57. Howard J. Parad and Libbie Parad, "A Study of Crisis-Oriented Planned Short-Term Treatment," Parts 1 and 2, *Social Casework* 49 (June and July 1968):346–55, 418–26.

damage. According to Cumming and Cumming such ego-damaged persons will experience even simple problems as crises.[58] It is very likely that from the psychoeconomic point of view the crisis, accidental or self-generated, and the response to it are not maladaptive but, in fact, are an attempt at adaptation (although admittedly self-defeating and generating more problems) which serves to ward off deep unconscious depression, anxiety, or an underlying psychotic process. We usually characterize such people as suffering from character disorders or borderline states. These clients are generally not the ones we can help significantly with brief crisis intervention as we have defined it. They often do need emergency and first aid help. Workers consistently complain, however, that when the emergency has been weathered these clients are no longer available for any kind of sustained work. They do not stand still long enough to be available for work between "crises," so to speak. For such clients a different model and set of expectations must be developed. Periodic intervention with emergency provisions and ego conservation as a goal may be the treatment of choice. When agency skills and resources warrant it, more long term approaches and serious commitment of sustained treatment efforts may yield results in the direction of ego growth and adaptation, as Reiner and Kaufman noted in working with character disorders,[59] or through the adult socialization approaches described by McBroom.[60]

The kinds of people for whom crisis-oriented brief treatment is not appropriate are those disordered individuals and families with character disorders or those in borderline states where acting out and flight are major mechanisms of adaptation. It is also not the treatment of choice for people with extremely marginal or low functioning of a chronic nature who need some form of constant, though not necessarily intensive, support as a kind of lifeline—such as certain chronic patients discharged from mental hospitals. For the latter,

58. John Cumming and Elaine Cumming, *Ego and Milieu* (New York: Atherton Press, 1963), p. 55.
59. Beatrice Reiner and Irving Kaufman, *Character Disorders in Parents of Delinquents* (New York: Family Service Association of America, 1959).
60. Elizabeth McBroom, *Adult Socialization: A Basis for Public Assistance Practice* (California: State Department of Social Welfare, 1966).

support is conceived of as similar to an orthopedic appliance, but in a psychological sense. A goodly number of social workers' caseloads are made up of such persons. Both goals and techniques have to be formulated differently for them. Institutional supports and contributions by other caretakers may also have to be provided in new ways.

There is no way to categorize people for whom brief treatment is the method of choice. It cannot be done along the lines of symptoms, syndromes, or diagnostic categories. Of greater significance is the person's integrative capacity or ego strengths, which means, among other factors, the availability of a resilient repertoire of coping mechanisms. When brief treatment is placed in the context of crisis formulations, we have a better way of sorting things out, provided we can identify the crisis state. In this context we presume there has been a prior state of adaptive functioning with some degree of satisfaction. Thus, in general people with acute conflictual problems, or neurotic responses that are immediately reactive to the environment, are more amenable to brief intervention. These are people with an essentially good ego who are under considerable external stress. But chronically disordered persons in acute stress can also respond favorably to brief treatment. For example, brief treatment has been surprisingly effective with persons of borderline character who may be on the verge of a psychotic episode with breakthrough of primitive impulses. Here, active intervention can often restore crumbling defenses and return the person to a previous level of functioning. It appears, therefore, that people at widely separated ends of the mental health–mental illness continuum can make good use of brief treatment. For both, the goal is restoration of prior adequate functioning within the limits of present capacities and opportunities. We have also noted that brief treatment has the potency to do more than restore functioning. It can produce profound changes in personality by facilitating some rapid reorganization of psychic structure and energy. This is most likely to happen at times of maturational crises, such as at adolescence, when the personality is in a greater state of flux.

We have not been able to distinguish sharply, except in broad terms, the types of clients for whom crisis brief treatment is a method of choice. As to social problems or fields of practice, the approach cuts across all areas and seems to be relevant in all kinds of settings. Family agencies and out-patient psychiatric services have moved toward this approach. Older and newer types of psychiatric emergency services are very committed to this method. Other emergency services under nonmedical auspices, such as suicide prevention centers, also use this approach. Medical social work settings are very familiar and comfortable with crisis-oriented brief treatment by virtue of the nature of the problems in such settings. However, they have not, by and large, conceptualized their rich clinical experience in terms of crisis theory. Public welfare workers find this approach highly relevant and congenial. Protective services are very sensitive to the concept of crisis and have turned to crisis theory for help. The tendency, however, has been to misconstrue the nature of crises and the power and limits of brief intervention and to misapply this theory in work with clients for whom life style crises are most frequently operative. Agencies working with unmarried mothers also respond to these ideas and approaches. The agency most comfortable and experienced with the crisis brief treatment approach has been Travelers Aid, which has developed both a descriptive literature and some conceptualization regarding its work.

In essence, we have taken the position that crisis brief treatment has extensive utility with a wide variety of clients and patients, cutting across traditional diagnostic typologies, social problem areas, and a spectrum of agency services.

UNSOLVED PROBLEMS

There are many unsolved and unknown problems to be defined in a newly evolving framework such as crisis-oriented brief treatment. The most glaring problem of all is that as yet there is very little systematic practice that consciously employs the model as it has emerged to date. There are a few services committed to this mode of practice throughout the country, mostly mental health services. Elsewhere the practice is partial, not designated or set apart from other approaches. Thus, crisis brief treatment tends to be hit or miss. Consequently there exists as yet no systematic study of outcome at termination or of long term effects. There is a need for both practice and study of experimental efforts with attention to variables such as target groups, social problem groups, and use of differential time dimensions.

From a conceptual point of view, we need a definition of crisis that can be more easily operationalized. As was pointed out, practitioners have difficulty identifying a state of crisis as well as the precipitating stress factors. We also need definitions of the concept of "brief" and these can only be achieved by consciously experimenting with time factors. We need greater clarity about the kinds of people for whom this approach is the treatment of choice, since at present there is little consensus. Another area which has not been sufficiently conceptualized is a framework for diagnosing a family unit in crisis. It has been suggested that crisis brief treatment is relevant to individuals and families, but little has been done to conceptualize the nature of the crisis as it manifests itself in a family system or to develop relevant methods and techniques for treatment of the family as a whole.

We also need better understanding of the dynamics that bring about change. In crisis theory, the dynamic force for change is made possible by the disequilibrium of a crisis that produces a fluid ego as well as an altered environmental state. The goal in crisis brief treatment is action and the furtherance of rapid behavioral change with positive reinforcement. This involves complex processes which should be based on understanding of psychodynamics. In other models, the dynamics of change are conceptualized differently. They may be based on self-understanding or insight, or the freeing of latent energies formerly tied up with defenses of the infantile neurosis. These concepts need reexamination, testing, and some reformulation in the light of new insights developed.

We also need greater clarity regarding the conceptual underpinnings and what is necessary by way of a knowledge base for crisis treatment. For example, what aspects of psychoanalytic theory, learning theory, social role theory, family interaction theory, and ego psychology are relevant and useful in crisis brief treatment? A major task is to blend and integrate these theories with the knowledge of various conditions of stress. As indicated earlier, there is an urgent need for more knowledge of the specific effects of particular crises and the requisite psychological problem-solving tasks necessary for healthy crisis resolution.

In regard to techniques, it has been suggested that new techniques may need to be developed in addition to those with which casework practitioners are very familiar. It may be useful to experiment with selected aspects of behavioral modification and with a socialization approach; there may be a need to develop more nonverbal action models, as well as a need to develop more of an ecological approach instead of almost total reliance on the person-to-person approach.

Crisis brief treatment raises questions which require some modifications in conventional casework theory. We have already touched on the relevance of the nature and kind of diagnosis required, and modification in the concept and use of relationship. The concept of self-determination may also need to be reexamined in the light of the client's need for both self-direction and autonomy or guidance and protection in crisis brief treatment work. The concept of motivation needs clarification in regard to defining the level and nature of motivation necessary for change.[61] Motivation for relief of suffering may be a better starting point than motivation for change in behavior or feelings as it is traditionally conceptualized.

From the point of view of education and training, several issues are unanswered. Is this an approach that can be successfully used only by the seasoned and experienced clinician who knows the long term process and has an understanding of depth phenomena and can therefore find his way more readily to shortcuts? There is observable evidence that some beginners are very skilled in this approach, whereas seasoned clinicians often have great difficulty reorienting themselves if they suffer from "trained incompetence." Can this approach be taught in professional schools of social work? And if so, at what point in the casework sequence can it best be introduced?

Another issue has to do with how the social work profession as a whole conceptualizes its operations and major com-

---

61. Genevieve Oxley, "The Caseworker's Expectations and Client Motivation," *Social Casework* 47 (July 1966):432–37.

mitments and subsequent deployment of manpower. In essence, the question is how much of the professional effort
and enterprise should be committed to remedial work and
how much should be geared to more systematic efforts at prevention. Crisis theory leads to two levels of intervention—
the generic and the specific.[62] The specific level is the clinical
level of intervention, designated as early diagnosis and treatment of the casualties of crises which can be dealt with
through the methods of brief treatment, as described. The
generic level of application, which is more in keeping with
a primary prevention effort, can be aimed at various target
groups, populations designated to be especially vulnerable
or at risk. Here, community caretakers, professionals and
nonprofessionals, are the primary helping agents, assisted
with knowledge and techniques through methods of consultation and education by mental health professionals. The
generic knowledge applicable to people in specific crisis
states can be utilized in this fashion both for strengthening
coping efforts and for screening failures. In addition to work
with other professionals and nonprofessionals who deal with
specific populations, social workers can also apply generic
knowledge of crisis to work with community agencies and
basic institutions in order to sensitize such institutions to
basic human needs and to special needs of people in times
of crisis, and to help bring about greater responsiveness.

In sum then, crisis-oriented brief treatment is a most useful approach for intervention and help to many kinds of
people who turn to social and mental health agencies. It is
not a radically new effort, but builds on many values and
tested components of knowledge and theoretical frames of
reference. It is consistent with the major social casework
goals of restoration and enhancement of personal and social
functioning. It is an approach which takes into account the
multidimensional factors of causation and problem solution.
It can also contribute to the greater understanding of the
complex forces of interrelationship between social environment, stress, and individual response which might eventually

62. Gerald Jacobson, Martin Strickler, and Wilbur Morley, "Generic and
Individual Approaches to Crisis Intervention," *American Journal of
Public Health* 58 (February 1968):338–43.

lead to a more ecologically oriented effort and the creation
of sounder institutions.

Bibliography

Bellak, Leopold, and Small, Leonard. *Emergency Psychotherapy
and Brief Psychotherapy.* New York: Grune & Stratton, 1965.

Bloom, Bernard. "Definitional Aspects of the Crisis Concept."
Journal of Consulting Psychology 27 (December 1963):498–502.
Also in *Crisis Intervention: Selected Readings,* edited by Howard J. Parad. New York: Family Service Association of America,
1965.

Caplan, Gerald. *Principles of Preventive Psychiatry.* New York:
Basic Books, 1964, chap. 2.

Cumming, John, and Cumming, Elaine. *Ego and Milieu.* New
York: Atherton Press, 1963.

Jacobson, Gerald F. "Crisis Theory and Treatment Strategy: Some
Sociocultural and Psychodynamic Considerations." *Journal of
Nervous and Mental Disease* 141 (August 1965).

Kaplan, David M. "A Concept of Acute Situational Disorders."
Social Work 7 (April 1962).

Klein, D., and Lindemann, E. "Preventive Intervention in Indi-
vidual and Family Crisis Situations." In *Prevention of Mental
Disorders in Children,* edited by G. Caplan. New York: Basic
Books, 1961.

Lindemann, Erich. "Symptomatology and Management of Acute
Grief." *American Journal of Psychiatry* 101 (September 1944).

Malan, D. H. *A Study of Brief Psychotherapy.* London: Tavistock
Publications; Springfield, Ill.: Charles C. Thomas, 1963, chaps.
1–3.

Parad, Howard J., ed. *Crisis Intervention: Selected Readings.* New
York: Family Service Association of America, 1965.

Rapoport, Lydia. "Crisis-Oriented Short-Term Treatment." *Social
Service Review* 41 (March 1967).

Sarvis, Mary A.; Dewees, Sally; and Johnson, Ruth F. "A Concept
of Ego-Oriented Psychotherapy." *Psychiatry* 22 (August 1959):
277–87.

Selby, Lola G. "Social Work and Crisis Theory." *Social Work
Papers,* vol. 10. Los Angeles: University of Southern California,
1963.

Wolberg, Lewis R. *Short-Term Psychotherapy.* New York and London: Grune & Stratton, 1965.

8 | Socialization and Social Casework

Elizabeth McBroom

INTRODUCTION

In 1959 a United Nations social affairs officer in a Latin American country cited a popular anthropological study, *Five Families,* by Oscar Lewis[1] as evidence of his contention that social casework, United States style, should not be taught or practiced south of the border. The problems in the five Mexican families, he said, typified all those in the geographic region: they were economic and therefore would yield only to economic solutions. Certainly, four of the families suffered extreme poverty. The officer, however, was ignoring the fifth family, that of the "new millionaire." The Castro family, like the other four, was need-ridden, miserable, and vulnerable. Money had not solved their problems.

Economic remedies, however desperately needed, are not panaceas for human problems. Social casework, however skilled, is not designed to meet the whole range of human need. Casework has not usually been taught or practiced as though it were the total answer, but this has sometimes been the received message. Students still dichotomize social reconstruction and individual treatment as either-or propositions, disregarding their complementarity as differentiated social and professional responses to need.

For these reasons, a presentation of practice theory must identify the context and range in which practice is expected to be effective. Gladwin[2] has set forth three strategies to deal with problems of poverty: (1) changes in deep-seated attitudes and values held by society at large; (2) new expectations, behaviors, and skills to be learned by the poor whose life styles are at issue; and (3) extensive alterations in the economic and political structure so that newly opened avenues of opportunity will remain open in the future.

The specific role of social caseworkers employing a practice model based on adult socialization theory would be concerned with the second of these strategies: teaching new be-

Elizabeth McBroom is professor of social work, School of Social Work, University of Southern California, Los Angeles.
1. Oscar Lewis, *Five Families: Mexican Case Studies in the Culture of Poverty* (New York: Basic Books, 1959).
2. Thomas Gladwin, *Poverty USA* (Boston: Little, Brown and Company, 1967), p. 15.

haviors, attitudes, and skills. Gladwin's address is to the poor whose life styles are at issue. In addition to the poor, there are other groups of adults whose life styles are at issue as they face new demands associated with changes in the self and altered relationships in their social networks.

Many of these challenges will be met with personal and family resources already available. For others, professional help will increase the probability of preventing damage, preserving human values, and extending opportunity. The professional help occurs not in a vacuum, but in relation to attitudes and values held by society at large and to opportunities established by the economic and political system. The commitment of social caseworkers is to develop theory and practice for helping those who need individual aid to be able to function in full human dignity. Presumably, their numbers will decrease when basic income and social opportunity are guaranteed for all.

SOCIALIZATION THEORY AND CASEWORK PRACTICE

A beginning point in extending theory lies in relating it to the already accepted and tested body of knowledge. Here is a dilemma by no means unique to social work. Grinker,[3] who undertook to summarize conceptual progress in psychoanalysis up to 1968, stated that a criterion for preparing to describe any frontier was the assumption that the main body or consolidated area could be defined as structure and process in development. He found, however, no coherent package of psychoanalytic theory: the literature confused rather than clarified definitive trends, and discarded concepts were viewed as integral, rather than historical; the jump-steps of progress were difficult to follow, and some ideas had appeared ahead of their time. For a discipline to advance from movement to science, he maintained, it is necessary to identify and learn from error and to value capacity for change. In social work, the same self-evaluation and open-

3. Roy R. Grinker, Sr., "Conceptual Progress in Psychoanalysis," in *Modern Psychoanalysis*, ed. Judd Marmor (New York: Basic Books, 1968), pp. 19–20.

ness are called for to improve the record of the profession in serving populations at risk.

The exploration of socialization theory has been stimulated by professional and public concern with the extent of family dysfunction found in mass social welfare programs, especially public assistance, probation, and social service departments in public hospitals. Social casework has had relatively small influence on these client populations. Problems persist and multiply from generation to generation. The numbers of skilled workers have never been adequate to the volume of the task. In addition, traditional psychotherapeutic techniques have proved to be poorly adapted to problems of these families.[4]

During the sixties the profession has made a concerted effort to extend knowledge and develop appropriate new techniques, and to reorganize professional education in order to disseminate relevant knowledge and skills more widely. Adult socialization theory, with a rich interdisciplinary scholarship directed to understanding personal change through social interaction, has offered one potential for extension of practice knowledge. To date, the theoretical contributions have been virtually untapped in social work. Their fit and usefulness in underpinning practice remain untested.[5]

---

4. Rudolph and Cumming presented a persuasive account of this dilemma based on their community survey in New York State. (Claire Rudolph and John Cumming, "Where Are Additional Psychiatric Services Most Needed?" *Social Work* 7 [1962]:15–20.)

5. I have undertaken one study and reported additional observations. (Elizabeth McBroom, "A Comparative Analysis of Social Work Interventions in Two Types of AFDC Families," Doctoral dissertation, University of California, Berkeley, 1965; "Helping AFDC Families: A Comparative Study," *Social Service Review* 39 [1965]:390–98; *Adult Socialization: A Basis for Public Assistance Practice* [Sacramento, Calif.: Department of Social Welfare, 1966]; "The Socialization of Parents," *Child Welfare* 46 [1967]:132–36; "Social Workers as Agents of Socialization," paper read at Student-Alumni Meeting, 1968, School of Social Service Administration, University of Chicago.) Louise Bandler described social work in Boston's North Point project under the title, "Casework: A Process of Socialization," in *The Drifters,* ed. Eleanor Pavenstedt (Boston: Little, Brown and Company, 1968).

An essay by Lippitt, in a recent publication of the Social Science Research Council, deals with socialization agents and agencies, problems,

A coherent "package" of theory specifically related to social work practice is not available. However, one means for extending existing theory that promises to explain dynamics and advance the understanding of process is to use it as a guide to practice and to evaluate its effectiveness in achieving the declared purpose. Social workers who have made tentative efforts to test concepts of adult socialization in practice or training have reported, for example: "I operated many times on a pragmatic basis, and had not been aware that I was hewing to anything as reassuring as a theory," or "The concrete helping acts necessary to practice need to be sanctioned. They are valid in meeting the professional demand to be fully helpful."

The essential philosophical or ethical rationale for socialization was set forth by Clausen,[6] who pointed out that human society depends on some consensus about present and emergent goals and the means for achieving them, that society is possible only as individuals willingly accept the ways of their groups and continues only as members do what they must do to make society function. Social norms, in Clausen's view, are neither monolithic nor coercive; indeed innovative behavior is demanded. The concept of socialization emphasizes acquisition of knowledge of self and others in social interaction rather than universal requirements or demands made on individuals by society.

Merton,[7] who used the concept of adult socialization to analyze the social process by which a medical student becomes a physician, defined socialization as "the process by which people selectively acquire the values and attitudes, the interests, skills, and knowledge—in short, the culture—current in the groups of which they are, or seek to become, members. . . . Socialization takes place primarily through social interaction with people who are significant for the individ-

---

and practice. He mentions the recreation association, leisure time programs, socialization engineers, social practice, and group workers, but not social casework or social workers. See Ronald Lippett, "Improving the Socialization Process," in *Socialization and Society*, ed. John A. Clausen (Boston: Little, Brown and Company, 1968).

6. Clausen, *Socialization and Society*, p. 6.

7. Robert K. Merton et al., eds., *The Student Physician* (Cambridge: Harvard University Press, 1957), p. 287.

ual." Parsons[8] maintained that the socialization process involves reward and punishment[9] by a socializing agent who adopts the role of teacher and becomes an active model for imitation. Attitudes, as well as discrete acts, are crucial. An indispensable condition is that the recruit acquire a stake in the favorable attitudes and approval of the socializing agent.

Studies of child-rearing conceptualized as a process of socialization have analyzed parent-child transactions with the parent in the role of socializing agent and the child as a recruit to be socialized to important roles in his social group. Operationalizing the model for social work practice with adults involves viewing the worker as agent of socialization and the agency as a nontotal institution[10] that serves as a setting for developmental socialization (normative for the client's age-stage), compensatory socialization (role learning missed because opportunities—including agents or models—were not available at the appropriate age-stage), and resocialization (efforts to alter deviant behavior).

The process of socialization is conventionally analyzed by identifying agent, aim, techniques, timing, and transition rituals. In a casework model, the worker is the agent and the aim is enhancement of the client's competence to function in family, work, or community groups. The worker, therefore, helps him to acquire behaviors adequate to the demands of his social roles. Major techniques are teaching, modeling, inviting participation, giving feedback, and enlisting cooperation. The client would be internalizing new expectations, developing new self-conceptions, observing, participating, and taking roles. He would be aware of the role of the worker as a socializing agent, and motivated as actor in the process (in contrast to being a passive recipient of care).

The worker perceives the client (or the client presents himself to the worker) as unprepared for the performance

---

8. Talcott Parsons, *The Social System* (Glencoe, Ill.: Free Press, 1951), p. 205.

9. The terms "reward" and "punishment" have been almost entirely supplanted by the concept of feedback, the information and aids to self-evaluation that come from others as results of one's actions.

10. Some caseworkers practice in total institutions (mental hospitals, prisons).

of an adequate repertoire of adult roles in his society. The worker, as agent of socialization, is active in providing alternative opportunities, giving explicit explanations, providing feedback on client's response and performance, and offering himself freely and consciously as a model for identification.

To summarize, the socialization model for casework practice has been conceptualized as follows: The focus of change is the client's self-concept, internalized values, behaviors inadequate to social role, and expectations of self and others. The milieu must provide opportunities to improve role performance and interact in new kinds of situations. The worker, taking the role of "socializing agent," actively teaches, models, and invites participation. Communication is explicit. Feedback and consensus on meaning are essential. Mutual responsibilities and expectations are defined. The client is perceived to be suffering because of limited opportunities for role performance. The worker helps actively toward the explicit goal of the client's accelerated learning and competence in adult social roles.

The worker functions as a change agent. Knowledge is incomplete about how the worker's interventions articulate with different problems in families served. The effort of preliminary analysis has been to identify "bridging concepts" between personality theory and practice theory when the *major* problem focus is perceived as inadequate opportunities for social role learning in the client's past or present social network.

MAJOR SOURCES IN BEHAVIORAL SCIENCE THEORY

Socialization theory has developed in the United States mainly within the social science disciplines of anthropology, psychology, and sociology.[11] Specific aspects of role-learning have been studied as facets of a larger social process which

---

11. John A. Clausen has presented "A Historical and Comparative View of Socialization Theory and Research" in the recent volume of papers written by members of the Committee on Socialization and Social Structure of the Social Science Research Council. (Clausen, *Socialization and Society*, pp. 18–72.)

includes all child-rearing and all education. In the currently accepted sense of the term, derived from studies of behaviorism, education, empirical research in sociology, and influences from anthropology, the focus is on social development of the person, with socialization as an organizing principle. It is usually taken to mean the processes of training a human being for social participation in his group. These processes involve his incorporating the group's beliefs and customs. Broadly, therefore, it is the acquisition of knowledge of self and others in social interaction,[12] the process by which the human being attains his most fully human potential and level of functioning.

A central concept of socialization theory is the concept of the self. George Herbert Mead's influence was "sharply directed to basic aspects of socialization—to the rise of meaning and of selfhood in the process of social interaction."[13] Erikson's epigenetic model presents realistic self-esteem as a result of the many development steps in which physical mastery coincides with cultural meaning and functional pleasure with social recognition.[14]

Behavioral scientists are extending knowledge of cognitive processes and applying principles of organization, purpose, differentiation, growth, communication, and control to the study of living organisms. Under the broad umbrella of system theory, this approach takes in the idea of self-regulation as the core of human conduct. The source of these ideas is found in the writings of John Dewey and George Herbert Mead. Mead conceptualized behavior as a series of self-correcting adjustments to changing life conditions. Modern theorists are rediscovering the cogency of connecting human motivation with the course of events or a general direction

---

12. Ibid., p. 47.

13. Anselm Strauss, in his introduction to a recent edition of Mead's writing, argues that Merton and Parsons, functionalist theorists in sociology, made a restricted selection from Mead's writing which pertained mainly to self-control as a reflection of social control and was much less dynamic than Mead's treatment of the self as a process. George Herbert Mead, *On Social Psychology* (Chicago: University of Chicago Press, 1964), p. xii.

14. Erik H. Erikson, *Identity: Youth and Crisis* (New York: W. W. Norton and Company, 1968), p. 49.

of human conduct, rather than remaining preoccupied with isolated incidents.[15]

An understanding of these aspects of human behavior and this theoretical framework has important developmental aspects. Recent studies of child development emphasize that the cognitive aspects are inseparable from overall maturation and the personal and social skills for living which have been labeled functions of the ego.[16] These approaches are in accord with a social learning theory of personality which takes into account goal-setting and expectancy, related to motivation in which there is realistic hope for success.

In recent years system theory has become basic in social science research and interdisciplinary communication. The system theory concept of feedback, in the context of socialization, would apply to making a person aware of how his actions affect other people and giving him guidance for the control of acts that lead to failure. Autonomy depends on feedback. Otherwise, the person is at the mercy of drift, impulse, and external controls. In this light, conduct is viewed as depending on the individual's responses to inner states, perceptions, reactions of others, and his own reactions as he moves into novel experiences and seeks new solutions. All purposeful and self-correcting behavior requires feedback which results in new information and thus makes possible modification of behavior. Success reinforces patterns which become the basis for values. Prolonged and persistent failure leads to alienation and dysfunction. It is also recognized that many objectives as well as many gratifications are interpersonal rather than individual.[17]

Grinker[18] has pointed out that in classical psychoanalysis personality was originally regarded as an integrated, open, biopsychosocial system with components and determinants which were biological, psychological, and social. Contemporary psychoanalysts also recognize the person as a biologi-

15. Tamotsu Shibutoni, "A Cybernetic Approach to Motivation," in *Modern Systems Research for the Behavioral Scientist,* ed. Walter Buckley (Chicago: Aldine Publishing Company, 1968), p. 330.
16. Eleanor Pavenstedt, ed., *The Drifters: Children of Disorganized Lower-Class Families* (Boston: Little, Brown and Company, 1967), p. 5.
17. Shibutoni, "A Cybernetic Approach," p. 333.
18. Grinker, "Conceptual Progress," p. 21.

cal system in transaction with the environment and with potentials which are adaptive to reality and which prepare him for an average expectable environment. The prototype for the biological processes is the recently discovered principle in molecular biology that information is coded, transmitted, and encoded, and that man behaves in accordance with the basic concepts of information and control which characterize system theory.[19] The human organism shares fundamental aspects of all organized systems: being or structure; acting, behavior, or function; and becoming or development.

Further, many psychologists have pointed out that the developing person is motivated by the feedback he gets about the environmental consequences of his own action. This is not a one-way process; the person is active—not merely reactive—in his participation and interaction with his environment.

Applying the biological concept of information to studies of development would dictate search for distortions in the ways in which information is communicated to the developing child. For example, actions and reactions of infant and mother establish a transactional feedback relationship which is at first symbiotic, but later operates between separated organisms. In this relationship, the mother is influenced by her own personality, ethnicity, and culture values, and has her own problems. She is moved toward the mother role by her baby's needs, but personal, social, and material resources may be deficient. In such instances, learning through new identifications may become an important factor in her adaptation.[20]

Understanding the processes of growth and development is essential to socialization theory. Adult socialization is primarily concerned with the study of behavior and the possibilities of behavioral change when chronological maturity is reached and growth has stopped or slowed; that is, with changes in the self after childhood, in different settings, and in response to changes in those in reciprocal roles.[21] Psycho-

---

19. Ibid., p. 25.
20. Ibid., p. 29.
21. Howard S. Becker, "The Self and Adult Socialization," in *The Study*

analysis, too, is directing more study to behavior, since behavior reveals the needs, problems, and dilemmas of the person in action.[22]

Social scientists in the War on Poverty have pushed to find ways for all citizens to become capable of full participation in society. They have devoted much attention to the concept of competence and have identified this particular quality as the outcome, or goal, of socialization.

Competence has a biopsychological basis in the organism which influences development from infancy. The sociological concept, however, refers to the ways in which the individual participates in communication in his social systems. Smith[23] identified the important area of study in socialization as the ways in which the gap between the organic basis and social aspects of competence may be bridged with explicit conceptual links as well as evidence from empirical research.

A basic assumption about competence is that a core of interrelated personal attributes plays a crucial role in determining how effectively each person interacts with his environment. Developmental progress or deficit proceeds in circles that tend to be cumulative in benign or malignant effects. This is the contemporary view of causation, in contrast to an effort to isolate or pinpoint clear-cut effects of single causes. In other words, once the individual is launched on a given trajectory, either success or failure tends to be cumulative, and the problem of intervention is often to correct the course of that trajectory. Current investigators conceptualize the normative course of development as progression from a primarily impulsive orientation, through an opportunistic or conformist one, to an orientation that is conscientious, autonomous, and integrative.[24]

In summary, socialization theory is derived from sociology, social psychology, and anthropology, and from the current work in all behavioral science on system and communica-

of Personality: An Interdisciplinary Appraisal, ed. Edward Norbeck et al. (New York: Holt, Rinehart and Winston, 1968), p. 197.

22. Grinker, "Conceptual Progress," p. 34.

23. M. Brewster Smith, "Competence and Socialization," in Clausen, Socialization and Society, p. 277.

24. Ibid., p. 278.

tions theory. Major sources are found in the formulations of George Herbert Mead[25] on social development of the self in interaction with others, and in the current work of those who have built on Mead's theories. Concepts of role-learning and the goal of social competence represent major aspects of the theory. It is assumed that the demands of society are not monolithic, the goals are always emergent, and the adult is active and innovative as well as being reactive.

The knowledge most directly relevant to social work practice includes an understanding of adult identities and role functions, and criteria for observing and assessing cognitive and affective patterns in relation to family life styles. Interventive activity demands an understanding of the processes of change in adult life, the effects of interpersonal influences and gratification on role-learning, and the effects of differential resources and opportunities in social networks.

CANDIDATES FOR ADULT SOCIALIZATION

Adult socialization has been described as the process of teaching and learning social roles, with increased social competence as the goal. Clients, therefore, will be men and women whose limited opportunities for learning any given role have impaired current function so seriously as to produce problems for self and others, including life styles which fail to meet the needs of family members. The social roles may be those that all adults are expected to assume as members of work groups, families, and communities. They may also be special roles dictated by social change, individual loss of function, or increased opportunity.

Social casework based on adult socialization theory has been tried principally in families in which parents have multiple difficulties in carrying out their responsibilities. The family is conceptualized as a social system (specifically a small group) functionally related to external systems and to its individual members. Interrelated changes in structure and function occur over time and with changes in the external systems and the family's relationship to them. As the nuclear family replaces the extended kinship group, individual re-

25. Mead, *On Social Psychology.*

sponsibility for certain functions, including infant care and management of tensions, increases. The family also has an important new responsibility: maintaining relationships with the social institutions which carry out those economic, educational, and other functions which families formerly performed directly.[26]

Lack of competence or failure to fulfill these responsibilities is the concern of social work, as is attested by the volume of professional literature which attempts to explain the etiology of family problems and suggest appropriate treatments. Parsons[27] saw a possible historical trend toward disorganization of the family as a social system. Such a trend seems also to characterize certain individual family cycles. The tendency toward disorganization may be explained in part as the response to psychological stress identified by Horvath:[28] a decrement in goal-oriented behavior, marked by confusion and inappropriate activity. Later stages bring impairments in function. This describes the multiproblem family in which there has been progressive deterioration and discouragement to a stage of exhaustion, with depleted motivation for adequate performance in family roles. Many families known to social agencies have long histories of poverty with related handicaps: physical neglect, poor self-image, social isolation, limited school attendance and marginal literacy, lack of work skills, and chronic or recurrent unemployment.

Stein[29] identified as a common factor in troubled families in the North Point project the lack of generational differentiation between parents and children: parents related to their children on a sibling or rival basis; they were impulsive, punitive, unable to teach, discipline, or differentiate among their children. He attributed the most serious and

---

26. Norman M. Bell and Ezra F. Vogel, "Toward a Framework for Functional Analysis of Family Behavior," in *A Modern Introduction to the Family,* ed. Norman W. Bell and Ezra F. Vogel (Glencoe, Ill.: Free Press, 1960), p. 7.

27. Parsons, *Social System,* p. 3.

28. Fred E. Horvath, "Psychological Stress: A Review of Definitions and Experimental Research," *General Systems* 4 (1959):209.

29. Maurice R. Stein, "Sociocultural Perspectives on the Neighborhood and the Families," in Pavenstedt, *Drifters,* p. 312.

persistent dysfunction to this lack and believed that it also served as an indicator of dysfunctioning families in all types of societies.[30]

The following sections on the beginning phase, diagnosis, and treatment are principally concerned with describing caseworkers' activities (and the underlying rationales) in identifying, engaging with, and helping families characterized by the difficulties outlined above.

THE INITIAL ENCOUNTER

The initial encounter in the socialization approach, which is limited to the first contact rather than the several interviews of the traditional beginning phase, has two possible positive goals: further engagement, if indicated, or mutual decision (involving minimal rationalization) that further engagement is not indicated.

The first encounter is crucial, and the emphasis is on prompt and timely activity, because a sluggish or delayed response can in itself be frustrating to the client whose need is urgent. From this first contact, moreover, worker and client have a need for mutual feedback that will affirm that they have in fact made a start on a vital connection with each other, that they have embarked on a potentially helpful or useful enterprise which will be furthered in ensuing encounters.

Efforts of professional workers to engage the most deprived families in casework treatment have not been marked by extensive success. In fact, several recent research and demonstration projects have taken as their starting point groups of families abandoned as "hopeless" by established commu-

---

30. Further evidence is suggested in a recent study which found that the most seriously disturbed youth from upper- and middle-class families were those whose parents, failing "to preserve the essential asymmetry and the indelible generational separation," had placed them in a peer relationship or made them, during childhood, unwilling confidantes or witnesses of their own sexual or marital difficulties. Fads and misinterpretations of personality theory had contributed to confusion, permissiveness, and parental insecurity. Thomas J. Cottle, "Parent and Child: The Hazards of Equality," *Saturday Review of Literature* (1 Feb. 1969):17.

nity agencies after more or less heroic efforts to involve them in change. The negative outcome of an unsuccessful first meeting is a barrier to continuance despite evidence or conviction of a family's need for a type of help which worker and agency are prepared and expected to extend. The result is frustration (for client, worker, agency, and community). The client experiences alienation or discouragement because he has experienced another disappointment or failure. This section undertakes to set forth those insights, attitudes, conditions, and acts which will extend chances for the favorable outcome.

Socialization theory suggests some techniques that promise special usefulness for the initial phase. If the "target" is an adult who is unsocialized to his parental role and therefore relates to his children defensively as a peer or rival, the social worker acting as an agent of socialization meets him at this level of need. The extremely deprived parent, as Pavenstedt[31] has noted, is need-oriented; he understands the concrete but not the abstract, and acts mean more than words to him. The need for feedback is immediate, the capacity for delayed gratification (related to an impaired sense of trust) is low. Relationship is established by *active* response to client's requests and by explicit communication of acceptance: those words and deeds which say plainly to the client, "You are a valuable person with dignity that is your very own. I listen and respond to you. You really can trust me and the agency I represent to carry out our contract, to keep our promises, and to promise all we can." This message acknowledges that the individual is important to society in his own right and status as an adult, as well as in his role as parent.

Since trust is an early achievement of human development, it may be assumed that those who survive and function even minimally have begun to establish trust and can develop further. Such rudimentary or impaired trust has often occurred in family settings and social environments where trusting was unrealistic and sometimes dangerous, and future expectations were low. The initial phase, therefore, involves relating to and building on elementary trust. A rapid focus on the problem, with direct engagement of the client through

---

31. Pavenstedt, *Drifters*, p. 38.

active explanations and straightforward answers, communicates interest and concern. This means that the worker takes a position, rather than merely reflecting or absorbing the client's feelings. He lets the client know exactly who he is and what is the purpose of his contact. Early encounters are likely to entail sharing personal experiences and exchanging information to support the feeling of genuine acceptance which helps to make the initial encounter the beginning of a mutually defined undertaking rather than an abortive, mutually frustrating ending.

Bandler[32] found that once the relationship of trust had been established, the worker could proceed to help families establish a priority of problems to bring more order to their lives. Through this process, the worker provided feedback by reaction and response, and by use of language to name, identify, categorize, and explain. He helped the client to recognize what was important, immediate, and feasible. He gave for real needs and crises. The joint endeavor of worker and client became a form of reality testing in which the client gained increased ability to discriminate.

The question has been raised, Does the worker who moves too fast in the initial phase lose the client? Sensitive timing is a reflection of empathy with the client's need and capacity which is of highest importance. Workers can and do confuse clients by racing ahead of them, but many clients have also been lost in the initial phase by discouragement because "nothing happened." The principle invoked involves starting where the client is, but with the assumption that he wants and needs to participate more competently in his social network. Perception of the family system as the primary target, as well as recent additions to knowledge of child development which explain irreversible damage by failure of imprinting at critical stages in deprived environments, suggest a new urgency for timeliness in casework treatment.[33] Re-

32. Louise S. Bandler, "Casework: A Process of Socialization," in Pavenstedt, *Drifters*, p. 263.
33. Ambrose maintains that there are good grounds for the hypothesis, yet to be tested, that there is an early critical period (from the fifth to twelfth week of life for family infants, fifth to eighteenth week for institutional infants) in the development of the human infant's social responsiveness. J. A. Ambrose, "The Concept of a Critical Period for the

ports (as in child guidance literature) of gains in the "third treatment year" may be already too late. The social worker with the deprived family is dealing with life styles and capacities. His concern is to start immediately and build toward protective, nurturant, concerned, effective, and appropriately stimulating parenting. This is a cumulative process in which early perceptible results hearten both worker and client family for the long pull.

This all indicates experimentation and innovative ways of reaching the families, without undue anxiety about norms and constraints of traditional professional roles. Giving the client a concrete experience of active help may be the most important way to communicate with him. Bandler[34] describes adaptations of technique to achieve initial involvement. These are usually carried out in the home with the worker participating in activities, virtually as a member of the family, finding the basis for return in the parents' immediate realistic need, and moving toward a solution of the problem before identifying it.

Many effective techniques have been used but not reported in social work literature. Rudolph and Cumming[35] recommend close attention to the successes of untrained workers in public assistance who helped to stabilize troubled families. Some of their techniques fit into a socialization framework and will become available for theory-building and training programs when they are identified, conceptualized, and tied to their rationales, so that they can be evaluated according to purpose and outcomes.

The development of techniques, however, is not the most difficult task. All techniques are used in the context of relationship. In a more general observation, Brim[36] has noted that it is a human relationship, with information, emotional support, and expectations, that encourages and stabilizes an

Development of Social Responsiveness in Early Human Infancy," in *Determinants of Infant Behavior II*, ed. Brian Foss (London: Methuen and Company, 1963), pp. 201–25.

34. Bandler, "Casework: A Process of Socialization," p. 260.

35. Rudolph and Cumming, "Where Are Additional Psychiatric Services Most Needed?"

36. Orville G. Brim, Jr., "Adult Socialization," in Clausen, *Socialization and Society*, p. 194.

adult's own efforts to change. In social casework, the essential problem is to meet need with timeliness and adequacy—even generosity—and with direct, effective communication that makes regard for the person and intent to help unmistakable to the client from the first moment of encounter.

ASSESSMENT OF THE CLIENT IN HIS SETTING

Diagnosis, most broadly, locates the client in his milieu, accounts for that location, and assesses the chances for movement or change. It identifies sources of stress, coping modes, and potentials. It explores the frustration that arises from expectations which are not supported by resources for achievement. Extremes of frustration are experienced as futility, a common syndrome in the client groups with whom this paper is concerned. A more serious condition from the standpoint of potential for change is the client who has formed no expectations, or who has abandoned expectations formerly held.

Bruck[37] notes that locating the individual in his culture involves an evaluation of the total social environment, including the supports or reinforcements that are available or may be brought into play.

Since the client's social competence is the end in view, the diagnosis would evaluate or grade his competence, or undertake to identify specific roles in which his incompetence creates problems. Exact scales for competence have not been developed. Competence, though complex, can be analyzed by partializing overall functioning and assessing performance in major social roles. The deficits can then be examined in relation to barriers to competent functioning (internal and external) with consideration of how worker and client might deal with the barriers. In other words, if multiple role deficiencies are apparent, it is necessary to select specific roles as high priorities. These are usually related to "islands of competence" that can be extended by enlarging the repertoire of attitudes and behavioral skills for performance, especially in certain roles which will bring immediate rewards from family and community.

---

37. Max Bruck, "Behavior Modification Theory and Practice: A Critical Review," *Social Work* 13 (1968):44.

Brewster Smith[38] has offered an interesting analysis of the "incompetence syndrome" as manifested in many children who grow up in colony, ghetto, or slum. Their attitudes that work does not bring success and that they are foredoomed are firmly based in past experience and social reality. The failure of these children to attain competence because they have not had sufficient positive encounter with their milieu is a social loss that leads to mounting social crisis and, if not checked, to the decay of open society. This problem is not encountered in simpler societies where there is more equal opportunity and ritual support that insures every individual a sense of his own worth. The most deprived members of contemporary urban society exist at a near jungle level where it would be foolish to trust others, and where self-respect is difficult to achieve. Thus, the pattern is set for a fatalistic attitude toward one's own endeavors and their consequences, and for snatching instant gratification.

Smith has described the developmental experience of many parents. As Bandler observes,[39] their deficits in experience, education, personality, and community connections make them unable to take the adult role or serve as models to their children. This group represents severe deficiency in the repertoire of attitudes and behaviors they bring to learning the parental role. She reports that response to the initial meeting of basic needs is an important diagnostic differential between those mothers who could develop more mature behavior when reality needs are met and schizophrenic mothers in whom narcissism is essentially fixated and repressed.

Roberts[40] has suggested an ordinal rank for diagnostic classification of adults with deficient socialization: the unsocialized, who were severely neglected and deprived as children, and who consequently internalized few social values and have poor control of impulse; the inadequately socialized; and those adequately socialized to a subculture in which they learned to carry specific roles which are dysfunctional for themselves or for other family members in their present social setting.

---

38. Smith, "Competence and Socialization," p. 287.
39. Bandler, "Family Functioning," p. 231.
40. Robert W. Roberts, personal communication, June 1968.

The unsocialized in this classification scheme are those without basic trust, lacking, in Bandler's terms, "islands or vestiges of intact ego functioning from all developmental phases."[41] This diagnosis can be made on the basis of history, plus current life style and response to helping efforts. An example is Mrs. Glenn, age thirty-five. She has been diagnosed as diabetic, uncontrolled, and suffers periodic comas associated with excessive intake of alcohol. She was abandoned by her parents at age three and grew up in a succession of "orphanages" and reform schools. Her school attendance was irregular, and she did not attain functional literacy. She lives with her three single teenage daughters and five small grandchildren in a house virtually devoid of furniture. There are no routines of care or feeding, and the children are usually crying or apathetic. Mrs. Glenn's behavior is destructive of self and others, antagonistic to family members and to would-be family helpers. She is unmotivated for self-care, and shows rapid physical and mental deterioration. The extreme unsocialized state is often correlated with or complemented by emotional disturbance, or mental retardation, growing out of the same developmental experiences.

The inadequately socialized would be prime targets for what has been termed compensatory socialization; this category includes persons who have missed the teaching and opportunities to learn from adequate role models that normally occur earlier in life as part of the gradual preparation for adult status and social roles. They have some capacity and motivation for current learning and can improve role performance and take on new attitudes and values as a result of efforts. The consistent help of a socializing agent becomes important to them, provided that there are adequate instrumental and material supports for achieving competence.

As suggested earlier, diagnosis takes into account both persons as actors and the adequacy of their external resources. Diagnosis of the person is more precise after the environment has been stabilized. In any case, diagnosis focuses on the interplay between problem behavior and the range of generating conditions. It also involves agreement on specific be-

---

41. Bandler, "Family Functioning," p. 251.

havioral indicators of favored global constructs (rejection, dependency, weak ego). Bruck[42] makes the point that specification of behavioral indicators increases clarity of communication, helps identify the problem to be treated, and suggests ordering of priorities and selection of treatment techniques.

Another facet of differential diagnosis is impairment of parenting in relation to the age of the child. It is now recognized that parents have different capacities, probably associated with their own socialization experience, for relating to and sustaining successive stages of child development. The severest parental disturbance (the most "unnatural") leads to neglect or active abuse of the small infant. The growing child and competitive, emancipating adolescent put increasing demands on the parent's maturity and on his ability to deal with his own frustrations and aggressions and to find gratifications in the development of the child as a separate, autonomous, and unique new individual.

Brim[43] notes that the rates of certain social events are indicators of man's relationship to society and of strains or failures in that relationship. The incidence of divorce, suicide, illness, alcoholism, school failure, crime and delinquency, truancy, desertion, and neglect also serve as diagnostic indicators within a given family.

History furnishes additional indicators. It is important to know to what extent the parent had opportunities to function as part of his family of orientation, how consistent were the role relationships, and how gratifying was the interaction.

The response to current opportunity is an important point of diagnosis. For example, responses to the worker's modeling may be indicators of an individual's capacity for control and flexibility, discrimination and self-perception, and therefore of his potential for growth and change. The client's use of the worker as model should be both selective and temporary, as a means toward the end of autonomy.

Since the concerns of this particular scheme of assessment is with life styles and efforts to initiate life style changes, several crucial "maintenance" questions must be answered:

42. Bruck, "Behavior Modification Theory," p. 53.
43. Brim, "Adult Socialization," p. 206.

What maintains the given life style? (Are there gratifications involved that can be identified, or is there no escape? What "mix" of these two influences has developed over time?)
Can actual dangers involved in continuing this life style be identified?

Finally, if a worker takes a teaching role with client, the question of educational diagnosis arises. Short of a formal, assembled test, the worker may need more dependable and standardized tools for assessing a client's learning power, pattern, and problems, and the "disabling" gaps in normative learning.

The considerations which enter into casework diagnosis related to socialization theory as discussed in this section are summarized below. This diagnostic classification is a hypothetical formulation as yet unsupported by systematic observation or correlated with treatments. Diagnostic indicators include history, location in milieu, environmental supports, stress sources, role deficits and coping modes (including parental competence by child's age-stage), and factors maintaining current life style.

1. *Unsocialized.* The parents (or single parent in a family with serial transient mates or substitute parental figures) have had minimal family and social opportunities, lifelong. They are distrustful, functionally illiterate, have major health problems (usually associated with neglect), are isolated or unrelated to neighbors, do not use health or educational resources, and respond to children on a competitive peer level. There is possible ability for nurturant care of infants, but stimulation is usually inappropriate. There is intolerance of autonomy strivings at toddler age, combined with inability or indifference toward training. The household is chaotic; children are neglected, are often ill, and attend school irregularly. The family appears to be in a "no exit" situation because of cumulative developmental and situational deficits which impair competence, make the family unacceptable in the immediate milieu (neighbors are concerned for the children's safety or survival), and frustrate professsional helping efforts.

2. *Inadequately socialized.*[44] There is more stability of

---

44. There are probably few "optimally socialized adults," and "over-

family structure than in group one. (For example, two parents are present during significant periods of the children's development; or the single parent or substitute parental figures demonstrate potential or competence in parental roles.) The family has some (possibly sympathetic or "grudging") acceptance in the neighborhood and school. The parents have functional literacy or can compensate for its lack. They hold and can express expectations for children's achievement, though expectations may be unrealistic and unrelated to daily behavior of parents or children. They can learn and carry out adequate care and response with infants and preschool children and make use of resources, if available. The development of the parents may have held many deficits, but damage is not so severe as to prevent relationship, response, and new behavioral learning. They are able to perceive and use feedback from community and professional helpers, and to trust and use the worker as a model.

3. *Socialized to specific subculture.* The family is migrant: especially rural to urban, or South to North or West.[45] Family roles, adequate to other expectations and opportunities, become inadequate. The family takes little initiative to find or use opportunities designed to help them adapt to changes in social or economic circumstances. Expectations and hopes are low. Mobility and the demands of a new subculture may increase family strains. (For example: the father, lacking minimal skills for employment in urban industry and past the age for training programs, deserts the family.) The family does not protect against new dangers or alter its life style to adapt to the new milieu. In large numbers of client families, the polarization of social and economic classes makes socialization to the most deprived group increasingly dysfunctional for children who will be expected to fill complex social roles.

---

socialization" is dangerous and undesirable. The focus of *social* concern is role performance so inadequate as to be prejudicial to the client's safety or self-esteem or to the development of others, especially children or other dependent family members.

45. Harriette Arnow presented a moving fictional account of a family destroyed in the move from a subsistence Appalachian farm to the inflating economy and harsh living of wartime Detroit. Harriette S. Arnow, *The Dollmaker* (New York: Macmillan Company, 1954).

THE SOCIAL CASEWORK PROCESS AS SOCIALIZATION FOR COMPETENCE

Caseworker and client never embark on a course of intended change in a social vacuum. Before beginning to define, describe, rationalize, and project the intended results of the dyadic transactions, it should be repeated that immediate and remote systems impinge and partly determine outcomes. The method employed[46] is continuously in interaction with personality characteristics *and* with the social conditions under which the effort at change is made.

This section outlines direct, face-to-face procedures of the social caseworker intended to change the attitudes and behaviors of clients. The major focus is on work with families who present deficits sometimes carried over from one generation to another, those who have not been able to escape from one generation to another, and those who have not been able to escape from the entrapments of social neglect and resulting debilities. It is therefore assumed that parallel efforts at social change are extending conditions under which all persons can pursue their own development, and that such changes in the social environment will make possible experience in the real world that will reward effort. Work with the individual should enable him to maximize his opportunities. An underlying assumption is that opportunities will be available or that the individual will acquire the skills and motivation to join with others in creating them. The attitudes of hope and self-respect essential for competence are fostered in the worker-client relationship. They are maintained only as the client perceives evidence of the respect he wins in the wider world, and as opportunity and shared power makes his hopes realistic.[47]

Socialization has been considered an interpersonal process leading to the goal of competence, and competence has been considered adequate performance in the roles one is expected to fill, or to which one aspires. In work roles, this usually means meeting competitive demands in urban industrial

---

46. Brim, "Adult Socialization," p. 187.
47. Smith, "Competence and Socialization," p. 313.

society. In family roles, it means giving protective, nurturant, appropriately stimulating care to children, especially in the preschool years, and ensuring use of schools and other major social institutions. It also means meeting physical, expressive, and certain social needs of adult family members.

If the role of social worker is conceptualized as agent of socialization, it is, like the teacher and parent roles which are prototypes, characterized by activity, nurture, stimulation, setting of explicit expectations, providing feedback on performance, and modeling.

In the parental role, the caseworker accepts the client, conveys acceptance outspokenly as well as by the range of responses which communicate feeling, and limits behavior by direct feedback. In his warm acceptance of the person, he fills the expressive parental role; in modeling skills, attitudes, and behaviors necessary to function in the wider society, he is acting in the instrumental parent role.

A teaching or educational function has at times been depreciated or considered inappropriate for the caseworker. This was congruent with interpretations of a personality theory which placed almost exclusive emphasis on man as a feeling or sentient being, and compartmentalized or relegated to formal institutions of instruction and control direct concern with man as thinker and actor. Since all helping professions today address themselves more responsibly and knowledgeably to the whole person, there is less fear of "overintellectualizing." Lack of knowledge is recognized as a contributing cause of incompetence. The caseworker deals with lack of knowledge by teaching his client how to attain and perform in varied social roles, by teaching new expectations and behaviors. The teaching task involves presenting information at appropriate language levels, and acknowledging the client's gains promptly and generously.

The significance of the worker as teacher and the client's trust in him are central to continuance and enlargement of the undertaking: internalizing of new expectations and confidence, maximum autonomy, and innovation on the part of the client. This is essential to the client's self-actualization because competence in the modern world means ability to cope with change rather than with the status quo. A range of cognitive and communication skills are necessary for coping with change.

The content of role-teaching and role-learning has numerous variations in specific situations; for example, different age-stages of children imply differential expectations and responsibilities of parents; adaptations are called for when the parental role must be reconciled with the sick role or shared for other reasons.

Bandler[48] has found that worker contacts are greatly increased during crisis and may involve, for example, "good-grandmother" energy, free of rivalry or seduction. This energy may be directed to bringing order out of household chaos, providing transportation, giving direct expressions of value for parent and children, or to immediate involvement in daily problems. Such activities are evaluated as furnishing corrective family experiences which create trust and enhance social functioning.

Many beginning caseworkers express anxiety that activity, position-taking, and expression of differences will somehow interfere with developing a good relationship with the client. Perhaps it requires a degree of sophistication and security to recognize that relationship grows out of facing and resolving differences that arise rather than out of avoiding issues basic to a joint enterprise. Evasion is a denial of mutuality or partnership in problem-solving.

The social worker's function as model for his client has not received full attention in theory.[49] He does function as

---

48. Bandler, "Casework: A Process of Socialization," p. 270.

49. Raymond W. Swan and Wynn Tabbert, doctoral candidates at the University of Southern California, have made contributions to clarification of the concept of modeling in social work practice.

Psychoanalysts and social psychologists have explored at length the process of learning through identification as a factor in adaptation. (Urie Bronfenbrenner, "Freudian Theories of Identification and Their Derivatives," *Child Development* 31 [1960]:15.) Bronfenbrenner's search of the literature revealed that the term identification has described *behavior* (A learns to act through taking as his model the overt acts of B); *motive* (A tries to emulate B); and, most common, *process*, the psychological forces that impel the learner to emulate a model. He also found that theory abounded in elaborate explanation for apocryphal phenomena. (Bronfenbrenner, "Freudian Theories of Identification," p. 38.)

model, whether acknowledged or not, and the best use and safeguard lies in exercising this aspect of relationship with full awareness and purpose.

In the most planned and concrete aspect, the worker consciously and purposefully demonstrates specific acts of social competence for and with the client. The acts are goal-directed and are openly discussed between worker and client. They may include role-playing in areas of immediate concern to the client. The worker may also demonstrate acts of social competence to the client in "real life" in the community and may combine such demonstration with social advocacy. This has occurred in planned three-way meetings with worker, client, and landlord (or housing project director), in which the worker has effectively presented the need and justification for repairs or larger quarters, if the client's own request has been futile or when negotiations have become uncontrolled and deteriorated to inaction or abusiveness on one or both sides. It has also been used in three-way conferences with schoolteachers and principals when parents have been unsure of how to present themselves, ask the important questions, or get needed direction in carrying out family supports to children's school achievement. The intended purpose of such modeling is that the client handles future similar encounters and presentations independently, and with increased assurance and effectiveness.

There are additional opportunities for workers to model as responsible, competent adults who find gratification in their work role. Such modeling can be of high importance to youths who have never had a regularly employed parent. Workers may also model in the parental role by referring to their own children, as well as by direct transactions with client's children. Bandler[50] has described the caseworker as a parental figure who provides a new model for carrying out the tasks of child-rearing and family life, especially for mothers who have lacked such models in their own early years. Workers in the Boston study engaged in discussion, information-giving, precept, and demonstration.

Modeling has greatest meaning when there is enough continuity to make the relationship important, to give the client

---

50. Bandler, "Casework: A Process of Socialization," p. 260.

a stake in pleasing another whose esteem he values. The prototype is, again, the parent as agent of socialization for the developing child. The importance of the basic relationship is recognized, along with the techniques of information, feedback, and expectation-setting. It is not only specific acts that are modeled, but attitudes as well; for example, the worker demonstrates an attitude of respect and concern for the infant and young child, or the attitude that acknowledges the masculine dignity of an unemployed or disabled father. Such attitudes must underlie all acts if they are to be more than empty rituals.

A British psychologist and social work educator, Derek Jehu,[51] stresses this point in a discussion of the "imitative learning" that occurs in the context of the warm, affectionate, nurturant relationship which characterizes any effective social work model. He considers that the client's perception of the worker as expert or authority is also relevant, since the model's high status, prestige, competence, and control of resources increase the gains to be realized by imitating him. The most immediate value lies in his modeling adaptive, problem-solving behavior in the parental role. The worker may do this directly by demonstrating appropriate behavior to children in the presence of parents, and by arranging other models in the environment. This is a major rationale, for example, of the casework process in providing homemaker service.

In short, all that is subsumed in the discussion of modeling implies that a relationship of mutual trust has been established with a worker who is at once warm and responsible, which will admit of the worker functioning as model and sometimes modeling in the advocate role. He allies himself with the parent's basic wish to function, and identifies and fills knowledge gaps. These activities are based on the following assumption: Knowledge and confidence, newly opened channels, and feedback from children and other family members all enhance the client's image of himself as parent and reinforces newly acquired, newly tried behaviors. The mother who can begin to act as a parent and find gratification in that

---

51. Derek Jehu, *Learning Theory and Social Work* (London: Routledge and Kegan Paul, 1967), p. 102.

role, who can experience being appreciated and valued by others, has less need to be a rival of her own children.

Modeling must also identify and meet the client's conceptual readiness. What is essential to learning is phase-specific, rather than enduring or perpetual. The client's response to the expressed expectation of increased competence is of high importance. As was noted above, the expectation finds no anchor in the client unless his own basic wish for better function, pushed by the stressing effects of incompetence, is recognized. All worker-client activities flow from, reinforce, and are intended to fulfill this wish. The listing below summarizes treatments in relation to diagnostic groups identified in the preceding section. The treatment classifications, like the diagnoses, represent hypothetical propositions not yet systematically tested.

1. *Unsocialized*
   a. The unsocialized parent has little ability to respond to others or to fill the parenting role, even with maximal available nurture, social supports, and resources. Children are in danger of abuse or neglect. It is necessary to interrupt the cycle by separation of parents and children and to assist parents to find substitute social roles.[52] Treatment is based on a judgment and prediction that parents will be actively harmful to children.
   b. The parent gives evidence of potential ability to respond and provide some care and protection to children. The indication is for support and enhance-

---

52. Professional literature and personal documents contain numerous accounts of successful contact and influence with profoundly withdrawn and alienated persons. These include Frieda Fromm-Reichmann's work with schizophrenic patients, experimental assignments of borderline retarded young adults to care for autistic children, Annie Sullivan's teaching of the primitive child that Helen Keller was when she first encountered her, the work of religious orders in caring for mentally retarded persons, and Eldridge Cleaver's description of Chris Lovdjieff as prison teacher. (Eldridge Cleaver, *Soul on Ice* [New York: Dell Publishing Company, 1968], pp. 31–39.) All are characterized by a single-minded, nearly monastic dedication to the task which is directly opposite to the change agent as an adult rooted in his own network and functioning competently in multiple social roles. These reports suggest that treatments for parents separated from their children might have aims and processes very different from those of adult socialization.

ment of parenting ability with maximal direct aids, such as compensatory preschool programs or home-maker service. Treatment implies a judgment that parental care will not be actively harmul to children, but must be heavily supplemented by secondary social resources.

2. *Inadequately socialized*

These parents are major targets for social casework based on the socialization model and using modalities described in this section. Treatment is a nurturant relationship, demonstration of trustworthiness through a long testing period, modeling with open sharing and revelation, direct action, and simple direct verbal communication; mutual expectations are made explicit; adequate, prompt feedback, maximum instrumental provision, and direct work are employed to extend the client's skills and use of (connection with and contribution to) resources and social movements in the community.

3. *Socialized to specific subculture*

Major treatment focus is on opening channels for significant and rewarding connections in the new milieu: training, orientation—with attention to perception—information, and learning behaviors appropriate and effective in new situations. Treatment in peer groups organized specifically for socialization may supplement all efforts noted in treatment of the second group, designated as "inadequately socialized."

ADDITIONAL TARGET GROUPS

In addition to the multiproblem or multideficit families considered above, there are other "target groups" of clients for whom social casework based on the theory of socialization may be the treatment of choice. They include individuals whose previously attained social competence has diminished either because of changes in the self[53] or because of altera-

---

53. Many activities encompassed in "rehabilitation" may be conceptualized as socialization. Social workers who participate in this process with physicians and educators are uniquely concerned with client's changing

tions in social expectations with passage of time, changed location, or shifts in technology and associated cultural values. Such changes affect all people at some time during the life cycle. Some individuals achieve a solution by mobility or by initiating changes in self (including learning new roles); many weather the strains of transition with the ongoing support of family and other primary groups. At major turning points in their adult careers, other people need professional help, including the help of social workers.[54]

Those who come to the attention of caseworkers are those who need resources beyond self and natural social networks; specifically, they need professional help and adequate instrumental supports in order to learn new roles. Clausen[55] has described (but not labeled as potential social work clients) this latter group of adults: they encounter an identity problem or crisis with the onset of chronic disability, infirmities of old age, or failure in an important role. In such a crisis, an individual must come to terms with altered self-capacity which interferes with action and pursuit of goals to which he holds a high commitment. The process of socialization supports him in making an adaptation by assisting him to make an acceptable redefinition or transformation of identity. Brim[56] pointed to a general lack of knowledge about the social processes which account for varieties of adaptations to realities and stresses of the middle years, including the impact of the family and the pervasive necessity to reconcile achievement with aspirations.

Adult socialization as a casework activity can support upward mobility aspirations. The activity may take the form of teaching attitudes and interpersonal behavior for higher level employment opportunities, or teaching work-role demands to women who enter the labor force after the child-rearing years. Adults may also seek and initiate casework help for socialization out of interest in self-growth, or out of

---

self-images and self-expectations, and with their responses to altered expectations from others.

54. At the present stage of organization, identification of need and provision of service remains haphazard.

55. Clausen, *Socialization and Society*, p. 9.

56. Brim, "Adult Socialization," p. 223.

discontent with current relationships and functioning, desire for change, or inability to cope with change.

Socialization to the parental role may require outside help even in families who have met needs adequately during most of the family life cycle. Brim[57] has suggested the role reversal that occurs when middle-aged sons and daughters must assume (often as a legal requirement) parentlike responsibilities for their own aging parents. The change may seem to occur abruptly, with intolerable conflict that leads to failure in filial behavior and in the role of old person and to rupture of family ties. Urban industrial societies accord minimal acceptance or function to the elderly. Casework in such families may therefore be needed, but not adequate to solve the problems if material supports are insufficient and general social attitudes depreciate and place a low value on old age.

Persons entering new social roles after the normative age or resuming interrupted roles may need professional help. The patient recovering from a physical or mental illness associated with social isolation often needs encouragement to give adequate care to self and presentation of self; he needs feedback on unacceptable behavior as well as on important gains, and help in reestablishing connections with community groups. Mobile persons, migrants, and immigrants newly arrived in a technological society may be best helped by a socialization approach, with the caseworker teaching ways of becoming oriented to the new community and of participating in social movements and political activities related to survival.

People at or past middle age who undertake parental responsibilities by adoption or resume them by caring for grandchildren often need social work help. Casework based on socialization theory has been evaluated as highly effective with parents who have adhered to role models for self or child that have become anachronistic for the third generation (for example, a completely passive, submissive feminine role).[58] The problems will be compounded if two or more of

---

57. Ibid., p. 214.
58. An analysis of casework activity with such a family using this model has been reported by Sylvia Mitchell, a student at the University of Southern California.

these conditions occur simultaneously, as when grand-parents take in one or more children and move from their rural home to a city in a different part of the country.

The diagnostic classification scheme might be adapted to these additional client target groups. For example, the role changes initiated by aging or loss of function in adult life may also be assessed differentially by dimensions of milieu, personal resources, history, and the availability of measures for stabilization or prompt meeting of deficit. The classification scheme for these target groups is extended, with indicators, also speculative, in the groups listed below.

1. *Unsocialized*

   The client has not had a significant work role, and there is no distinct critical or traumatic dividing line between productive life and later life. His life experience has led to low expectations. The onset of exemption from the expectation that he fulfill a work role may come early because of impaired (neglected) health.

2. *Inadequately socialized*

   The client has been socialized to a prior work role which becomes unavailable because of the individual's loss of function, or structural changes in the work place.

   The client is socialized to some family roles, but undertakes or resumes a demanding role "out of phase." (Married couple beyond child-bearing age adopts a child or takes orphaned grandchildren into the home.)

3. *Socialized to subculture*

   A highly institutionalized life style becomes unavailable, as in retirement of career officers from military service in middle life which brings enforced departure of the family from the military enclave with its structured expectations and supports.

SOME UNSOLVED PROBLEMS

The foregoing sections make it obvious that efforts to apply a theoretical model from behavioral science to social casework raise many questions related to practice theory. Before naming several of these questions, it is important to mention certain ethical or philosophical issues which inevitably arise. These issues were well presented at the 1968 National Con-

ference on Social Welfare by Henry Miller,[59] who expressed
shock and dismay at most of the literature on multiproblem
families. He labeled reaching-out efforts to change family
patterns as welfare colonialism, clinicalism, uplift, and paternalism. Men are not children, he said, echoing Fanon[60]
and his latter-day disciples. The only issue is the right to
self-determination, however bad the outcome, for each must
choose his own life style and destiny.

Overlooking the echoes of cultural relativism (presumably,
it fell with the Third Reich, which had made it an untenable
scientific position), this is a persuasive argument. It suggests
dangers most social workers fear and hypocrisies they decry.
It invokes visions of deadening oversocialization, the imposition of arbitrary goals, and the construction of rigidly controlled environments. It is on the side of minority groups who
also perceive the welfare effort (if carried out according to
the intent of its leaders) as a vast process of homogenization.
We will do our own thing, cry the chicanos, and not as part
of a WASP society.[61]

These protests are valid, but they are somewhat beside the
point made in this paper. One faces the question of the extent to which self-determination is individual and absolute,
or limited by social systems and the order of nature. Having
seen Mrs. Glenn's grandchildren, one is haunted by questions
about *their* right to self-determination, and the extent to
which it may be foreclosed in infancy. This is a way of saying
that on ethical grounds socialization is appropriately a basis
for casework treatment of individual disabilities in a role
function which may occur in any group, rather than a
modality for influencing or eliminating group differences
rooted in varied cultures.

The stance of the worker as model raises additional ethical
questions, since it introduces structural asymmetry in the
dyad, which is not between equals, but to which the in-

59. Henry Miller, "Social Work in the Black Ghetto: The New Colonialism," *Social Work* 14 (1969):65–76.
60. Frantz Fanon, *The Wretched of the Earth* (New York: Grove Press,
1963).
61. Ruben Salazar, "No Middle Class Illusions: New Types of Leader
Arising among Latins," Los Angeles Times, 3 February 1969.

equality of status between agent-recruit, teacher-student, or parent-child is essential. Professionals are prone to perceive elements of coercion, manipulation, or condescension in a structured relationship thus conceptualized, and to be repulsed. Parentalism, derogated as paternalism, arouses critics who would erase all structural hierarchies in favor of totally egalitarian relationships. The evidence is beginning to come in that in the family structure difference between parents and children is denied at great cost.[62] Attacks on teachers and other authorities are prevalent. Outcomes for learning and socialization are in the balance. One supposes that actions aimed against extreme rigidity and authoritarianism will swing wildly past the mark to produce increasing disorder, at least in the immediate future.

These ethical issues are inseparable from treatment goals. Jehu[63] pointed out that decisions about how people *ought* to behave, what their conditions of life *should* be, are still moral, rather than scientific, and that on moral questions social workers cannot be morally neutral. The social worker's obligation is recognition of value differences and of his influences on the client, and acceptance of responsibility for his activity intended to produce change.

Important theoretical problems deal with gaps in knowledge about behavior and practice, the competence of the worker, and the extent to which society and social casework itself are open systems.

Bruck[64] has inquired whether modifications of simple behaviors lead to modification of complex behaviors, or whether they are separate, of different orders, and under different influences. He suggests that socially acceptable behaviors can be learned through role playing, modeling, and reinforcement, and that such treatments will change impulsive, inconsistent, frustrating interaction patterns in deprived and disorganized families. Others contend that the changes described represent only a surface conformity. Indeed, this was Stein's[65] evaluation of "successful" treatment in the North

---

62. Cottle, "Parent and Child," and Stein, "Sociocultural Perspectives."
63. Jehu, *Learning Theory*, p. 112.
64. Bruck, "Behavior Modification Theory," p. 54.
65. Stein, "Sociocultural Perspectives," p. 313.

Point project. He concluded that these mothers had only learned to turn another face to the worker.

It is not known whether increased competence in primary family roles is self-rewarding. Data from significant numbers of families in which such changes have occurred are not available. A related question deals with the extent to which behavioral change may create heightened self-esteem. This question has not been answered from experience of large numbers of parents, for example, who gained competence in family roles. Very little systematic knowledge is available about the effects of different backgrounds and capacities of clients, the time investments indicated, effects of continuous or intermittent help, and different indications for the two sexes (in this instance, for mother and father roles). Presumably these are influenced by differing experiences and expectations in boyhood and girlhood.

The gap between the theoretical model and effective practice is wide. The questions above have yet to be operationalized by behavioral indicators which will make assessment of client and situation more precise and dependable. Much is unknown, or yet to be adapted from more abstract or simply controlled contexts, about the interplay of the immediate situation and what the individual brings to it from the long course of his development. This knowledge is crucial to assessing the extent of change that can be expected in adult life, the circumstances and frequency of change, and the kinds of environments that support or precipitate change.[66] Techniques derived from socialization theory await testing in social work practice.

Personal qualities of workers are of the highest importance. The need to be punitive or controlling is perhaps a less frequent hazard than low levels of competence and motivation. Problems are related directly to recruitment and professional education, as well as to the climate of social agencies and staff morale.

Modeling is potentially promising. It is threatening to some supervisors, who have expressed fear that workers will use relationships with clients inappropriately to meet their own needs. Workers can be good models, not overly needful,

---

66. Brim, "Adult Socialization," p. 222.

if they are well rooted in their own networks, performing adequately in several adult social roles, and if their own life experience has not been too limited. Caseworkers who model incompetence or disaffection in their work role are doing double disservice to clients.

This chapter has not dealt with the timing of adult socialization or with transition rituals as part of casework practice. Both are potentially of high significance and suggest, for example, that the thrust of adult socialization to parental roles should be carried out increasingly in agencies equipped to do preventive work.

In closing, it may be repeated that the caseworker's achievements are related to the availability of resources necessary for all people to become full members of modern industrial society. If an individual prepares for a work role but finds employment closed to him, his chances for success are slight, and others in his network may see as their alternatives abandonment of hope or determination to change the system. If the only goals that society holds for some members are dehumanizing, changes in the system are indicated.

Grinker[67] analyzed psychonanalysis as an open system. If social casework, too, is an open system in a rapidly changing society, future developments will include the replacement of some traditional functions, experimentation with new roles, and redefinition of old roles to meet social needs. For social casework, competence is more effective help extended to more people who need it.

MAJOR REFERENCES

The literature on socialization is extensive and, like most scholarly and other kinds of production today, increasing at an explosive rate. The selection of twelve references demands arbitrary and subjective decisions. One criterion for the following list was a balance of various orientations, sources, and applications of theory. Included are a recent collection of essays (with comprehensive bibliographies) by leading theorists in sociology and social psychology (Clausen); two treatments of competence as the goal of socialization (Gladwin,

---

67. Grinker, "Conceptual Progress."

Inkeles); an analysis of the process and conditions of change in adult life which constitutes socialization in professional education (Merton et al.); an exploration of preparation for the parental role (Brim); the work of a philosopher whose ideas made a special contribution to interactionist theory in social psychology (Mead), with an example of a text (Shibutani) and a book of readings (Rose) which expound this theory and its relation to socialization; the statement of a psychiatrist oriented to socialization theory (Sullivan); two reports which relate socialization to social casework practice (McBroom, Pavenstedt); and a volume of two essays, one of which presents socialization as a social development of the individual, whereas the other analyzes formally organized socialization settings (Brim and Wheeler).

Bibliography

Brim, Orville G., Jr. *Education for Child Rearing.* New York: Russell Sage Foundation, 1959.
Brim, Orville G., Jr., and Wheeler, Stanton. *Socialization after Childhood: Two Essays.* New York: John Wiley and Sons, 1966.
Clausen, John A., ed. *Socialization and Society.* Boston: Little, Brown and Company, 1968.
Gladwin, Thomas. *Poverty USA.* Boston: Little, Brown and Company, 1967.
Inkeles, Alex. "Social Structure and the Socialization of Competence." *Harvard Educational Review* 36 (1966):265–83.
McBroom, Elizabeth. "A Comparative Study of Social Work Interventions in Two Types of AFDC Families." Doctoral diss., University of California, Berkeley, 1965.
Mead, George Herbert. *On Social Psychology.* Chicago: University of Chicago Press, 1964.
Merton, Robert K., et. al., eds. *The Student Physician.* Cambridge: Harvard University Press, 1957.
Pavenstedt, Eleanor, ed. *The Drifters: Children of Disorganized Lower-Class Families.* Boston: Little, Brown and Company, 1967.
Rose, Arnold M., ed. *Human Behavior and Social Processes: An Interactionist Approach.* Boston: Houghton-Mifflin Company, 1962.
Shibutani, Tamotsu. *Society and Personality: An Interactionist Approach to Social Psychology.* Englewood Cliffs, New Jersey: Prentice-Hall, 1961.
Sullivan, Harry Stack. *The Interpersonal Theory of Psychiatry.* New York: W. W. Norton and Company, 1953.

9 | Social Casework Theory:
An Overview

Bernece K. Simon

INTRODUCTION

Social casework burgeons in many forms from its firmly
planted roots. It takes sustenance from the profession and, in
return, gives significant purpose and immediate connection
to people, the central concern of the profession.

In a society of paradoxes of poverty and affluence, of over-
population and brilliant technology, of deeply disturbing
contradictions that arise from accelerated complexity that
produces dehumanization, social casework makes its contribution by its commitment to the individual in society. The
commitment to understand, to differentiate, to act for and
with the individual gives social casework crucial importance
in alleviating the human suffering related to society's problems. The agony of the individual is seen in his search for
autonomy, self-realization, and productive, decent living
with his fellowmen. Never has our society had such profound need for institutionalized concern for, and competence to deal with, individual development, purposes, and
problems. Traditionally, the role of social casework in a
profession has been to promote individually satisfying and
socially constructive living. Thus, it has taken a unique place
among disciplines dedicated to the development of a humane
society that values each of its members.

Charlotte Towle frequently described social work at its
best as the "conscience of society," and called for a renas-
cence of the unity of cause and function in the profession.[1]
In recent years, society has had to arouse the social conscience
of social work. It is now reawakened, and the profession is
convulsed with the effort to define and unify cause and function. As part of social work, social casework finds its cause in
the promotion of the welfare of the individual in society
and its function in the implementation of this cause. Social
casework serves as one aspect of the conscience of society
insofar as it is proud, competent, and passionate in its dedication to the individuality of all persons.

Bernece K. Simon is professor of social work, School of Social Service
Administration, University of Chicago.
1. Charlotte Towle, "Social Work: Cause and Function," *Social Casework* 42 (October 1961). Also in Helen Harris Perlman, ed., *Helping*
(Chicago: University of Chicago Press, 1969).

Commitment, pride, and passion can be developed in the individual practitioner by his interpretation of, and conviction about, the cause of social casework. Competence is necessary to unify cause and function, to give reality to pride and direction to passion. Competence requires knowledge, understanding, and a coherent guide for its enactment in the service of cause. What is the basis for competence in social casework? What is available to social caseworkers to enable them to undertake disciplined, professional responsibility in relation to individuals? What is there to direct passion, make pride real, and implement commitment?

The reader, having read this far in the volume, will undoubtedly have his own opinion of the significance of the seven approaches to social casework theory. He will also have come to some conclusions as to the utility for practice inherent in them and may even have made a decision to put one or more of them to the acid test of practice. In what follows, an attempt is made to arrive at the overall significance of these casework approaches for the current state of social casework theory and for its future development. Analysis and synthesis of these rich materials will be undertaken for this purpose. The analysis will focus on the major aspects of casework theory: behavioral science foundations, and casework practice theory—initial phase, assessment, and treatment. This will be preceded by suggestive frameworks for study and appraisal of theory and followed by a presentation of the issues, questions, and problems that evolved in the symposium discussions and were sparked in me by the entire enterprise.

THEORY STUDY AND APPRAISAL

A General Framework

Germain's paper on the history of our efforts to find a rational basis for practice that encompasses both the science and the art of professional practice sets the stage for efforts to understand how the necessary systematic work can be undertaken. One aspect of the work is the development of a framework for analysis and appraisal of various approaches to casework. The general plan for evaluation of casework systems presented below is a guide that might lead to more detailed and rigorous ones. The general framework seemed useful to derive an overview of casework theory as presented in these papers, but it was not used for a detailed comparative study of the several position papers.

The guiding criteria for systematic examination of theories for practice are consistency and coherence—consistency in the use of a behavioral science base throughout a theory and coherence of the parts into a whole that serves as a guide for practice.

In order to evaluate consistency and coherence it is necessary (a) to understand the conception of man-in-society that is propounded by the theoretician, as evidenced in the behavioral science base as well as in its implicit dimensions, (b) to identify the theoretician's implicit and explicit view of the function and goals of social casework and of its place in social work, (c) to understand the connection of the goals of social casework to the theory of the phases of the casework process, and (d) to identify the relationship of the conception of man and the goals of social casework to the principles of operation in the theory; that is, the necessary interactions of client and worker and the techniques or procedures by which the theory is applied.

This general framework can be elaborated in many ways for study of specific aspects of a casework theory or theories. One of the aspects of any casework theory that it is most important to understand is its behavioral science foundations. These foundations portray the theoretician's conception of man and, in turn, exert a profound influence on practice theory. It is also important to understand these foundations in order to distinguish clearly between the practice theory and the frame of reference in which it is cast. The significance of this distinction is best exemplified by the problems caseworkers have accrued over the years by blurring the lines between Freudian personality and behavior theory, psychoanalytic practice theory and principles, and social casework practice theory. Finally, it is important to study the behavioral science base carefully, because our frequent warnings about the uncertainty of knowledge for practice are warnings essentially about the behavioral science basis for practice. It is, therefore, important to know how uncertain the knowledge is, where the uncertainties are, and how these might influence the development of theory and practice.

A Specific Framework: Behavioral Science Base

This framework[2] is essentially a series of questions to be applied to the examination of the behavioral science underpinnings of a casework theory. These questions are directed toward a critical analysis of the nature of the behavioral science base as well as toward its use in casework theory. The questions are arranged in order of their general to particular significance for casework theory.

1. What is the state of the behavioral science theory or theories?[3]
   a. Is it a theory, or some organization of concepts?—e.g., small group concepts, role concepts.
   b. What empirical validation, if any, is there for the theory?
   c. What differences exist among scholars in the particular behavioral science area? What is the nature and importance of these differences?
   d. What appear to be the difficulties of relating the generalizations of the theory to casework theory and practice?
2. What purpose or purposes does the theory serve for casework theory?[4] Is it a way of thinking or a way of operation?
   a. Is it useful as field or background for the casework theory?

2. See Donald H. Ford and Hugh B. Urban, *Systems of Psychotherapy* (New York: John Wiley & Sons, 1964) for sophisticated and complete systems for analysis of theories for practice.

3. Ruth M. Butler, "An Orientation to Knowledge of Human Growth and Behavior in Social Work Education," in *Curriculum Study of the Council on Social Work Education* (New York: Council on Social Work Education, 1959), 6:59–60.

4. Bernece K. Simon, "Borrowed Concepts: Problems and Issues for Curriculum Planning," in *Health and Disability Concepts in Social Work Education*, Proceedings of a workshop, School of Social Work, University of Minnesota (Minneapolis: Department of Health, Education and Welfare, Vocational Rehabilitation Administration, 1964), p. 32.

b. Is it useful as major focus for assessment or treatment, or both?

1) Does it enrich the general understanding of man in society, or does it serve as a specific guide to understanding individuals in society as explicated in the assessment phase of the practice theory?

2) Does it aid in a general therapeutic attitude and approach, or does it lead to principles for treatment?

3. What is the consistency of the influence of the behavioral science base on the practice theory?

The questions about the state of the behavioral science theory and the nature of its purpose and use in casework theory are important not only for the theory but also for the way in which the ideas from the foundation theory will be integrated in practice.[5] If the behavioral science concepts are too abstract, too general, or too philosophical and, therefore, cannot be translated for application in any part of the casework theory, it is likely that practitioners will abandon, in whole or in part, the behavioral science base and the social casework theory in favor of a search for techniques that work, unconnected to any frame of reference that can guide professional operations. This, in turn, affects analyses and conceptualizations of practice that should serve, along with behavioral science, the development of casework theory.[6]

These frameworks for study and appraisal of theory were used to address the question, Where is social casework theory in 1969? But to deal concretely with this question several additional subquestions were considered.

1. Do the seven papers constitute one practice theory, or several?

2. What are their significant similarities and differences:
   a. In behavioral science base?

---

5. See, for instance, Harriett Bartlett, "The Place and Use of Knowledge in Social Work Practice," *Social Work* 9 (July 1964). Martin Bloom, "Connecting Formal Behavioral Science Theory to Individual Social Work Practice," *Social Service Review* 39 (March 1965). Edwin J. Thomas, "Selecting Knowledge from Behavioral Science," in *Building Social Work Knowledge: Report of a Conference* (New York: National Association of Social Workers, 1964).

6. *Building Social Work Knowledge: Report of a Conference,* pp. 4–5.

    b. In the theory for the initial, assessment, and treat-
    ment phases of casework?
  3. How have the authors addressed themselves to practice
    tasks and problems in their statements of theory?
  4. How are values dealt with in the theory expositions?
  5. What are the general trends and emphases in the several
    approaches? What are the implications of these trends
    for the current casework scene and what do they por-
    tend for the future?

Analysis and appraisal of theory are not suggested as an
intellectual game or as an effort to gain status among disciplines. They are necessary for the development of a casework theory that is consistent, coherent, and usable in
practice. Finally, detailed appraisal of theory permits examination of the efficacy of casework theory for practice and
the formulation of research questions that may validate and
improve theory, and may contribute to the significance and
utility of the foundation theories and concepts.

SOCIAL CASEWORK, 1969

Social Casework Theory or Theories?

The vitality and creativity in casework thinking are evident
in these chapters and need no elaboration here. It is also
evident that serious and vigorous work has been undertaken
to find new ways to combine the "scientism and humanity"
of the social casework tradition. There is an equally serious
and vigorous effort to enrich, broaden, and deepen social
casework theory to encompass the various developing ideas
of the complex interrelationship and interaction of man and
society. Commitment to the individual is clearly expressed
by the authors and it is a commitment that takes into account
new interpretations of the idea that "no man is an island
entire unto itself."

    The position papers show that there is, at this time, no
unitary social casework practice theory, and it is debatable
whether any one of the presentations is a complete theory,
entirely coherent and consistent in the relationship of its
parts and in potential applications to practice. It is likely
that what is contained between these covers is, in fact, seven

"approaches" to the development of social casework theory. These seven approaches are not distinct theories in the sense that they each can serve as guides to any and all kinds of social casework practice or that they each represent a separate "school of thought" in casework thinking. Rather, some of them represent well-developed "schools of thought" and are considered by their authors to be general practice approaches; some are concerned with special or unique kinds of problems and people; some are embryonic; and some are eclectic in their behavioral science base whereas others are built on a less mixed foundation.

It has been commonly assumed that the approaches explicated by Hollis, Perlman, and Smalley represent "schools of thought" in social casework theory—diagnostic, problem-solving, and functional, respectively. Insofar as there are basic differences among these authors, it is important to note that these are differences within a dynamic psychological frame of reference. The "school of thought" that each represents must be identified by the differences among them of the purposes, objectives, and processes of social casework. One of the developments in social casework theory highlighted by the symposium papers is that these three schools of casework thought seem to have more areas of similarity now than formerly. There is similarity not only in the purposes and objectives, but also in some important aspects of the processes of casework. In some respects, the differences seem to be in degree and in emphasis rather than in substance. What is difficult to discern with any certainty is whether differences in degree and emphasis are of such magnitude as to constitute differences in kind. For instance, the question may be asked whether the different emphases in the initial phases in these three approaches are so different as to affect other phases of the casework process, the content and process of the interaction between the client and the worker, and, most important, the outcome of the work that is undertaken by the client and the worker. Perhaps, the "school of thought" quality of each derives more from the conception of man held by the theoretician and from his ideas of the objectives of social casework than from the other aspects of the theory—those aspects that serve more specifically as guides or framework for practice. The conception of man and the generally stated objectives for casework are concepts that cover so many ideas and implicit assumptions that it is possible that they have a partially unknown but powerful impact upon the practice elements of the theory. We may still have three schools of thought in these approaches, but it is more difficult than it once was to pinpoint the basic differences or to be sure of their derivations.

The approaches set forth by McBroom, Rapoport, and Scherz seem, on the other hand, to be new developments derived from various aspects of the common core of casework theory and practice. These approaches seem to be evolving treatment approaches in casework rather than new general casework theories. It is possible, for instance, to conceive of these three theoretical positions as being incorporated as treatment options within the more generally stated and universally inclusive theories of Hollis, Perlman, and Smalley. For instance, there seems to be a very close theoretical and practice affinity between "crisis-oriented brief treatment" and "problem-solving." There are evidences in these three "treatment theories" of a kind of eclectic reorganization and differing emphases of various aspects of current casework theory.

Arranging these three approaches into one group cannot be carried too far, however, because they are in different stages of development, they have not been equally promulgated or tried in practice, and their roots in "traditional" casework theory are not the same in quality or quantity. For instance, it is possible that McBroom's approach, which is in a very early stage of development, might develop as a distinct casework theory largely based on learning theories and concepts of adult socialization and could be expressed as a more universally inclusive approach than it now appears to be. Rapoport has suggested that some of the theoretical problems in her approach have not been worked out either, because the theory has not been fully applied in practice in sufficient quantity or because there have been idiosyncratic interpretations of some of the most basic aspects of the approach. The varying definitions of "crisis" by caseworkers using a "crisis" approach is one such example. Family treatment, of course, has many variations on the theme, as Scherz notes, and there are many practitioners as well as academicians who consider family treatment the only effective treatment modality in casework. Scherz also suggests that there may be rather far-reaching developments in family treatment theory related to further examination of system theory and of ideas about "family life style." Thus, these three treatment approaches are examples of theory-building in process. They are in various stages of development and they may prove to be treatment modalities accessible for use in any more general casework frame of reference; or any one of them may be an embryonic school of thought. Their future development depends upon how they are used in practice, the methods used to study such practice, and some clarification in casework thinking about the differential uses of various casework approaches.

It is more difficult to place behavior modification in these theoretical approaches to casework. The behavioral science foundation of this approach sets it apart from the others. Comparison is further complicated because Thomas has confined himself to only one aspect of sociobehavioral theory as it relates to casework treatment. That is, he has lifted out and adapted laws and principles of operant behavior and operant conditioning and set forth a guide for their use in casework service. On the basis of the behavioral science underpinning and the principles and laws of operation, this approach can probably be classified as a distinct, separate system of casework treatment. Lifted from the larger framework of sociobehavioral concepts, it is less clear that it is a separate, developed, universally applicable theory for casework. Another question, but one that must be dealt with, is whether the techniques in this system can be used in a cluster, or individually, in other casework approaches based on a different conception of man, different general and specific objectives, and a different idea of the processes of treatment. There is no question, however, that behavior modification techniques, combined with the larger sociobehavioral approach, constitute a distinct school of thought for casework.

Regardless of how these theoretical approaches might be classified, they are similar and different in ways that warrant consideration. The agreements and divergencies are both quantitative and qualitative. For instance, there are agreements among most of the authors at the general level of values and purposes of casework and at the particular level of principles for practice. Between these there are differences of emphases within a point of view and differences about the casework process that seem to be differences in degree. When these are taken together, it is not easy to ascertain whether these different emphases make for a distinctly different casework approach. Thus, the location, degree, and kind of similarities and differences in theories are important for understanding their implications as theory and as guide for practice.

Similarities and Differences in Theoretical Approaches: Behavioral Science Foundations

There are wide variations in the specificity and detail with which the authors identify the behavioral science basis for their practice theories. There are also differences in the analysis and descriptions of the nature of the debt owed the foundation theories. All the authors, except Thomas, have drawn from a broad range of the behavioral and natural sciences and disciplines. Thomas has confined himself to presenting and discussing only that foundation theory that has relevance for behavior modification in its relation to casework. He addresses himself to those aspects of Pavlovian and Skinnerian psychology, and the "variant emphases" that have developed from these, that are directly influential in the treatment system he presents. This is in contrast to most of the other papers, in which a range of sources that have varying kinds of relationship to a comprehensive practice theory are presented as undergirding that theory. The authors who present a specific treatment focus also identify a more limited range of foundation sources, but, even so, less specifically than Thomas.

All the casework approaches except behavior modification have a central connection to a form of dynamic psychology that postulates a theory of personality—personality development, structure, and function. Behavior modification postulates certain laws and principles of human behavior and behavior mechanisms. It specifically eschews a theory of personality. Although some personality theory is central to most of the approaches, none of the practice theories is undergirded solely by personality theory. Nor is classical Freudian personality theory the universal core of these approaches.

These two factors are significant evidences, among many, of the evolutionary development in the thinking of several of the authors.

A careful reading of the most well known of the practice theories shows considerable change over the last few years. These changes, particularly in relation to personality theory, are expressed in the ways in which the authors have incorporated the developments in ego psychology into their view of the nature of man and into the explication of individual behavior that is relevant for social casework. Thus concepts of conflict-free areas in ego development and function, of autonomy, and of drive for mastery and competence are included—although with varying degrees of emphasis and detail—in most, if not all, the dynamically oriented practice theories. This is of great importance not only for the evolution of casework theory but also for the theoretical basis that these ideas provide to supplant the beliefs and assumptions of early writers[7] about the "push" for the biopsychosocial growth and development that is available in all men.

In addition, these aspects of ego psychology may serve as the basis for the development of specific principles of operation for the general treatment tenet that social casework treatment is allied with the "healthy" aspects of the personality or with the "healthy" defenses. A thorough integration of these ideas from ego psychology may, perhaps, continue the development of a model for social casework assessment and treatment that is realistically balanced to take into account health, illness, and the wellsprings of strength in most people. Finally, understanding and integration of concepts of ego autonomy, drive for mastery, and competence may aid in the development of specific ideas and principles that will rescue the elusive doctrine of individual self-determination from its limbo between philosophy and psychology to take its place in the real world of principles of operation in social casework, and, indeed, in social work.[8]

---

7. Gordon Hamilton, Kenneth Pray, Bertha Reynolds, Virginia Robinson, Lynton Swift, Jessie Taft, Charlotte Towle, as well as others, exemplify this assumption or belief in their early writings.
8. For a major stride in this direction see Helen Harris Perlman, "Self-

The emphasis on the utility of ego psychology concepts for social casework theory must take into account that these concepts are postulates—hypotheses about individual human development and functioning that have not been validated. They are theoretical expressions of expert observations that, perhaps, can achieve one kind of validation through efforts to put them to use in social casework practice as well as in theory. In addition, these ideas about ego origins and functions may serve as one of several bridges from man's psyche into his environment and, thus, contribute to the development of operative conceptualizations of the interrelationship of man and his environment within a framework that permits individualization of the person.

The various ways in which the authors have identified possible sources for understanding the interrelationship of man-in-environment are interesting and exciting, and provide a wide latitude for specification of the meaning and implementation of "social" in social casework.

Generally, the authors identify a wide range of sources that are related to their practice theories. Most indicate that their thinking has been affected by theoretical and empirical developments in sociology, social psychology, cultural anthropology, biology, and some aspects of ecology. For many years we have referred to a biopsychosocial view of man, being grandiloquently general about what we have derived from these three areas, but we have, alternately, emphasized one more than the other two. We have always given short shrift to the biological aspects of man except for the now frequent use of concepts of stress and homeostasis. It is not of great moment for the development of social casework theory to find this listing of sources. What is of import for understanding where we are now and what lies ahead is the specification of concepts that have more than a general or courtesy connection to a practice theory.

Among the specific concepts, role concepts have the firmest place among the social science ideas thought to have immediate and specific relevance for social casework. One of the attractions of role "theory" is that the usefulness of the con-

Determination: Illusion or Reality?" *Social Service Review* 39 (December 1965):410–22.

ceptualizations does not depend upon their validation as "truths" about the behavior of man but rather that they can be used as a way of thinking about and organizing observations of, and knowledge about, man. It can serve as a frame of reference to focus ideas about man's interpersonal, intergroup and intersocietal relationships, functions, and behavior. It can be, and is, used on a continuum—from a specific way to understand people in their life situations to a general way of looking at human social activity. It is, perhaps, an already operative bridge between individual psyche and individual interaction with environment. Perlman goes further to suggest that the role frame of reference offers a rich source for the development of goals, methods, and procedures for individual and family treatment specifically connected to the use of role concepts for observation, assessment, and understanding of people in their intimate role relationships.[9]

Following this relatively well-established integration of a social science contribution are variously detailed and explicated others. Among the more interesting and suggestive contributions are various kinds of learning theories, the concept of adult socialization, small-group concepts, the development and function of cognition in behavior, and system theory. These ideas are not all of the same order of business and do not have equal potency for the practice theories which claim them as undergirding. They are listed, however, as examples of the thrust in casework theory toward establishment of a base for theory and practice that clearly identifies the individual in interaction with his environment as the area of observation and of work for the social caseworker. They are also examples of progressive movement from a single personality and illness frame of reference to a more existential, dynamic idea of man in movement with his life. It is this thrust that widens horizons for the development of a pluralistic view and variegated practice of social casework without our old hierarchical notions about that practice.

It would be unnecessarily repetitive to point out the potential relevance for practice theory of each of the "new" behavioral science concepts presented by the authors. How-

---

9. Helen Harris Perlman, *Persona: Social Role and Personality* (Chicago: University of Chicago Press, 1968), pp. 197–203.

ever, one of these constructs commands special attention. The surprising, almost sudden references to "system theory" is significant even though other new ideas may be equally or more important to the development of practice theories. System theory seems noteworthy not only because it appears to be an evolutionary groundswell (after lying dormant since the idea was first developed in relation to casework),[10] but also because it has potential either as a neatly synthesizing idea or as another episode of imperfectly understood but passionately espoused or rejected doctrine. It is useful, also, to consider system theory as one example for analysis of the purpose and utility of a behavioral science concept for casework theory.

As presented in these papers, system theory seems to have some of the advantages of the function of role concepts. It seems to offer a frame of reference for thinking about and organizing ideas that have long been important to social casework theory and practice, especially ideas, principles, and data about man in interaction with society. In my opinion, the most important necessity for the development of a theory for social work as well as casework is the development of descriptions, analyses, and specifications of this interaction. The philosophical and social implications of a detailed mapping of the mutuality between man and environment are crucial for the future of mankind if one considers the problems of environmental pollution, the possibility of worldwide famine, and the ultimate terrors of war. On a less cosmic plane, precise delineation of man-environment concepts might lead to a definition of the purposes and functions of social work that could encompass a commitment to the individual and to social work responsibility for societal change. From such a definition, it might be possible to specify the knowledge and competence necessary to practice in relation to such a commitment.

It may also be possible to use the system concept to render manageable, in both theory and practice, the myth of casework responsibility for the "whole man." A frame of reference for definition of the "whole man" and for the de-

---

10. Werner Lutz, *Concepts and Principles Underlying Casework Practice* (Washington, D.C.: National Association of Social Workers, 1956).

tail of the interrelationship of the parts of the whole might make it possible for the casework practitioner to move flexibly between and amid man-in-environment, man-as-a-whole, and problematic parts of both these aspects of man. A system frame of reference might broaden and deepen the conception of personality beyond the common architectural version of its structure that originally was never intended. This broadening and deepening could be facilitated by an interactional view of personality structure and development that could make a more coherent and more practically useful idea of the totality of the individual in any moment in time, as partial product of his past, living in the present and becoming for his future. System concepts may offer a general, unifying frame of reference that might lead to solutions of some of our conceptual problems, but they may obscure or create other problems.

Is the usefulness of system theory confined to that of a frame of reference for organizing the ideas of social casework into a more coherent and consistent theory for practice? Does it have a secondary, but limited, utility in that it substitutes precision and economy of language for elaborate descriptive expressions? Are system concepts such that with careful use they might contribute to greater precision and realism in the process and content of assessment? That is, will the concepts help us to delineate the relationships between the various aspects of the person and his situation that we examine in the assessment process? Will system ideas contribute to elaboration of the treatment process, and equally important, to the clarification of the interrelationship of assessment and treatment? Is it possible to examine system theory for some solution to diagnostic and treatment typology issues, particularly their relationship to each other? Finally, how does system theory need to be studied, understood, and tested for its compatibility with the almost universal emphasis in casework theory on the crucial importance of the individual as moving, changing, and adapting within the context of changing relationships with other people, institutions, and environmental conditions? That is, will a system frame of reference enhance and support the widening of the meaning of "dynamic" as used in these chapters? Or is there the possibility that the concepts and special language of system theory might produce a new kind of stereotypy and an unforeseen static and oversimplified quality in thinking about the complexity of living people in life situations? Obviously, answers to these and the other questions will be derived only from study and use of the theory and from carefully worked out integration and adaptation of it to the specific needs of casework theory and practice.[11]

The behavioral science underpinning of the social casework practice theories presented here is one aspect of the development of theory that demonstrates the evolutionary leap that has taken place in casework thinking. In spite of the different emphases given to underlying theories by the authors, it is clear that, taken together, they offer many avenues for investigatory and developmental travel for the enrichment of social casework. It is possible, now, for practice-oriented theoreticians and theory-oriented practitioners to choose areas of behavioral science and casework theory of particular interest and relevance for future study, testing, and elaboration. The diversity that is available will fulfill its potential for contribution if choices are made on the basis of some system of analysis of compatibility, accessibility, and utility, instead of on a variety of visceral responses.[12] This kind of evaluation can help us to develop immunity to the bandwagon virus. It also can assist in our mature identification of real differences in casework theories and in the acceptance of such differences as natural.

Careful, integrated understanding of the relationship of the specific behavioral science theory to casework theory is important, further, because it may be possible for social casework to make a long overdue return contribution to the "basic sciences" that undergird its theory and its practice. This return can be in the form of verification or repudiation of behavioral science theory by empirical study and organization of how people do, in fact, behave in response to the problematic situations that bring them to the attention of

---

11. Since this chapter was written I have become aware that this approach to system concepts has been dealt with in some detail by M. P. Janchill, "Systems Concepts in Casework Theory and Practice," *Social Casework* 50 (February 1969):74–82.

12. Simon, "Borrowed Concepts," pp. 32–33.

caseworkers. A contribution may also be made by conceptualization, in a mutually understood frame of reference,[13] of the enormous body of data from casework practice that sets forth the origins, accompanying conditions, development, and responses of people in an endless variety of real-life situations. Scrutiny of the applicability of underlying behavior theory in the casework context may also identify questions for study of the casework processes that would, in turn, help to clarify the substance and methodology most pertinent for the validation of casework theory.

Initial Phase

For a long time a crucial difference between casework theories was found in the conceptualizations of the initial phase. Certainly, this phase was a critical distinguishing factor in the three major schools of thought in casework. The differentiation was possible not only because, as Charlotte Towle described it, the initial phase is "pattern-setting" for the entire process, but also because it held within it the objectives and focus of the work to be undertaken. In the past casework approaches could be separately identified, for instance by the stated purposes of the initial phase, by the amount, depth, and range of longitudinal history that the theory required, by the explicit and implicit roles assigned to the applicant in this phase, and by the interpretation and implementation of the maxim propounded by Charlotte Towle—"Treatment starts with the first interview." These distinguishing factors in the initial phase also gave clues to, or concrete manifestations of, the theoretician's view of man as well as of his implicit assumptions about the purposes and function of social casework.

In these current statements of casework theory, there is a surprising similarity in the authors' exposition of the initial phase. This similarity is a specific example of the evolution of casework thinking. But the initial phase presentations also highlight the nagging problem of degree and kind of difference.

All the authors identify the engagement of the client in the helping process as an important goal of the initial phase.

---

13. Ford and Urban, *Systems of Psychotherapy*, pp. 8–9.

However, there are differences among them as to the content and interaction considered necessary for this engagement to occur. There are also differences as to the relative importance of this goal, among other goals for the initial phase. All authors make clear the necessity for the presentation and elaboration of the problem (or problems) as the client sees it. There are degrees of difference as to what the caseworker does with the client's view of the problem. All the authors except Thomas state that some aspect of treatment is present in the initial phase. The differences in the purpose and implementation of the treatment aspects in the beginning phase are quite clear.

All the authors disclaim, more or less specifically, the requirement for a "complete" longitudinal history. There is general agreement among them that the "here-and-now" situation—and its immediate antecedents, current implications, and effects—are of prime importance. There are, however, clear-cut differences of degree in this particular area. Since one of the central purposes of all the approaches in the initial phase is the engagement of the client, there is general agreement that the client is an active, full participant in this phase and that his purposes of making himself understood and understanding what he is "in for," are to be served as well as the worker's purposes. There are differences, however, as to the nature of the client's participation and whether this participation is a product of the initial phase, a necessity for its operation and continuance, or some mixture of both. All the authors but two disclaim a "study" period, as such (Hollis, pp. 46–49; Thomas, pp. 195–97).

The puzzling questions posed by the similarities and differences in these initial phases are whether the similarities are more important than the differences, and whether the differences make for such contrasting modes of operation that the results of the initial phases will be quite distinct and thus affect all other phases. This is an example of how apparent differences of degree might produce difference in substance. For instance, treatment in the initial phase ranges among providing immediate, concrete services, affecting clients' perceptions, palpable affective investment by the worker, and the establishment of a generally therapeutic atmosphere. Within this range there are differences in objectives, in interactions between client and worker, and in the content of these interactions. Do these constitute theoretical contrasts in the initial phase, or do these differences arise from special cases of casework problems and endeavors? Finally, what differences do they produce in other phases of the casework enterprise? If the differences suggested here are real, do they make of the similarities a witness of faith, or is there something of substance in the similarities?

Even though there is meaningful, operational diversity in the seven approaches to social casework, the similarities in the initial phase seem to point to some important developments in casework. There seems to be a common core in the casework method, no matter what the differences in theoretical elaboration. Perhaps one of the major sources of this core is the value base of social work. Many of the similarities seem to evolve from efforts to implement our hard-to-live-by beliefs and values. For example, the emphases on real participation by clients in the initial phase, on the signal importance of understanding the client's view of himself in relation to his problem or problematic situation, can be seen as an application of the concept of the dignity and worth of every man and the unconditional respect due him. In the facilitation of the client's participation, this respect is demonstrated not only by the intangible atmosphere of the casework encounter and by the worker's equally intangible attitudes, but also by the worker's open, concrete activity in the interaction that enables and encourages the client's involvement in his behalf. The change in the purpose, focus, range and level of "history-taking" that is universal in these approaches, and the requirement that whatever "history" is elicited be relevant to the client and his view of his situation is an attempt in theory to make possible in practice active self-determination on the client's part. These factors, taken together, can facilitate the application of the idea of the work of casework as a mutual undertaking of the client and worker in which there are equal but different responsibilities and in which the worker is, indeed, at the service of the client.[14]

---

14. Since writing this chapter, I have heard these ideas better and more fully developed by Helen Harris Perlman in an unpublished paper, "Changing Views of Man in Social Casework."

These similarities in the initial phase seem to be another aspect of the evolution in casework from concentration on individual illness to an image of man in constant interaction with the universal, but unequal, demands of life which he cannot always meet on his own. The incorporation of these ideas and values in the theories provides a universal framework for a cooperative, collaborative endeavor with the client.

Presumably, other sources for what is common to most of the theories are clinical experience and the recently burgeoning studies of man, as well as the existential demands of any helping process. The similarities in the initial phase seem to be directed toward a guide for the application of ideas in the behavioral science foundations. Theoretical recognition of client participation, relevance and focus of history, emphasis on the here-and-now, respect for and work with the client's view of his situation, and the freedom for self-determination all require principles for practice that take account of the gradual movement away from a morbidity orientation. It makes possible the application in practice of the principle of alliance by the worker with the available, accessible, mastering ego functions of the client.

This discussion of the initial phase has been directed toward the development of an overview of casework theory in 1969. The similarities and differences among the theory statements have been used as tools to arrive at this overview rather than to identify and examine all details. Helen Perlman has said that the initial phase is the prototype of the entire casework process.[15] On this basis, it would be possible to leave discussion of the theory at this point and to assume that the overview from the initial phase would hold for the other phases. But a discussion of the other phases seems indicated because they have long been the focus of debate as to the relative merits of casework theories, with particular reference, of course, to the three major schools of thought.

Assessment and Treatment

Diagnosis has been the height of the storm in this debate.

---

15. Helen Harris Perlman, *Social Casework: A Problem-solving Process* (Chicago: University of Chicago Press, 1957), p. 111.

Perhaps there is significance for the current climatic conditions in social casework that the symposium uses the word "assessment" instead of "diagnosis" and most of the authors accepted this term as understandable and useful. The purposes of diagnosis and its relationship to treatment have been knotty theoretical issues arising from the apparent differences in diagnostic theory in social casework. The symposium papers, however, reveal that there are some startling similarities in the assessment-treatment phases, as there were in the initial phase.

All authors identify as a major purpose of assessment knowledge and understanding of the client in his situation to predict and guide treatment or intervention. In and of itself, this is not as startling as is the similarity in elaboration of this purpose by the theoreticians. In the elaboration, the authors make the point that the assessment process is not an exercise for its own sake but a process necessary for true individualization of the individual-family-situation in order to arrive at a differential treatment. There is an effort throughout toward a dynamic, fluid approach to assessment that is exemplified by careful consideration of the utility of classifications as part of assessment. The developmental aspect of this trend in the various approaches is, perhaps, demonstrated by the extensive discussion on assessment undertaken by Smalley, even though she holds firmly to the principle of assessment directed toward understanding of a person-in-a-process rather than toward an organization of observations into a classification. Hollis undertakes an extensive discussion of the necessity for understanding the person-as-he-is-now-in-a-situation, even though she holds firmly to the differential necessity for various kinds of classification, particularly a clinical one. This is not seen in Thomas's exposition because behavior modification requires, in both theory and practice, the specific narrowing of assessment to enable the practitioner to zero in on a specific, discrete "piece of observable behavior" to be modified.

The general relationship of assessment to treatment, as delineated by the authors, is one of the clearest examples of evolution in casework theory. That is, there seems to be agreement that assessment must be continuous throughout the casework process and that the "truest" assessment is derived from and built upon treatment. There is a quite different quality in this agreement from earlier protocol, often honored in the breech, that "diagnosis is always tentative." This conception of the relationship between assessment and treatment seems to have developed from a clearer perception of the mutuality of the client-worker endeavor and from an experiential recognition that the client makes himself and his situation known and understandable through the work that he and the worker do together. There is implicit in all this a true renunciation of "doing-to-and-for" for "doing-with."

Another area of general agreement is the idea, variously expressed, that attention must be directed to, and data gathered about, the "problem(s)" that the client considers brought him to need help or considers to be important. The substance of this agreement varies according to the authors' ideas of what brings people to grief. System dysfunction in families, inadequate adult functioning, problematic situation, deficient or impaired coping mechanisms in response to hazardous events, and inability to manage some aspect of one's life, are examples of the differing substance. The variety is interesting because underlying it seems to be a shared idea that no matter what the origins of trouble, it will be felt and expressed by people in relation to their current life situations.

Some glimpse of the future of casework theory development may be seen in the systematic relationship between the initial phase, assessment, and treatment as delineated by most of the authors. The diminishing importance of a "study" period makes this possible. Another possible portent for theory organization and more detailed conceptualizations of the content and process of the initial phase and assessment is the "systems" thinking that is explicit in some of the conceptualizations of assessment and implicit or embryonic in others. Scherz and McBroom apply these ideas rather specifically in relation to families as systems and family and environment as system; the potential for this kind of organization of concepts is seen in Rapoport and Smalley. Hollis and Perlman have made a beginning use of system ideas for organization of their respective areas of observation. The stimulus-response, operant-consequence concepts in behavior modification seem also to lend themselves to system organization. The trend in the use of system theory to organize ideas about assessment as well as to organize the data of assessment seems to indicate a common need among the theoreticians for organizing principles to limit and focus the work and data of assessment. The differences among the theories for assessment are related to differences among the authors in their respective ideas about the focus of treatment or the area for work. The area for work dictates the area for observation.[16] The way focus of treatment dictates the focus for assessment is seen in all the approaches. It is most clearly and economically seen in those theoretical statements that identify a specific kind of treatment, or treatment for a specific kind of situation: McBroom, Rapoport, Scherz, and Thomas. The effect of treatment focus on assessment is seen in a more general and generalizable form in the other three approaches. The differences in areas of observation and in focus for assessment among the authors are differences in kind insofar as focus of treatment is different among them. In this respect, there is a more or less clear theoretical connection between assessment and treatment in the seven approaches.

The statements on assessment demonstrate the amount of thought and work that has been invested in this phase of the casework process, whether the work is for or against assessment or diagnosis as we have known it in the past. In spite of differences in focus, content, and possibly process, the assessment phase in each approach is well organized, well conceptualized, and detailed enough to provide implicit or explicit principles for operation, along with some ways in which the necessary observations can be interpreted. Each approach has a framework for assessment derived from the major behavioral science underpinning, from the casework model, or both, and is more or less clearly related to the general focus for treatment propounded by each theoretician. This depth in development of assessment theory is interesting in comparison with the state of treatment theory in casework.

---

16. Bernece K. Simon, *Relationship between Theory and Practice in Social Casework*, Social Work Practice in Medical Care and Rehabilitation Settings, monograph 4 (New York: National Association of Social Workers, 1960), p. 11.

Treatment theory as presented in the seven approaches, always with exceptions, is confined to expositions of the general goals and focus of treatment, general principles for operation, and more or less explicit description of the function and quality of the casework relationship. Identifications and elaborations of techniques of treatment are uneven. In general, these approaches do not provide a complete statement of treatment methodology. Insofar as this is true, it might be said that there is only rudimentary treatment theory in social casework. There are, however, some provocative areas for pursuit of such a theory in the various statements and in the questions that arise from them.

All treatment approaches have a goal of change, modification, or improvement in relation to the situations that come to the attention of caseworkers. Within this global goal, however, there are differences in the extent of change envisioned, in the focus for change, and in the definition of change. The variations in the concept of change will be discussed at greater length later, but it may be that basic differences among the theories are found in the ideas about change. The idea of change itself may be the heart of the difficulties in the formulation of treatment theory. For instance, the ambiguity in the interconnections and overlaps in change extent, change focus, and change definition become apparent when identification of similarities and differences is undertaken. As is seen from study of those approaches directed toward individuals, change focus ranges from modification of the person to modification of a specific behavior of a person.[17] These focuses have in them, implicitly or explicitly, a continuum of the extent of change envisioned. Family treatment focuses on modification in the family system. There is, however, a broad spectrum of the extent of change envisioned, from change in specific aspects of role learning and performance in the family to change relating to the family's understanding of the underlying motives of its transactions, communication, and behavior processes.[18] It is interesting

---

17. For comparison, it can be said that change ideas are on a continuum from those identified by Hollis through the ideas of the other authors to the ideas of change found in Thomas's exposition.

18. This range for family treatment can be seen in that available from McBroom to Scherz and that within Scherz's discussion of change and change objectives (pp. 244–48).

that, in spite of differences in perspective on change, most of the authors make clear that treatment is focused or partialized and that there is no goal for treating all problems, nor a goal of "cure" in any absolute sense. There is an obvious concern in all the approaches to avoid any hierarchy of goals of treatment and to aim for truly differential treatment with each theoretical position. These agreements are expressed in various ways but are, nevertheless, important areas of consensus. The major differences about treatment center on the ideas of change and on the appropriate areas for focus of treatment from among the array of human troubles.

In the general principles of operation there is more evidence of a common core among most approaches, and, indeed, several of the authors say that principles for operation that are well known in casework hold for their approaches as well. The differences among them, as Rapoport points out in her discussion (pp. 294–303) of treatment principles, are a matter of reordering, recombining, and differing emphases of these common principles. These variations among the authors are related to the amount and kind of activity the worker is expected to undertake, the directness of approach to the problems that need attention, the quality and uses of the casework relationship, and the circular or linear relationship between the initial phase, assessment, and treatment. Some of these differences, in combination, make for a quite different look and "feel" in the casework operations described by the several authors. For instance, the worker activity described by McBroom and Rapoport is quite different from that described by Hollis and Smalley. The continuous, dynamic relationship of initial, assessment, and treatment phases is most clearly explicated in Perlman, although McBroom, Rapoport, Scherz, and Smalley describe a comparable relationship. There is considerable agreement among the authors that the "here-and-now" of clients' lives is the area for treatment work. This agreement is an important development in casework theory and is an anchoring point for the appraisal of the nature of the relationship of initial, assessment, and treatment phases in any specific theoretical statement.

The casework relationship is variously described and elaborated by the authors. Except in behavior modification, there is no doubt that the relationship remains the keystone of the casework process. The uses and quality of that relationship have undergone changes of expansion, specificity, and flexibility. McBroom's classification of the major characteristics of the relationship in socialization—parenting, teaching, and modeling (pp. 337–43)—is an interesting example of specification of the uses of the relationship for specific treatment purposes. These relationship roles also demonstrate expansion and flexibility in use of the casework relationship. Rapoport is working in this direction, too. The range of ideas about relationship that is presented in the seven papers offers fertile ground for further examination of the casework relationship and for movement of this concept beyond its traditional mystique. The trend in most of the presentations is to specify the quality and use of the relationship necessary for the kinds of person-situations and for the goals of the treatment.

The functionalist approach to the entire treatment process is distinct from the others, since it is shaped by the use of the relationship, the use of the function and policy of the agency, and the use of time and of structure in the process.[19] This is perhaps best illustrated by Smalley's definition of treatment of any kind as the use of a social service by a person or group (large or small) toward his (its) own and the general social welfare. The definition of social casework is specified as the use of a social service for release of the individual's power for improved social functioning in relation to a special problem or purpose (pp. 80–82). The differences in functionalism are real in spite of its forceful impact on all of casework thinking. The impact has been in respect to the importance of agency function to the casework operations, the recognition of time as an important dynamic in life, the practical meaning of self-determination, and the crucial importance for assessment and treatment of "process" between the worker and the client.

It is not necessary to point out the variations in the discussion of techniques in these theoretical approaches. Many of the problems in the definition and identification of tech-

---

19. See the explication of the five principles as presented throughout Smalley's paper.

niques that we have long been aware of in social casework[20] are, apparently, still with us. Some of the approaches specify certain techniques as of prime importance to treatment in that approach and in so doing identify a kind of cluster of techniques that seem most relevant for the objectives and the general principles of the treatment.[21] This is a needed development in social casework theory. It is needed for purposes of the theory itself and for research into that theory, providing that the development of specific techniques for specific purposes does not increase the yearning in all of us for never-fail recipes for the complex business of helping others. The distrust of "how-to" technology is appropriately deep within most of us. This is demonstrated by the statements of some of the authors that any or all of the techniques available to caseworkers are usable in relation to the general principles and objectives of the treatment phase in the theory. This is not the place to elaborate on Hollis's research and that of the others she cites (pp. 63–69) into the actual use of techniques or "procedures," as she uses the term. It is self-evident, however, that such research is necessary to link techniques to the rest of the theory.[22] The most important aspect of such research, of course, is its potential for the expansion of theory validation. Hollis's work, and that of others interested in the study of techniques, is a major contribution to the evolution of casework theory.

It is important to give special consideration to behavior modification because of its outstanding differences in the matter of treatment and because it raises the issue of the importance of technology to casework theory. One of the elements in this approach is the assertion that the techniques used in behavior modification have been derived from numerous experiments that have been published, widely disseminated, and cross-validated. The important aspects for our purposes, however, are the differences and similarities of this approach to the other approaches in terms of its objectives and use of its special techniques.

---

20. Simon, *Relationship between Theory and Practice*, pp. 28–30.
21. McBroom, Rapoport, Scherz, and Thomas variously present specific techniques for specific treatment objectives.
22. Ford and Urban, *Systems of Psychotherapy*, pp. 86–106.

One similarity is that there is no framework or taxonomy for use of the techniques, although Thomas says that some organizing principles can be articulated and presents some that seem to constitute a taxonomy (pp. 204–14). This is a similarity that has a difference in that the other approaches have a framework of general principles (but no taxonomy that holds up) from which techniques probably could be developed. It is important to keep in mind, however, that the scientific underpinning of behavior modification is such that validation of technology is a first priority and is necessary for the development of a taxonomy. That is, general principles are derived from validated particulars insofar as they will lend themselves to grouping.

The major differences in Thomas's approach for this aspect of theory development are: (1) that there is a direct, linear relationship between the specific, identified behavior, the modification objective, and the technique required by the kind of behavior and the modification objective—that is, the assessment identifies the specific piece of behavior to be modified from which the modification objective is derived and, thus, techniques are specifically chosen for the specific function they serve in the modification of behavior; and (2) that it is therefore possible to develop criteria for selection among techniques. This is a clear difference from the interconnecting, overlapping, simultaneous, and relatively universal functions of techniques in other casework approaches. It is also different because, at this stage of development, the use of technique in behavior modification has no theoretical or actual relationship to the nature of the worker-client relationship, although Thomas assumes a positive one. The worker's "style" and the kind of person the client is are also unrelated to use of technique in this system. Use of technique is governed by the specific modification objective. In this respect there is similarity to Hollis's study of the "change objective" of the techniques used by workers.

Examination of specific techniques in behavior modification reveals that the objectives of some of them seem identical with the objectives of several techniques or procedures in other casework approaches. The techniques involved in reinforcement seem to have objectives that are like those for the use of support, education, and advice in other theoretical frameworks. This has, of course, been pointed out and commented upon in various discussions of sociobehavior theory as well as of behavior modification. The fact of these similarities is less important than their meaning for use in practice. Techniques seem interchangeable among the other casework approaches, but we must remember always the potential difference that may be significant for their use and outcome through reordering and varying emphases. Within the reordering and emphases, however, the common techniques are used within frameworks that have in common a dynamic psychological base, a theory of personality, and a primary dependence on the casework relationship to give meaning and impact to the use of techniques.

In addition, the casework frameworks seem to be moving in the direction of an interconnected system in which the parts and their uses affect each other. The clear development in the theories of the constantly moving, interlocking, mutually affecting relationship between diagnosis and treatment is one example of this. The question in relation to apparently similar techniques in behavior modification is, Does the similarity of objectives render them usable within basically different theoretical frameworks? Would the reinforcement techniques, for instance, have the same effect in another theoretical context? Another question about use of techniques from behavior modification in other frameworks is the influence of the casework relationship on the effectiveness of any technique. Since at this time relationship considerations are not primary in the investigative and developmental work in the various "schools" of behavior modification, and other casework approaches have done little about investigating the impact of the relationship, this may be an academic question. Nevertheless, it seems important. On the basis of the logic of the approach, as presented by Thomas, it seems that identification of the specific behavior to be modified and concomitant identification of the objective of modification is sufficient for selection of the technique that serves the objective regardless of the context in which it is used. The criteria for selection of techniques listed by Thomas (pp. 214–15) give one pause to think in relation to the interchangeability of behavior modification techniques in the other approaches. This is another aspect of the question of the relation of technique to the other parts of a theoretical framework. That is, in addition to questions of worker "style," client receptivity, and the nature and quality of the casework relationship in the use of techniques, there is still the question whether the total conceptual framework has any power or relevance in the choice, use, and outcome of techniques or procedures.

The issue of values inherent or explicit in any theoretical framework may also be important in the choice of technique. It does not seem possible to grapple with that issue here because the problem is universal and there is no evidence except that of subjective response that this problem is not as worrisome for the practice of behavior modification as it is for other approaches, or, more important, that the value base of behavior modification is markedly different from the others. Nevertheless, the relation of values to technology remains a question for further examination and work.

The general level of treatment theory, its gaps and uneven development as discussed here, is, perhaps, characteristic of the theoretical and empirical problems in social casework. It is puzzling, nevertheless, that treatment theory is comparatively less explicated than assessment theory. And it is difficult to be sure why this is so or even to hazard valid conjecture about it.

One inhibiting factor in treatment theory development might be our inability or unwillingness to consider theoretical and empirical problems separately. That is, we have not developed a complete theoretical system because the validation process is fraught with such formidable conceptual and methodological difficulties. The conceptual problems for both research and theory formulation are in turn affected by problems of, and concerns about, values, goals, and professionalism, as Germain has suggested in a historical context. For instance, in the attempt to identify the reasons for the state of treatment theory, it is almost impossible to separate the theoretical and the empirical from the value or ideological issues.

The questions about the place of technique in the theory make a case in point. There was a time when questions of technical "how-to" posed by students and practitioners were uniformly answered by "it depends on the case." We all know there is some truth to this response. Perhaps this equivocation was undertaken to guard against any thought or operation that would dilute the individualization of the client. Thus, classifications of all kinds have been suspect on this basis, especially classifications of techniques and generalizations about their use. Now there is evidence that worker's "style" is apparently a primary factor in the use of technique.[23] This research-based knowledge is important, but it is only one step in understanding treatment processes and procedures in relation to theory. But in either case, the value of individuality is powerfully at work. To develop the example further, the concept of professionalism enters in the notion that it is intellectually more respectable to promulgate theory and principles for practitioners to develop into whatever techniques would make principle and theory operational than to identify and organize techniques in the way that is being attempted in current study and research. There was conviction that a truly professional practitioner could develop technical competence by thorough understanding of theory and principle. Of course this is true too; but this conviction may have been based less on certainty as to what constitutes professional competence and more on the vicissitudes of the battle to move from apprentice-learning and technician development to professional status. Thus scientific attitudes and activity are melded with a valuable ideology, to the possible dilution of both.

Another aspect of the effect of these problems on both theoretical and empirical questions is possibly seen in various "outcome" studies where there was an attempt, for lack of concepts and substantive organization for our procedures, to study outcome without reference to "As the result of what?"

Another example of a possibly inhibiting factor in theory development as well as the theory-ideology problem is the various, essentially useful, but misused efforts at classifications of treatment. The usefulness of these efforts is obvious, but it seems to have been distorted by the hierarchical values that were attached to the classifications. Status and effectiveness of treatment "methods" became identical on the basis

---

23. William J. Reid, "Characteristics of Casework Intervention," *Welfare in Review* 5 (October 1967):11–19.

of attachment to a set of ideas rather than on validation of usefulness and effectiveness in relation to objectives of treatment. The incorporation of treatment classifications into practice seemed to have been affected by the largely unacknowledged differences between stated treatment goals in any given case and the private, implicit treatment goals of the worker in the case. These differences derived from ideas of status and ideological convictions. That this was afoot has been evident from some of our early and recent researches into continuance.[24]

The issue of the relationship mystique has already been cited but merits repetition here as another area where theory, validation, and ideology are enveloped in a Gordian knot that needs considerable unraveling if treatment theory is to advance and enrich practice.

Solution of problems for the development of treatment theory lies only partly in the area of research conception and methodology. Solutions are also needed for the problems of separating the study of values, treatment goals, treatment methods, and treatment procedures in order to arrive at a synthesis in treatment theory that constitutes a guide to practice at these various levels. A strong case was developed in the symposium discussions that as a first order of business the theoreticians must pursue the position and the detail of technology in their several approaches. This was thought necessary for further theory development and imperative for testing such theory and for the progressive development of casework research. For practice, specificity of treatment procedures might make for worker flexibility and creativity in relation to individual clients because the worker would have options, a repertoire, and a guide available for his choice.

---

24. See Margaret Blenkner, "Predictive Factors in the Initial Interview in Family Casework," *Social Service Review* 28 (March 1954). Margaret Blenkner, J. McV. Hunt, and Leonard S. Kogan, "A Study of Interrelated Factors in the Initial Interview with New Clients," *Social Casework* 32 (January 1951). Leonard S. Kogan, "The Short-Term Case in a Family Agency," *Social Casework* 38 (May, June, July 1957). Lilian Ripple, Ernestina Alexander, and Bernice Polemis, *Motivation, Capacity and Opportunity: Studies in Casework Theory and Practice*. (Chicago: School of Social Service Administration, University of Chicago, 1964). Ann W. Shyne, "What Research Tells Us about Short-Term Cases in Family Agencies," *Social Casework* 38 (May 1957).

Issues, Questions, and Problems

In addition to the issues, questions, and problems presented so far, the symposium discussions also brought forth important ideas not readily apparent in the written papers. What follows are some highlights and analyses of the symposium discussions and some integration and reemphasis of significant areas already identified as needing further work.

There were exciting discussions in the symposium sessions on the conception of man held by the theoreticians, on the concept of change and change objectives, and on the boundaries of social casework, both within any theoretical system and in relation to the profession and society.

The major point for discussion in relation to the conception of man was the idea of the "whole" man. As would be expected, those theoreticians working on a base of dynamic psychology agreed that the whole man is important to the psychological-casework framework. The difference among them was the way in which the whole man concept is used for assessment and particularly for treatment. There seemed to be agreement, in discussion, that the concept of the whole man serves as a backdrop for both assessment and treatment of a segment of the man in interaction with a problematic phase of his life. The differences seemed to be in how wide or narrow a segment is considered appropriate by each of the theoreticians. Appropriateness was derived from individual definitions of the whole man and from the individual's position about the focus of assessment and treatment in his theory. It is interesting, in view of the varied use of system theory in most of the approaches, that there was only beginning work on defining the whole man as a man-environment system. The extent to which the theoreticians view the appropriate problematic segment as a man-environment problem is more or less elaborated in the various theoretical expositions.

Behavior modification theory does not have a conception of the whole man. The whole man idea is regarded as a philosophical issue that has no place in behavior modification theory. It is also seen as an idea that arises from a personality orientation. From the behavior modification point of view, consideration of the whole man conception is an example of the inappropriate mixture of ideology and science. Although

Germain identified this tendency as a problem in the historical development of casework, the symposium discussion revealed that many of the theoreticians conceived of values as crucial to theory formulation in that they serve as boundaries for the theoretical structure and as basic guidelines for the development of operational principles within the theory.

Discussion of the conception of man and of the place of the idea of the whole man in a theoretical system for casework practice gave rise to the conception of change held by the theoreticians and the definition of change objectives in the several theories. The concept of change is not clearly dealt with in the various approaches, and so the change objectives are relatively elusive. The discussion did not elucidate a conception of change.[25] It did, however, reveal the complexity of this idea for an interpersonal process such as casework. It seemed that the idea of change could only be approached through consideration of change objectives. There was general, but not complete, agreement that personality change is not the central objective in the theories. The inclusion of the behavior modification approach in this agreement must be considered in the context of the fact that such an objective is irrelevant to and incompatible with that theory.

Within the general disclaimer of a personality change objective, there was intensive discussion of the potential effects of various kinds of change or modification on personality. The discussion did not clarify whether the theoretical effects are related to personality structure, personality functions, and functioning, or only the subjective perceptions of the individual or any combination of these. There was a common conviction among most symposium participants that change or modification in one area of an individual's life affected other areas. This belief was accompanied by uncertainty as to how or whether this conviction could be translated into

---

25. Scherz suggested, in discussion, that change is the basic fact of life to which people must adapt. She thought, therefore, that a major objective of family treatment, and perhaps casework, should be to enable families and individuals to develop ways to deal with and incorporate change. For this reason, and because we do not know the extent of human capacity, she thought that the concept of limited change goals is a constricting idea and does not sufficiently take into account the creativity inherent in the human being.

theory. The uncertain nature of this aspect of the discussion was expressed by the question, How can it be ascertained that change or modification in the area of treatment focus does or does not effect change in other areas of the person-situation configuration?

The question of permeation of change in various areas of life, or a chain reaction of change, was of intense interest to all the theorists. It is a phenomenon that is observed in behavior modification treatment and was described by Thomas in discussion as "spread" or an "avalanche" effect, needing considerable study. For behaviorists it is an example of the complexity of behavior and the rudimentary nature of the laws that have been developed about it; for dynamic psychology adherents it is an example of the complexity of the human personality and its many unknown facets. It may be that some kind of system idea may offer a way of analysis of this phenomenon beyond the obvious, descriptive one of systemic interaction.

The question of the limitations or boundaries of expectable change led, as it should, to consideration of man-in-environment. In this context the problem was expressed in terms of the effect of environment on personality and personality change and the question of whether environmental forces are internalized by the individual and become part of the personality. There was agreement among most that environment has a crucial impact on personality. The nature of this impact was not specified in terms of personality development, structure, functions, functioning, or any combination of these. There is some specification of environmental impact on personality in that aspect of socialization that deals with adult learning (McBroom: pp. 316–20). There was agreement that environmental change produces psychological change. This was not developed in discussion beyond the depth of detail which Towle has elaborated, particularly in *Common Human Needs*. The level of generality at which this discussion proceeded, combined with the sparseness of consideration of environmental aspects of treatment in the exposition of theory,[26] attests to the concept of man-in-en-

---

26. For exceptions to this statement, see McBroom and Rapoport. In these theoretical statements there is detailed consideration of the person-environment interaction.

vironment as a most compelling area for study, examination, research, and theorizing in casework, if not in all of social work. There is no doubt that there is a surge of effort to rid our thinking and attitudes of the man-environment dichotomy. It seems that we lack the conceptual tools to produce a man-environment unity that will serve casework theoretical frameworks and provide for principles of casework operation or practice. There are, for instance, wide variations among the approaches in the way in which man-in-environment as an interaction is dealt with in the various phases of the casework process. McBroom's certainty about the absolute necessity for societal supports necessary for adult socialization is one approach to the needed conceptualizations. Perlman's use of motivation-capacity and opportunity as the interrelated area for assessment is another start for such conceptualization. Opportunity, in this formulation, needs considerable elaboration of its components, and especially of its specific relationship to motivation and capacity.

Conceptions of man, change objectives, change outcomes, and serendipities inevitably led to questions about the boundaries of the casework process within the specific theories and within the profession and society. The whole man issue raised the question of the boundaries of casework assessment as well as of casework treatment. This question was dealt with along the lines delineated by Hollis (pp. 49–56) and was not pursued as vigorously or as intensively as it, perhaps, should have been. One reason, among many, that it was not discussed further was the urgency of the subject of casework boundaries in the profession and in society.

The questions of environmental effects on personality and environment as a dynamic in change led to the issue of the caseworker as advocate. The discussion centered on the distinction between "case advocacy" (caseworker as advocate for the individual and his welfare) and "policy advocacy" (caseworker as advocate of societal or agency policy change.)[27] It was agreed that caseworkers have been and continue to be advocates for their individual clients. It was further agreed that in the recent past this kind of advocacy has not been a

---

27. This clarifying idea was formulated by Robert Roberts in the symposium discussion.

specified aspect of treatment theory as it is now presented. But it has been an ingredient in treatment throughout the history of casework.

Policy advocacy that involves the client with the caseworker (as contrasted to social caseworkers' undertaking policy advocacy as social workers and as citizens) was thought, in the discussion, to need careful examination. Policy advocacy, in which the caseworker is a community mover and shaker in which the client must take an active part with him, such as appearances in courts, before legislative bodies, in public media and in protests to agencies or governmental bodies, raises questions, in a new context, of ethics, self-determination, and the imposition of values and standards of behavior on clients by social workers. The use of clients by caseworkers in policy advocacy could develop into conscious as well as unconscious exploitation of clients' misery and helplessness as surely as the goal of "adjustment to his environment" (which was never a theoretical goal of casework) is alleged to have done. This exploitation will develop unless there is careful work with clients as to what they want for themselves and how much they want to and can involve themselves as citizens, not clients, in societal and policy change. This is a concrete example of the interrelation of values and theory development. Insofar as individual advocacy and policy advocacy constitute an expansion of the relationship concept in casework, it appears that the usual ethical considerations and criteria for the use of the professional relationship must be applied.

Hollis suggested that, if policy advocacy by caseworkers in relation to their clients is also an expansion of the caseworker's professional function, instead of an unquestioning move into this function there might be consideration of a continuing division of functions within the profession. That is, when the client's role in policy advocacy is worked out as described above, the client might be referred for his part in such activity to other professional sources for the resources, support, and help he might need. There are important implications in this discussion for future theory development and for study of what, in practice, is actually undertaken in advocacy along with how it is undertaken and its outcome.

These issues, not specifically addressed in the formal ex-

positions, are of utmost significance to the future development of social casework theory and practice. Of equal significance are some other gaps in the formal presentations
that were also not approached in the symposium discussions.
The most important of these, in my view, is the concept of
prevention as it might be incorporated in casework. Mc-
Broom and Rapoport are more specific about this than other
theoreticians. Inherent in the discussion of change permeation is a notion of prevention. And a kind of prevention—
arrest or deterrence of continuing deterioration or disability
development—has been implicit in the caseworker's general
goals of treatment throughout our history. The possibility
that primary or secondary prevention could be conceptualized as a general goal for casework is an area that is wide
open for work and a desperately needed expansion of theory.
It is likely that this is an area where practice might feed de
novo into theory. Family life education is one such source.
Use of professional social workers in settings where casework has not been incorporated, or which have not been considered sources for theory development, is another possibility. Day-care centers, maternal and child health clinics, as
well as other medical facilities related to acute illness, and
schools are examples of settings that could be first-hand
sources for the development of prevention theory for social
work to which caseworkers can make a primary contribution.
Community mental health settings constitute another potential source of raw material for theory development and
validation, providing there is sufficient clarification of the
function of social work in these settings. Crisis-oriented brief
treatment may serve as a conceptual model for some of this
essential work.

Another area that is covered in the formal statements but
not considered in the symposium discussions or in this paper
is the "target" groups of the various theories. It seems to me
that this subject must be accepted as the individual theoreticians see it because there is no basis, either theoretical or
empirical, upon which to dispute or to refine their assertions.
The theoretical basis for either corroboration or negation of
the opinion of the theoreticians about the appropriate people-problem-situation configuration for their theories is not
available because, among other reasons, it is likely that none

of the approaches has ever been applied in the whole. The empirical basis for corroboration or negation will probably not be available until some of the empirical problems in treatment discussed above are solved. Even McBroom's approach, which is specifically addressed to a specific people-problem-situation set, remains to be fully tested in practice as well as tested by research methods.

The unsolved problems are available for study and thought as they are presented by the seven theoreticians and therefore are not dealt with here.

Summary

This presentation was directed, by general comparisons and contrasts, to the present status of social casework theory, to identification of the significance of outstanding similarities and differences of the seven theoretical approaches to social casework, and to suggesting ways to study and appraise theory.

There is great diversity in casework theory. The symposium concluded that this is good and that a goal of a unitary theory is probably not appropriate or healthy for the development of practice that must address itself to a myriad of difficult, baffling, and little-understood human problems. There was a deep-felt hope on the part of most symposium participants that the diversity in theories for practice not produce new "schools" of casework that would garner passionate ideological adherents. Rather, it was hoped that diversity would encourage intellectual ferment, clashes of ideas that would result in rigorous practice, and research efforts based on specification of the general aspects and tangible utility of the several theories. For me, the meaning of the diversity is not entirely clear because the recurring similarities across and between the various approaches suggest a common core in all the theories, with the possible exception of behavior modification.

The problems for the future growth of social casework theory and practice are: (a) the development of a middle-range conceptualization of man-in-environment that can be applied in practice; (b) the explication of the concept of change and change objectives in social casework; (c) work on the feasibility of developing and incorporating applicable concepts of prevention specific to social casework; (*d*) concrete elucidation of treatment theory, including development of techniques specific to a particular theory so that practice validation of the utility of the theory and research validation of the theory itself are possible; (*e*) separation of ideological and scientific problems in social casework so that each can serve its rightful function in relation to the development of both theory and practice and the solution of the many theoretical and empirical problems; and (*f*) recognition that a humanistic-scientific profession must build its knowledge both by accretion and by new breakthroughs.

This rich, valuable volume is but a way station to our future. It will serve its purpose best if it is regarded as a map of the work that is cut out, in the "here-and-now" and in the long future ahead, for all disciplines and professions dedicated to the development of the humanity of man in his environment.

PARTICIPANTS IN THE CHARLOTTE TOWLE MEMORIAL SYMPOSIUM ON COMPARATIVE THEORETICAL APPROACHES TO CASEWORK PRACTICE

Planning Committee

Dorothy Aikin
Rachel Marks
Robert H. Nee
(co-chairman)

Robert W. Roberts
(co-chairman)
Bernece K. Simon

Participants

Dorothy Aikin
Ernestina Alexander
Sylvia Astro
Edwin Brown
Elizabeth Butler (Recorder)
Laura Epstein
Carel Germain
John Goldmeier
Mary Gyarfas
Florence Hollis
Philip Hovda (Recorder)
Janet Kohrman (Recorder)
Rachel Marks
Friedericka Mayers
(Recorder)

Elizabeth McBroom
Robert H. Nee
Helen Harris Perlman
Lydia Rapoport
William J. Reid
Walter Rest
Lilian Ripple
Robert W. Roberts
Frances H. Scherz
Bernece K. Simon
(Discussion Leader)
Ruth E. Smalley
Mary L. Somers
Marian Tillotson
Edwin J. Thomas

Index

Behavioral science foundation
—*Cont.*
functional casework, 83, 85–
96; for problem-solving, 169–
78; for psychosocial casework,
39–40; for socialization the-
ory, 320–25
Biology, molecular, 323
Birth, premature. *See* Prema-
turity
Birth, significance of, 91–92, 94,
99
Borderline states, 305
Boston School of Social Work,
10 n
Bowen, Murray, 234
Brackett, Jeffrey, 10 n
Brewer, William, 11 n
Bribing, Grete L., 39, 64
Brief treatment. *See* Crisis inter-
vention; Short-term treatment
Brim, Orville G., Jr., 330, 334,
344, 345
Bronfenbrenner, Urie, 339 n
Bruck, Max, 331, 334, 348
Bruner, Jerome, 18 n

Cabot, Richard, 13
Cannon, Ida, 13
Capacity, client, 135, 146, 158,
166–68
Caplan, Gerald, 267, 269, 287
Case history. *See* History-taking
Casework: contribution of, 355,
370–71; danger of obsolescence, 28–29; definition of,
81, 380; direct and indirect,
63–64; functional (*see* Functional casework); history, 5–
32, 356; limitations on, 61–
62; medical, 13; as a profession, 12, 14, 21, 385; and science, 5–32, 38, 156, 177; relation to social work, 15–21,
126–28, 134, 355. *See also*
Social work

Caseworker: as advocate, 119,
390–91; as agent of socialization, 318–20, 338; attitude of,
42, 199, 288–90; authenticity
of, 290, 300; character of, 73,
94–95, 203 n, 349–50; education of, 14, 95, 116, 124, 126–
28, 262–63, 309; as evaluator
of policy, 126; in family therapy, 248–50; functions of, 63,
80, 119–20, 215–16, 300, 329;
number of, 249–50; parental
role of, 338, 340–41; qualifica-
tions of, 127–28; responsibilities of, 121–25; as role model,
250, 300, 320, 334, 339–42,
347–48, 349–50; style, 73, 162,
237, 249, 382, 384, 385; as
teacher, 216, 335, 338
Casework theories: behavioral
science foundations of, 357–
59, 364–71; evaluation of,
356–60; initial phase in, 371–
74; relationship in, 379–80; as
schools of thought, 361–62;
similarities and differences,
360–63; sources of, 366; as
theory-building, 362–63, 384–
87
Causation, 15, 16, 160, 178
Challenge, 277
Change: dynamics of, 142, 273–
74, 308, 388–89; objectives,
60, 79, 261, 349, 388
Character disorders, 72–73, 305
Charity. *See* Philanthropy
Charity Organization Societies,
8, 9 n, 10, 13
Children: in family therapy,
253, 257–58, 262
Choice. *See* Autonomy
Classical conditioning. *See* Conditioning, respondent
Classification: and assessment,
24–25, 52, 53–56, 166–67, 332–
36, 346, 375; in family ther-

Lock, Sir Charles, 8 n
Loss, 277, 285–86
Lovdjieff, Chris, 342 n
Lowry, Fern, 38
Lutz, Werner, 40
Lynd, Helen Merrell, 89

McBroom, Elizabeth, 305, 362–93 passim
Malan, David H., 270, 289
Man, concepts of, 79–80, 86–88, 90–94, 144–45, 221, 322–23, 361–62, 365, 387–90
Man-environment concept, 323, 324, 366, 367, 387, 389–90
Manpower problem, 127
Marital pair, 237–38
Marriage, 226–29, 230, 284
Maslow, A. H., 88
Mastery, drive for, 38, 144, 272, 291, 292, 365. See also Autonomy; Effectance
Mead, George Herbert, 83, 85, 173, 177 n, 321, 325
Medical model, 13, 15–16, 21, 55–56, 79, 135, 138, 275–76, 295
Meliorism, 11
Mental hygiene movement, 16
Mental illness, 55–56, 62, 72, 166–67, 258–59, 279, 305, 306
Mental Research Institute, 223
Merton, Robert K., 318, 321 n
Method. See Treatment, method of
Meyer, Carol, 28
Middles, significance of, 101–2
Migrants, 336, 345
Milford Conference (1929), 14, 15
Millenson, J. R., 206 n
Miller, Henry, 347
Miller, Irving, 5 n
Miller, N. E., 184
Mitchell, Sylvia, 345

Mobility, upward, 344
Model presentation, 213
Modification, 216, 297
Motivation, 56–57, 72, 146, 309, 321–22; assessment of, 158, 164–66; stimulation of, 43, 134–135
Motives, underlying, 247
Moustakas, Clark, 88
Mowrer, O. H., 185
Mullen, Edward J., 67, 69
Murphey, Lois Barclay, 160
Murray, Henry, 39

Narcissism, 71
National Conference on Charities and Corrections, 9
National Conference on Social Welfare (1968), 9 n, 346–47
National Conference of Social Work, 9 n
Needs, of client, 36, 47, 58, 72, 85, 300
Negative practice, 211
Neo-Freudianism. See Ego psychology
Neurosis. See Mental illness
Newtonian physics, 10
New York School of Social Work, 10 n, 15, 38, 82
Nondirective therapy, 152
Norms, social, 318
North Point project, 326, 348

Objectives. See Change objectives; Goals
Object relationships, 229, 232, 233, 241, 252
Observation, direct, 196, 225
"Open door" policy, 303
Operant behavior, 187–88, 193, 204
Operant conditioning, 185, 190, 192–93, 205–8, 274
Opportunity, 135, 158–61